W9-CND-901

Protesting Affirmative Action

RECONFIGURING AMERICAN POLITICAL HISTORY

Ronald P. Formisano, Paul Bourke,
Donald DeBats, and Paula M. Baker
Series Founders

Protesting Affirmative Action

The Struggle over Equality after the Civil Rights Revolution

DENNIS DESLIPPE

The Johns Hopkins University Press
Baltimore

The Johns Hopkins University Press
2715 North Charles Street
Baltimore, Maryland 21218-4363
www.press.jhu.edu

Library of Congress Cataloging-in-Publication Data

Deslippe, Dennis.
Protesting affirmative action : the struggle over equality after the civil rights
revolution / Dennis Deslippe.
p.   cm. — (Reconfiguring American political history)
Includes bibliographical references and index.
ISBN-13: 978-1-4214-0358-8 (hardcover : alk. paper)
ISBN-10: 1-4214-0358-7 (hardcover : alk. paper)
1. Affirmative action programs—United States—History. 2. Equality—United
States—History. 3. Race discrimination—United States—History. 4. United
States—Race relations—History. 5. Affirmative action programs—Law and
legislation—United States. I. Title.
HF5549.5.A34D427 2012
323.173—dc23   2011019911

A catalog record for this book is available from the British Library.

To Therese and John

CONTENTS

When I began this project, I worried that I would receive little support for such a polarizing topic. As you can read in these acknowledgments, this concern was unnecessary. I am pleased to thank the institutions and people who assisted me over the past decade. I could not have written this book without the generous research funds I was given by the American Philosophical Society, the Australian National University, the Gerald R. Ford Presidential Library, and the Schlesinger Library at Harvard University. A National Endowment for the Humanities Fellowship in 2005 was crucial in moving the project along.

Librarians and archivists were indispensable in facilitating my research, especially those at the American Jewish Archives, the American Jewish Committee Library, the American Jewish Historical Society, the Bentley Historical Library at the University of Michigan, the Jimmy Carter Presidential Library, the George Meany Memorial Archives, the Gerald R. Ford Presidential Library, the Historical Society of Pennsylvania, the Hoover Institution Library and Archives at Stanford University, the Library of Congress, the National Archives, the New York Public Library, the State Historical Society of Wisconsin, the Walter P. Reuther Library at Wayne State University, the University of Washington Library Special Collections, and the Yale University Library. Tom Karel, Michael Lear, Christopher Raab, Mary Shelly, and Scott Vine at the Franklin and Marshall College Library provided skilled assistance along the way.

My thanks to those scholars who read, offered suggestions, and encouraged me: Martha Biondi, Kevin Boyle, David Colman-Lewis, Jeff Cowie, Jonathan Goldberg-Hiller, Laura Kalman, Greg Kaster, Linda Kerber, Matt Lassiter, Sophia Lee, Nancy MacLean, Jack Metzger, Alan Petigny, and Tom Sugrue. Although some of our interpretations differ on affirmative action, their scholarship is manifest on every page. In addition to these readers, I have presented selections from the manuscript at conferences, including those of the American Society for

Legal History, the Australia-New Zealand American Studies Association, and the Law and Society Association; audience members and fellow panelists at these gatherings and at the Newberry Library Seminar of Labor History, the Policy History Conference, and the North American Labor History Conference pushed me to think more carefully about my argument. I wish to offer a special note of thanks to Robert Gordon, Lawrence Friedman, and the participants in the University of Wisconsin Law School's 2003 J. Willard Hurst Legal History Institute.

The labor of anonymous readers of journal manuscripts often goes unheralded, so I appreciate especially their careful readings of my essays. Portions of chapters 1 and 5 appeared in "'Do Whites Have Rights?' White Detroit Policemen and 'Reverse Discrimination' Protests in the 1970s," *Journal of American History* 91:3 (December 2004): 932–60, and chapter 2 and 3 in "'We Must Bring Together a New Coalition': The Challenge of Working-Class White Ethnics to Color-Blind Conservatism in the 1970s," *International Labor and Working-Class History* 74 (Fall 2008): 148–70.

I owe a great debt to Robert J. Brugger at the Johns Hopkins University Press for his early and steady enthusiasm for this project. His emails and telephone calls with questions about my progress with the manuscript as well as specific advice on its organization and argument were well timed. He and the other staff members at the Press are professionals, and I am pleased to have worked with them on this book. I profited enormously from the anonymous reader's report as well as Martin Schneider's excellent and thorough copyediting of the work.

Colleagues and friends sustained me in countless ways. Just as I conceived this project, Sally Kenney, now at Tulane University, provided me with office space at the University of Minnesota while I was on sabbatical. Dave Cohen, a friend from my days at Wayne State University, brought his sharp legal skills to bear on a draft of chapter 4. Franklin and Marshall College has been a wonderful intellectual home for the book's completion. My thanks to my supportive colleagues in American Studies: Dan Frick, Greg Kaliss, Alison Kibler, Eliza Reilly, David Schuyler, Louise Stevenson, and Carl Willard; although disperesed across the campus, my Women and Gender Studies colleagues have enriched my research and teaching with their impressive scholarly work and teaching as well.

Alison Kibler's name belongs in nearly every paragraph of these acknowledgments. She is a great colleague, constructive critic, and consistent ally. I am in awe of the energy and love she brings to our life together. I dedicate this book to our children, Therese and John. They experienced the researching and writing of this project firsthand from the time they were small children ("Just a few more paragraphs and I'm done!"). They give me hope that we will find the right words and deeds.

AAAA	American Association for Affirmative Action
AAUP	American Association of University Professors
ADL	Anti-Defamation League of B'nai B'rith
AFL-CIO	American Federation of Labor–Congress of Industrial Organizations
AFSCME	American Federation of State, County, and Municipal Employees
AFT	American Federation of Teachers
BCTC	New York Building and Construction Trades Council
CANI	Committee on Academic Non-Discrimination and Integrity
CBTU	Congress of Black Trade Unionists
CEEO	President's Committee on Equal Employment Opportunity
CETA	Comprehensive Education and Training Act
CLUW	Coalition of Labor Union Women
CORE	Congress of Racial Equality
CRD	AFL-CIO Civil Rights Department
CUNY	City University of New York
DOJ	U.S. Department of Justice
DPOA	Detroit Police Officers Association
EEOC	U.S. Equal Employment Opportunity Commission
HEW	U.S. Department of Health, Education, and Welfare
IBEW	International Brotherhood of Electrical Workers
IEB	United Automobile Workers International Executive Board
IUE	International Union of Electrical Workers
LSA	Detroit Lieutenant and Sergeants Association
NAACP	National Association for the Advancement of Colored People
NAS	National Association of Scholars
NLRB	National Labor Relations Board

NUL	National Urban League
OCR	U.S. Office of Civil Rights
OFCC	U.S. Office of Federal Contract Compliance
PLF	Pacific Legal Foundation
UAW	United Automobile Workers
UCD	University of California, Davis
USCCR	U.S. Commission on Civil Rights
USW	United Steel Workers of America
WEAL	Women's Equity Action League

Protesting Affirmative Action

Introduction

The newspaper headlines in the summer of 1965 were thick with reports on the bloody struggle for voting rights in the South and on the urban riots in Harlem and Watts. It was a pivotal moment in the history of the nation's race relations: in the two years since the iconic March on Washington for Jobs and Freedom, a great many Americans had looked with pride on the advances in civil rights. The U.S. Congress passed the Civil Rights Act of 1964, which, among other things, banned employment discrimination; legislators then shepherded the Voting Rights Act of 1965 through Congress. Just as southern segregation seemed to be crumbling, however, fissures appeared within the civil rights coalition in the form of rising black anger in the North and an accompanying white backlash. As black nationalists, impatient with the pace of change, shook up the civil rights movement, white support for further civil rights legislation began to waver.

It was easy, then, to overlook a *Wall Street Journal* article about three white musicians in Chicago complaining that they had been fired on account of their race. The musicians, part of the twenty-five-piece, all-white CBS Orchestra, found themselves out of a job when the network replaced them with three black musicians. This was necessary, explained a CBS executive, because the network's participation in the federal government's voluntary "Plans for Progress" obligated it "to take affirmative action to offer employment to members of minority groups on a company-wide basis." The newspaper's editors were sympathetic with the three white musicians. They warned that "the zeal CBS . . . and others are bringing to the struggle to stamp out a century of wrong sometimes obliterates good judgment." After two of the musicians returned to work, the remaining one lodged a discrimination complaint with the Illinois Fair Employment Practices Commission. We do not know the resolution of what may have been the first "reverse discrimination" legal action, since state officials have destroyed the records from that period, and there is no evidence that the musician went on to file a lawsuit.[1]

This seemingly minor news item indicated a new direction in the struggle for equality. It was one thing to end discriminatory employment practices, as Title VII of the Civil Rights Act of 1964 had done, but it was quite another to take proactive steps to train, hire, and promote workers from underrepresented groups. Although there had been pilot programs such as "Plans for Progress" since the early 1960s, affirmative action as we recognize it today emerged as a fully formed program in 1969, when the federal government required federal contractors in Philadelphia to meet certain goals for hiring African Americans to combat institutionalized discrimination in the city's skilled building trade unions; this became known as the "Philadelphia Plan." The next year the government issued guidelines for affirmative action in higher education. Some Americans at the time rejected the rationale for affirmative action. "Is it morally defensible for a company to fire an employee solely because of his race?" wondered the *Wall Street Journal* in an article about the CBS Orchestra story. The Chicago incident occurred less than three months after President Lyndon B. Johnson had delivered his bold challenge at Howard University for the nation to make "not just equality a right and a theory but equality as a fact and equality as a result." But the newspaper's editors concluded that the moral and social costs of pursuing this goal were too high: "For as long as men are hired and fired on the basis of color alone, America's racial tensions will not subside. Anything that preserves such tensions we call 'negative action.'" Suddenly, the hope generated by the achievements of the civil rights movement seemed to be imperiled. "The year 1965 is seeing the racial issue snarled in conflicts between one right and another," wrote Charles Abrams, creator of the New York Housing Authority. "Equality under laws is confronted by the claim that the long subordination of the Negro's rights demands preferential treatment, which in turn is attacked as 'discrimination in reverse.'"[2]

We are accustomed to thinking that opposition to affirmative action arose in 1978 with the U.S. Supreme Court decision in *Regents of the University of California v. Bakke,* not right alongside the earliest programs in the 1960s. In considering the case between Allan Bakke, a white man and unsuccessful medical school applicant, and the University of California at Davis, the justices approved of preference programs as long as they served to create a diverse campus and did not involve the imposition of quotas. The court was divided on the matter, however, and the narrow "diversity" justification signaled to rising activists and politicians of the New Right an opening for future anti–affirmative action litigation and lobbying. Commentators have since fixed on opposition to race- and gender-sensitive programs as wholly within the realm of conservative ideas and politics. The passion, the energy, and the resources mobilized today against affirmative action come entirely from the political right.[3]

This book considers the longer, more varied history of affirmative action in the nearly fifteen years before *Bakke*. This was a period when opponents of various political and ideological stripes transformed federal equal employment opportunity policies, local and national politics, and social relations on the nation's campuses and workplaces. During this period they filed "reverse discrimination" charges with the U.S. Equal Employment Opportunity Commission; brought lawsuits in the local, state, and federal court systems; and worked, using formal and informal means, to change the stance of government, businesses, labor unions, and institutions of higher education on this divisive issue. "There is, perhaps, no area of employment law that so brings the tensions inherent in Title VII into focus as that called 'reverse discrimination,'" wrote the authors of a primer on equal employment law at the time. Opponents did not simply resist new programs for advancing the economic status of minority men and women of all races, they also harnessed "rights talk" to their own ends, making far-reaching claims about equality, justice, and citizenship in the post–civil rights era.[4]

Despite being a formidable presence in law and politics, these opponents did not constitute a single social protest movement or represent one political stance. Rather, during this first generation, they came from three sources: what I call labor unionism, colorblind liberalism, and colorblind conservatism. Moreover, far from serving as a phalanx for the New Right, it was labor unionists and liberals—not conservatives—who led the opposition. Although all three groups shared some of the same arguments (and often found themselves on the same side of "reverse discrimination" litigation), they engaged in their own brands of opposition to affirmative action, which were built on unique class positions, views of the state, and understandings of the "rights revolution." To be sure, they did not engage in open conflict with each other, but the three strands of opposition tended to work independently. I argue that, in the long run, this lack of unity diluted their strength and capacity. In the decade and a half before *Bakke*, when affirmative action was conceptually, constitutionally, and politically up for grabs, however, they made their mark on emerging policies.

We know little about their efforts. This is surprising, given the regular diet of anti–affirmative action commentaries on talk radio and cable news networks as well as the large output of books and articles (a quick search in the Education Full Text Data Base from H. W. Wilson, a publisher of reference materials, generated 1,569 hits on the subject). Much of the content, however, is polemical in nature or given over to the study of specific cases or legal developments. Until recently, historical works on affirmative action examined almost exclusively judicial and executive branch developments in explaining the emergence of race- and gender-sensitive programs. With renewed interest in political history in the last few years, scholars have turned their attention to the origins of affirmative action by focusing on the grassroots pressure of civil rights activists and feminists on policymakers and judges. The study of affirmative action is now in full bloom: some books deal with its pre-1960s roots, others look at the shifts in political and partisan culture that made preferential policies possible in the late 1960s, and still others consider how political and legal institutions helped to frame policies.

For all the variety of their contributions, these works offer only a fleeting treatment of this early opposition, usually folding "reverse discrimination" protests into the rise of the New Right. A full consideration of the range and significance of affirmative action opposition before *Bakke* eludes us. Some older works offer the "Nixon hardhat" as the archetypal opponent of equal opportunity; studies of "white backlash" of the 1960s and 1970s take opposition to liberalism seriously but focus on the neighborhood, not the workplace or campus, as the locus of discontent. The few historians in the last decade who consider the opposition to affirmative action beyond the textbook accounts of *Bakke* tend to work within the confines of "whiteness studies." They claim that opponents drew on their "white" identity and the privileges it bestowed in the form of psychological and economic benefits as an underlying reason for opposing affirmative action. Where pre-1965 forms of "whiteness" were visible in the raw racism of segregation and violence, "whiteness" scholars argue that, in recent U.S. history, it has taken a more hidden, but powerful, form in appeals to colorblindness, meritocracy, and individual rights. "The racialized nature of social policy in the United States since the Great Depression has actually increased the possessive investment in whiteness among European Americans over the past five decades," writes historian George Lipsitz. The calls for individual rights and colorblindness, Lipsitz contends, served as "a cover for coordinated collective group interests." For all their flashes of insight into the workings of race and gender in the writing of policy, however, there is surprisingly little room in this approach for exploring the context in which opponents put forth their argument. The reasons for their opposition are frequently assumed rather than demonstrated.[5]

The diverse reactions to affirmative action that I analyze in this book should warn us away from dismissing opponents as simply agents of "whiteness" or defenders of masculine privilege. Many Americans, even white Americans, were quite undecided about the matter. In fact, the majority of the public over the course of the last forty-five years remains conflicted about the validity of preference programs. While some opponents were motivated to preserve their privileged status, others understood the seriousness of discrimination's effects and sought to find an alternative to existing affirmative action policies. This perspective would not fit well with the rigid nature of today's organized opposition, but it does reflect the American public's more nuanced views on equal employment opportunity. In a study of public opinion polling on affirmative action from 1970 to 1995, two sociologists report that, far from positioning themselves clearly on either side of the affirmative action debate, Americans generally backed strong remedial affirmative action measures—known as "soft" affirmative action—while tending to reject the "hard" affirmative action of quotas. But even in these cases, they have hesitated to reject programs outright, choosing instead to look for openings in the wording to allow for programs that address inequality. Over the decades, poll respondents viewed affirmative action measures in higher education admissions more favorably than those in hiring and promotion schemes. Their support increased significantly if the recipients were not restricted to African Americans. Therefore, the tendency to present social relations in what Vron Ware has called a "stark duotone imagery" does not sufficiently capture the ways differently situated opponents reacted differently to demands for equality. Just as there were various forms of affirmative action, so, too, were there various campaigns of opposition. This, in turn, forces us to consider the roots of the varying levels of support Americans give affirmative action today.[6]

Although the affirmative action debate drew in increasingly large numbers of Americans during these years, the protests themselves were narrower in two ways. First, despite claiming such a large share of our politics and law, those claiming to be victims of "reverse discrimination" were in only two kinds of employment: unionized labor and higher education employment and admissions. In these workplaces with a focus on aptitude test scores, promotion exam results, grades, apprenticeship training credentials, and seniority ranking, the ideal of meritocracy was treated as inviolable. Rebuffed applicants, presenting themselves as victims of affirmative action, argued that preferences constituted a kind of favoritism that diluted the importance of individual rights and qualifications. They could file discrimination charges and lawsuits, lobby administrators and policymakers, and generally complain about their situation. These avenues of complaint were considerably less available in other kinds of employment. In the military, for example, promotions boards since the 1970s succeeded in instituting what many experts consider model affirmative action programs through a military system of command that operates largely outside the civil court system. So too in the nonunion private sector, affirmative action "victims" have had little recourse to make their case. "The company which determines that it should employ more Negroes can make its own choice of how to go about this," explained one legal scholar in 1966. Unlike in unions and higher education, there was far less transparency or use of quantifiable methods for assessing hiring and promotion applications. In practice, the corporate world has embraced affirmative action both in order to avoid discrimination lawsuits from minority men and women of all races and to benefit from the positive effects that diversity brings.[7]

Second, although affirmative action regulations have, over time, included Native Americans, Asian Americans, Hispanics, women, and—more recently—the disabled, opponents tailored their legal challenges around the legitimacy of African Americans as recipients. This is not surprising, argues sociologist John Skrentny, given that the perception of government policymakers in the mid-1960s was that African Americans were severely disadvantaged compared to whites and were morally worthy of antidiscrimination laws. Thus, they designed affirmative action for African Americans. This explains why opponents, who did not ignore other recipient groups entirely, looked to the history of black and white relations in developing their foundational understanding of equality. I do not mean to slight the important place in the history of affirmative action of recipients who were not black. On occasion, the struggle veered into debates over which of the other recipient groups was deserving of preferences. Although these served in an immediate way as a strategy to divide affirmative action supporters, they did reveal barely concealed anxieties about the effects of the dramatic reordering of social relations begun in the tumultuous 1960s. This was true especially for women, since feminists led the way in pushing for the creation of strong affirmative action guidelines, particularly in higher education. Where "reverse discrimination" protests took the form of hostility to women hired or promoted in a specific program, however, the debates in the media, the lobbying of policymakers and politicians, and the anti–affirmative action litigation focused for the most part on the admissions, hiring, or promotions of African Americans.[8]

Protesting Affirmative Action is structured in a chronological fashion around the various efforts, beginning in the 1960s, of labor liberals, colorblind liberals, and colorblind conservatives to oppose affirmative action. Despite their considerable differences, all three opposition strands wore the imprint of mid-twentieth-century liberalism. The first part of the book takes up the origins of labor union opposition. Postwar liberals decried racial inequality and condemned irrationality, in general, embracing individual rights and procedural protections for citizens as paramount to a just society. Many labor leaders and other New Deal liberals had preferred a more vigorous political program that would have undertaken structural economic reforms and pursued the redistribution of wealth and power. With the resurgence of Republican support and the rise of more moderate liberalism within the Democratic Party by the late 1940s, the likelihood of such ambitious change was gone; in its place came government measures to spur mass consumption accompanied by measures to protect consumers and a modest welfare safety net for those Americans who did not benefit from the long period of strong economic growth in the two decades following the end of World War II. After the passage of the aggressively antiunion Taft-Hartley Act in 1947, a series of bruising strikes, and the effects of Cold War anticommunism, American labor leaders settled for the generous contracts the rank and file enjoyed and the political power they still wielded within the Democratic Party.[9]

The public face of a chastened but still robust labor movement masked major divisions between "labor conservatives" and "labor liberals." Labor conservatives, especially those in southern local union branches, as well as the members of the skilled and construction trade unions affiliated with the American Federation of Labor, recoiled at the social turmoil of the 1960s. They looked with resentment on claims for racial and gender equality in the workplace, and they resisted ending exclusionary labor practices as required by the law. Labor conservatives experienced affirmative action as a loss of privilege, status, and traditional family and ethnic mutualism. Within labor and the Democratic Party, they contrasted sharply with labor liberals, many of whom first came together in the 1930s through the Congress of Industrial Organizations. Once the merger of these two labor federations was achieved in the mid-1950s, liberal unionists were usually successful in steering the American Federation of Labor–Congress of Industrial Organizations (AFL-CIO) to back strong civil rights and, later, feminist demands in the areas of job assignment, pay, and seniority arrangements. The labor movement was then at the zenith of its power, with about one-third of the nation's nonagricultural workforce belonging to unions. Labor leaders, including AFL-CIO president George Meany, were national figures and held a prominent place within the Democratic Party.

This book begins by telling the story of how labor liberals embraced civil rights legislation in the belief that it would clear away pockets of discrimination at the local level while leaving routine labor relations undisturbed. Labor support—both from the AFL-CIO as well as from constituent unions like the United Automobile Workers and United Steel Workers—was critical in pushing bills through Congress. These unions did yeoman duty in lobbying legislators and educating rank-and-file unionists. Their most important contribution to shepherding Title VII to passage was in countering Alabama Senator J. Lister Hill's suggestion that it would result in quotas. "The bill does not require 'racial balance' on a job. It does not upset seniority rights already obtained from any employee," promised the federation's legal department. Lister's interpretation of the bill, in this view, was a "figment of the imagination . . . or result[s] from misunderstandings of the bill and existing law."[10]

When, just a few years later, Hill's forecast seemed to be coming true, labor liberals nevertheless endorsed affirmative action programs. They did so haltingly, often in the face of pressure from activists both inside and outside unions as well as of executive orders and court orders. On a certain level it was not difficult for them to back affirmative action: outside of construction and skilled trades unions, few labor organizations oversaw the hiring of employees. They were, in effect, giving their approval for something outside their purview. Still, some labor liberal leaders needed prodding, since their unions contained small but influential sections of skilled workers who resisted affirmative action mandates. Moreover, labor leaders worried about the effect of race- and gender-sensitive programs on a diverse labor movement where worker solidarity, not targeted preferences, was still a powerful unifying code. They spent their lobbying resources on labor law reform and full employment legislation, not affirmative action. Unionists had a general unease with the way that the judicial and administrative machinery of affirmative action operated separately from the industrial relations regime as overseen by the National Labor Relations Board. This left them to deal with two administrative systems, the one familiar and geared toward traditional collective bargaining practices, the other new, regulatory in nature, and often hostile to these practices and likely to make unions as much as employers liable for legal judgments.

The debate that raged in those early years—over where the rights of unionists ended and those of affirmative action recipients began—left labor without a clearly established rationale for opposition. The most dramatic part of the opposition campaign came in the face of massive layoffs in the recession of the mid-1970s, as labor liberals positioned themselves alongside labor conservatives when affirmative action advocates, in an effort to avoid the discharge of recently hired affirmative action recipients, attempted to modify the seniority principle of "last hired, first fired." Suddenly, the labor liberals switched sides, claiming that policymakers were violating time-honored principles that benefited all workers, irrespective of race. They pressed the federal government to abandon plans to establish "reverse seniority" policies and mounted legal challenges to those local efforts that were already under way. During these middle years of this first wave of opposition, a united labor movement put the future of affirmative action in serious doubt.

The focus of the book then shifts to the concurrent attack of colorblind liberals on the use of numerical goals in institutions of higher education. At the core of their anti–affirmative action message lay a belief that racial or gender differences should have no effect on the prospects of a job applicant. Colorblind liberalism was grounded in defense of individual rights and the premise that an applicant's merit should be the basis for his or her rewards. Its foundational text was Gunnar Myrdal's *An American Dilemma,* a book that, when it appeared in 1944, came to define the mainstream liberal view of equality and race relations in postwar America. Its author, a Swedish economist, explained the nation's record of persistent racism as in conflict with its ideals of individual freedom and democracy. The force of these positive qualities, he argued, was destined to extinguish inequality. "The conquering of color caste . . . is America's own innermost desire," Myrdal assured his readers. "People are all much alike on a fundamental level. And they are all good people. They want to be rational and just."[11]

This perspective suited the political and economic conditions of the postwar era: there was no place for discrimination in a period with a rapidly growing middle class, an unprecedented expansion in higher education, and a tense struggle for security against the Soviet Union. With discrimination against Catholics and Jewish "white ethnics" disappearing rapidly and suburban growth washing away old prejudices, so too with race discrimination. Many colorblind liberals found Myrdal's reduction of racial inequality to pockets of bigotry and individual racist attitudes to be a bit too simplistic, but they nevertheless held that strong federal and state civil rights measures, combined with robust economic growth, would defeat what were, to many liberal Republicans and Democrats, irrational and unpatriotic tendencies. There was a deep-seated optimism to this perspective, one that revealed itself in the hundreds of "intergroup relations committees" that sprang up in communities across the country. Even though few local and state governments passed substantial fair employment laws during the years leading up to the passage of the Civil Rights Act of 1964, civil rights allies were feeling the wind at their back as they set forth to eradicate racial inequality.[12]

As a matter of liberal faith, they supported broad welfare state policies as a means of opening up opportunity and reducing inequality. This was what British sociologist T. H. Marshall at the time called the "social rights," to distinguish from the older civil and political rights of eighteenth- and nineteenth-century liberalism.[13] During this high water mark of postwar liberalism, colorblind liberals rejected policies that relied on racial identity or proportionality. According to the National Association for the Advancement of Colored People's Jack Greenberg, "The chief problem with quotas ... is that they introduce a potentially retrogressive concept into the cherished notion of equality." Thurgood Marshall, the NAACP's chief counsel until he became a federal appeals court judge in 1961 (and, in 1967, a U.S. Supreme Court justice), confirmed that the organization "strongly oppose[d] any idea that would distinguish colored citizens as a unique or separate group apart from the rest of the American people." Many of these notable civil rights figures would come to endorse "hard" affirmative action, including the NAACP's labor director, Herbert Hill, who had once characterized quotas and preferential treatment proposals in the late 1950s as "a sugar-coated form of segregation."[14]

This consensus held as late as 1963. In an article that year in the Jesuit weekly magazine *America* entitled "Rights, not Ratios," the author reminded readers that African Americans had a right to expect strong federal antidiscrimination measures, "but what he cannot ask is discrimination in his favor or that other workers be dismissed to provide a job for him." Myrdal weighed in on the issue that same year at a roundtable discussion on "Liberalism and the Negro": "I don't think Negroes are going to be given preferential treatment. ... I think it would be most unfortunate if they were." Affirmative action won few converts at first. The U.S. Commission on Civil Rights, which by the late 1960s would become one of the staunchest supporters of "hard" affirmative action, joined labor unions and other supporters of civil rights legislation in insisting that the bill "only requires that employers, labor unions, and employment agencies treat all persons on the basis of their merit and ability and without regard to their race, color, religion, or national origin."[15]

When this postwar consensus broke, it put much of the leadership and rank and file of American Jewish civic and religious organizations at the forefront of the colorblind liberal opposition. This was not surprising, since American Jews, individually and organizationally, were an important part of postwar liberalism. They had provided key support to the civil rights movement and other liberal causes. Although there was still labor market discrimination against Jews during this period, anti-Semitism saw a decline alongside a booming economy and rapid growth in the higher education system from which they benefited greatly as they took up faculty positions and participated fully in the professional occupations. American Jews rejected affirmative action programs, especially those in higher education, on the grounds that it would return the country to the exclusionary practices that had kept religious and ethnic group members out of the most prestigious institutions for so long. Affirmative action, they argued, was a retreat from individual rights and the rewarding of merit. It was bad for the economy and a grave injustice.

Nevertheless, colorblind liberals saw themselves more as reformers than as affirmative action opponents per se. They rejected programs that contained numerical goals or quotas but promoted the wide range of remedial programs that became known as "soft" affirmative action. This was a difficult position to hold by the end of the 1960s, a period of mounting unemployment and increased competition for college and university admissions and faculty positions. Amid the growing strength of identity politics, colorblind liberals struggled to find the right formula for ensuring equality of opportunity but not equality of outcome. It became even thornier as more Americans stepped forward, including "white ethnics," to demand that the government include them in hiring and admissions policies. In the late 1960s and early 1970s, Jewish organizations lobbied the federal government to revise affirmative action guidelines, forwarded the "reverse discrimination" complaints flowing into their offices over to the government, and engaged in fierce debate with affirmative action supporters over where to draw legal and ethical lines when addressing inequality. At the same time, some opponents softened their position, allowing that numerical goals might be used on a limited and temporary basis. The old liberal and civil rights alliance faced implosion, as the two sides became locked in conflict over the specific wording of affirmative action policies and the larger significance of compensatory justice.

As the book's two case studies illustrate, the challenges of colorblind liberals and labor unionists in the mid-1970s to correct what they understood to be affirmative action's flaws were only partially successful. The first case study looks at *DeFunis v. Odegaard*, a lawsuit considered by the U.S. Supreme Court in 1974 and the first "reverse discrimination" case. The simmering conflict between the higher education affirmative action supporters and opponents was exposed when Marco DeFunis, an unsuccessful law school applicant, filed a lawsuit against the University of Washington charging the university with denying him admissions while welcoming some two dozen minority students with lower test scores. A host of organizations and individuals rushed to file amicus briefs of support for both sides. These included especially Jewish American organizations whose ranks were split over whether the university's program was unjust and whether the cost of opposing old allies was worth defending the colorblind principle. The adversarial nature of the lawsuit, however, left little room for a thorough airing of the nuances of the colorblind liberal position. Although they did not retreat from their general outlook, the *DeFunis* case was a bruising experience that revealed the fuzziness of the anti–affirmative action stance within Jewish groups.[16]

The second case study looks at the "reverse discrimination" protests in the Detroit Police Department, one of the many by police officers and firefighters that cropped up across the country at the time. If the Detroit protests garnered more media attention for their intense, occasionally violent nature than other such actions, it was nevertheless representative of the growing portrayal of white men as affirmative action victims. Where just a half-decade earlier they might have dismissed the resistance of labor conservatives as a crude expression of disgruntlement, many Americans, troubled by bad economic times, began to take more seriously the placement of merit examinations and seniority over race- and gender-sensitive criteria. Significantly, men and women unionists of all races in Detroit and elsewhere lined up in defense of white police officers against civil rights leaders and feminists. Although the white and male-dominated police unions failed to thwart most municipal affirmative action plans, they persevered over the course of the second half of the 1970s and the 1980s and succeeded in limiting affirmative action programs to hiring and promotion and not firing.

Colorblind conservatism's gradual eclipse of labor liberalism and colorblind liberalism in the second half of the 1970s was largely rooted in the inability of affirmative action opponents to gain a foothold in a Democratic Party that had become closely identified with public interest organizations and centrist politicians who had little affinity with the ambitious legislative spirit characteristic of the New Deal and Great Society years. During the presidential administrations of Richard Nixon and Gerald Ford, moderate Republicans staved off attacks on affirmative action; despite his strained relationship with civil rights leaders and feminists, Jimmy Carter put his administration solidly behind affirmative action in *Bakke*. Carter was a new kind of Democrat: his brand of post-1960s politics joined conservative fiscal policies and support for deregulation and what political scientist Jeffrey Berry calls "post-materialist" liberalism centered on such elements as environmentalism, good government, consumer protection, and social rights. Labor liberals and colorblind liberals may have reflected better the public's outlook on the contentious issue, but their ambiguity concerning race- and gender-sensitive programs did not translate well in Congress and presidential administrations during this period.[17]

As they faded in influence, in their place came the colorblind conservative ideology with its clear and powerful message. It emphasized market forces and meritocracy over what conservatives viewed as unconstitutional public policies predicated on a kind of racial and gender "spoils system." They rejected the open racism of the extreme right but refused to accept the proposition that underlying structures of inequality had persisted in a significant way after the demise of Jim Crow. Before focusing on affirmative action, colorblind conservatives had honed their message in campaigns in the suburban "New South" against busing in the early 1970s. This message increasingly drew support from the growing electoral fortunes of the New Right and was taken up by a network of conservative law professors, economists, politicians, and foundation heads, who began to bankroll "reverse discrimination" litigation. Their natural constituency was the suburban middle-class professional who had embraced consumerism, home ownership, and bans on de jure discrimination—not southern white vigilantes or sullen northern white workers. Where colorblind liberals sought to chart a middle path that was attentive to racial and gender inequality, their conservative counterparts rejected any policies that implicated them in remedying past and present inequality.[18]

There has been no other controversy in modern American history quite like affirmative action. This is true not just on account of its duration but also for the multiple ways it has shaped our understanding of the rights revolution. Americans have been fond of professing support for equality, especially since the mid-twentieth century. That they could not fix on an exact means to achieve this goal—or even what it might look like once it had been secured—can be seen in the variety of opposition that cropped up after 1965. Affirmative action gave rise to a "unique moral debate," writes philosopher Michel Rosenfeld, since, unlike other vexing issues such as abortion, supporters and opponents alike have used remarkably similar legal and ethical vocabularies. As this book makes clear, this "intramural debate among partisans of equality" manifested itself in hard-fought struggles over jobs, promotions, and admissions. It revealed as well the conflicting ways in which affirmative action opponents attempted to put their stamp on law and policy at the end of the civil rights era.[19]

CHAPTER ONE

"The Best 'Affirmative Action Program' Is Creating Jobs for Everyone"

Organized Labor Responds to Affirmative Action, 1960–1974

Even as the first recognizable affirmative action programs were emerging in the mid-1960s, the American labor movement was engaged in a more public and longstanding effort to address racial and gender exclusion, segregation, and inequality in the nation's workplaces and union halls. The history of the Chicago musicians' union was typical. As the laid-off members of the CBS Orchestra protested their layoffs, the leaders of the American Federation of Musicians (AFM) union locals were facing serious challenges to their routine practices from black members and civil rights advocates. White musicians, complained a black AFM member in Detroit, received "all of the choice jobs with little or no efforts being advanced by the local to remedy a most disgraceful economic situation." In some cities, there were separate locals for black and white musicians. This was a practice that AFM leaders, assisted by staff members at the American Federation of Labor–Congress of Industrial Organizations (AFL-CIO), had worked to end since the 1950s. "The situation is a fairly complex one," admitted one federation staff member in 1962. "In some cases there has been great difficulty in convincing both the white and Negro locals to merge." This was especially true in Chicago, where the AFM invoked trusteeship supervision over the merger process. At the ceremony marking the completion of the merger in 1966, a Chicago priest told unionists and distinguished guests (including Mayor Richard J. Daley) that their success was "an example for the nation as . . . [it] makes its way toward an integrated society, where all people will be judged on merit and fitness."[1]

While much of the nation's attention remained fixed on the segregated South, policymakers and civil rights activists had long considered the racially exclusive skilled trades and construction unions to be significant obstacles to improving the economic status of African Americans. The effort to remove these obstacles required a long struggle, one that lacked the kind of drama that makes newspaper headlines and was intermittently punctuated by the promise of strong, antidiscriminatory measures. In many unions there were only a few black members (in some, none at all), and they usually worked at the lowest-paid jobs and received the worst referrals. The National Association for the Advancement of Colored People's (NAACP) Herbert Hill reported in 1959 on "a broad exclusion of Negro youth from apprenticeship training programs jointly conducted by industrial management and labor unions in the North as well as in the South." Despite its limitations, civil rights supporters welcomed the ban on race and sex discrimination contained in Title VII of the Civil Rights Act of 1964 as an important legal tool to right this exclusion and unequal treatment.[2]

Although affirmative action advocates viewed race and gender hiring and training programs as a reasonable extension of these antidiscrimination efforts, labor leaders in these early years of affirmative action offered multiple reasons for rejecting plans containing numerical goals or quotas. They claimed that such plans diluted skill levels by bringing poorly trained workers on jobs, frustrated the practice of recruiting family members, burdened the current workforce for the past misdeeds of others, and failed to create new jobs or increase wages. Alongside this mix of principled and parochial objections was the notion that, in its enforcement of equal opportunity, the government had created an administrative and judicial framework hostile to labor unions. When legislators were drafting what would become Title VII, union leaders had lobbied for an equal employment agency that would be located in the Labor Department and would have strong enforcement powers along the lines of the National Labor Relations Board (NLRB), which oversaw industrial relations disputes. What they received instead was the considerably weaker Equal Employment Opportunity Commission. The EEOC, housed in the Justice Department, could hold hearings, investigate discrimination complaints, and issue findings, but it could not issue cease-and-desist orders. Complainants then had the option of filing a lawsuit against the offending employer or union. The new law also placed the legal means for charging discrimination out of the familiar industrial relations realm. According to political scientist Paul Frymer, many of the lawyers representing aggrieved minorities were often "tied to corporate power" since they were representing their clients pro bono alongside their normal corporate practices. The judges, Frymer notes, "ignored labor laws, and thus issues such as collective bargaining, majority representation, seniority, and security agreements that were not addressed in anti-discrimination laws." Unions scrambled to adjust to this new layer of government oversight. "The once tight little ship of private adjudication," one industrial relations expert observed in 1971, "is indeed becoming a leaky vessel."[3]

This chapter deals with the efforts of labor leaders in the early years of affirmative action to reconcile race- and gender-sensitive plans with the prevailing industrial relations order. In a widely distributed pamphlet, the AFL-CIO Executive Council in 1966 called the EEOC "a new and vitally important tool to strengthen labor's program to ensure fair and equal employment opportunity." Nevertheless, they insisted that the primary means of ensuring workplace equality would be by "negotiating non-discrimination clauses in all collective bargaining contracts and utilizing these clauses in all stages of the collective bargaining procedure." As the number of race and sex discrimination complaints piled up and costly litigation drained their coffers, concerned labor leaders argued that expansionary fiscal policies and legislation to boost workers' employment and income levels were superior to affirmative action. "We take the position that the best 'affirmative action program' is creating jobs for everyone," William Pollard, the head of the federation's Civil Rights Department (CRD), told U.S. Assistant Attorney General Drew Days in the mid-1970s.[4]

The labor movement was badly divided on the issue. Skilled trades and construction unions rejected a series of Johnson administration pilot "city plans" requiring affirmative action in all federal contracts. This opposition became a political flashpoint when, in 1969, the Nixon administration put one of the proposed plans, the Philadelphia Plan, into action. Industrial unions were more welcoming of affirmative action. This receptivity was rooted in the fact that industrial unions, unlike skilled trades and construction unions, did not, for the most part, oversee the hiring process. Their rank-and-file membership consisted largely of agricultural and factory workers whose elected officials and staff members were committed to the "social unionism" of the 1930s and 1940s in which the labor movement played a defining role in promoting political and economic democracy. Although labor's postwar success in securing generous wages and benefits for its members through a routinized collective bargaining regime sapped social unionism of its vitality, industrial union leaders such as Walter Reuther of the United Automobile Workers (UAW) remained at the forefront of the struggle for civil rights, antipoverty programs, urban renewal, and education reform. Even Reuther and like-minded unionists faced criticism from their members to move more forcefully against pockets of workplace discrimination (especially the skilled workers they represented) and to practice affirmative action in hiring union staff and running candidates for executive board positions.[5]

Labor liberals were very slow to address gender inequality. In the two decades following World War II, union leaders (and many women unionists) continued to support the protective laws for women passed early in the twentieth century. These measures may have helped women workers avoid the worst aspects of industrial labor in some cases, but they also prohibited them from drawing overtime pay and securing higher-paying jobs. Industrial—not to mention skilled trades—union leaders were largely resistant to pleas from the growing number of women members that their organizations revise their stance on protectionism and that they include women in staff and leadership positions that reflected their increased workforce participation. Women pressed their demands by filing Title VII discrimination complaints over job typing by sex, unequal wage rates, and separate seniority lists. No labor union was immune from sex or race discrimination charges. Startled labor liberals, noted the NAACP's Hill, "did not anticipate the extent to which labor unions would come under attack once Title VII went into effect." Determined activists formed interunion organizations such as the Coalition of Black Trade Unionists (CBTU) and the Coalition of Labor Union Women (CLUW) and brought their own unions as well as the AFL-CIO to support, among other things, affirmative action.[6]

Liberal unionists' support for affirmative action, however, was not openended. Although they differed with conservative unionists in the late 1960s and early 1970s, they closed ranks with them in the mid-1970s when policymakers attempted to expand affirmative action beyond hiring and promotion to include a reversal of the hallowed seniority precept of "last hired, first fired." Industrial unionists had forged the seniority system in the crucible of the Great Depression. Union members had come to see it, as historian Nelson Lichtenstein puts it, as "part of the moral economy of the work regime"; it represented the most important "property" interest a worker held in his job. To be sure, union leaders and employers violated the seniority principle on occasion—most notably in regard to women workers at the end of World War II when they created departmental or unit seniority to shut women and minorities out of high-paying jobs. Challenges to seniority systems after the passage of Title VII, however, led to modifications in procedures for counting years of service and for granting retroactive seniority to specific classes of discrimination victims. Unionists might disagree with each other about what form "last hired, first fired" should take, but they were steadfast in their loyalty to seniority. The issue caught fire when the media reported on the clash—at a time of mounting unemployment—between the "rights revolution" and "labor rights." The conflict over seniority challenged both labor's vitality and the future of affirmative action.[7]

Union Discrimination and the Growing Force of Antidiscrimination Law

Shortly before the implementation of the "Philadelphia Plan," Herbert Hill reviewed labor's intransigence to civil rights initiatives for members of a congressional committee on federal contract compliance. Hill's focus that day was on the building trades. "These 'manly' jobs with their high status implications are especially important for Negro male workers who are so frequently either denied employment or permitted to work only in low-paying menial 'dead-end' jobs," he reported. Hill and others argued that unions had made little progress in this area. In the early 1960s in Pittsburgh, for example, African Americans made up nearly 17 percent of the city's population but held only 4.7 percent of construction industry jobs. (Of those, 65 percent were workers in low-paying laborer and plasterer jobs.) In the wake of demonstrations, meetings with city officials, and a Pennsylvania Human Relations Commission order that the city's seven all-white locals begin admitting blacks to membership and apprenticeship training, only four minority applicants took the apprenticeship examination. Of that group, two passed, but one of them ended up leaving the training program. Pittsburgh's dismal record was similar to other cities across the country. In 1961, the U.S. Commission on Civil Rights concluded that "most international unions have failed to exhibit any profound concerns over civil rights."[8]

Union officials promised to end discrimination. According to a report compiled by the Labor Department, Pittsburgh labor leaders went so far as to "allow an impartial observer to verify the administration of [apprentice] skill tests, to furnish on request written reports on the number and disposition of applications by non-whites." In Cincinnati and St. Louis, the heads of skilled trades unions agreed to establish a fair practices committee with civil rights representatives; in Chicago, they promised to work with vocational education departments at area high schools in order to increase the pool of potential apprentices. For the most part, union officials promised little more than to end discriminatory practices (although in Trenton, New Jersey, they did accept five black journeymen and two black apprentices). Many unions refused even to provide basic information on the racial composition of their memberships. More than two-thirds of the labor organizations contacted by the federal government for such information did not submit their survey, and those that did left out important information. In response to this slow pace of change, civil rights activists launched protests against building trades unions at publicly funded construction sites in New York City, Philadelphia, Cleveland, and Elizabeth, New Jersey. "Union discrimination against Negroes appears to be leading to a crisis," warned the *New York Times* in 1963.[9]

Industrial union leaders faced sharp criticism as well. Before the merger of the two labor federations in 1955, the CIO and its constituent industrial unions carried the social unionist banner against segregationist legislators, recalcitrant employers, and some of their own members who had engaged in work stoppages to keep African Americans out of coveted jobs. Although their record of integration and promotion of racial equality was superior to almost every other public institution or organization—including the AFL—their civil rights record did not match their rhetoric. In the late 1940s, industrial union officers worked hard to bring rank-and-file members into the NAACP and lobbied the NLRB to refuse union certification to any local that either barred or segregated workers on the basis of their race. Their relationship with some civil rights leaders, however, soured in the 1950s. This may have been due, in part, to clashing personalities as well as the effects that Cold War anticommunism had on each movement. In a few cases, NAACP staff members intervened in fierce elections among CIO, AFL, and independent unions. Despite industrial unions' impressive civil rights record, disparities between black and white industrial workers persisted. In the UAW, for example, the proportion of African Americans in skilled trades departments stood at 2 percent, the same as in AFL-based unions. (Black UAW staffers dubbed these departments "the Deep South" of the UAW.) Although several industrial unions, including the United Packinghouse Workers and the Transport Workers, had black officers on their highest governing bodies, not a single African American served on the UAW's twenty-two-person international executive board (IEB). Labor leaders explained that they were making steady progress on union race relations; to many black unionists, the commitment seemed shallow. White union officers "preached liberalism to us," observed one black union activist, but then offered only their NAACP membership as proof of their dedication to civil rights.[10]

Civil rights critics of the labor movement greeted with optimism the wave of federal equal employment opportunity measures in the first half of the 1960s. One of the first was President John F. Kennedy's 1961 Executive Order 10925, which instructed federal contractors to take "affirmative action" in assigning contracts. Kennedy created the President's Commission on Equal Employment Opportunity (CEEO) to enforce his order. Two years later Kennedy issued EO 11114, which extended EO 10925 to cover employment on federally financed construction projects. That same year, women activists—with considerable labor union support—succeeded in bringing Congress and the Kennedy administration to pass the Equal Pay Act of 1963. Then came Title VII. That the EEOC received some ten thousand complaints during its first year in existence (about 25 percent dealt with sex discrimination) underscored the persistence of workplace discrimination. Just two years after it became law, the EEOC investigated charges of labor union discrimination in 658 cases—the number would nearly double by 1971. It was proof to many that the problem was widespread but solvable.[11]

Even before the government enacted Title VII, some civil rights leaders proposed hiring measures that resembled affirmative action. "Token integration and pilot placement in business, industry, and government is not enough," insisted the National Urban League's Whitney Young in 1963. Since employers had failed to consider black applicants for so long, Young reasoned, "their institutions must now recruit qualified Negro employees and give preference to their employment." In effect, he concluded, they should "employ Negroes because they are Negroes." Just a few months before Young made his comments, the Congress of Racial Equality's (CORE) national council instructed its local chapters to make "very specific demands which far exceed tokenism." They explained that "we used to talk simply of merit employment. . . . Now, National CORE is talking in terms of 'compensatory hiring.'" Although such an idea was out of step with the dominant colorblind liberalism of the period, this form of proto–affirmative action was rooted in protests dating back to at least the "Don't Buy Where You Can't Work" campaign against chain stores of the 1930s. The attention to racial proportionality in employment consideration persisted in the demand of the "Progressive Citizens of America" in the late 1940s that Lucky Stores in California create a workforce whose racial composition matched that of their customers; in the "Harlem Liquor Boycott" a decade later; and in the Philadelphia boycott of the early 1960s organized by some four hundred black ministers against Sunoco Gas, Pepsi, Breyers Ice Cream, and the Tasty Baking Company, producers of Tastykake. Even the members of Dwight Eisenhower's Committee on Government Contracts in 1960 encouraged contractors to hire black workers on a "limited preferential basis."[12]

At a time when civil rights supporters were fighting against racial violence and working to provide formal access to public accommodations, schools, and the voting booth, this perspective on equal employment opportunity garnered little official support. Young denied that he wanted quotas. Nevertheless, he did argue that it was "essential that there be conscious preferment to help them catch up." Kennedy, the first U.S. president to use the term *affirmative action*, dismissed any notion of quotas or numerical goals at an August 1963 press conference: "I think it is a mistake to begin to assign quotas on a basis of religion, or race, or color, or nationality. I think we'd get into a good deal of trouble." What was needed, he went on, was to give "everyone a fair chance. But not hard and fast quotas." When a group of protestors brought construction of the Downstate Medical Center in Brooklyn and the Rutgers Housing Project in Manhattan to a standstill after officials rejected a demand that 25 percent of the construction jobs go to black workers, the *New York Times* characterized it as a " 'quota system' [that] disregards qualifications, at best leads only to token jobs and is obviously discrimination in reverse." One New York councilman from Manhattan wrote to the newspaper that "the current wave of 'head counts' on employment according to race is to be deplored." Labor leaders weighed in on the issue as well. "If the Negroes were asking for something more than equal opportunity, I think that would be crazy, and I would oppose that," stated Walter Reuther. A. Phillip Randolph, veteran union leader and head of the Negro American Labor Council, said that the idea smacked of "Jim Crowism in reverse."[13]

Ironically, the policy rationale for race- and gender-sensitive programs was set by the CEEO's colorblind antidiscriminatory efforts. In order to demonstrate compliance with EO 10925, government offices and the affected contractors submitted comprehensive data on the racial composition of their workforce. The CEEO's review and publication of the collected data drew policymakers and employers away from the task of processing individual complaints and toward a consideration of broad employment patterns and, in the parlance of the early 1960s, the underutilization of manpower. Although the meaning of "affirmative action" remained fuzzy, some public officials and employers were gravitating toward the view that setting hiring goals or quotas was appropriate. Kennedy himself began to push cabinet members to explain their lack of progress in appointing African Americans to senior positions. In the wake of CEEO hearings, some businesses began to hire more black job applicants for fear of losing government contracts; in the commission's first year alone, federal agencies hired almost eleven thousand blacks.[14]

As social unrest in northern ghettoes grew, so too did calls for more aggressive affirmative action. "What is daily becoming harder to see is how, if quotas and preferential treatment are disallowed, anything which will be accomplished for Negro employment," cautioned editor and liberal author Edward Chase. Some advocates addressed in a more tentative manner the need for "hard" affirmative action. Loren Miller, a Los Angeles municipal judge, began an article on the subject by making the unremarkable recommendation that the government "should embark on an intensive program to encourage Negro application for jobs." Miller pushed further, however, suggesting that the government encourage employers ("'pressure' is probably a better word") to hire these applicants as a way of "undoing . . . a century of wrong doing." Civil rights leaders understood that the shape and character of the struggle for equality was about to change. "The proposal for preferential employment for Negroes will undoubtedly be overwhelmingly opposed by the average white person," warned NAACP general counsel Robert Carver.[15]

For all the importance historians rightly assign Lyndon Johnson for his shepherding of civil rights legislation to passage and his eloquent Howard University commencement address, his administration's understanding of affirmative action was ambiguous. In January 1964, just a month after Johnson took office, one of his White House staff members produced a summary statement on the meaning and scope of affirmative action. It was, the staff member wrote, a "relatively new concept" that meant "positive or firm or aggressive action as opposed to negative or infirm or passive action." Most of the examples offered dealt with the ban on discrimination Congress was hashing out in the Title VII legislation. There were a few "soft" affirmative action recommendations, including a call for improved schools and better vocational education programs for minorities. For the rest of the Johnson years, officials alternated between articulating the case for compensatory justice and insisting that race-neutral programs were the norm. "If an employer or union had in the past discriminated against applicants for jobs or membership on the basis of their race, it is not enough for that employer or union now just to stop discriminating," Secretary of Labor W. Willard Wirtz told community leaders in Philadelphia. "There is an affirmative responsibility to counteract the effects of the previous policy." In another speech soon after, however, Wirtz explained that he did not support a "job preference idea": "Any talk or thought about a quota kind of employment . . . would be terribly, terribly misguided."[16]

Even those at the head of federal agencies charged with overseeing affirmative action refused to subscribe to this notion. Edward Sylvester, director of the Office of Federal Contract Compliance (OFCC), was typical. President Johnson created the OFCC in September 1965 through Executive Order 11246. In doing so he dissolved the CEEO and transferred authority over government employment to the U.S. Civil Service Commission and contract compliance operations to the Labor Department; the two divisions formed the OFCC. Executive Order 11246 (amended in 1967 with EO 11375 to include "sex") promised to deliver expanded affirmative action mandates. In addition to prohibiting discrimination by federal contractors and federally assisted construction contractors and subcontractors doing over $10,000 in government business in one year (Kennedy's order had covered those doing over $50,000), it required them to "take affirmative action to ensure that applicants are employed, and that employees are treated during employment, without regard to their race, color, religion, sex, or national origin." That was not all: it also obligated contractors with fifty or more employees and contracts of $50,000 or more to implement plans to increase the participation of underrepresented minorities and women. Sylvester insisted that "there is no fixed and firm definition of affirmative action." The best he could offer—"in a general way"—was that it meant "anything you have to do to get results." He concluded that this was not necessarily a job for the federal government. "We really prefer that the contractor determine himself what affirmative action he can take," the OFCC director told a gathering of contractors in 1967.[17]

Not all administration members shared Sylvester's unwillingness to intervene. Daniel Patrick Moynihan, the Labor Department's special assistant secretary for research and policy planning, was an early advocate of the "hard" affirmative action approach. The future U.S. senator from New York attracted considerable criticism from race-conscious liberals at the time for his use of "damage imagery" as an explanation for black poverty in *The Negro Family: The Case for National Action* (1965). In his focus on the "culture of poverty" and its effect on black urban males, however, Moynihan looked to innovative hiring programs to help create black economic mobility. "The Negroes are asking for unequal treatment," he wrote Labor Secretary Wirtz. "More seriously, it may be that without unequal treatment in the immediate future there is no way to achieve anything like equal status in the long run." By the end of Johnson's presidency, there were others who defended this newer kind of affirmative action, including Anthony Rachal, a special assistant to the chairman of the U.S. Civil Service Commission. Rachal took on critics who warned that aggressive implementation of EO 11246 would destroy the merit system. "This is not the case," he insisted in a 1968 speech. "The intent is to make the merit system whole—a true merit system, one which recognizes that all groups . . . are competent and worthy and that their inclusion . . . is essential to the mandates of the merit system." Rachal pushed further, arguing that aptitude and knowledge tests were insufficient to gauge merit. He told the audience that "our determination to identify the talents of all citizens has brought about new and revised techniques and approaches for determining who is the best qualified applicant for a given job."[18]

Others in the executive branch shared Moynihan and Rachal's view. The U.S. Commission on Civil Rights (USCCR), led by Father Theodore Hesburgh, a stalwart liberal and president of the University of Notre Dame, generated a significant body of evidence on the nature of race discrimination in employment beginning in the late 1950s using public hearings and survey data. Although Hesburgh and his fellow commissioners had little formal power to address inequality, their use of the bully pulpit helped to shape the Kennedy and Johnson administrations' equal employment opportunity policies. As the 1960s wore on, the USCCR turned its sights on recently instituted policies meant to counter systemic inequality. At a November 1968 meeting, for example, the USCCR's research director shared with the commissioners the results of a study of Detroit, Philadelphia, Atlanta, San Francisco, and other large cities that showed the continuing relegation of minorities to low-paying jobs. Federal government merit criteria guidelines had failed to increase minority job opportunities. USCCR commissioner Maurice Mitchell suggested that the lack of progress was rooted in the fact that "most merit system procedures . . . are based on tactics and expectations that go back 20 or 30 years." What was needed, Mitchell concluded, was "a modernized set of systems installed which take into account the realities of contemporary existence."[19]

The EEOC, more than any other government agency at the time, took on the job of advancing race- and gender-sensitive policies. At first glance it seemed ill suited to the task, because it was hamstrung by the lack of enforcement power, faced a crushing backlog of complaints, and experienced a near-constant turnover of its commissioners during its first decade. Moreover, unlike most executive branch departments and agencies, the EEOC did not have a constituency to give it visibility, as, for example, the Labor Department did with organized labor. Federal equal employment opportunity enforcement took place across a number of executive departments, thus weakening the EEOC further. Instead of these factors rendering the new commission peripheral to equal opportunity efforts, however, its members made creative use of them to forward bold remedial proposals. Faced with Title VII's seemingly strict ban on race-based preferences or quotas, the EEOC, in the words of policy historian Hugh Davis Graham, crafted "a counter-appeal to a kind of higher-law doctrine." Congress, they argued, had a broader purpose in mind than a narrow legislative proscription would allow. Just one month after opening its doors in July 1965, EEOC representatives told a White House conference on discrimination that complaint processing and case-by-case litigation was secondary to finding solutions to patterns of social and economic disadvantage.[20]

EEOC senior staff members were instrumental in creating "hard" affirmative action. Most were self-identified liberals and trained in law or economics; few had personal or professional connections to the labor movement. Many, such as Rutgers University law professor Alfred Blumrosen, moved between federal government service and academic employments, where they had the time to develop innovative policies. Blumrosen, often working with his wife, scholar Ruth Blumrosen, combined a passion for justice alongside a sharp critique of existing state and federal civil rights enforcement mechanism. In the 1965–67 period he helped organize the EEOC and then served as its first chief of conciliation and director of federal-state relations. After only two weeks at the commission, Blumrosen proposed that the government organize a uniform national standard for reporting compliance. "The history of the period 1945–1965 makes it clear that the use of numerical standards is necessary if there is to be significant improvement in the employment opportunities," he wrote. "Milder medicine will not work."[21]

EEOC staff members who advocated for the aggressive enforcement of the prohibition on sex discrimination also helped develop an expanded definition of affirmative action. Perhaps the most important was Sonia Pressman, a Polish Jew who had fled with her family from Nazi Germany and had graduated from Cornell University and the University of Miami Law School before coming to the EEOC. At the commission she helped document disparities in employment patterns that would indicate discriminatory intent. Specifically, Pressman drafted an influential memo in 1966 that suggested that the commission use statistical data on an employer's workforce as evidence of discrimination patterns. "Statistics help us to determine the effect, if any, of laws against discrimination," she informed the "Women's Caucus" at the American Statistical Association's 1971 meeting. "They point the way towards the priorities which need to be set if change in employment patterns is the result."[22]

The various components of affirmative action came together at the EEOC. Beginning in 1965, the commission required employers to submit an "EEO-1," a single reporting form containing a breakdown of the workforce by occupation, race, and sex. Employee testing guidelines came the following year: the EEOC rejected the position that professionally developed tests were adequate on their face. Now they must focus on the specific job (or class of jobs) under consideration, not just assess "general ability." In 1968 the EEOC created grants for state and local governments to identify "disparate minority employment patterns." Once found, offending employers could face discrimination charges, hearings into their practices, conciliation efforts, and referrals to the EEOC. By 1971 some 350 state and local representatives were attending regional training sessions. The EEOC became an influential force in affirmative action litigation by providing amicus briefs and, after congressional action in 1972, filing class action lawsuits. Finally, they worked with employers, unions, and judges in crafting large-scale consent decrees that resulted in mandatory payouts as well as hiring and promotion timetables for affirmative action recipients. "We believe that the achievement of results in employment is the only adequate measure of affirmative action," EEOC chairman Clifford Alexander Jr. told Secretary of Treasury Henry Fowler in 1968.[23]

Despite all this preparatory work, the Johnson administration never instituted hiring plans with numerical goals. Much to the chagrin of labor leaders, Labor Department officials proposed a series of policy experiments for the construction industry in St. Louis, San Francisco, Cleveland, and Philadelphia. The requirements varied in each city. Philadelphia had the most far-reaching plan in its specification of how many minorities must be hired and into which positions they were to be placed on federally funded projects. This came to be known as the Philadelphia Plan. Labor Secretary Wirtz appeared before an AFL-CIO Building and Construction Trades Department convention to calm union leaders: "I want to make it dead clear that I think it is an error to approach this problem . . . in terms that mean a required number of people, one or more Negroes or whites or anybody else as being required on every single situation . . . is simply the wrong approach to the problem, and we have got to find a better one." Faced with labor union resistance, as well as a declaration by U.S. Comptroller General Elmer Staats that it violated Title VII, Labor Department officials shelved the Philadelphia Plan.[24]

The new Republican administration of Richard Nixon dusted it off in June 1969. In order to get around Title VII's ban on quotas, government officials required that employers meet numerical goals that would raise the percentage of minorities in affected trades from the then-meager 1.6 percent to at least 4 percent the next year and 19 percent by 1973. Scholars have correctly connected Nixon's embrace of affirmative action as part of his shrewd campaign to destabilize the Democratic Party's already-fraying New Deal coalition. He pursued this goal by stoking the resentment of conservative blue-collar whites against blacks, feminists, counterculture youth, and others and by pitting blacks and whites against each other on the job. (Nixon announced steep cuts in federal spending on construction as well.) "The NAACP wanted a tougher requirement; the unions hated the whole thing," remembered John Ehrlichman, Nixon's counsel and presidential assistant for domestic affairs. "Before long, the AFL-CIO and the NAACP were locked in combat over one of the passionate issues of the day and the Nixon Administration was located in a sweet and reasonable middle." Veteran civil rights organizer and labor ally Bayard Rustin came to a similar conclusion. As a result of the president's machinations, Rustin acknowledged, Nixon "weakens his political opposition by aggravating the differences between his two strongest and most progressive forces—the labor movement and the civil rights movement."[25]

This was more than one politician's grab for power. The central role of moderate Republicans such as Labor Secretary George Shultz in pushing for affirmative action demonstrates that some contractors, business leaders, and economists saw it as a way to undercut the economic power of labor unions. As a trained economist and head of the University of Chicago's Business School, Shultz was one of the Nixon administration's most articulate affirmative action supporters. Shortly before taking up his government post, he spoke to the Industrial Relations Research Association about the need for "special measures . . . to expand the quantity and quality of labor market information available." Up until then, he told his fellow scholars, "there has been little systematic effort to analyze the relationship between hiring standards and actual job requirements." Shultz called for a serious consideration of the way industry designed jobs and the employment criteria they used, but he warned that this would "clearly . . . impinge upon collective bargaining practices," as the accepted procedures were "certain to come under new scrutiny." Once in his new position, Shultz oversaw the implementation of the Philadelphia Plan and then, in February 1970, issued "Order No. 4," which required all businesses holding federal contracts to adopt hiring plans so that the composition of their workforce mirrored that of the community in which it was located. The NAACP leadership was delighted. In a statement aimed clearly at unions, it argued that "it is no good to pile plan upon plan . . . as long as all of these are under the sole control and direction of organizations whose main purpose is to keep down the supply of skilled labor in order to maintain a job scarcity situation." It lauded the Philadelphia Plan since "it goes to the heart of the problem: *getting black workers on the job*." After a decade of flawed programs and slow progress, they welcomed measures that promised to bring equal opportunities.[26]

Rank-and-File and Leadership Resistance to Race- and Gender-Sensitive Programs

While civil rights leaders cheered aggressive affirmative action in the workplace, unionists fretted. Many had resisted the forces of change wrought by the rights revolution; others had sought an accommodation and attempted to meld union principles and practices with challenges to race and gender disparities.

The heads of the skilled trades and construction unions were the most hostile to these programs. They continued to insist that their own voluntary measures were working and that mandates such as those contained in the Philadelphia Plan would fray the social fabric of the close-knit workplace as well as dilute productivity and impose burdens on unions that other sectors of American society would not share. "The backlash and the whipping boy concept centers on the building trades unions," complained Herrick Roth, president of the Colorado AFL-CIO Labor Council, to Nixon in December 1969. Roth touted the union-sponsored Labor Education Advancement Program in his state for increasing the number of skilled black workers: "YET THERE IS NO QUOTA SYSTEM! And what's even more important—they are learning and performing skills. . . . [E]very fifth face [is] Black!" Furthermore, he chastised Nixon for being "a bit hypocritical" for cutting construction funds and imposing affirmative action simultaneously. "You Mr. President with one hand are making it harder for those already working in the construction industry to stay at work," Roth wrote. "You are making it doubly hard for anyone of any skin color or racial background to enter new employment."[27]

Unionists tried, and failed, in the years leading up to the Philadelphia Plan to interest civil rights organizations as well as state and federal government agencies in affirmative action plans overseen largely by labor unions. The AFL-CIO's Donald Slaiman, for example, contacted the executive director of Kentucky's Commission on Human Rights in 1966 about adopting a program begun in New York City by the Workers Defense League. Slaiman, a staff member in the federation's CRD, characterized the program as "one of the most successful operations we know of for recruiting more qualified minority group youngsters into the trades." The same year he asked officials in Kansas and Minnesota to modify their procedures for processing discrimination complaints so that the AFL-CIO might receive copies of complaints. The head of the Minnesota Commission Against Discrimination agreed but would only share complaints after investigations into the charges had begun. Meanwhile, the director of the Kansas Commission on Civil Rights refused outright. "To them, it may appear that we are weakening their case by informing you since you are, at least in their eyes, the same union against which they have lodged their complaints in the first place," he explained.[28]

Federation officials did not fare better at the national level. When C. J. Haggerty, president of the AFL-CIO Building and Construction Trades Department, wrote to Labor Secretary Wirtz in February 1968 to tell him of their plan for a program to create "qualified applicants for apprenticeships" and to give "special attention to deficiencies affecting the full qualification of Negro and other minority group applicants . . . and remedy the same if practical," Wirtz was guarded in his reply. He informed Haggerty that he was "gratified" and commended him "for the forthright position you have taken." He, however, proposed "to continue carrying out anti-discrimination provisions concerning apprenticeship." In an effort to head off a growing number of discrimination lawsuits, the federation's William Pollard asked the NAACP Legal Defense Fund's Robert Belton that they meet to discuss two pending court cases involving the United Paper Workers and the Oil, Chemical, and Atomic Workers unions. Belton begged off, explaining that "in neither case do we feel that we have sufficient information . . . which will allow for meaningful discussion." He added that he believed "it will be necessary for the respective courts . . . to make some ruling on the refusal of the companies and/or unions to supply us with some information pursuant to the appropriate rules under the Federal Rules of Civil Procedure." It was clear that the NAACP had little faith in labor's ability to solve workplace discrimination: they sharply criticized a plan by the Building and Construction Trades Council of Greater New York, along with contractors, as "just one more effort to pull the wool over the eyes" of black and Puerto Rican workers.[29]

Unionists were adamant that they were making real advances. At a press conference in 1969, Slaiman announced that the percentage of minorities enrolled in apprenticeship training programs had increased from just over 2 percent in 1960 to 7.2 percent in 1968 and then to 9.4 percent in the first half of 1969. He noted that the AFL-CIO was supporting "compensatory preparation to make up for educating gaps and access gaps," but more initiatives along the lines of the Johnson administration's ambitious federal urban aid program, known as the Model Cities Program, were necessary. Unfortunately, he said, "very little actual money is going into construction programs in Model Cities." Critics hammered away at the slow and uneven progress in unions, even after Title VII went into effect. One industrial relations scholar noted that, of the first eight EEOC complaints lodged against building trades unions, five locals refused to implement any remedial measures or even admit that discrimination had occurred. This conciliation process, this author argued, would be "incapable of eradicating deeply rooted and institutionalized union practices of discrimination." Even a sympathetic Bayard Rustin reminded labor leaders that "statements in themselves, no matter how excellent, are not enough. . . . There has been foot-dragging and evasion. There must be forthright action. Now there must be visible results."[30]

The most hostile skilled white workers feared that affirmative action programs would eliminate a work culture shaped by ethnic and family ties. Many unionists viewed nepotism as an appropriate practice rooted in the notion of skilled work as a kind of property right. (Forty percent of applicants accepted by the Philadelphia Plumbers Union were sons of union plumbers.) "It is natural that sons and relatives, as well as friends, receive preferential treatment. It is not accidental that early trade unions were closely tied to ethnic groups," the author of an article on discrimination in the Pittsburgh construction industry instructed readers. One *New York Times* letter writer captured the class and familial context of skilled employment:

> Some men leave their sons money, some large investments, some business connections and some a profession. I have none of these to bequeath to my sons. I have only one worthwhile thing to give: my trade. . . . For this simple father's wish it is said that I discriminate against Negroes. Don't all of us discriminate? Which of us when it comes to a choice will not choose a son over all others? . . . Why should the government have any more right to decide how I dispose of my heritage than it does how the corner grocer disposes of his?

In defending this view, white unionists were careful not to profess racial animus. "When I was a young man, [the union] discriminated against everybody," quipped George Meany, federation president and longtime member of New York Plumbers Local 2. "It had an even-handed policy of discrimination—they wouldn't take anybody in."[31]

They saw no contradiction in supporting this old-fashioned preference system and in objecting to affirmative action on the grounds that only the best qualified should work in skilled jobs. "There seems to be a belief that anybody can be a plumber, anybody can be a sheet metal worker, anybody can be an electrician with very little preparation or training," Meany complained to a National Press Club audience in 1970. When U.S. Assistant Attorney General Stephen Pollak met with representatives from the AFL-CIO's Building and Construction Trades Department in 1968 and informed them that "there would have to be acceptance for a limited period of time for Negroes who had no experience," a union officer present "pointed out that such a procedure could result in a flood of applicants whose expectations would become frustrated since employers would not hire them." In the process of undermining the skill levels of individual trades, they believed, affirmative action would weaken the labor movement. Writing to Nixon in 1970, a cameraman working in Los Angeles characterized affirmative action recipients as "so-called minorities . . . [and] inexperience [*sic*] men who in most instances will not even be paying union dues." He protested that "throw[ing] qualified men off their jobs for the benefit of someone else is *not* the American Way." As the criticism against unions intensified, so too did the feeling among unionists that the labor movement was being treated unfairly. "You don't attack an institution or an industry and say 'change your methods,'" a journeyman electrical worker scolded *Washington Post* columnist Hobart Rowan. "I would not think of implying that you and the newspaper industry don't know best how to run your industry."[32]

This defensiveness was at the center of the "hardhat" rebellion as skilled trades and construction unionists decried the cultural and radical changes sweeping the country. In the spring of 1970, it captured national headlines. In early May, hundreds of construction workers converged on Wall Street and disrupted an antiwar rally, injuring scores of protestors. Less than two weeks later, New York's Building and Construction Trades Council—with Nixon administration encouragement—sponsored a large prowar demonstration festooned with American flags. The photograph of BCTC president Peter Brennan presenting Nixon with a hardhat that appeared in newspapers soon afterward illustrated the rising "white backlash." Commentators at the time explored the class and racial resentments of white working-class men. In *The Troubled American* Richard Lemon noted that the "Middle American" was "basically sympathetic to black aspirations" but "jealous of their union membership, because it is the only security they have, and they are resistant to Negro demands which seem to threaten that equity." There was no denying that racism had pervaded their ranks. Sociologist E. E. Masters observed through his research at a working-class bar that white patrons "still subscribe to folk beliefs about blacks: That they are lazy, not as bright as white people, more childlike, more primitive, more highly sexed, etc." Moreover, they viewed their labor unions in practical terms: "They do not think of the union as an instrument for social change or social reform."[33]

Working-class whites came to think of themselves as victims. "The white worker feels economically threatened, personally imperiled, politically suckered," explained Garment Workers vice president Gus Tyler in 1972. Although there was a lack of precision about what constituted class identity in "backlash" talk (they were "forgotten," "working," and "blue collar" Americans), Andrew Levison argued in *The Working Class Majority* that they self-consciously separated their interests from that of middle-class whites. "Where workers see a common working-class issue, they respond 'tolerantly,'" Levison wrote. "But when the issue poses the needs of the blacks as a whole against all whites, workers often became incensed at being lumped together with the affluent and seeing their problems ignored." And the people doing the "lumping" were liberals. Union leaders struck back with charges of hypocrisy. John Lyons, president of the Bridge and Structural Iron Workers Union, told those gathered at an AFL-CIO conference on equal employment opportunity in 1969 that he was "sure that white collar areas and especially job categories not covered by union agreements compared very unfavorably" with organized labor's record. Nevertheless, he continued, the press "keep writing of the systematic exclusion of Negroes from the segregated apprenticeship programs of the building trades."[34]

Labor's hostility to the "new liberalism" was evident in George Meany's decision to withhold the federation's endorsement of Democrat George McGovern in his 1972 presidential bid. Meany's bitterness toward McGovern and the party was rooted in his distaste for the young activists—some of whom represented the counterculture—gaining influence within Democratic ranks. These new power brokers in the party were disdainful of organized labor. Although the labor leader shared McGovern's stance on economic issues, he rejected the nominee's position on busing, welfare, and foreign policy. The changes put in place for delegate selection to the national convention and other internal party policies following the 1968 loss to Nixon reduced greatly the power of labor in the Democratic Party (overseen by McGovern as chairman of the committee drafting new rules). Political scientist Bruce Miroff observes, "Rarely in American history had a major interest group suffered such a rapid drop in power as did organized labor between 1968 and 1972." Labor unionists and their supporters fared badly at the 1972 convention in Miami Beach, where the credential committee refused to seat stalwart supporters such as Chicago Mayor Richard J. Daley and all but shut labor leaders out of the writing of the party's platform. Labor unionists may have become, as Meany characterized it, "second class citizens," but the Democratic Party paid the price on Election Day with Nixon's landslide victory. "Though liberals did not consciously set out to drive workers into the arms of [George] Wallace and Nixon, the appalling fact is that is precisely what they did," Levison wrote. Although this is a somewhat limited explanation of the rise of white working-class conservatism, Levison accurately highlighted a significant factor in the growing marginalization of unions in liberal circles.[35]

Local skilled trades and construction unionists dug in against affirmative action. At first they attempted to stop African American applicants by adding a "grandfather clause" to the eligibility requirements in the form of extra points on the entrance examination to applicants whose fathers had worked in the trade. They initiated confidential interviews for admissions as well. The most resistant unionists moved on to work stoppages, protest rallies, and violence. In 1966 St. Louis construction workers launched a "hate strike" over the awarding of a

Gateway Archworks contract to nonunion plumbers, many of whom were black; the strike lasted five months and involved five skilled union locals. When Assistant Labor Secretary Arthur Fletcher appeared at a Chicago meeting to speak on affirmative action, five hundred unionists jammed into the room and created sufficient noise to postpone his talk. The next day, two thousand construction workers turned out to battle four hundred policemen. Union protestors in Pittsburgh were especially bold: in response to the mayor's push for unions to accept more black members, four thousand furious white workers marched to City Hall with signs reading "Wallace in '72" and "We Are the Majority." Fifty people were injured and over two hundred arrested. "Unless and until this country wakes up to the fact that these things pose very serious problems, we're going to have very serious confrontations, probably to the point of bloodshed," predicted EEOC chairman William H. Brown III in response to a question about the Pittsburgh protest.[36]

Labor union resistance did not impede the institutionalization of affirmative action. AFL-CIO leaders had hoped that Congress would follow the lead of Everett Dirksen, the Republican minority leader in the U.S. Senate from Illinois, and thwart the Philadelphia Plan for violating Title VII's ban on quotas. When Dirksen died in September 1969, however, his replacement was Pennsylvania's Hugh Scott, an affirmative action supporter. The federation's chief lobbyist, Andrew Biemiller, then worked with Comptroller General Staats and Senator Robert Byrd of West Virginia to add a rider to a minor supplemental appropriations bill that would prohibit any government funds from being spent on contracts not approved by Staats's office. After clearing an initial Senate vote, the measure seemed on its way to final approval until intense pressure from the White House in December stopped its momentum in the U.S. House of Representatives. The Senate soon dropped this rider from the final version of the bill.[37]

A string of federal court decisions during the same period was most damaging to labor's hopes of stopping affirmative action. Union officials had long feared the growing influence of the judiciary and the Justice Department in workplace discrimination matters. When Assistant Attorney General Pollak asked labor representatives at the 1968 meeting why unions objected to this, one unionist "pointed out that unions could not expect something less than impartial treatment from the courts in certain areas of the country and also from the DOJ which might be in the hands of another administration." The courts soon struck down, among other things, nepotism and ordered unions to develop aggressive outreach campaigns to bring minorities into apprenticeship programs. Many of their decisions were geared to remedial actions. These included a case in Louisiana, in which they ordered the Asbestos Workers Union to admit three African American workers immediately on the grounds that they had discriminated against them; in New York City, in which they mandated that minorities make up at least 25 percent of the membership of the newspaper and publication delivery unions; and in Seattle, in which they required building construction unions to recruit enough black workers to fill at least 30 percent of their apprenticeship programs. In 1971 the U.S. Supreme Court refused to consider a lower court ruling upholding the Philadelphia Plan's legality. Union coffers emptied quickly to meet the rising cost of litigation. The amount that labor organizations spent defending themselves in court doubled between 1966 and 1973, doubled again between 1973 and 1979, and then quadrupled between 1979 and 1983.[38]

Union leaders did not have a viable strategy to reverse these trends. When they looked to their usual places of support in the federal government, they discovered that, in Graham's words, "the executive branch was united, the Congress was divided, and the courts appeared to be supportive of affirmative action." The EEOC, in particular, troubled them. "EEOC is dabbling far too much in labor relations problems like plant-wide seniority and job-testing beyond what is necessary to prevent racial discrimination," fumed Peter Schoemann, head of the Plumbers Union in 1967. Congress increased the EEOC's authority when it allowed, through the Equal Employment Opportunity Act of 1972, the commission to file its own lawsuits. With this change, recalled an EEOC staff member, "you had an enormous club with which you could walk into federal court."[39]

Despite the hostility of Schoemann and others, the federation's CRD staff worked with the EEOC to reduce union liability. At times the CRD cooperated with the EEOC's efforts to root out discrimination, as in the Louisiana Asbestos Workers case. This particular legal action began in 1966 when several black workers and at least one Mexican American (as well as a sympathetic white worker) filed a discrimination complaint charging "a pattern of practice . . . wherein the common slogan to be seeking membership is THAT ONE MUST BE WHITE AND KIN." When conciliation efforts failed, the CRD's Doris Gibson traveled to Louisiana and reported back that the business agent there insisted that the local "had never had a Negro member nor was he going to be the one to try and break this tradition." Gibson noted that she "got the distinct impression [that] he had no wish to cooperate with us or the EEOC." Although this reaction was fairly common, many union officers did work with the CRD to resolve complaints or to prepare for their testimony at EEOC public hearings. "Our records indicate that we have been involved in many, many conferences with the representatives of the Commission, International and local unions for the purpose of obtaining successful conciliation agreements," wrote William Pollard. Training unionists in CRD "compliance awareness" programs, he boasted, had played a significant role in reducing the number of lawsuits.[40]

The CRD's staff members frequently found themselves in a difficult position as they sought to defend union practices and to obey equal employment opportunity mandates, all without alienating union rank-and-file members. William Pollard, responding to an NAACP invitation, arrived in St. Louis to help conciliate a dispute between black and white firefighters over a promotion scheme that was on the verge of becoming dangerous. "If the men are not promoted properly there will be killings," warned the local firefighters union president, who was white. Pollard listened as black firefighters told him about being harassed, isolated, and punished for minor infractions. He sympathized with their plight, but when they threatened to take unspecified action against the union, Pollard reported that he "advised them that he was a 100% union man & would not be intimidated by those because he was a union man."[41]

Still, the relationship between the CRD and the EEOC was strained. Some of this came from the federation's frustration with the EEOC's complaint backlog as well as its inability or unwillingness to provide them with complete copies of discrimination complaints lodged against unions in a timely manner. It was rooted as well in their fundamental difference about the role of the labor movement in advocating for workplace equality. After informing Donald Slaiman of meetings with EEOC staff at several regional offices, Pollard complained that "many of the new [EEOC] hires were young and in many instances had no affection for the labor movement." There were a few exceptions to this characterization, including Winn Newman, who would later hold positions as counsel to several unions and worked with the EEOC in its early years, and deputy general counsel Richard Berg. Both lawyers tried unsuccessfully to create close working arrangements between the commission and labor unions. For the most part, however, EEOC commissioners and staff believed that unions were as culpable for discrimination as employers. "Every sign indicates that the Commission is desirous of increasing the number of lawsuits or raiding our treasuries through back pay awards," Pollard concluded.[42]

While the CRD struggled, unsuccessfully, to gain a place in government policymaking, union leaders continued to resist "hard" affirmative action. Calling programs that contained numerical goals "quota democracy," AFL-CIO secretary-treasurer Lane Kirkland reminded a Jewish Labor Committee audience in 1972 that the federation was "in opposition to quotas, calls for open doors and the total destruction of barriers without regard to percentages or numbers." Kirkland's view did not prevail, but unionists insisted that the significant increase in minority skilled unionists (their share of apprenticeship and journeymen slots jumped from 4 percent in 1964 to over 15 percent in 1975) had come as a result of union-sponsored efforts and not government policies. Robert Georgine, head of the Building and Construction Trades Department in the mid-1970s, made just this claim before echoing the AFL-CIO's position that, above all, full employment was needed. Such a focus "would help minorities without at the same time penalizing other workers and exacerbating social tension." Without it, Georgine feared, "we will have . . . a situation where workers are divided against each other like a pack of wolves fighting over a bone."[43]

Georgine had a point, since affirmative action did not result in large-scale gains for working-class Americans. For those victims of longstanding discrimination, however, the ability to vie for higher-paying, skilled jobs was justice long overdue. Still, for all the discord surrounding preferential programs, the returns in private sector employment were slim, as some of its strongest supporters acknowledged. Richard Levin, director of Philadelphia's Commission on Human Relations, pointed out in 1969 that, at most, the Philadelphia Plan would secure only around two thousand jobs for minorities. "In several ways the amount of time and effort being spent on the construction industry is unfortunate," he complained. The 1970s were, in fact, a period of decline for construction unions. While conservative hardhats celebrated Nixon's appointment of one of their own, Peter Brennan, to the post of secretary of labor, large contractors and corporations were in the process of undermining craft wages and organizing efforts. By mid-decade the practice of "double-breasting" allowed construction firms to set up nonunion subsidiary workforces at project sites across the country. A series of deep recessions and high unemployment further compounded the decline of labor strength.[44]

Industrial Unions and Their Accommodation to Affirmative Action

At first glance, the history of industrial unions and affirmative action is similar to that of skilled trades and construction unions. Leaders of both kinds of unions faced a large number of discrimination complaints; had few minority men or women of all races in higher-paying, skilled jobs; and promoted their own affirmative action plans in the hopes of avoiding government mandates. Like the old-line AFL unionists, industrial unionists denounced numerical goals and quotas. In the heat of the battle over the passage of the Civil Rights Act of

1964, the UAW's Walter Reuther waved aside the objections of Senator Lister Hill of Alabama that Title VII legislation would require "unmathematical apportionment of jobs" along racial lines, insisting that "we do not believe it to be the import of the pending Federal measure." In April 1966 the UAW joined other unions, including the United Rubber Workers, the United Steel Workers, and the United Packinghouse Workers, in the interest of "creating dialogue and working together" with state and federal equal employment opportunity commissions. Their focus was on "soft" affirmative action, including "the employment of Negroes and other minorities where they are not now employed, working toward establishment of effective training programs to raise their *qualification levels* to a standard that will meet the requirements of our complex economic society."[45]

Even if they wanted to hold off the calls for changes in the way unions and the workplace operated, however, they could not. The nation's blue-collar workforce was in the midst of one of the most difficult periods since the Great Depression. Unlike the mass organizing of the 1930s, the labor movement in the 1970s lacked a dominant narrative. The "hardhat rebellion" was only one part of this story: it was also a decade marked by a significant jump in unionization rates for service sector workers and public sector employees and the founding of the CBTU and the CLUW. As Meany's leadership at the helm of the AFL-CIO in Washington, D.C., maintained the public face of "Big Labor," a new generation of working-class black, Hispanic, and white men and women lashed out against workplace alienation and diminished opportunity through absenteeism, workplace sabotage, and wildcat strikes. "An amalgam of politically complex, and at times quite contradictory, forces defined the blue-collar revival of the 1970s," notes labor historian Jefferson Cowie.[46]

The most dramatic transformation to affect organized labor was its newfound support for gender equality. Despite the EEOC's initial unwillingness to enforce Title VII's sex discrimination ban fully, union women unleashed an avalanche of charges over job typing by sex, separate seniority lists, unfair restrictions due to state protective laws, and unequal employment benefits. "Some of the early EEOC cases were filed by working-class women who were victims of discrimination and who I consider heroines," recalled the EEOC's Sonia Pressman in 1990. Sometimes rank-and-file members expressed their dissatisfaction to local and international union offices. "As an unprotected 'man' I work a little more than women and I earn almost twice as much money," wrote one Communications Workers woman from the West Coast to George Meany following her entry into a "male" job. "'Protective laws,' sir, I do not need." They resorted to the courtroom as well, especially when their local leadership proved unyielding. The first case that dealt with Title VII's contravention of protective laws to reach appellate court, *Weeks v. Southern Bell* (1969), began when Lorena Weeks's employer refused her bid for a telephone switchman's job on the grounds that women were not permitted to work in this position. When Weeks complained to her local union president, he informed her that she did not get the job "because the man is the breadwinner in the family and women just don't need this type of job." Weeks prevailed, as did women across the country in their push for higher-paying jobs and union leadership positions.[47]

In response to this activism, some industrial union leaders such as Walter Reuther shifted their thinking to one of support for affirmative action. Reuther did not come to this point easily: he was a social democrat by upbringing and embraced the growth liberalism of postwar American, not numerical goals and quotas, as the most legitimate way to bolster workers' economic status. After the passage of the landmark civil rights legislation in the mid-1960s, Reuther continued to champion civil rights and other social justice causes. He spent much of his energy in the years leading up to his death in 1970, however, determining the UAW's place within a Democratic Party and labor federation that was badly divided, especially over U.S. involvement in the Vietnam War (Reuther joined other unionists in the National Labor Committee for McGovern-Shriver). He struggled to stave off the growing strength of white backlash among members as well as the radical ferment of Black Power, which he thought divisive. "If you are part of a minority how do you expect, if you isolate yourself from the majority, ever to gain access to political power?" Reuther wondered. Like those around him, however, he warmed to race- and gender-sensitive initiatives. Reuther's initial resistance to designating IEB seats to members of underrepresented groups melted away in the 1960s, first as black representatives took their places early in the decade and then in 1966 when Olga Madar joined the top leadership. Reuther pushed for the hiring of minorities for staff positions too. " 'You've got to have at least one black on your staff,' " black unionist and UAW vice president Marc Stepp remembered Reuther telling regional directors. "If it weren't for Walter pushing we probably wouldn't have" any minorities on staff, Stepp concluded.[48]

Reuther's change in thinking was evident at a lengthy IEB meeting in October 1969. Board members spent much of their time considering the small gains made in bringing black workers into skilled positions and apprenticeship programs. "We have made some progress. We have not made sufficient progress," Reuther declared. Relying on outreach programs would not longer suffice: "There is a new urgency here. You kid yourself if you believe you can go on in our union, business as usual, with the skilled trades. We have got to get some new ideas." The UAW president and others at the meeting pushed aside the arguments against affirmative action. Reuther considered worries that it would lead to less qualified workers in skilled positions as "pious hogwash," noting that "these people want to maintain these jobs on a monopoly basis"; UAW vice president (later president) Douglas Fraser suggested that "we could prove that tests are not an accurate predictor of who is going to be a good skilled tradesman." Martin Gerber observed that "many women desire to work in skilled trades. They are perfectly qualified to do the job but many obstacles have been working against them for years."[49]

"Nobody likes quotas because you cannot solve basic social problems by quotas," Reuther noted. But the union must "move ahead more effectively and aggressively," he said. The biggest obstacle would be employers: Ford Motor Company executives had not replied to UAW proposals for establishing proportional goals for the hiring of skilled workers—"a very reasonable proposal," Reuther thought. The one bright spot was an agreement with North American Rockwell ensuring that black and Mexican American workers would hold half of the apprenticeship positions. "I think that begins to reflect what I call the new dimension of this crisis," Reuther concluded. Paul Schrade, liberal activist and Reuther's assistant, was pleased: "What you . . . are agitating for here Walter is a very dangerous, radical and revolutionary approach."[50]

Despite Reuther's bold pronouncements, labor leaders by and large accommodated more than converted to a pro–affirmative action stance. And they usually did so in a halting, inconsistent manner. They often found themselves forced to respond to litigation they had not initiated. This was true for the United Steelworkers of America (USW) in *Griggs v. Duke Power* (1971), the first Supreme Court decision to address affirmative action. The case began in 1966 when fourteen black employees at a North Carolina power plant failed to qualify for higher-paying positions because they lacked certain educational credentials. With the NAACP's assistance, they filed an EEOC complaint and then a lawsuit. By an unanimous vote the Supreme Court found in their favor: the justices stated that employers could not set requirements that were unrelated to the satisfactory performance of jobs. Furthermore, they held that the burden rested on the employer to show that these requirements fit the "business necessity" demand set forth in Title VII. The most far-reaching element in the decision was the notion that the "impact" of employer actions—and not just their "treatment" of workers—determined whether discrimination had occurred. In the USW amicus brief in support of the black plaintiffs, union lawyers argued that the test was unfair because it was not job-related, not because it had a disparate impact. "No union that held both black and white members could embrace disparate-impact reasoning," explained Judith Stein in her study of race, public policy, and the steel industry. "The union evaluated employment practices as good, bad, or indifferent on the basis of their impact on workers in general, not simply when they affected blacks adversely."[51]

Even groups such as the CLUW observed the delicate balance between affirmative action support and defending union principles and priorities. "Remember, we are not each other's enemies," CLUW vice president and black unionist Addie Wyatt of the Amalgamated Meatcutters Union told those in attendance at the organization's founding convention in 1974. "Our unions are not the enemies, because we are the unions. . . . We are telling our unions that we are ready and capable to fight." CLUW feminists supported affirmative action but placed most of the blame for inequality with employers who, they asserted, "profit[ed] by dividing workers on sexual, racial and age lines." While they were opposed to a "feminist union" because they "already have the structure to make change," as CLUW officer Gloria Johnson put it, "if unions don't do the right thing these women can first pursue their grievance procedure . . . then cases can be filed." CLUW president Olga Madar suggested in the group's newsletter that women workers hold men "accountable through the political process in union elections."[52]

When policymakers addressed the exclusion of minority men and women of all races in the skilled trades and construction unions, they turned their attention to challenging the many work rules that had developed in industrial labor over the decades. These served to regiment minorities and women to lower pay and less desirable jobs and made them prone to more frequent layoffs than white men. Industrial union leaders correctly pointed to their scarce influence over hiring decisions. Union negotiators had considerable influence, however, over the details of promotion, transfer, and seniority. These were treasured parts of collective bargaining agreements, with seniority being the most important. "What makes seniority a sacred cow to labor is its all-embracing influence on the worker's job and income," explained one journalist. "A small difference in seniority rank may determine whether the employee works days or nights, whether he is promoted or demoted, and whether he is laid off early, late or not at all in a slump." The use of unit or department seniority rather than plant seniority determined much of this "difference." It worked against those in vulnerable jobs—even those with many years of service. Many of these jobs were in departments affected by automation. To make matters worse, the fine print in

some labor agreements permitted workers in skilled jobs to avoid layoffs by forcing out workers in lower jobs disproportionately held by women of all races and
minority men. The seniority system tended to lock in the effects of job typing by
race and sex that predated Title VII. A survey of furloughed steel workers at one
large plant in the mid-1960s, for example, revealed that while 11.5 percent of the
total workforce was out of a job, 38 percent of the black workforce lost their positions. With Title VII's ban on discriminatory seniority systems, however, these
arrangements came under scrutiny.[53]

Those workers with the most to lose under the new law resisted it the most.
In midwest locals of the United Packinghouse Workers union, black and white
women united to force the union and employers to open "men's" jobs to them
and to create single seniority lists. Male unionists, faced with unemployment
due to rapid automation, variously ignored, ostracized, and threatened protesting women. "I've always been a believer that if the man's the head of the house he
should have the job," said one packinghouse union officer. Unionists elsewhere
struggled over seniority as well. White steelworkers, for example, fought hard to
maintain their old seniority system. In one instance, an equal employment officer with the U.S. Army reviewed in 1966 for the CRD's southern director how
an employer and the local union leadership at a Georgia mill "resisted a joining
of jobs into one line on the grounds that when the Negro qualifies for jobs. . . .
[H]e could replace a white man in the event of a cutback if his seniority was
greater than that of the white man." Management and union, he confided, "considers this a potential source of agitation, discontent, and possible violence."[54]

A body of case law soon emerged from these conflicts that would reshape
seniority practices. In the very first reported case challenging a seniority system,
a federal judge in Virginia ruled in 1968 in *Quarles v. Philip Morris, Inc.* that the
departmental seniority system built up over the decades in the South's tobacco
industry was not a bona fide seniority system, because "its genesis [is] in racial
discrimination." Lawmakers mandated that bona fide systems were those seniority arrangements that were not created with the interest to discriminate or
that somehow involved discriminatory treatment of some workers in its opera-
tion. The judge rejected company and union pleas that the system established
before Title VII's passage was still valid: "Congress did not intend to freeze an
entire generation of Negro employees into discriminatory patterns that existed
before the act." The next year, the Fifth Circuit Court of Appeals in *Papermakers,
Local 189 v. U.S.* tackled the thorny issue of what relief, if any, was due seniority discrimination victims. Although they rejected the argument that plaintiffs
could not claim "fictional seniority" and obtain compensation for the number of

years elapsed since Title VII's effective date (that "would comprise preferential treatment rather than remedial treatment"), they should receive "rightful place" relief when they documented their earliest application or transfer efforts. Finally, in *Robinson v. Lorillard* (1971), the Fourth Circuit Court of Appeals declared in another case involving tobacco workers that the use of a "business necessity" defense was not acceptable if the practices it entailed carried forward the efforts of past discrimination.[55]

The consent decrees that came into force in several major industries in the 1970s went even further than these court decisions. These were affirmative action plans meant to address in a wholesale fashion race and gender inequality in seniority and job assignments. The 1974 Steel Consent Decree was especially far-reaching. It came after years of EEOC complaints and lawsuits that brought little progress for minority men and none at all for women, whose share of the steel workforce actually dropped from around 1.4 percent in 1965 to 0.5 percent in 1971. Government officials began to craft an industry-wide decree when, in 1973, both the Labor Department investigating Bethlehem Steel's Sparrows Point plant in Baltimore and a federal judge hearing a case about U.S. Steel's Fairfield plant in Birmingham, Alabama, found discriminatory seniority systems in place. In the out-of-court settlement, steel manufacturers paid $31 million in damages to black, Hispanic, and women workers. They also agreed that 20 percent of all newly hired workers would be affirmative action recipients. The decree mandated more transparent job application procedures and the use of plantwide seniority.[56]

Policymakers and activists continued to view labor unions as obstacles to equal employment opportunity. "Despite the protestations of innocence for them by their apologists, the unions are in federal courts a great deal these days," chided William Gould, a Stanford law professor and former EEOC consultant. Industrial union leaders scrambled to position their organizations so that they would avoid crippling penalties. The Steel Workers leadership characterized its participation in the decree negotiations in mostly practical terms. Without the decree in place, they "recognized that an industry-wide lawsuit could lead to unworkable and inconsistent seniority rules written by judges, a complete reshuffling of employees, and a severe crippling of the International." Notwithstanding the defensive nature of their participation, union leaders also thought that the decree would "not only vindicate the just and lawful rights of our minority members, but they also yield substantial improvements to *all* our members in areas which have long been a matter of union concern." In many ways the decree delivered on these promises: neither the steel companies nor the union had to admit violating workers' rights, it exempted them from further class action lawsuits, and the companies paid the USW's share of the damages. Minority men and women as well as white women came into the steel mills in greater numbers, taking jobs that had once been the preserve of white men. Just as in the building and construction unions, it was a pyrrhic victory, however, since a dramatic increase in steel imports and a stagnant economy thinned the USW's ranks. The 1970s alone saw a net loss of some thirty thousand jobs in the industry.[57]

As union leaders began to endorse affirmative action, they faced off against disgruntled white men who picketed and took legal action to counter consent decrees and other preferential hiring and seniority programs. Complaints of reverse discrimination—never more than 1 percent of the complaints the EEOC received—shot up in the first six months of 1974 as an economic recession deepened. The commission logged 335 such charges in those months, and judges began to turn their attention to claims of discrimination against those who historically had been favored in employment. Rank-and-file steelworkers, who pointed out that they were not asked to vote on the consent decree, were among the sharpest affirmative action critics. Some three hundred USW members picketed the union's headquarters soon after it was signed. "I can't imagine going along with such an agreement," declared a local union officer. One steelworker filed an EEOC complaint claiming that he had waited for years to obtain an apprenticeship spot, only to see a nineteen-year-old black woman get the position instead. (She should have had to "wait her turn," he noted.) Another USW member, this one in Kansas City, Missouri, told the EEOC that black workers with less seniority were gaining admission to apprenticeship programs: "I believe that the Blacks are receiving more favorable treatment." And still another worker, this one at the Jones and Laughlin Steel mill in Cleveland, filed his discrimination charge after female employees with less seniority used consent decree provisions to "move around men" into the most desirable jobs.[58]

Other unions received similar criticism. "Considerations such as seniority and job qualifications have not been equally evaluated. The Union appears unable to represent White on an equal basis with Blacks," wrote a Communications Workers unionist working for a Memphis telephone company. The narrative thread running through most of the complaints was of a unionist gaining the necessary seniority level and credentials, only to be blindsided by a union-sanctioned affirmative action plan. On behalf of such workers, John Mele lodged his reverse discrimination complaint in October 1973 against the U.S. Justice Department and a New Jersey local of the Electrical Workers (IBEW). He did so when his efforts to become part of an apprenticeship program failed due to an "unjust quota system" in which thirty of the thirty-five available positions were earmarked for minority applicants. Mele took his case to federal court. He alleged that the Justice Department and union were using "an illegal minority recruitment program which was involved in quota systems, proportional representation, and discrimination in reverse." Federal judge Lawrence Whipple informed Mele that he was "not unsympathetic to the plaintiff's plight and recognizes the seeming inequities imposed on him." The problem, Whipple continued, was that affirmative action programs "have been held to constitute a valid exercise of executive power and this Court is duty bound to follow the Federal policy."[59]

Industrial unionists as well as public and service sector unionists were more receptive to affirmative action than workers such as Whipple. Some, including those in the American Federation of State, County, and Municipal Employees (AFSCME) union, were enthusiastic supporters. At its 1974 convention, AFSCME delegates backed a resolution supporting "all feasible means, including programs of affirmative action to overcome the effects of historic discrimination so that throughout our society, and particularly in the workplaces in America, we can truly achieve 'unqualified equality.'" At the same time they denounced the "misleading labels" of "reverse discrimination" and "quotas" as efforts meant to undermine affirmative action's objective to "undo the legacy of discrimination." With the abolition of departmental seniority arrangements, labor liberals hoped that disruptions to collective bargaining practices had come to an end. "There have been in the past seniority systems that were discriminatory on their face, but thank God they are gone," the UAW's general counsel, John Fillion, reported to the union's IEB in 1975. Civil rights groups acknowledged these changes in labor's ranks as well. The usually critical Urban League praised the "major efforts and advances" of the AFL-CIO's CRD and "many international unions." The work of the CBTU, the CLUW, and the A. Philip Randolph Institute, which "show and reflect tremendous influence in their programs toward making affirmative action objectives a reality within the union structure," was even more significant.[60]

Affirmative Action and the Seniority Crisis of the Mid-1970s

Just as this support was solidifying in many quarters of the labor movement, a fresh demand by policymakers, civil rights activists, and feminists that the nation's unions suspend the "last hired, first fired" cornerstone of seniority placed labor liberals squarely in opposition to affirmative action. The severe economic recession in the mid-1970s brought the issue into focus, as industrial workers bore the brunt of an 11 percent national unemployment figure. In 1974 General Motors, Ford, and Chrysler laid off a staggering 225,000 workers as imports doubled their U.S. market share. The recession's impact weighed most heavily on minority men and women of all races. The jobless rates for whites stood at 6.4 percent in 1975; for African Americans it was 12.8 percent. In the durable goods manufacturing sector, 11.2 percent of all women workers lost their jobs, compared to 7.7 percent of all men. These cutbacks hit some local unions especially hard. The General Motors assembly plant in Fremont, California, for example, shed twenty-three hundred workers in January 1975, including nearly all five hundred of their women employees; the year before, General Motors let go of twenty-four hundred workers in Linden, New Jersey, including all three hundred women hired since the auto maker brought them into production positions in 1970.[61]

The crisis over seniority captured national headlines. Nina Totenberg reported in the *New York Times* that "resentment among minorities and women is growing. They feel that just as they were finally getting a foot in the door of employment opportunities, it is being slammed in their faces." Many affirmative action supporters outside the labor movement were hostile to the seniority system in general. "There are some who argue that seniority is a vested right. This, of course, is sheer nonsense," the NAACP's Herbert Hill fumed. "The argument that white men have a prior right to a job and that black people must wait until there is full employment before they can work is the essence of racist mentality." The scope of affirmative action must widen, they argued. "Affirmative action programs have upset the traditional rules of hiring. They can upset the rules of layoffs as well," insisted Columbia law professor Harriet Rabb. Alfred and Ruth Blumrosen explained that the "disparate impact" ruling in *Griggs* should guide government and management layoff policies: "If the burden is allowed to rest on the weak, the recently emancipated minorities and women, there is a genuine risk it will remain there permanently." There was an array of alternative schemes that would soften the blow of layoffs, including shorter hours, sharing jobs, rotating layoffs, and—most controversially—reverse seniority. "We're going to have to get . . . [unions] to be more innovative and to be more flexible," EEOC chairman Lowell Perry informed Urban League convention delegates in 1975.[62]

Buffeted by these challenges, labor leaders mounted a far-ranging defense of seniority. They characterized "reverse seniority" as an attack on workers' fundamental rights. "*Bona fide* seniority systems protect every worker, black or white, male or female," William Pollard said. "To destroy seniority systems would not create a single job, but would permit management to pick and choose workers without regard to date of hire—the very thing seniority was established in 1900 to prevent." Union members would fiercely resist any changes, since seniority was "one of the most highly prized possessions of any employee." Federation president George Meany was incensed by the suggestion to scrap seniority, even on a temporary basis. "What justice is there in that? What becomes of the right of contract? What becomes of the sanctity of a contract?" he lamented. AFL-CIO leaders rejected work sharing and shorter hours, characterizing them as "share the poverty" schemes. They steeled themselves for a possible EEOC policy change. "The problem caused by the recession has kept our department working on the double. The attack on seniority has been endless," Pollard reported to his colleagues in December 1975.[63]

The unionists most responsive to affirmative action offered some of the most targeted criticism. They warned of a rights-based model of social regulation that was growing out of control. AFSCME's president, Jerry Wurf, acknowledged his union's support for affirmative action but noted that "it is unfair and outrageous for administrators to hide behind affirmative action requirements as an excuse for circumventing seniority rules." To Winn Newman, counsel for the International Union of Electrical Workers, changes to seniority would "penalize workers for the discriminatory acts of the employer." That union's president reminded the membership that "the answer to equal opportunity is the creation of more jobs so that workers won't have to fight over those jobs that are left." The UAW confronted civil rights leaders at an "Ad Hoc Hearings and Strategy Session on 'Affirmative Action in Employment' " convened by the Congressional Black Caucus in November 1975. Looking out on an audience filled with members of the Urban League, the NAACP, and other civil rights groups, UAW Vice President Marc Stepp declared that "the real villain of the unfortunate predicament . . . is an increasing lack of sensitivity by the current Administration [of Gerald Ford] to come to grips with the basic problems of unemployment and inflation." Stepp was clear about the UAW's position: the remedy chosen to deal with unemployment "should not affect the status or impose a burden . . . on the incumbent employees who are members of majority as well as minority groups and women."[64]

African American unionist men and unionist women of all races in such industries as textiles, steel, paper, electrical products, meat packing, and automotive products offered their firm support for seniority systems. CBTU and CLUW convention delegates passed resolutions supporting seniority throughout the 1970s. Charlie Hayes, CBTU vice president and a Chicago packinghouse unionist, defended seniority on race-neutral terms: "The seniority system has come to be the backbone—indeed, the lifeblood—of trade unionism in this country. A threat to the seniority system is tantamount to a threat to the collective power of workers and trade unionism itself." In a press release on "Full Employment: Our Central Focus," CBTU officers reasoned that "if there were enough jobs . . . Whites would not need to be pitted against Blacks." Bayard Rustin told an Urban League gathering in 1975, "No union could exist without maintaining lines of seniority." Turning the matter back on his detractors, Rustin put it in personal terms: "I've never met a black man with high seniority who would agree to let a newly hired black woman take his job in case of layoffs, even if the woman got the job because of past discrimination against women."[65]

CLUW members echoed these points, decrying seniority critics as, in Olga Madar's words, "supportive of management's long opposition to seniority systems and a return to the law of the jungle at the workplace." Working-class feminists such as Madar attempted to negotiate between feminism and gender-neutral goals of social unionism by emphasizing equal treatment of all workers: "I am not about to let the leftists, the corporate managements [sic] and the women's organizations destroy the seniority systems. I am for affirmative action and yes, quotas, if necessary; but I think that can be done without injury to a current workforce. . . . The only official CLUW position is a statement saying that 'Brother and Sister workers should not be penalized for the past discrimination of management.'" In a letter to NOW's president, Karen DeCrow, Madar defended her position by drawing on her work experience in the 1940s, when women strove to gain their place in the seniority system. "You may be too young to recall what happened to working women after World War II," she lectured to DeCrow. "The seniority systems were violated in both organized and unorganized workplaces and affected both women and older men." Catherine Conroy of Communications Workers spoke for many union women when she asserted that "you cannot just stomp on seniority."[66]

The threat to undo the "last hired, last fired" practice was evidence of organized labor's vulnerability in the mid-1970s. Although they still held out hope for passage of labor law reform legislation, unionists had lost considerable influence in the Democratic Party. In urban areas, their traditional stronghold, they became locked in conflict with a generation of new black mayors over dwindling resources. Imported goods took a bite out of industrial union membership, and increases in nonunion construction workers undercut the strength of the building trades unions. Labor leaders' most immediate concern was over the fate of seniority systems in the face of proposed EEOC guidelines and an onslaught of lawsuits. In the first of these lawsuits, a federal district judge in *Watkins v. Steelworkers, Local 2369 and Continental Can Co.*, about a Louisiana employer and union local's history of race discrimination before the Civil Rights Act of 1964, addressed the near-total absence of black employees when the "last hired, first fired" policy came into play. The judge ordered that the layoffs be undertaken so that the ratio of blacks and whites on the payroll would be maintained. In their appeal, the Steelworkers Union argued that, although black workers faced a grim prospect of rehire, "Congress in its wisdom determined that there were countervailing considerations of social policy dictating against granting preferential seniority to a new generation of blacks to cure the discrimination which was visited upon a prior generation." The appellate court reversed the lower court's ruling, but new seniority cases appeared in quick succession, involving workers in a Connecticut shipyard, a California automobile plant, a New Jersey public utility, and a New York–based airline.[67]

If affirmative action in the 1960s focused on who should be hired, in the challenging economy of the 1970s it tended to deal with who should be fired. As affirmative action's meaning appeared to change, the distance between those unionists who resisted it and those who accommodated it through changes in collective bargaining agreements and consent decrees narrowed somewhat. Labor liberalism's compatibility with the rights revolution had stretched to the breaking point. Even as union activists pushed their organizations to embrace race and gender equality, they did so deftly, anxious not to diminish the central role of the labor movement in shaping workplace relations. As the recession deepened and the number of reverse discrimination complaints climbed, the nation's workplaces became increasingly tense and, in some places, violent.

While opposition within the labor movement solidified around the defense of seniority, another front in the struggle over affirmative action, one that had quietly been gathering steam since the late 1960s, began to draw increased attention on colleges and universities. This challenge involved the impassioned pleas of colorblind liberals to adhere to admissions, hiring, and promotion criteria based on the qualifications of individuals irrespective of their race, ethnicity, or gender. Their championing of the meritocracy ideal came in response to the push for strong affirmative action just as competition for coveted places within higher education intensified. Many middle-class Americans, worried about their own future and that of their children, came to view affirmative action as a stumbling block to equal opportunity.

CHAPTER TWO

"This Strange Madness"

The Origins of Opposition to Higher Education
Affirmative Action, 1968–1972

In his address to the Republican Party faithful at the annual Lincoln Day Dinner in Chicago in February 1970, Vice President Spiro Agnew delivered a blistering critique of the new affirmative action programs in America's colleges and universities. Much of the speech was standard Agnew fare: using characteristically bombastic language, the vice president denounced "supercilious sophisticates" for mandating "ethnic quotas" in admissions and faculty hiring. As he proceeded in his analysis, however, Agnew became less coarse. "The first and highest obligation of a university is to perform its own function well, according to the laws of learning itself," he lectured his audience. "For it is in the institutions of higher learning that the arts of civilization in their higher reaches must be preserved, enhanced, and transmitted." The use of proportionality as a criterion, he went on, was "repulsive to the liberal philosophy." Two months later, at a fundraiser in Des Moines, Iowa, Agnew developed his arguments further when he criticized a plan by University of Michigan administrators to have minorities constitute 10 percent of the student body. This, he concluded, was a violation of Thomas Jefferson's notion of a "natural aristocracy" as exemplified in the meritocratic system that had dominated higher education since World War II.[1]

Agnew's comments were significant for their attention to higher education when the struggle over affirmative action seemed to be concentrated in the exclusionary skilled trades. Recalcitrant hardhat workers and their union leaders, not graduate students and professors, were usually considered the face of "reverse discrimination" protests in the early years of affirmative action. The vice president, however, understood that colleges and universities were equally important sites of contestation over equality. The wide range of considerations he addressed concerning, as he called it, "this strange madness" captured the mix of principles and bare-knuckle politics at play in debates over affirmative action in the late 1960s and early 1970s. Agnew asserted that Michigan's plan was a "callow retreat from reality," since it lessened the value of a college diploma. The solution was not in offering "open enrollment" either, since he believed that colleges and universities were already filled with students who were "restless, purposeless, bored, and rebellious." Still, Agnew worried about a "dilution of opportunity." He called for increased financial assistance and more remedial services for the disadvantaged, but deserving, student irrespective of race.[2]

The swift reaction to the vice president's comments reveals the already-established support for affirmative action. In a group statement, admissions officers from twelve elite colleges and universities, including Harvard, Yale, Oberlin, Carleton, and Pomona, informed Agnew that the admissions process—they called it an "art"—was a flexible and sensitive approach to assess the potential of individual applicants. According to the University of Kentucky's registrar, by venturing outside of the confines of aptitude tests and grades, affirmative action was "not a lowering [but] a broadening of standards." In responding to his criticism of the University of Michigan's plan, the state's governor, moderate Republican William E. Milliken, reminded Agnew that "by admitting more black students the university will not be lowering its standards, but will be meeting its constitutional obligation to provide equal access to educational opportunities." Affirmative action backers offered as proof of support for their position survey results of 60,447 of the nation's faculty members; it showed that fully 40 percent of them favored admitting more minority undergraduates "even if it means relaxing normal academic standards of admission."[3]

Agnew's views, however, resonated strongly with many in and around higher education. That 60 percent of faculty surveyed did *not* support modified admissions criteria was the most obvious indication of considerable opposition, or at least wariness, to affirmative action. Some opponents offered firm rejection to both "hard" affirmative action plans that included numerical goals or quotas and "soft" affirmative action plans that offered special recruitment and remedial programs; others wavered in the level of their opposition, often willing to consider some kinds of affirmative action. Together, they constituted something less than a mass movement. In fact, most did not join anti–affirmative action groups, support "reverse discrimination" lawsuits, or make visible efforts to counter affirmative action in their institutions. That did not mean, however, that they did not influence the shape and direction of affirmative action policies. Their simmering resentment surfaced in their interactions with students and colleagues. It was manifest as well in difficult-to-detect ways such as search and tenure committee decisions and approval for research grants and new courses and degree programs. Those who did offer public opposition became a significant counterforce to civil rights activists, feminists, higher education administrators, and government policymakers. Over the course of affirmative action's prolonged and turbulent history, supporters and opponents alike claimed to be the true practitioners of equality, "the most emotive and powerful metaphor in American political discourse," according to historian J. R. Pole.[4]

This chapter focuses on the early opposition to higher education affirmative action beginning with the development of mild, or "soft," affirmative action in the early 1960s. These initiatives came primarily in the areas of new recruitment, financial assistance, precollegiate preparatory institutes, and tutoring services for African Americans. In the heyday of "growth liberalism" and the "rights revolution," the arguments for affirmative action were compelling to many higher education administrators, who saw it as a means of addressing both "manpower underutilization" and demands for racial equality. They launched unprecedented admissions and retention programs with foundation support. In retrospect, these efforts appear modest, but they helped to destabilize the routine workings of admissions as well as of faculty hiring and promotion by revealing what many came to understand as significant barriers to success.[5]

It then traces the emergence of, and opposition to, "hard" affirmative action. By the late 1960s, colleges and universities began to introduce more aggressive measures, including admissions and hiring goals. In some institutions, these took the form of quotas. Feminists on campuses and in organizations such as the National Organization for Women (NOW) and Women's Equity Action League (WEAL) were instrumental in instituting this new kind of affirmative action. They filed hundreds of complaints against colleges and universities for sex discrimination and lobbied federal agencies, especially the Department of Housing, Education, and Welfare (HEW), to force colleges and universities to increase the proportion of women in graduate and professional schools and in faculty positions, especially at the tenure level. Federal policymakers, who had already traversed the path of "hard" affirmative action in the skilled blue-collar job sector, were largely sympathetic to their demands.

Opponents were an influential counterforce, but they differed sharply among themselves about the appropriate role of the state in improving the status of minority men and women of all races. Advocates of colorblind liberalism were at the forefront in opposing policies predicated on the notion of proportionality. Many of these liberals were faculty members; a large number were Jewish. They braved the sting of racism charges, even as they sought to burnish their liberal credentials by lobbying for enhanced enforcement of antidiscrimination laws as well as urging new government measures in employment, housing, and education.

The conservatives who joined these disgruntled liberals were just emerging as a political force. They offered a vision of colorblindness grounded in economics, law, and philosophy that emphasized the damaging effects of equal opportunity policies. Where colorblind liberals continued to explore legislative and policy proposals to ensure race and gender equality, colorblind conservatives balked at new initiatives and focused instead on the virtues of limited government. Their explanations for lingering inequality focused on the wide range of differences in individual talent as well as the cultural deficiencies of minority groups that government action created—or at least worsened. Many opponents occupied a place between liberal and libertarian positions. The most significant were neoconservatives, a large number of them Jewish, who emerged in the mid-1960s as critics of the Democratic Party's foreign policy stance and, increasingly, of student activism and identity politics. Working in new organizations and in older ones such as the American Jewish Committee, the American Jewish Congress, and the Anti-Defamation League of B'nai B'rith (ADL), they leaned toward more conservative positions on affirmative action, even as liberals in the same groups sought creative ways to square the colorblind idea with ambitious admissions and hiring schemes.

For all their differences, colorblind liberals and conservatives were united in their view that affirmative action upset a meritocratic order that many Americans had come to believe helped create postwar prosperity and improved social relations. A new class of "mandarins," as Nicholas Lemann calls them in his history of meritocracy, moved into business, professional, and civic leadership positions in the 1950s and 1960s, secure in the belief that their ascent was due to pure talent. Meritocracy especially captured the loyalty of higher education faculty and students, many of them Catholic and Jewish and the children of immigrants. Before the 1950s these "white ethnics" found their way to the most prestigious institutions blocked by a quasi-hereditary white elite. In a meritocratic order, an individual's racial or gender identity was not supposed to matter. Affirmative action proponents argued, however, that such information played a key point in ensuring equal opportunity and in creating diverse campus populations. The long and complicated debate that is still with us today ensued: supporters pointed to meritocracy's uneven application, especially in the already visible unfairness in the treatment of women on account of gender as well as the still-hidden discriminatory effect of aptitude testing on minority men and women. Opponents, even those who admitted to the system's flaws, insisted that it was superior to race- and gender-sensitive criteria.[6]

As this chapter makes clear, "reverse discrimination" protests blended the defense of parochial interests and the advancement of principles. Affirmative action foes deployed a wide range of high-minded legal and philosophical objections in the nation's newspapers, magazines, and television talk shows that were missing from the blue-collar protests. The perception, however inaccurate, that colleges and universities were meritocratic institutions, unsullied by ethno-religious or white neighborhood job networks, legitimized affirmative action opposition for some middle-class whites. The importance Americans placed on higher education provided yet another reason. Most Americans had not attended a college or university, but their children were doing so—or at least aspired to attend. The route to personal and financial success was increasingly passing through the halls of higher learning. The immediate impact of affirmative action might be felt in a rejected application to an undergraduate program or to a law, medical, or some other professional school. As admission to professional and graduate programs became intensely competitive and as faculty positions open to the growing ranks of doctoral recipients all but dried up, many whites came to blame affirmative action for their failures. Although their belief about why they had not been admitted or hired might have been untrue, their losses were very real. By the mid-1970s, nearly every center of political and legal power, including Congress, the president, and the Supreme Court, was drawn into the struggle over the shape and character of equality in higher education.

Inequality in the "Golden Age of the University"

The twenty years following the end of World War II were marked by unprecedented growth in higher education. Colleges and universities became central to the national economy and cultural life. The increase in student enrollment was dramatic: almost 497,000 Americans received university degrees in the 1949–50 academic year, compared to 216,500 in 1940. Young people arrived on campuses in great numbers thanks to the Servicemen's Readjustment Act of 1944 (more commonly known as the GI Bill). This new law provided, among other things, financial support for veterans engaged in postsecondary studies. The skyrocketing postwar economy made higher education an affordable and desired commodity, as generous state and federal legislators embraced education as essential to continuing economic growth and winning the Cold War. The total figure for degree-seeking students shot up from 2.3 million in 1950 to 3.6 million in 1960, and then up to 7.9 million in 1970. By that year, nearly 48 percent of eighteen-year-olds were enrolled in some kind of postsecondary institution.[7]

The pace of change on campuses was dizzying. Married student housing, new dormitories and research buildings, the establishment of new state universities and two-year institutions accompanied a general loosening of regulations over students' lives. The sheer increase of student populations contributed to the establishment of large admissions operations. Applicants' scores on newly developed aptitude tests such as the Scholastic Aptitude Test, the Law Schools Admissions Test, and the Medical College Aptitude Test guided admissions staffs in making their decisions. Although never considered solely in admissions decisions (sometimes it was not even the most important factor), these tests came to symbolize a new era of impersonal, streamlined efficiency characteristic of large organizations. Universities, noted Christopher Jencks and David Riesman in their encyclopedic study of higher education published in the late 1960s, were "pace setters in the promotion of meritocratic values." They noted that "localism, sectarianism, ethnic prejudice and preference, class background, age, sex, and even occupational plans [were] largely ignored." Although student activists began to complain in the early 1960s about the impersonal nature of the "multiversity," affirmative action opponents would remember this period in wistful, almost emotional, terms as the years of unmatched scholarly and scientific advancements.[8]

Even as sophisticated assessment tests came into widespread use, applicants usually found it easy to gain admission. Many public institutions accepted any resident holding a high school diploma. In California, Chancellor Clark Kerr's "Master Plan" guaranteed that every high school student had a legal right to higher education at the public's expense. When aptitude tests came into general use, they often did not serve to exclude many applicants. This was true even in professional and graduate schools. Some medical schools in the 1950s and early 1960s, for example, were unable to fill all available seats for their incoming classes and, in effect, offered open admissions. It was not especially difficult to gain admittance to the most prestigious institutions: in 1960, for example, the University of California's Boalt Hall Law School accepted 517 of its 700 applicants. Stanford University in the 1950s accepted seven of every eight undergraduate applicants.[9]

Catholics and Jews, previously thwarted by official and unofficial Ivy League quotas, welcomed these new opportunities. In the nineteenth century, administrators and trustees of elite colleges and universities worried little about European immigrants challenging their gentlemen's club–like institutions. In the early twentieth century, however, they became alarmed as white ethnics, especially Jews, appeared on campuses in appreciable numbers. In offering support for a plan to limit the number of Jews admitted, Harvard's president, Abbott

Lawrence Lowell, offered the justification that, as a group, Jews "form a distinct body, and cling, or are driven, together, apart from the great mass of undergraduates." Yale's director of recruitment complained in 1929 that the list of incoming freshmen "might easily be mistaken for a recent roll call of the Wailing Wall." College administrators busied themselves developing regional quotas, formed preferences for alumni sons, and methods to examine the "whole" applicant. It was an imprecise science. At Harvard, Jewish applicants were categorized J1 ("conclusively Jewish"), J2 ("indicatively Jewish"), or J3 ("possibly, but not probably, Jewish"). Their efforts to cull their student ranks were successful: the percentage of Jews in their interwar years fell dramatically, from 15 to 20 percent of many Ivy League campuses to 10 percent of Harvard's student body, 8.2 percent of Yale's, and a mere 2.6 percent of Princeton's. The exclusion of Catholics was less systematic but very real at schools such as Princeton, where there were only 30 Catholics (most with Irish surnames) among the 629 students in the Class of 1927. Twenty years later, the authors of the report issued by the "President's Committee on Civil Rights" noted that one member of a medical school's admissions committee in New York City "admitted to a prejudice against Irish Catholics which affected his judgment." Catholics often chose to attend institutions sponsored by religious orders instead, such as Georgetown University and the University of Notre Dame.[10]

Anti-Semitism and anti-Catholicism were common within faculty ranks as well, particularly in disciplines such as history and English. There were four identifiable Jewish historians in American colleges and universities before World War I, which grew to only a modest number by midcentury. Savvy faculty advisors tended to steer aspiring Jewish students into industrial relations, economics, and the social sciences. Few Catholics taught at non-Catholic institutions. "A Catholic cannot teach history and be a true Catholic," announced one Protestant historian in the interwar period. The roots of such a sentiment, fed by the legacy of colonial and nineteenth-century anti-Catholicism and nativism, ran deep. Even in the midst of the postwar meritocratic university, the antipathy lingered: at least one young Catholic historian seeking academic employment sought his mentor's advice on choosing an appropriate Protestant affiliation to place on job applications. In the waning days of such bigotry, Carl Bridenbaugh, in his American Historical Association presidential address in the early 1960s, attacked the new generation of "urban-bred" historians for their "environmental deficiency." These scholars, Bridenbaugh judged, were "products of lower middle-class or foreign origins and their emotions not infrequently get in the way of historical reconstruction."[11]

In this period of rising expectations, the educational status of minority men and women of all races lagged significantly behind that of white men. Where women had once attained more years of formal schooling than men on average, in the postwar period, thanks in large part to the GI Bill, men were much more likely than women to pursue postsecondary education. In 1920 women received half of the nation's bachelor's degrees; by the mid-1950s they were receiving only 24 percent of the degrees. Women on campuses encountered administrators and faculty members who discouraged them from entering professions outside the traditionally female-dominated fields such as teaching and nursing. Historians have noted the steady rise in women's permanent workforce participation rates and survey data from the postwar years that indicate women's increased employment aspirations, but the sentiments of such public officials as Democratic Party standard-bearer Adlai Stevenson, who told Smith College graduates that he knew no better vocation for women than that of the "humble role of the housewife," provided a significant counterweight to proto-feminist sentiments.[12]

Women who did go to graduate or professional school were less likely than men—by half—to complete their studies. Once credentialed, they could not find adequate employment in many professions. In 1940 women received 13 percent of all doctorates, a figure that declined to 10 percent by the mid-1950s. Women in male-dominated fields faced humiliating job searches that usually ended in appointments to less lucrative specialties, part-time work, or unemployment. In a 1968 sample study of law firms, researchers found that men filled a whopping 93 percent of partner or partner-track positions. Women who sought positions in higher education encountered a similar fate. Female academics toiled in part-time or fixed-term appointments as their male colleagues received the higher-paying and more secure tenure-track lines. Outside of women's colleges, few women held tenured positions. The same study of the legal profession revealed that, of 2,550 law school faculty surveyed, 2,500 were men. Those women fortunate to take up faculty positions clustered in disciplines such as home economics, where they made up 96 percent of the nation's faculty, and library science, where they held 71 percent of the positions; they constituted less than 5 percent (often less than 1 percent) of the engineering, philosophy, agriculture, and physical science department faculties. The few who successfully traversed the tenure process were considered "honorary men." Male academics were uncomfortable with women's presence. "'She acts as though she were a man, like the dog who thinks he is a human being,'" one woman in the early 1960s quoted her male colleague describing a typical female academic.[13]

Black men and women faced legal and informal exclusion and segregation.

The historically black colleges educating the majority of black students struggled in the face of financial difficulty: in the late nineteenth and early twentieth centuries, some of the most prestigious institutions, like Fisk and Atlanta, scrambled to remain open. Their teaching staffs were stretched thin and drew on meager resources. The Association of American Universities accredited only about 5 percent of these schools. A special issue of *Life* in 1937 devoted to higher education did not indicate, in either the text or accompanying photographs, the existence of black students. The number of black students in white-dominated southern institutions in the early 1950s numbered less than five hundred. And although most colleges and universities outside the South admitted minorities, the campuses were overwhelmingly white. From 1940 to 1950 black enrollment grew from five thousand to sixty-one thousand students, but this accounted for only about 3 percent of the total enrollment at these institutions. At the time of the *Brown v. Board of Education* U.S. Supreme Court case in 1954, 4.9 percent of the undergraduate population was African American; in 1965 that figure was unchanged. Blacks existed on the margins of mega-universities awash with white students.[14]

This racial inequality existed at the graduate and professional school level as well. Few southern states before the 1950s provided equal access to African Americans, and historically black institutions lacked the resources to match other public and private colleges and universities. Black students could study law, dentistry, pharmacy, and library science at one or two southern institutions; most could not pursue graduate work in engineering or architecture anywhere in the South (the truly persistent left for schools elsewhere). The National Association for the Advancement of Colored People (NAACP) challenged the norm of "separate but equal" in graduate education during the 1930s and 1940s with some success. In their *Sweatt v. Painter* and *McLaurin v. Oklahoma State Reagents for Higher Education* decisions, the Supreme Court in 1950 (on the same day) prohibited states from setting up all-white graduate schools and from segregating graduate schools in public institutions. The pace of change, however, was slow. In the early 1950s, less than 1 percent of the entering classes at white-dominated medical schools were black. The majority of African Americans pursuing law degrees did so at black institutions such as Howard University. Although no comprehensive study exists for the first half of the 1960s on the racial identity of law students, Harvard University Law School officials estimated in 1965 that no more than seven hundred blacks were among the nation's sixty-five thousand men and women studying for law degrees, a percentage of roughly 1 percent. Very little had changed since the turn of the century.[15]

The Development of Early Higher Education
Affirmative Action Programs

The roots of higher education affirmative action ran deep, fed by the same civil rights and liberal currents of support for equality and economic growth that underpinned the development of affirmative action elsewhere. Although policymakers' earliest concern was with employment, they viewed education as the gateway to individual success. In its rawest form, the inequality inherent in segregated educational systems had galvanized activists in courtrooms and communities across the South. The history of the civil rights movement is filled with milestones meant to improve African Americans' educational status: the Supreme Court's *Brown v. Board of Education* desegregation decision in 1954, the Little Rock Central High School desegregation crisis in 1957, and the confrontation with Alabama Governor George Wallace over the registration of black students at that state's flagship institution in 1963. "Let us march on segregated schools until every vestige of segregated and inferior education becomes a thing of the past, and Negroes and whites study side by side in the socially healing context of the classroom," Martin Luther King Jr. urged civil rights activists at the end of the 1965 Selma March.[16]

Away from the glare of television cameras, scholars, activists, and government officials engaged in intense discussions in the late 1950s and early 1960s over how best to improve access to higher education. Those committed to addressing "women's issues" tackled the importance of education in the postwar era. Members of the American Council on Education's Commission on the Education of Women released the first of several reports in 1954. In *How Fare American Women?* they noted that women's postsecondary education had not kept pace with social and economic changes. Women, they lamented, were unequipped to deal with financial and other challenges. The report's authors were sparse in their far-reaching recommendations (they insisted that women consider home and family as their primary duties), but they did acknowledge an emerging discourse that encouraged women to pursue wider career and educational options. Nearly a decade later, the members of the education committees of the Presidential Commission on the Status of Women were more supportive of gender equality. They echoed the earlier report's call for improved educational opportunity. For the first time they embraced the notion that education could be a tool for social change. Although many of their recommendations did not make it into *The Presidential Report on American Women,* issued by the commission in 1963, administrators, policymakers, and activists took note of its emphasis on the educational needs of older American women, increased financial assistance, and the establishment of a federal office of research on women. By the mid-1960s, higher education institutions like the University of Minnesota, the University of Michigan, and Sarah Lawrence College had established continuing education programs for women who had dropped out of college.[17]

During the peak of the civil rights movement, most of the attention was on bolstering black enrollment. "Much remains to be done to make higher education fully available for qualified youth in minority groups," the Education Policies Commission, a group sponsored by the National Education Association and the American Association of School Administrators, noted in 1957. Foundations led the way in studying the problem, offering solutions, and funding early affirmative action programs. The Rockefeller Brothers Fund brought together several hundred experts in 1956 to explore the economic, social, military, foreign relations, and educational challenges the United States would face in the 1960s. Its 1961 report, *Prospects for America,* warned that "denial of opportunity to the Negro results in the loss of potentially creative and skillful manpower." The report's authors went beyond a simple "growth liberalism" analysis and explored possible deficiencies in the way colleges and universities were considering applicants' qualifications: "Decisions based on test scores must be made with the awareness of the imponderables in human behavior. We cannot measure the rare qualities of character that are a necessary ingredient of great performance. We cannot measure courage, vitality, or determination." While acknowledging the need to look beyond narrow meritocratic criteria, however, foundations also called for educators to devote more resources to nurturing bright students with high IQ scores and grades. "The education of outstandingly able young people, including the top few of genius caliber, is a major responsibility of colleges and universities," insisted the members of the Education Policy Commission.[18]

By the mid-1960s, higher education institutions of varying sizes and reputations were able to report on the establishment of what were known at the time as "compensatory programs." In a 1964 survey of 610 colleges and universities, 37 percent of the respondents claimed to have special recruiting, financial assistance, precollegiate preparation, or tutoring programs. Some institutions had more than one kind of program. The depth of commitment, particularly in terms of resources, however, was unclear. Selective liberal arts colleges and Ivy League institutions were at the forefront of these efforts. Fifteen east coast colleges and universities created the "Cooperative Program for Educational Opportunity" to recruit talented students who qualified for admissions but who would not likely apply without encouragement. Summer programs for high school students were popular: Yale, Dartmouth, Princeton, Columbia, Mount Holyoke, Oberlin, and Georgetown developed them; so too did Rutgers University, the University of Pittsburgh, and the University of Toledo. The Ford Foundation funded plans by, among others, Duke University, Cornell University, the University of Michigan, and the University of California to provide financial assistance to these newly recruited students. Except for isolated cases of institutions modifying their admissions criteria to bring in minority students (Williams College received a Ford Foundation grant for this purpose), there was little of the "hard" affirmative action that would emerge by decade's end.[19]

The early results were impressive. Harvard doubled its admissions of black students in 1969, to 109 students; Dartmouth increased the number from 50 to 120 in the same period; Princeton had 11 black students and 30 other minority students in its 1969 freshman class of 1,346 students; and the Seven Sisters colleges admitted new classes where, on average, black women made up 13 percent of the student body. Schools in the Big Ten system such as the University of Illinois and Indiana University created affirmative action programs as well. The University of Michigan admitted 200 minorities (mostly black applicants) in 1969, which pushed the total minority student body to around 1,000 students.[20]

Still, the numbers were small, and most early affirmative action addressed undergraduate, not graduate or professional school, admissions. None dealt with the underrepresentation of women and minorities in faculty ranks. A few institutions allowed students to draw out their undergraduate years with additional foundational courses in order to prepare them for the rigors of postgraduate study. Columbia University and Brown University, for example, joined with Tougaloo College, a historically black institution in Mississippi, in this purpose. The nation's law schools led the way in drawing black students to advanced degree programs. In 1965 Harvard Law School—with Rockefeller Foundation money—set up a "Special Summer Program" for forty juniors and seniors from southern black colleges. Dozens of other law schools instituted similar programs. That same year, New York University's law faculty authorized its admissions committee to "admit approximately 10–15 students who predictably will succeed in law school, even though their test scores and college grades place some below our predetermined cutoff line for admissions." Faculty members there were sensitive to the potential anger of rebuffed white applicants, so they stipulated that "in order to prevent the displacement of students who might otherwise have been admitted, we suggest that the first-year class be enlarged by the appropriate number."[21]

Medical schools soon followed with similar far-reaching plans. In 1968 the leadership of the American Association of Medical Colleges recommended that medical schools "admit increased numbers of students from geographical areas, economic backgrounds and ethnic groups that are now inadequately represented." The association offered precise goals the next year, suggesting that 12 percent of first-year students admitted for the 1975–76 academic year should be black students. By 1970 two-thirds of all medical schools and one-half of all law schools had some type of affirmative action in place. And it seemed to be working: between 1968 and 1974, the number of black students enrolled in first-year medical classes increased from 266 (2.7% of the total) to 1,106 (7.5%). In that same period, the number of Native Americans went from 3 to 71, Mexican Americans from 20 to 227, and mainland Puerto Ricans from 3 to 68. As the percentage of African Americans attending one of the two historically black medical schools dropped from 76 percent to 18 percent, other medical schools reported marked increases in black enrollment. In 1968 there were five black students among the 570 students working fulltime for a medical degree at Harvard; by the mid-1970s there were fifteen black students, along with three Native Americans, five Asian Americans, and seven Hispanics.[22]

The debate on how best to increase the number of black students, and how to assist them in graduating, had begun. "Do universities have the social right at this time to regard their admission criteria as sacrosanct?" asked political scientist and executive director of the Southern Regional Council Leslie W. Dunbar in 1966. Dunbar thought that they did not, but he warned that "extreme and knowing care must be taken to respect the dignity of those who require special guidance and training, and the universities have a social obligation not to lower or dilute their existing criteria." Edmund Gordon and Doxey Wilkerson, two Yeshiva University faculty members and authors of a 1966 study on compensatory education for the College Entrance Examination Board and the National Scholarship Service and Fund for Negro Students, acknowledged that higher education affirmative action "tend[s] to collide with recent trends toward higher and higher admissions standards." They noted that "most institutions resolve the conflict by restricting their recruitment efforts to disadvantaged with already demonstrated talent." Gordon and Wilkerson argued, however, that "full commitment to the compensatory principle calls for increased efforts to enroll and help risk candidates among disadvantaged high school graduates." This was already becoming an informal practice, at least in law schools. Duke University law professor Ernest Gellhorn observed in 1968 that the practice of passing black students on an easier scale was "quietly applied by at least one major law school, and probably the rule of more." For Gellhorn, this was "temporarily acceptable" while schools made "an adjustment of the entire grading scale so that the grades of other students fairly measure relative success."[23]

Campus activists helped shape new policies. They came to demand admissions and hiring plans by way of larger protests over governance and curriculum changes. At Cornell University in 1969, black students took over a campus building in response to what they argued were racist incidents. The rifle-carrying students insisted that the university create "black studies" courses and establish an African American student center. Between 1966 and 1972, higher education institutions inaugurated nearly five hundred black or "Afro-American" studies programs. White scholars, such as prominent historians Kenneth Stampp and Herbert Gutman, faced angry minority students and faculty who challenged their competency to speak and write on black culture. Although the issue never rose to the intensity of the large-scale protests over the Vietnam War, many activists turned their sights on incorporating numerical goals in admissions as a way of addressing the underrepresentation of minorities in colleges and universities. These developments marked the shift from "soft" to "hard" affirmative action.[24]

Race-conscious admissions became most visible at the City University of New York (CUNY). Administrators and public officials of a municipal college system unrivaled for its tuition-free, high-quality education for generations of working-class New Yorkers faced off against activists frustrated with the slow pace of increasing the small number of minorities. In 1969 only 14 percent of the student body was black, and 6 percent was Puerto Rican; at City College, the premier institution in the system, nonwhites made up only 13 percent of the student population. In February of that year, black and Puerto Rican students demanded, among other things, that City College's student body reflect the racial composition of the city's high schools, that black and Puerto Rican studies departments be established, and that all teacher education majors study the Spanish language as well as black and Puerto Rican history.[25]

To press their demands, activists occupied a campus building and engaged in vandalism and violence. In May 1969 the administration and faculty acceded to the demands. They created a "dual admissions" system whereby one-half of the incoming class would be assessed on the basis of the old system and the other half would be chosen from designated high schools in poverty-stricken neighborhoods. These applicants would not be required to meet a set grade standard. A firestorm of protests erupted from all sides of the conflict, including from white opponents. Two months later CUNY officials introduced an "open admissions" system and promised entry to one of the city's higher education institutions to all high school graduates. Of the one hundred thousand students admitted in the first three years under the new plan, forty-eight thousand applicants would not have qualified under the old standards.[26]

Student activists also pressed colleges and universities to retain minority students with failing grades. At Temple University, law school officials expelled fourteen black and Puerto Rican students for academic failure in September 1971; eleven of these students filed discrimination complaints with the state and federal government, charging the law school with failure to offer adequate support services such as tutorial assistance. School administrators readmitted all the students. A year earlier, Wayne State University's administration faced student protests when fourteen African American students flunked out of its law school. The "Wolverine Law Student Association" members insisted that not only must the students be allowed to return but the law school also "must be sensitive and responsive to the demands and rights of Black people" or else "face the wrath of the Black community and suffer serious political consequences." When negotiations dragged on, student protestors barricaded themselves in the library until the law school dean, Charles Joiner, agreed to readmit all of the students in question. Joiner had insisted to the faculty that "we have not and will not readmit en masse. . . . This special action is not discrimination in reverse. It is simply an effort to consider all facts with regard to re-admissions and to make judgments tailored to individual cases." It did not look that way to many on campus and metropolitan area residents when the local press reported that the students in the library "unchained the doors . . . and walked out to a rousing chorus of black power salutes from about 30 supporters outside."[27]

As administrators, faculty, and students grappled with how best to increase the number of minority students, federal officials pressed higher education institutions to submit affirmative action plans for faculty employment. Although they were not initially considered applicable to higher education, presidential executive orders provided much of the legal authority for the affirmative action launched in the late 1960s. Executive Order 10925, issued by President John F. Kennedy in 1961, prohibited contractors receiving federal money from discriminating on the basis of race, color, religion, and national origin; EO 11246, issued by President Lyndon Johnson in 1965, extended Kennedy's order by requiring "affirmative action." Johnson expanded his ban on discrimination to include sex discrimination with EO 11375 in 1968. In addition to executive orders, the Equal Pay Act of 1963 and Title VII of the Civil Rights Act of 1964 offered redress to women academics who believed that they faced salary and other kinds of discrimination. State lawmakers and officials in forty-two states enacted fair employment and equal pay laws as well. The first significant federal measure to include higher education came in February 1970, when the U.S. Department of Labor issued "Order No. 4," which required government contractors to develop hiring goals and timetables for minorities. The Labor Department turned over higher education enforcement of the order to the Office of Compliance Review (OCR) in HEW. While the Equal Employment Opportunity Commission (EEOC)—created as a result of the Civil Rights Act of 1964—would receive individual complaints, the OCR would deal directly with colleges and universities in developing affirmative action plans and in addressing class action suits. Noncompliance became a potentially expensive prospect for higher education institutions, as OCR officials were empowered to withhold federal research grants. At large institutions such as the University of Michigan, which received $60 million in federal funds, and the University of California, which received $70 million, the loss of federal money could spell disaster.[28]

Feminists—not civil rights activists—were the most instrumental group in getting the federal government to take seriously the goal of equality in higher education. By the late 1960s, women were regaining their share of doctoral degrees lost in the postwar period, but they found themselves shut out of many academic posts. In 1970 women accounted for half the number of humanities doctorates, but the slowdown in faculty hiring coupled with continuing discriminatory practices left them with less than 5 percent of the professorships across the country. Women academics formed caucuses in professional associations such as the Modern Language Association (1969) and the American Philosophical Association (1970); they passed resolutions at their respective annual meetings calling for daycare facilities on campus, pregnancy and parental leave, and the development of alternatives to the traditional career tracks. The authors of a 1975 Carnegie Council report on higher education affirmative action noted that by the late 1960s, there was "growing evidence of organized groups of women" conducting surveys of the gender composition of faculties and pressing for new policies, especially regarding faculty hiring procedures. Much of the activism occurred on individual campuses, such as the University of Michigan, where Jean King and Mary Yourd formed the "Ann Arbor FOCUS on Equal Employment for Women." King, a local lawyer, and Yourd, the widow of a former law school dean, lobbied legislators and filed formal complaints with the federal government. They wrote to U.S. Secretary of Labor George Shultz in May 1970 to tell him that, while Michigan awarded 11 percent of its PhDs to women, they only made up 6.6 percent of the university's faculty. King and Yourd informed the secretary that "this fact is especially important with regard to women students, for in order to find her own style and identity in the academic world a woman student needs a variety of women models."[29]

At the national level, the National Organization for Women (NOW) and the Women's Equity Action League (WEAL) coordinated the efforts of local chapters. NOW's Lucy Komisar advised chapter leaders that, despite the legal office's lodging of a "blanket complaint" of sex discrimination at colleges and universities, "your chapter should file individual complaints for all colleges in your area—just take a college catalogue and count the numbers of men and women on each academic level. . . . [G]et Congressmen and Senators to write the OFCC [Office of Federal Contract Compliance] asking for action." In May 1970 the organization's Boston chapter charged Harvard University with discrimination in faculty hiring; the next April, it publicly urged HEW to require higher education institutions to set goals and timetables for admitting more women into graduate programs.[30]

WEAL members proved even more effective than NOW in promoting higher education affirmative action. "In 1970 most men, and more than a few women, simply did not see sex discrimination as a problem on *their* campus, if indeed it was a problem anywhere," observed Bernice Sandler, director of the Project on the Status and Education of Women and member of the Presidential Advisory Committee on the Economic Role of Women. By 1973, WEAL, a small network of women activists, many of them in government, had filed over 360 class action complaints. Sandler herself could claim considerable credit for this effort. After receiving her PhD in 1969, the forty-one-year-old Sandler could not secure a permanent academic position. ("Let's face it, you come on too strong for a woman," one male academic told her.) When she noticed an obscure reference in a government publication that sex discrimination in higher education was illegal, Sandler mobilized her allies: working with Senator Harrison Williams (D-NJ) and WEAL members of Congress such as Martha Griffiths (D-MI), Edith Green (D-OR), Shirley Chisholm (D-NY), and Patsy Mink (D-HI), she lobbied policymakers to launch investigations into practices at the University of Michigan, Harvard University, and other institutions. After working in isolation for some months (the Ford Foundation agreed to cover her photocopying costs), Sandler was hired by HEW as an advisor.[31]

The effects of this activism underscored the link between feminism and emerging affirmative action policies. The federal government revised Order No. 4 in December 1971 to include women, and the Higher Education Act of 1972's prohibition on sex discrimination in any educational program turned policymakers' attention toward addressing inequality. "Affirmative action for women has become a priority issue in higher education," announced the author of a report for the American Association for Higher Education. HEW officials put college and university administrators on alert in 1972 that they must significantly revise their hiring and promotion criteria: "Goals should be set so as to overcome deficiencies in the utilization of minorities and women within a reasonable time. . . . Goals may be set in numbers or percentages." The routine workings of higher education seemed transformed. As affirmative action advocates studied the emerging affirmative action plans to ensure that they were far-reaching enough, a broad and influential opposition was already mobilized to promote colorblind policies and stop affirmative action in its tracks.[32]

The Emergence of Opposition to Higher Education Affirmative Action

American Jews, as individuals and in civic and religious organizations, offered the most significant opposition to affirmative action in the 1970s. They reacted most strongly to the changes affecting colleges and universities, where Jews, who made up 2.9 percent of the general population, held 9 percent of the faculty positions. The unprecedented growth in higher education came to an end as changing demographics and a worsening academic job market introduced the unfamiliar reality of scarcity. As the children born during the height of the baby boom completed their undergraduate educations, their applications to graduate and professional schools and tenure-track positions poured in to admissions and search committee mailboxes. Where once it had been relatively easy to secure, for example, a place in an incoming law school class, it was now fiercely competitive: by the early 1970s, the number of law school aspirants taking the Law School Admissions Test increased by a factor of ten over the course of the previous decade while the actual number of law students barely doubled. Affirmative action programs threatened to decrease applicants' odds even more. In his commencement address to the New School for Social Research in 1968, Daniel Patrick Moynihan, soon to join the Nixon administration as a policy advisor, offered an alarming prediction that "if ethnic quotas are to be imposed on American universities and similarly quasi-public institutions, the Jews will almost be driven out." Moynihan reckoned that "this would be a misfortune to them, but a disaster to the nation. And I very much fear there is a whiff of anti-Semitism in many of their demands." As affirmative action supporters filed complaint charges and lawsuits, lobbied government officials, and mobilized to articulate a rationale for race- and gender-sensitive plans, American Jews pushed back with equal vigor in defense of colorblind liberalism.[33]

The central contributions of American Jews to the civil rights movement made their opposition to affirmative action a particularly painful experience for all sides. Individual Jews offered steadfast, often heroic, moral, financial, and physical backing to the cause of racial equality. They did so in numbers significantly disproportionate to their share of the total population. Organizations that opposed affirmative action had been early and consistent supporters of antidiscrimination laws. In 1945, years before the U.S. Department of Justice had a civil rights division, the American Jewish Congress hired seven attorneys, who proceeded to file lawsuits against colleges and universities, landlords, realtors, and employers for racial discrimination. The American Jewish Committee published the celebrated "Studies in Prejudice" series in the late 1940s and sponsored Kenneth Clark's research on the damaging effects of segregated education, which became the backbone of the Supreme Court's reasoning in the 1954 *Brown* decision. The Anti-Defamation League was active in several civil rights efforts, including the campaign to integrate the armed forces. Jewish groups routinely filed amicus briefs in landmark civil rights cases and lobbied aggressively for the passage of the Civil Rights Act of 1964 and the Voting Rights Act of 1965. As a core constituency of postwar liberalism, American Jews welcomed a role for the state in targeting discriminatory acts and educating the public about racial justice.[34]

The now-standard narrative of the breakdown of this fabled alliance in the late 1960s obscures the roots of Jewish opposition to affirmative action that first emerged in the 1940s over quotas and the kinds of personal identity information the government was collecting. When the American Jewish Congress, the Congress of Industrial Organizations, the NAACP, and various Catholic and Protestant organizations formed the New York State Committee Against Discrimination in Education in 1945, its Jewish members faced off against other members who wanted antidiscrimination legislation to include an amendment allowing schools to consider race in order to "enrich the student body." Jewish leaders objected even to inquiries into an individual's racial, ethnic, or religious background. The American Jewish Congress explained its position on a 1957 government proposal to include a question about religious affiliation in its 1960 census: "We regard this proposal as unconstitutional and as an unwarranted invasion on the privacy of Americans." It did not modify this stance when it came to affirmative action plans in the 1960s. In an early statement arguing against a race-sensitive approach, American Jewish Committee leaders at a 1963 meeting announced that they "opposed any attempt to create a system of quotas as such for Negroes or anyone else in housing, employment, education and other areas."[35]

The rift that appeared between blacks and Jews after 1965 came over sharp disagreements about the shape and character of liberalism. Consensus melted away over issues such as the validity of black separatism, crime and other urban woes, and support for the state of Israel. "The American Negro is confused by the Jewish community," confessed black union leader Cleveland Robinson in 1966. "You initiated many of the programs against segregation and fought for equal rights of all citizens. Now, in the areas of housing and education, we see many Jews blocking our progress." The Ocean Hill–Brownsville School crisis in New York City in 1968 exposed further the fault lines dividing the two communities. When black activists, educators, and some parents demanded modification of teacher union seniority and promotion contract guarantees in order to devolve control of the city's schools to local boards, New York's teachers—60 percent of whom were Jewish—went on strike. This was much more than a battle over turf. According to historian Jerald Podair, the teachers and their supporters embraced a liberalism that was "integrationist, cosmopolitan, and humanist" and characterized by "individualism within a broadly pluralistic setting, equality of opportunity, and a race-blind, meritocratic approach to the distribution of societal rewards." African Americans were "deeply ambivalent" about these values. Many saw them as "fraudulent and hypocritical in their practical application." Black Power advocates chastised the prevailing notion of merit, calling it, as one correspondent for New York's *Amsterdam News* put it, "ridiculous." The fallout from the sometimes-violent crisis was dramatic: the political alliance uniting the city's black, Jewish, and white Protestant establishments imploded. In its place came a new coalition of "outer-borough" Jews and white Catholics.[36]

At the center of the Ocean Hill–Brownsville School crisis was Albert Shanker. The forty-year-old president of the city's United Federation of Teachers was Jewish, a dedicated unionist, and a proponent of colorblind meritocracy. Shanker answered his critics' charges of racism by pointing to the union's many efforts to bring about racial equality. These included a contract provision requiring the school board to recruit more teachers from the South, a new program to bring experienced teachers and white students to schools in minority and impoverished neighborhoods, and an internship program to assist minority teachers in qualifying for school principal positions. "We are not against affirmative action," he reminded one union member. "What we are against is quotas. The two things are really quite different." Shanker went on to become president of the American Federation of Teachers and continued to speak out against "hard" affirmative action, especially in his weekly *New York Times* paid column, "Where We Stand." "I think that quotas are essentially racist. . . . I think in the long run it will mean that minority groups who achieve positions will be viewed as being inferior. They will not be equal," he told a National Press Club audience in 1974.[37]

The outcry against CUNY's short-lived dual admissions plan, and then its open admissions policy, made visible on campuses the already fragile black-Jewish alliance. Disputes spilled out of classrooms and cafeterias and on to the streets. White students, shouting racial epithets, pursued black and Puerto Rican protestors who had broken windows at Queens College. Many of the city's residents, "for whom CUNY had been an important stepping stone to a better life," reported a contributor to the *American Jewish Yearbook*, had "strong reservations" about the open admissions plan, especially its effect on academic standards and the overall status of the system within the world of higher education. For older Jewish residents, the change at CUNY—where Jews once constituted nearly 80 percent of the student body—was a disaster. "City College has changed from a university to a high school. It's not even a high-grade school," lamented a man in his seventies. The CUNY degree, thought another man, had become "a fraud and is treated as such by the business community." The once unquestioned allegiance of American Jews to liberalism became more complicated. "Jews are not becoming illiberal," noted Milton Himmelfarb, director of information and research services for the American Jewish Committee. But, he continued, "the mass of Jews seem to have lost the confidence of a part of the liberal leadership."[38]

When American Jews complained about affirmative action, they did so in defense of colorblind principles and for more parochial reasons. One Jewish man in his fifties who was interviewed in the late 1970s for a study on Jews and affirmative action described its detrimental effect on the career trajectory of a "typical" Jewish-American teacher. This individual, he proposed, entered the profession in the 1940s with plans to become a school administrator. "The rules have suddenly changed on him," he said. "He's gone through all of this, he's worked for salaries that aren't all that big. He's gotten to the point where he has taken the exam for principal and he has passed it. And all of a sudden he is told, you can't have the principalship because we have to appoint a Black." At a conference on black-Jewish relations in Tarrytown, New York, in 1969, American Jewish Congress vice president Murray Gordon acknowledged the clearly different contexts in which the two groups viewed affirmative action: "The Jew was able to make it into American society by insisting upon merit as a value, as a test, and nothing else but merit. That's deadly for the black community if it wants to move rapidly. . . . [W]hat we found crucial to our development . . . works quite the other way for the black community, and we find it very hard to accept the notion that class or religion or race shall serve as a qualification rather than merit." This divergence created a longing for the old alliance. A Jewish woman in her forties understood the "move away from the assimilationist attitude . . . to a sense of pride; to a sense that we have to look out for ourselves." Still, she noted that it was "a real conflict . . . because we as an organization, and I think many of us as a people, were so liberal in the '50s."[39]

Alarmed parents from across the country wrote to Jewish organizations and newspapers to register their displeasure about affirmative action. Their complaints frequently took the form of stories about rebuffed family members denied college admissions or academic employment. These were anecdotal, but powerful, indications of affirmative action's effect on families. "I had four children with straight 'A' averages in high school and college and unable to attend the professional schools of their desires," a Valley Stream, New York, man wrote to the *Jewish Post*. He worried whether his fifth child ("verging on genius" he confided) would be admitted to medical school ("Our fears are real"). Another parent wrote to the American Jewish Committee to tell them that CUNY had rejected his two daughters—both with very high grades—from its doctoral English program. He urged that "this reverse discrimination must be stopped!" Politicians began to weigh in with stories as well: New York's gubernatorial candidate Howard Samuels revealed that "a Jewish boyfriend of his daughter was denied admission to a law school while minority students with lower grades were accepted."[40]

American Jews were becoming worried that, in the words of the heads of the Rabbinical Council of America, "merit is no longer the yardstick by which we measure success or the opportunity to serve." A member of the Detroit chapter of the National Council of Jewish Women complained about the black law student protest at Wayne State University and noted that "many members of the faculty freely admit to multiple standards, and many openly excuse it on the basis of 'affirmative action.'" A husband and wife academic couple from Baltimore (one had a doctorate in history, the other in English) believed that "incompetent, ill-prepared minority instructors have overshadowed the good work of other minority faculty. Better qualified white PhDs have not been hired or have been pushed aside for minority members." The correspondent reported that her department chairman "privately informed me that a less qualified black person was hired and conceded that I probably should have had the job." The letter was typical of many personal accounts that ended with the claim that affirmative action was destructive to higher education, that it was unfair to qualified blacks as well as whites, and, often, that the rejected applicant had received private assurances that they deserved the position.[41]

Although their reaction was often more measured that that of their rank-and-file members, Jewish organization leaders expressed alarm at affirmative action developments as well. Beginning in 1969, the American Jewish Congress, the American Jewish Committee, the Anti-Defamation League, and the National Jewish Community Relations Advisory Council took formal stands against preferential hiring and quotas. Prominent actor and folk singer Theodore Bikel of the American Jewish Congress reminded its executive committee members that "our young people are asking us to speak, and inaction on our part would be action and a particularly unbecoming form of action." In October 1969 the American Jewish Committee's executive board adopted a position from which they budged little in the years to come. While acknowledging the plight of "disadvantaged minorities," it nevertheless noted that "our sense of outrage for what they have endured does not cause us to lose sight of the needs and aspirations of other groups" (it mentioned "many Jews and members of other ethnic groups") and warned against "resorting to shortcut and dangerous solutions like quotas." For Benjamin Epstein, national director of the Anti-Defamation League, race-sensitive programs were "a reestablishment of a group percentage basis that destroyed the merit concept, which was the dream that made America so meaningful to the underprivileged Jew when he came to this country."[42]

As advocates of colorblind liberalism struggled to define their exact position on affirmative action, a small but influential group of scholars, journalists, and policymakers known as "neoconservatives" dedicated themselves wholly to defending higher education against threats to colorblind notions of merit and talent. It is difficult to define with precision what made one a neoconservative. They tended to be part of what Charles Kadushin, in his study of elite intellectuals, called the "Social Science-Literary Circle," whose members wrote for journals such as *The Public Interest* and *Commentary* as well as the *New York Review of Books*. The standard description of their origins is of a group of predominately Jewish leftists—some of them communists—who moved steadily rightward, first to anti-Stalinist Trotskyism and socialism in the late 1930s, then to liberalism in the 1940s and 1950s, and finally to a full break with liberalism in the late 1960s. Neoconservatism's ranks, however, were not as neatly constituted as this. Some, such as James Q. Wilson, Edward C. Banfield, and Ben J. Wattenberg, did not have leftist pasts: many were Christian, in particular Catholic, such as Jeane Kirkpatrick and Daniel Patrick Moynihan. The neoconservative label itself was a bit of a misnomer, since many eschewed the "conservative" brand. While Irving Kristol, widely described as the godfather of the neoconservative movement, defined a neoconservative as "a liberal mugged by reality," some resisted the label for years (Norman Podhoretz was a "centrist or centrist liberal"); others shunned it altogether (sociologist Daniel Bell described himself as a "socialist in economics, a liberal in politics, and a conservative in culture"). They were a diverse group, held together in foreign policy matters by firm anticommunism and in domestic concerns by opposition to the New Left and the drift of the Democratic Party to identity politics.[43]

Neoconservatives were not conservatives, or part of the New Right, at least not in the late 1960s. Irving Kristol considered *National Review,* the nation's foremost right-wing periodical, to be "too strident" and "insufficiently analytical"; he thought its editor William F. Buckley and its contributors "crackpotty" and their antiliberal rhetoric "sophomoric" and "simpleminded . . . in its 'anti-statism' in general and its contempt for all social reform in particular." Historian Gertrude Himmelfarb, Kristol's wife and a neoconservative as well, informed one interviewer, "We are children of the Depression . . . and are committed to the New Deal kind of welfare state. . . . Social Security is something we regard as a very good thing." Conservatives, in turn, did not know what to make of these brash new political actors. "They are insufficiently rooted in serious political realities . . . or coherent intellectual tradition," judged a *National Review* writer in 1970.[44]

In contrast to supporters of colorblind liberalism, however, neoconservatives were too horrified by what they saw as the cultural decadence rife in minority communities and in new social movements as well as wrong-headed policies offered by what Kristol called "the professoriate" to focus much attention on promoting liberal social programs. They denounced lenient professors, student protests, the countercultural lifestyle, and demands for curriculum changes to accommodate new minority and women's studies programs. "Here at Columbia . . . we have suffered a disaster whose precise dimensions it is impossible to state," wrote historian Richard Hofstadter in the aftermath of the student takeover of university buildings at Columbia in 1968. To Daniel Boorstin, campus radicals were "dyspeptics and psychotics"; Bruno Bettelheim dismissed them as "very, very sick." Renowned philosopher Sidney Hook, with the support of some two dozen distinguished scholars, organized the University Centers for Rational Alternatives (UCRA) in 1969 to counter these effects. Its leadership claimed to have some three thousand members spread over 350 campuses. "If the university is conceived as an agency of action to transform society in behalf of a course, no matter how exalted," warned Hook, "it loses its *relative* autonomy, imperils both its independence and objectivity, and subjects itself to retaliatory curbs and controls as the part of society on whose support and largesse it ultimately depends."[45]

The academics that joined Hook's new organization complained of campuses awash in permissiveness and diluted standards. At an UCRA conference held at Rockefeller University in February 1972, participants not only denounced "violent disruptions," "foul language," and "militant fanatics," they wondered as well whether colleges and universities had been too generous in their admissions policies. Fritz Machlup, an economist from Princeton and refugee from Nazi Germany, admitted to the "fear that longer education for more people may do more harm" because it encouraged "anti-intellectual revolts." Philosophy professor Paul Kurtz agreed, claiming that "many young people now in universities ought not to be there; they have neither the talent nor the motivation." The University of Pennsylvania's Glenn Morrow suggested that the quality of faculty members had declined as well. Morrow grumbled that the American Association of University Professors (AAUP) had eliminated the requirements that three members nominate applicants, that applicants receive the approval of two-thirds of the local chapter's leadership, and that applicants have three years of experience at an approved college or university. The AAUP, he mourned, "is no longer the elite organization that was envisioned at its founding." These faculty who lacked sufficient vetting, concluded Georgetown University economist Cyril Zebort, were responsible for passing as bona fide scholarship "cooked experiments" and "deliberately falsified assertions."[46]

Disillusioned liberal academics highlighted their commitment to the civil rights movement and postwar liberalism. Paul Seabury, a political scientist at the University of California at Berkeley and a member of what he called "the league of lost liberals," informed *Commentary* readers that since 1967 the federal government "has been experimenting with novel brews." Seabury wrote of the "single minded pursuers of an ideal of equity overrun[ning] and tramp[ling] the ideal itself, while injuring innocent bystanders as well." In the late 1980s, retired San Jose University president John Bunzel remembered with bitterness the "signs of authoritarianism and ideological intoxication" that had appeared on campuses two decades earlier. Campus radicals tested Bunzel's liberalism: he was a civil rights supporter, an American Civil Liberties Union (ACLU) member, and a Democratic Party convention delegate, but he soured on the direction of social protests when he faced classroom disruptions as a professor at San Francisco

State College in 1969. Then, as a new college president, he fought to defeat a faculty strike. Bunzel argued that faculty and administrators had embraced affirmative action as a way of showing "concern for the underdog and . . . eagerness to give their campuses a forward-looking image—in a word, that the university *was* relevant and responsive." Roman Pucinski, a Democratic congressman from Chicago, made the connection between campus activism and affirmative action when he told an audience in 1970, "Many who are now in the forefront of leading the rioting and unrest in our universities are the very people that have been admitted to these universities at lower standards."[47]

The UCRA's leadership created the Committee on Academic Non-Discrimination and Integrity (CANI), one of the most important organizations to oppose higher education affirmative action. It succeeded in attracting attention to the growing "reverse discrimination" protests. Led by such eminent scholars as Paul Seabury and Sidney Hook, reported *Newsweek* in 1972, the group represented "a male backlash . . . sweeping through academia, largely in response to the increasingly determined effort by women to secure more positions and promotions on college faculties." CANI members called for "soft" affirmative action that would include "a serious and massive increase in both remedial services and the number of places made available to qualified individuals." They focused their efforts, however, on developing philosophical and legal arguments against race- and gender-sensitive programs. "The historic irony in the demand for representation on the basis of an ascriptive principle is its complete reversal of radical and humanist values," warned Bell in the pages of *The Public Interest*. "The person himself has disappeared. Only attributes remain." Miro Todorovich, CANI executive secretary, raised the common grievance that the government had foisted on the higher education community a program designed for the business and industrial sectors, thus upsetting the admissions, hiring, and promotion processes. Todorovich wrote a sympathetic member of Gerald Ford's White House staff about the "disastrous effects" that might include "the abandonment of the PhD or publication of scholarly work as criteria for employment or advancement." Bell reflected the views of most neoconservatives when he informed readers that "there cannot be complete democratization in the entire range of human activities. . . . A meritocracy is made up of those who have earned their authority."[48]

Nathan Glazer was the most effective neoconservative figure against affirmative action. Born into a family of Jewish socialists and unionists, Glazer attended CUNY and then received his PhD from Columbia in 1962. Along the way he worked at the American Jewish Committee and the U.S. Housing and Finance Agency. Glazer was the author of several important works, including (with David Riesman) *The Lonely Crowd* and (with Daniel Patrick Moynihan) *Beyond the Melting Pot.* Glazer's scholarly passion in the 1950s and early 1960s was the relationship of the individual to his or her neighborhood and nation in postwar America. In 1964 he turned his attention to a defense of meritocracy, writing in *Commentary* that "we are moving into a diploma society, where individual merit rather than family and connections and group must be the basis for advancement, recognition, and achievement." A decade later, in his much-discussed *Affirmative Discrimination: Ethnic Inequality and Public Policy,* Glazer regretted the "new divisions and . . . new period of conflict and controversy" brought on by race sensitive programs. There was plenty wrong with affirmative action, he argued: the notion of "institutional racism" had not been adequately analyzed; many of the racial and ethnic categories such as "Spanish-surnamed American" were "particularly confused"; and the courts had played too dominant a role in affirmative action, Congress being best situated to oversee its development. "Facts are assumed . . . that are not true, but served as the basis to guide judicial decisions," he wrote. For Glazer, "soft" affirmative action was fine, but "hard" affirmative action was unprincipled and bad policy. Government officials and higher education administrators might try to fiddle with programs in the hopes of making them fairer or more efficient, but these were impossible tasks, as the very existence of goals and timetables marked a "withdrawal from the acceptance of common standards, a weakening of our sense of rightness or justice in making distinctions."[49]

Traditional conservatives of the period had neither a scholar of Glazer's prominence nor an organization such as CANI to battle affirmative action. Through the mid-1970s, their influence over the shape and direction of the opposition was modest. But conservatives did have definite positions on equality and the role government should play in addressing discrimination. In general they rejected federal and state civil rights legislation (including the Civil Rights Act of 1964) and embraced an orthodox neoclassical approach to inequality. *National Review* editors ridiculed the New York State Commission in 1964 for its new authority to initiate complaints: "In no time at all [it] will mushroom into six hundred threescore and six, and go up and down in the world peeping at keyholes and listening at transoms—all in the interest of protecting some people's rights at the expense of other people's." They came to accept existing civil rights laws but cautioned that, with this law in place, no further government action was needed. Conservatives weighed in early against affirmative action. Ralph K. Winter Jr., a Yale law professor and later a federal judge appointed by Ronald Reagan, wrote in 1967 that "preferential treatment" would have "great costs."

Winter railed against its supporters on the grounds that "instead of helping to eliminate race from politics, they inject it." When CUNY introduced its open admissions policy, *National Review* lamented that "demands for guaranteed diplomas are just around the corner." Affirmative action was unnecessary, since the free market corrected discriminatory treatment over time. Blacks had made significant progress, one *National Review* writer pointed out in 1973, as a result of economic growth: "Liberalism . . . is centrally concerned with failure. . . . Too many successes would put it out of business."[50]

Economist Thomas Sowell embodied this new version of colorblindness. Sowell told his life story in his *Black Education: Myths and Tragedies* in 1972. He wrote of how, as a young black Marine veteran, he worked in a federal civil service job and, with GI benefits, received undergraduate and graduate degrees. Sowell had disdain for the faculty members who supported campus radicals (it was "their only chance of playing a prominent, or even self-respecting role at the university") and for the African American community's receptivity to black power (blacks had "long been played by spellbinding orators"). He received offers for faculty positions but grew resentful when " 'token' black representation was sufficiently fashionable that there could be some cloud of suspicion over a black faculty member's appointment." The young scholar claimed no need for special consideration: "I had at this point published more than any of the other assistant professors in economics, and perhaps more than all of them put together." Sowell rejected affirmative action, even revisions of aptitude tests to make the wording of questions understandable to minority students. "Culture-free tests would be good predictors for someone who was going to lead a culture-free life, but that is impossible," he wrote. He rejected overt discriminatory treatment but insisted that little of that behavior remained in higher education institutions, since they were committed to rewarding pure merit. "As a man who had struggled hard against the odds to achieve success," notes historian Nancy MacLean, "he was a powerful messenger for the right's argument."[51]

Although colorblind conservatives were less central to the history of anti–affirmative action in the early years, the growing alliances of some neoconservatives with conservatives marked a partial fusing of a coalition that would come to the forefront only in the late 1970s. In most cases it was neoconservatives who made the intellectual and political journey rightward. Buckley brokered the liaison, especially with Kristol. By 1970 the onetime leftist was writing a column for *Fortune* and had joined a monthly lunch group with Buckley known as "the Boys Club." In its March 1971 issue, *National Review*'s editors extended an invitation to *Commentary* readers with the heading "Come On In, the Water's Fine." Some neoconservatives remained wary of conservative principles (Bell resigned from *The Public Interest* editorial board in 1973 because he believed the journal was becoming too conservative); others became affiliated with the growing number of right-wing foundations and think tanks such as the Hoover Institute, the Heritage Foundation, the Pacific Legal Foundation, and the John M. Olin Foundation. Some of these organizations served as funding sources for conservative intellectual movements, in particular the Olin Foundation, which provided money to Richard Posner, Richard Epstein, and other scholars in the law and economics movement. By 1979 the American Enterprise Institute, founded in 1943, had grown to a staff of 169 and had a $10 million budget. Irving Kristol became one of its long-term fellows.[52]

Colorblind liberals were at the helm of anti–affirmative action efforts. For all the reports at the time that American Jews were defecting to the Republican Party, Jewish leaders, for the most part, resisted the conservative message and continued to argue against affirmative action on the basis of colorblind liberalism. The American Jewish Committee's Institute of Human Relations, for example, launched what it characterized as "an intensive campaign" in 1973 to promote "positive action programs without 'quota systems.'" These included a greatly expanded federal government-sponsored jobs bank, increased job training, stronger enforcement of equal employment laws, and more open-enrollment programs at colleges and universities. That same year the American Jewish Committee approved the filling of amicus briefs against several municipal government affirmative action plans, "provided that the attack on the quota be coupled with espousal of such legitimate forms of affirmative action as may be appropriate in this situation." American Jews were aware of the difficult balance. "I'm not a fool. I realize that equal opportunity *per se* doesn't really mean anything if you don't have some real background opportunity," admitted one man. In the 1970s they would continue to struggle over the exact meaning of *opportunity* as they participated in litigation and lobbied the federal government, especially on higher education affirmative action. "Much soul-searching has been going on within Jewish organizations as they attempt to reach a principled position in a matter that touches close to home," observed one *New York Times* journalist.[53]

In this volatile period, it was difficult for these organizations' members to maintain good relations with civil rights allies. American Jewish opposition to higher education made headlines; the media didn't notice, much, that the American Jewish Committee and the American Jewish Congress joined with the NAACP and the American Civil Liberties Union in the early 1970s to file lawsuits in support of school busing, equalized public school funding, and increased food stamps allotments and against restrictive zoning ordinances that excluded multiunit housing. Some leaders attempted to relegate affirmative action to a secondary concern in order to highlight their common interests. In January 1973, for example, members of the National Jewish Community Relations Advisory Council's Committee on Equal Opportunity counseled that these protests be pursued "with a much lower profile than in the past," since there was the perception that it was "essentially a Black-Jewish confrontation rather than a matter of broad public concern and interest." The American Jewish Committee's Paul Perlmutter wrote from Boston, "The Jewish aspect should be 'decentered'— in fact, if there were no Jewish involved, the issue of quotas would exist and would flare up." Although the most public discord centered on race relations, Jewish leaders acknowledged tensions with feminists as well. The American Jewish Committee's Seymour Samet confided to the organization's Washington, D.C., representative Hyman Bookbinder that Bernice Sandler's denunciation of the Jewish opposition could "create misunderstanding and result in a polarization in which Jews would appear to be championing the rights of white males against the interests of women."[54]

If higher education affirmative action opponents did not speak in a single voice, they nevertheless articulated a passionate defense of equality based on colorblind meritocracy and individual rights. As new federal policy guidelines emerged, opponents would offer fresh challenges, which in turn generated increased public debate and lay bare the growing divisions among liberals. They held up the civil rights movement as the intellectual and ethical standard, one from which, they argued, affirmative action policies had strayed. A feature story in the *Philadelphia Inquirer* in 1974 told the story of Martin Goldman, a college student and civil rights volunteer a decade earlier and the victim of a savage attack by a gang of whites. The account focused, however, on how Goldman, a newly minted historian, had failed to obtain a tenure-track job in his specialization, African American history. When the head of Temple University's Institute of Pan-African Studies canceled his interview upon learning that he was white, Goldman sued and received a $5,000 settlement. The story's author was sympathetic to Goldman's plight: "He's became a victim. . . . Goldman was denied a job because he's white. It's a measure of how far the civil rights movement has come that Goldman now stands outside it, a victim of discrimination."[55]

CHAPTER THREE

"This Issue Is Getting Hotter"

The Struggle over Affirmative Action Policy in the
Early 1970s

Over the course of the 1970s, Americans debated affirmative action with increasing sophistication and unease. Compared to the antibusing movement, which generated a high pitch of controversy across the country over resistance to court-ordered plans, opposition to affirmative action appeared at first to be a series of spirited lobbying sessions involving union leaders, higher education faculty and administrators, and government officials. These initial quiet efforts, however, marked a rupture in support for the colorblind liberalism that dominated social policy in the United States after World War II. As the busing crisis faded from national headlines by the mid-1970s, "reverse discrimination" protests grew in significance. Affirmative action supporters and opponents staked claims over the meaning of equality, merit, compensatory justice, and diversity. The growing number of Americans who, in turn, joined the debate reflected new divisions in the workplace and on college campuses that were unimaginable just a decade earlier.

A May 1975 forum on affirmative action hosted by the American Enterprise Institute (AEI), a conservative think tank, captured the depth of the divisions. The participants on stage that evening represented, in a predictable way, a debate between opposing sides. The *Washington Post*'s William Raspberry defended race- and gender-sensitive programs since "institutions tend to reproduce themselves unless something interferes with that process. Build an institution white, for racist reasons, and it will continue . . . unless some thing interferes with that." Liberal columnist Vera Glaser added that affirmative action "is not aimed at creating preference. . . . [It] is aimed at ending the preference for white males which has always existed in the business and academic worlds." The charge that such efforts constituted setting quotas was unfounded, Glaser insisted. Goals—not quotas—were "more or less an attempt to estimate what an employer's workforce would be like if there were no illegal discrimination." But for University of

Chicago law professor Richard Posner, affirmative action was "wrong," "foolish," an "evil practice." Posner announced to the gathering, "Every time you discriminate against one group you are pushing out another group." Political scientist Paul Seabury joined Posner's side and complained that higher education affirmative action—run by "bureaucrats"—would destroy meritocracy: "Does the value of individualistic merit have any intrinsic meaning in a culture that is dominated by collective group rights?"[1]

The AEI forum also revealed the ambivalence of some opponents who were not prepared to make a blanket condemnation of affirmative action. Owen Fiss, a faculty member at Yale's law school, began his comments by warning that the collection of racial and gender identity data by institutions was "problematic" since "it looks like it's at odds with your obligation not to discriminate." Fiss went on to warn against the "over-enforcement" of nondiscrimination policies on the grounds that "you may . . . create incentives to hire on the basis of race or sex discrimination." He balked, however, at endorsing Posner and Seabury's view that existing antidiscriminatory measures such as Title VII of the Civil Rights Act of 1964 were sufficient. "You may, by using the traditional law enforcement technique, leave a great deal of race or sex discrimination undetected, unestablished, and uncorrected," he worried. By the end of the event, Fiss had endorsed aggressive programs that avoided numerical goals or quotas but addressed bias and structural inequality. "Sometimes you take a risk, sometimes you engage in very difficult judgment because you believe that the substantive principle that is at stake is worth exposing yourself to those types of difficulties." Fiss's unwieldy set of priorities represented the views of many Americans who could not quite make up their minds about affirmative action.[2]

Public officials and the national media began to notice both the intensity of opposition and the difficult balancing of principles. "This issue is getting hotter. . . . The affirmative action situation is snowballing," University of Denver chancellor and U.S. Commission on Civil Rights member Maurice Mitchell informed fellow commissioners at a 1972 meeting. There was no doubt that many Americans rejected affirmative action as a clear violation of constitutional and ethical principles of colorblind treatment. News stories reported that ill-conceived programs unjustly rewarded applicants on the basis of race or gender, not talent and hard work. When Washington University student pranksters prepared identical records for two fictitious graduate students—one white, the other black—and submitted them to 176 colleges and universities for open faculty positions, they reported to the press that the black "applicants" received positive responses from 44 percent of the institutions while the followup interest for the white counterpart stood at 9 percent. Critics pointed to the haphazard nature of programs that were poorly designed and lacked safeguards against abuse. One *New York Times* journalist, for example, related a "documented case" of trickery at the University of California at Berkeley in 1975 in which a rejected applicant who had used his father's surname reapplied under his mother's Spanish surname. On his second attempt he was admitted "with a large grant."[3]

Where middle-class whites had seemed untroubled by new training and hiring programs in exclusionary skilled trade unions, they now balked at plans to reorder the higher education system. The National Jewish Community Relations Advisory Council reported on the "considerable anxiety" in local Jewish communities. They noted that "Jews are finding it increasingly difficult, if not impossible, to gain admission into colleges . . . and employment opportunities for Jews in university faculties and various branches of government service are being limited or curtailed." Although the sense of concern was genuine, the evidence of "reverse discrimination" was often impressionistic and exaggerated. The organization's David Samet, for example, concluded that the Cleveland Jewish community's low spirits were "a consequence of 'horror stories' emanating from New York City and spread across the country by Jewish organizations." The result, Samet lamented, were "baseless anxieties" that "seriously jeopardized" relations with civil rights organizations. Meanwhile, affirmative action advocates argued that the newly established programs were insufficient: they referred to an American Council on Education study that revealed that the percentage of blacks in faculty positions rose from 2.2 percent of the total in 1968–69 to only 2.9 percent in 1973; the percentage of women crept up from 19.1 percent to 20 percent in the same period. More affirmative action, not less, was needed, they insisted.[4]

Even as the terms of the debate seemed to be crystallizing, Jewish leaders remained at the forefront of efforts to reconcile colorblind liberalism with the new liberalism of the post–civil rights era. They struggled to answer vexing questions: Which groups of Americans should be given affirmative action consideration? What exactly constituted a "quota"? Were numerical goals or quotas acceptable for some occupations but not for higher education? Should affirmative action "victims" be compensated? Where colorblind conservatives considered the template for the affirmative action debate established, these liberals were less settled in their understanding of preferential treatment. American Jewish organizations served two functions in the early years of affirmative action: they provided a forum for fierce debate over how hard opponents should come down on government and higher education programs, and they mounted the most effective campaign against affirmative action through the mobilization of resources and lobbyists. To be sure, young and talented conservative scholars contributed to this opposition, but conservative think tanks and foundations were not yet able to match the political strength and capacity for political action of Jewish organizations.

Politicians and policymakers became engaged in this issue so charged with constitutional, ideological, and electoral significance. Opponents began to gain political traction during the 1972 presidential race between Richard Nixon and George McGovern when a coalition of Jewish organizations publicly demanded that the candidates announce their positions on affirmative action. At the same time, Jewish American leaders initiated an extensive campaign for officials in the U.S. Department of Health, Education, and Welfare (HEW) to reduce significantly their requirements on higher education institutions. This came just as labor union leaders were rushing to defend the seniority principle of "last hired, first fired" in the face of calls for its modification in order to preserve recent affirmative action hires. It was a decisive moment in the history of affirmative action. Supporters scrambled to counter an opposition that, despite lacking consensus, seemed to be making inroads into the shape and character of policy. At this juncture the future of higher education affirmative action was very much in doubt.

"The Numbers Game": The Significance of "Quotas" in Affirmative Action Policies

No part of affirmative action met with more resistance than the requirement that colleges and universities meet numerical goals in their admissions, hiring, and promotion. To opponents, "goals" were simply a euphemism for "quotas." They were to be avoided since they undercut individual rights, diminished the importance of meritocracy, and threatened to usher in a new order of racism. Court-directed affirmative action offered the most public evidence of quotas. When federal district judge W. Arthur Garrity ordered in 1974 that, for every white teacher hired in Boston, a black teacher must be hired until blacks made up 20 percent of the teaching force, few observers doubted that this constituted a quota. Most guidelines, however, were not as direct as Garrity's order. To be sure, in addition to the requirement that institutions keep detailed records of the race and gender for all applicants, they mandated that a certain number or percentage of applicants belonging to targeted groups be hired or admitted with a specific period of time. The guidelines that HEW officials issued in 1972 for colleges and universities were typical: "Goals should be set so as to overcome deficiencies in the utilization of minorities and women within a reasonable time. . . . Goals may be set in numbers or percentages." This, too, seemed to be a quota, at least to affirmative action opponents. The parsing of "quota" and "goal" stymied many education leaders. Convention delegates to the 1972 American Association of University Professors (AAUP) meeting, for example, backed a resolution favoring "energetic and systematic attempts" to bring minority men and women of all races into their ranks. They insisted, however, that their support "should not be construed as a policy of 'reverse discrimination.'" The AAUP committee on academic freedom and tenure confessed that they were "unable to find appropriate language to incorporate a standard against discrimination in faculty appointments in a set of recommended regulations for colleges and universities." The report's authors added that some faculty members "evidently feel that their institutions are setting quotas in response to government pressure."[5]

Opponents scoffed at claims that affirmative action plans did not actually mandate quotas. "A quota does not cease to be one because it is undeclared, because it is subject to periodic adjustment, or because it is called 'reasonable representation,'" declared Larry Levinsky of the Anti-Defamation League of B'nai B'rith (ADL). When HEW used "numerical goal" instead of "quota," Sidney Hook, prominent philosopher and chairman of the Committee for Academic Non-Discrimination and Integrity, called the substitution of other words a "transparent semantic evasion." CANI leaders developed their critique further, maintaining that the use of poorly masked quotas not only corroded individual rights but also represented a misallocation of HEW resources away from legitimate enforcement of antidiscrimination measures. "Arriving at certain numerical proportions is not the same thing was putting an end to discrimination against individuals of any color or sex," insisted CANI. "It does distract from the effort to end discrimination . . . by giving the illusion that proportionality is a fit substitute for equal opportunity."[6]

In struggling to answer the quota charge, affirmative action supporters alternated between denying the existence of quotas and explaining their existence as violations of official policy. Brooklyn College's Gertrude Ezorsky reminded readers in the *New York Review of Books* in May 1974 that "for all their 'quota mongering' they have failed to show a single case where HEW has, in fact, imposed a quota on a university, i.e., refused to accept 'good faith efforts' in lieu of a goal unfulfilled." Still, on some occasions, Ezorsky admitted, school officials had used quotas. This occurred when government investigators, "carried away by their power[,] . . . exceeded their legal authority." In a debate with Miro Todorovich, CANI's director, Howard Glickstein of the University of the Notre

Dame Law School criticized those who "grossly exaggerate the nature and extent of abuses connected with affirmative action programs." Todorovich responded that the fault lay with the language of "goals," which had "created much ill will, cynicism, and no little injustice." This grouping of applicants created a predetermined fate for all: "It is good to be black, valuable to be a woman, and bad luck to be both white and male."[7]

The "quota debate" unsettled American Jews who belonged to organizations with strong antidiscriminatory programs that appeared to many to be using affirmative action as a matter of definition. One man, a self-identified Jew and college faculty member, argued in an interview in a late 1970s that calls for increasing the number of Jews in underrepresented white-collar occupations were hypocritical. "My dad tells me that the ADL was arguing in its early years . . . [for] more Jews, more Jews. Jews are forty percent of schools. We should be forty percent of teachers," he noted. "Now schools are sixty percent minority groups and [American Federation of Teachers president] Al Shanker . . . [and] the ADL and the *Commentary* crowd sing a different tune." Others pointed to the Israeli government's practice of favoring Jews over Arabs and Sephardic Jews over Ashkenazi Jews for certain jobs, noting that it undercut the contention that quotas were at odds with a Jewish sense of justice. How did they answer the charge that they too were playing the "numbers game"? "We have neither insisted upon proportional representation nor ethnic goals," proclaimed the American Jewish Committee. "Instead, we have demanded that Jews not be excluded because they are Jewish and that they be considered on the same basis of qualification and merit applied to others." The ADL defended its work with the Bell Telephone System, the New York City Police Department, and others as simply pushing employers "to make affirmative efforts to seek Jews as job candidates and then hire strictly on the merits." As they struggled with competing ethical and identity claims, at least a few arrived at the conclusion that numerical goals or quotas were unfortunate but necessary. David Haber, a member of the American Jewish Congress executive committee and the Rutgers University Law School faculty, thought that support for affirmative action without backing quotas was "unrealistic": "A school will only get a significant number of underprivileged if a significant number is fixed."[8]

The files of Jewish organizations from the period illustrate conflict and shifting positions. In 1969, for example, the National Jewish Community Relations Advisory Council opposed any policies that smacked of preferential hiring, numerical goals, or quotas; at its 1972 convention, however, the council's leaders modified their stance and proclaimed that, while they continued to oppose quotas, "we do not oppose . . . the setting of specific target goals and timetables for rectifying the imbalances resulting from past discrimination." Just two years later they had another change of heart and reverted to their original position: "We reject the proposition that race, color or ethnicity is a qualification or disqualification for any post. . . . We oppose the use of quotas and proportional representation in hiring, upgrading, and admission of members of minority groups." Few could engage in the debate in a detached manner. "Much soul-searching has been going on within Jewish organizations as they attempt to reach a principled position in a matter that touches close to home," wrote Walter Goodman of the *New York Times.*[9]

The leadership of the American Jewish Congress wavered as it attempted to balance self-interest with the two principles of colorblindness and equality. Rabbi Elmer Berger argued to fellow executive committee members in 1972 that numerical goals were necessary "during a transitional period until equality can be achieved." Diane Ravitch, future U.S. assistant secretary of education, countered that while "public and private institutions must work to improve the black man's ability to compete," this "did not mean that people should be hired because or their race of that the merit system should be abandoned." The Jewish leadership were concerned as well about affirmative action's effect on Jews. If they did not acknowledge this practical issue, warned executive director Naomi Levine, "she did not know what role the AJCongress could play in the Jewish community of tomorrow," according to the minutes of a meeting of the executive committee. Another member agreed: it was "chutzpah . . . for us to tell Jews that it was right and proper for them to make sacrifices." Berger chastised his opponents, telling them that the organization should not adopt an anti–affirmative action stance "simply because those who happen to be Jewish find themselves personally and individually aggrieved in the process of selection." In the end, the American Jewish Congress board did not overturn their earlier anti–affirmative action resolution, but they were uneasy with their official stance. Levine softened her opposition two years later when she agreed that goals or timetables might be permissible, but "only as guides or benchmarks to help administrators determine if their hiring procedures and requirements are in fact nondiscriminatory."[10]

The American Jewish Committee was the most divided Jewish organization. In 1969 its leaders opposed "the creation of a system of quotas for any group including the disadvantaged in education, employment or any other area of American life." They understood the needs of "disadvantaged minorities" and supported "special measures" for them but insisted that "our sense of outrage for what they have endured does not cause us to lose sight of the needs and aspirations of other groups." At a special meeting on affirmative action in 1972, they again rejected quotas, proportional representation, and goals. They warned of "the spectre of 'lowering of standards' by according preferential treatment to applicants from disadvantaged groups." Still, the participants wavered about the soundness of the merit system: "There was a general consensus that all established standards should be questioned and re-examined as they often constituted a denial of the very merit principle we profess to support."[11]

Despite efforts to present a unified front, the group's national leadership faced pressure from chapters across the country as well as its New York headquarters to alter their position. In an interview in the early 1970s, Executive Vice President Bert Gold observed that the American Jewish Committee's Social Action and Intergroup Relations Office, headed by Seymour Samet, was more sympathetic to the notion of "goals." The group's national officers met with a different resistance in Philadelphia, where its chapter president noted that "we are even more hard line"; national staff members, however, had to prod Cleveland officers to move more aggressively against affirmative action, in particular by publicizing reports of minority medical students' poor records compared to white students at Case Western Reserve University. They were battered from all sides. Jewish academics from Brooklyn College, Fairleigh Dickinson University, Temple University, Rutgers University, and Tufts Medical School attending a 1972 consultation with American Jewish Committee officers and staff "agreed that the problem of quotas was most serious and that AJC should involve itself with this issue." Two participants accused the organization with being "soft" on higher education affirmative action. The meeting concluded with the warning that "if the AJC did not maintain a strong anti-quota stance, independent Jewish faculty groups would 'steal' the issue from the Committee."[12]

The organization's Washington, D.C., lobbyist, Hyman Bookbinder, was the most critical of its official stance. Bookbinder, a former legislative representative for the AFL-CIO and assistant director of the Office of Economic Opportunity during the Johnson administration, cautioned the New York leadership that it was "unsatisfactory to rest my case on abstractions like 'quotas are improper.'" He insisted that "a certain amount of ambiguity, of flexibility, in this area" was "not only unavoidable, but perhaps even desirable." While putting the best possible reading of the group's position to civil rights allies, Bookbinder privately nudged his colleagues to "develop ways of monitoring programs so that numerical goals are used as measuring devices only rather than as primary methods of 'affirmative action.'" The difference between a "goal" and a "quota," he admitted, "is not great but sufficient to make it acceptable." Bookbinder worked behind the scenes—and perhaps behind the backs of the American Jewish Committee leadership—to support affirmative action, even going so far as to contact Nixon administration officials in 1972 to encourage them not to scrap existing programs.[13]

Bookbinder's colleagues scolded him. "The fine line between goals that are mandatory . . . and quotas escapes me, even when court ordered," the American Jewish Committee's Seymour Brief lectured him. "[Stanley] Pottinger may have tried to make the distinction, but I can't separate them and I think you haven't, at least for me." Both Bookbinder's views and the organization's 1972 statement on affirmative action opened its leaders to charges of equivocation. U.S. Civil Service Commission staff member Bernard Rosen informed Bookbinder that his position was "very troublesome to him and the Commission." Bookbinder summarized Rosen's views for Seymour Samet: "We've given away too much, he believes, by this explicit granting of preferential treatment. It runs contrary to the basic law to say that any preference may be racially or ethnically motivated." American Jewish Committee president Philip Hoffman assured *New York Times* readers, "We are firmly committed in our opposition to quotas in employment and other facets of American life. . . . We will continue to do everything in our power both to resist trends to a quota oriented society and to expand appropriate efforts to eliminate discrimination wherever it exists." Even then, the issue kept cropping up: in 1973 Hoffman wrote to John Morsell, the NAACP's assistant executive director, that his organization "agrees that the use of numerical data and statistical techniques can help assure the effectiveness of affirmative action programs with safeguards against any abuses."[14]

The spirited debate continued, but longstanding Jewish opposition to the collection of individual race and religious identity information by the government, employers, and educational institutions proved durable. By a vote of 18 to 8, the American Jewish Congress executive committee backed a resolution in 1973 on the "destructive effect" of such data gathering; in 1976 they asked the HEW secretary to destroy a form distributed to public school systems in five major cities (including New York City). Through the form, the government required teachers and administrators to identify themselves and their students by their racial and ethnic origins. When a federal judge sentenced the principal of the Long Island City High School to nighttime confinement in a community treatment center for refusing to complete or sign census directives, the Council of Jewish Organizations protested to President Gerald Ford that such classifications were "totally unscientific and frightening in their implications" as well as a "clear-cut invasion of privacy." In Los Angeles, ten parents—Jews, Native Americans, African Americans, and Hispanics—filed a superior court case in October 1976 in opposition to school district surveys requesting students' racial and ethnic information. The parents argued that it violated privacy rights guaranteed by the U.S. Constitution as well as federal and state laws.[15]

Affirmative action supporters dismissed the parsing of policy language of "goals" and "quotas" as a distraction from the fundamental challenge of securing race and gender equality. To them, such debates were an insincere cover for less principled opposition. "A goal is a quota only if you want very much to believe that it is," concluded Mordeca Jane Pollack, a Brandeis University professor and the National Organization for Women's university compliance coordinator. More guarded supporters were less dismissive. Clark Kerr and the other coauthors of the Carnegie Council's affirmative action report expressed their general support for admissions and hiring plans but criticized the "statistical games" they claimed administrators played. It should not, they wrote, "be allowed to degenerate into a 'numbers racket,' into a monstrous piece of fakery." Broad numerical goals for colleges and universities were acceptable, but "the finer the tuning, the grosser the result."[16]

Try as they did to present a coherent and consistent argument against affirmative action, opponents undercut their race- and gender-blind principles by supporting the use of numerical goals and quotas in blue-collar employment. They argued that working-class jobs bore little resemblance to the rarefied world of higher education. "Putting someone in a tenured position, which is capitalized at three quarters of a million dollars, is very different from hiring a black rather than a white plumber," insisted Daniel Bell. For all their concern over "hard" affirmative action, the American Jewish Committee backed a proportional hiring plan in the Memphis Fire Department. They did so, Sam Rabinove explained, because "college teaching is inherently different from firefighting, in terms of capabilities required and there is no evidence today that qualified blacks are 'underutilized' in college teaching or cannot find jobs commensurate with their capabilities." Even within the ranks of CANI—an organization especially unyielding in its defense of meritocracy—some members softened their opposition to affirmative action implemented away from campuses. In addition to urging open apprenticeship programs and heightened government scrutiny of union elections, for example, CUNY professor and CANI member Richard Gambino held that modifying traditional seniority arrangements was necessary to preserve the recent gains of affirmative action recipients.[17]

Affirmative action supporters pounced on these opponents and charged hypocrisy. Howard Glickstein denounced the "self-righteousness" of those who believed that there was "something special about higher education." They ought to acknowledge, Glickstein wrote, "that the same principles of nondiscrimination that apply to plumbers, policemen, and sheet metal workers also apply to professors!" David Sarnet explained that the "blind spot" was rooted in class bias: criticism of affirmative action seemed confined to fields in which Jews were heavily represented, such as higher education, "to the disregard of areas in which Jews are relatively few, such as the construction trades and fire departments." University of Texas economist (and secretary of labor in the Carter administration) Ray Marshall also noticed that "academic whites often see no inconsistency in demanding four-year requirements for B.A. degrees, while condemning electricians for requiring four years, mostly spent at work for apprenticeships." Marshall chalked this up to the fact that "few of them [academics] know much about the jobs they are criticizing." Not all higher education opponents were drawn into this two-track approach. The key was consistency in opposing affirmative action programs, the American Jewish Committee's Bert Gold concluded. This was necessary "even in the most egregious cases" of discrimination since "exceptions of this nature, in the long run, are likely to do more harm than good."[18]

"Dangerously Tribalistic": Debating Group Inclusion in Affirmative Action Programs

The most immediate challenge for affirmative action opponents was to contain the growing number of claims by members of ethnic and racial groups for inclusion in programs. This was no easy task, since pro–affirmative action activists seized on the capacious notion of "disadvantage" that politicians, policymakers, and economists employed at the inception of hiring and admissions programs in the 1960s. It was not clear who exactly belonged in this category. Some experts focused on refining the concepts of the "poverty line" and the "culture of poverty" and on identifying geographical poverty zones in the nation's urban centers and rural outposts. For Michael Harrington, author of *The Other America,* the disadvantaged were "non-white minorities . . . [and] the aged, the migrant workers, the industrial rejects, children, families with a female head, people of low education." They hesitated to equate the disadvantaged only with minority group members. "The answer to the question 'Who are the disadvantaged?' is more complicated than it seems," noted the Ford Foundation's Mario Fantini and Columbia University's Gerald Weinstein. "The disadvantaged cannot be defined by race, residence, jobs, or behavior alone." Doxey Wilkerson and Edmund Gordon, two African American scholars and the authors of a 1966 study on compensatory education, defined the "disadvantaged" as individuals "handicapped" by depressed social and economic circumstance. "In many instances, they are further handicapped by ethnic and cultural caste status," they wrote. Wilkerson and Gordon applied this definition to "predominantly Negro, Puerto Rican, Mexican, and Southern rural or mountain whites." Supporters sought to include as many Americans as possible in the early years of compensatory programs. In their encyclopedic study of higher education published at the time, Christopher Jencks and David Riesman argued that equal opportunity could best be achieved by "deliberately favoring applicants from working-class or lower-class backgrounds regardless of race."[19]

Leaders of "white ethnic" organizations rushed forward with data to prove the disadvantaged status of Polish, Italian, Slavic, and Irish immigrants and their children and grandchildren. This came as a surprise to affirmative action supporters and opponents alike, who believed that white ethnicity was characterized by resentment and insularity that usually took the form of support for reactionary populists such as former Alabama governor George Wallace and resistance to neighborhood integration and busing. It seemed unusual to them that white ethnics might support affirmative action. In fact, the white ethnic revival that swept the country in the late 1960s and early 1970s was an unwieldy phenomenon whose participants both celebrated immigrant success and complained of a continuing lag in economic progress for second- and third-generation ethnics. Scholars and journalists (often part of what anthropologist Micaela di Leonardo calls "the ethnic industry") wavered between shoring up the old "melting pot" assimilationist model and exploring newer claims of ethnic distinctiveness popularized in movies like *The Godfather* and in books with titles such as *Blood of my Blood, The Rise of the Unmeltable Ethnics,* and *The Decline of the WASP.* It was clear that there was no single entity known as "white ethnics." Although many came to craft their family and ethnic group narrative around a kind of "bootstraps" story of community uplift—music to the ears of colorblind conservatives—there existed as well support for government programs for urban, education, employment, and health care reform. In his study of Jews and Italians in Brooklyn's Canarsie neighborhood, sociologist Jonathan Rieder discovered, alongside the strong backlash to liberalism, "strain[s] of biracial populism." In cities across the country, white ethnic leaders allied their organizations with the National Center for Urban Ethnic Affairs, a group headed by civil rights veteran Monsignor Geno Baroni.[20]

Ethnic activists laid the blame for dismal economic gains at the feet of the media, the government, and corporations, whom they often lumped together as elites. "The Ethnic American is forgotten and forlorn," complained Baltimore city council member (and future U.S. senator) Barbara Mikulski. "We are 'near poor' economically. No one listens to our problems." Since the federal government did not conduct surveys on the economic and educational status according to ethnicity, there was little in the way of substantive data to prove Mikulski's claim. When neoconservative sociologist Nathan Glazer noticed an announcement for Ford Foundation grants on ethnic group research, he was told that "in the Ford Foundation's usage 'ethnic' meant members of racial minorities and of group that had their origin in some parts of Latin America." It fell to groups like the Congress of Italian-American Organizations, the Joint Civic Committee of Italian Americans, and the Polish American Congress to fund their own studies. Their conclusion was that white ethnics suffered from considerable discrimination in the worlds of business and higher education. "Those social classes which seem so committed to expiating guilt for injustices done to blacks are quite unconvinced about injustices and exploitations worked upon white ethnics and upon their ancestors," observed Father Andrew Greeley, a Catholic priest and University of Chicago sociologist.[21]

For Stephen Adubato, a thirty-eight-year-old former civics teacher and head of the Cultural and Education Center in Newark, New Jersey, the solution was to create "Displaced White Ethnics" in 1970 and develop alliances with the city's minority communities. That same year his group supported a black mayoral candidate over an Italian-American opponent. "We want no slowdown in the advancement of blacks or browns, but we don't want their advancement at the expense of the white ethnics," he explained. "Let's all share in the advancement with the same equality." Adubato and like-minded ethnic leaders pushed for enforcement of existing antidiscrimination laws and lobbied for additional legislative and executive orders. Title VII of the Civil Rights Act of 1964 was particularly important since it banned, in addition to workplace discrimination on the basis of race, color, creed, and sex, discrimination due to an individual's national origin. The Columbian Coalition, an organization of Italian-American professionals and business people, retained counsel to prepare legal briefs on behalf of coethnics claiming to be discrimination victims. Ethnic activists and sympathetic politicians were pleased when the Equal Employment Opportunity Commission—created to enforce Title VII—rendered a favorable ruling on national origins discrimination. Congressman Frank Annunzio, a Democrat from Illinois, cheered an EEOC decision in 1970 in support of a Polish immigrant's complaint: "Italian-Americans across the nation must be alerted to this decision . . . because the immigrant who has long been the butt of ridicule, exploitation, or discrimination . . . has the door of redress open to him." The percentage of national origins complaints, however, remained relatively small. Annunzio explained that this was a result of the "myth" that Title VII was "passed only for the purpose of eliminating racial discrimination."[22]

White ethnics began to demand that they receive affirmative action consideration. Scholars writing on the ethnic revival of the period emphasize the Republican courting of the white ethnic vote. This was more than a case of manipulating cultural anxiety— politicians often reacted to ethnics' varied demands. Richard Nixon's supposedly masterful manipulation of blue-collar and white ethnic culture and social defensiveness was in large measure as much a product of ad hoc policymaking in the face of direct lobbying. President Lyndon Johnson faced it first, including from his own special assistant Jack Valenti in 1965. "While you have made some spectacular Negro appointments . . . let us not forget that the largest ethnic group in this country (larger than the Negro) is the Italian," he reminded Johnson. By the time Nixon arrived in the White House, the demands for political appointments, ethnic studies legislation, and affirmative action were in full swing. "This ethnic thing continues to plague us as more and more letters come in from various unhappy groups," Nixon aide Tom Lias informed the president's special counsel and political strategist Harry Dent in 1970. "The head Pole went away from here mad last week, etc. etc. . . . With all this smoke there must be fire." Some Nixon advisors and cabinet members such as Charles Colson and Labor Secretary George Shultz pushed for white ethnic eligibility for affirmative action as well.[23]

In December 1971 HEW officials offered white ethnics some affirmative action consideration, but it fell short of mandating hiring goals or timetables. The watery policy language, however, did acknowledge that white ethnics suffered discrimination. They concluded that "experience of various religious groups, primarily Jews and Catholics, and members of certain ethnic groups, primarily of Eastern, Middle, and Southern European Ancestry . . . continue to be excluded from executive, middle-management, and other job levels, because of discrimination based on their religion and/or national origin." Under this directive, employers were required to undertake various activities to "remedy this underutilization of that particular religious or ethnic minority group."[24]

A few white ethnics even filed affirmative action lawsuits. Albert Maise, a rejected applicant to the University of Colorado Law School, argued in court that, as an Italian American, he should be given the same consideration as black, Native American, and Mexican American applicants. Colorado's law school faced a similar claim from Philip DiLeo, who asked that his application be included with minority applicants in the "Special Academic Assistance Program." DiLeo thought this was appropriate, since he was "of Italian-American heritage and a product of slum schools, [and] was educationally, socially, and economically disadvantaged." The judges hearing the cases ruled against Maise and DiLeo, but the chairman of the Italian American Foundation persisted in calling for compensatory preferences for white ethnics. Some legal actions in opposition to affirmative action seemed to contain backhanded arguments in defense of proportionality and consideration of applicants' racial and ethnic backgrounds. When Columbian Coalition attorneys filed charges against CUNY on the grounds that the institution's affirmative action program had resulted in the unfair advancement of minority candidates to permanent rank, they noted that, if the two rejected faculty members they represented had been promoted instead, they would be the first Italian Americans to hold such positions in their departments. In the case of one of the professors, the lawyers pointed out that Italian American students constituted over 25 percent of the department in which he taught. Other ethnic leaders made similar kinds of observations. Aloysius Mazewski, president of the Polish American Congress, told President Jimmy Carter in 1980, for example, of his disappointment that none of the seventy-nine minority judicial nominees had Polish surnames. "I abhor quotas but if that is the case, 5 percent of the population of the United States are Americans of Polish descent," he reminded Carter.[25]

American Jewish leaders were especially alarmed by this development. Most major Jewish organizations, including the American Jewish Committee, the American Jewish Congress, and ADL, were vocal opponents to the "hard" affirmative action of goals and quotas but were committed to the "soft" affirmative action of improved recruitment of minorities, compensatory education, and better financial assistance for underrepresented groups. They feared the spread of group- or identity-based affirmative claims. American Jewish Committee legal director Samuel Rabinove warned the organization's president in 1972 that "recent indications are that white ethnics (the Italians, for example) are also seeking to get into the act." Samet, the director of the group's national affairs department, told an interviewer a year later about a rumor that local Irish American applicants had approached Brandeis University administrators with a request for special admissions consideration, since Boston's Irish population was so large. Some Jewish Americans were even interested in modifying affirmative action programs to include themselves. At a meeting of the National Jewish Community Advisory Council in 1972, Rabbi Samson Weiss proposed that Jews be declared a minority, so, as he put it, "Jews can get in on preferential hiring." Samet fretted about "some evidence of Jewish organizations demanding preferential treatment for Jews and using language very similar to that of non-Jewish organizations whose efforts we decry." The city council of Englewood, New Jersey, in 1975 designated Jews as minorities, thus making them eligible for the municipality's affirmative action employment program. "The perils of contagion are manifest," warned Rabinove.[26]

This came as jarring news to colorblind liberals. "Breaking the white community into subgroups is the beginning of the end," reasoned the United Synagogue's Social Action Committee chairman, "because every ethnic group has its 'quota' and Jews, who are only 3% of the population [will] find themselves back where they were 30 or 40 years ago with Jewish quotas closing education and professional doors in their faces." Larry Lavinsky, chairman of the ADL's National Law Committee, argued that discrimination against white ethnics was proof that a colorblind policy should guide government officials and higher education administrators: "Such groups have only recently begun to enjoy the benefits of a free society and should not be exposed to new discriminatory bans, even if they are raised in the case of compensation to certain racial minorities for past injustices." Still, these colorblind liberals did not wish to dismiss the white ethnicity entirely and alienate their allies. American Jewish Committee leaders acknowledged that white ethnicity was still relevant and that there was "no incompatibility" between helping white ethnics "fulfill their authentic needs and aspirations" and their organization's "flat opposition" to quotas.[27]

The neoconservative and conservative response was to denounce calls for white ethnic affirmative action consideration as, in the words of Queens College's Richard Gambino, "dangerously tribalistic." They concluded that ethnicity was not a significant influence in the lives of second- and third-generation Americans. "We are a nation of immigrants, but we are not a nation of 'ethnics,'" Nathan Glazer pointed out. There was, they contended, little more than a devious "me-tooism" at work in the ethnic revival. "As this process of giving benefits of the basis of one's racial or national origin develops, more and more groups will spring into existence," promised Richard Posner. "People who had forgotten they were Croatian Americans will become conscious of their ethnic identity in order to assert their claim to a part of the pie."[28]

The fears of affirmative action opponents went unrealized. In 1973 the federal government released revised—and weaker—regulations covering white ethnics. The new guidelines required employers to "take affirmative action to insure that applicants are employed, and that employees are treated during employment, without regard to their religion or national origin." This was to be accomplished through "outreach and positive recruitment" and with "accomodation to religious observance and practice." The guidelines did not, however, contain the word *underutilization,* and enforcement was left to employers. It is not entirely clear how this policy came into being. Certainly, affirmative action supporters were largely unsympathetic to white ethnic appeals. "The plight of the white ethnics is not the result of discrimination . . . and should not be raised in the context of Title VII," the general counsel of New York City's Commission on Human Rights told the *New York Times.* According to sociologist John Skrentny, the definitional meaning of being African American had framed policy elites' understanding of other groups' eligibility. In this way, Native Americans, Asian Americans, and Hispanics were "definitionally and morally analogous to blacks" in the eyes of policy elites. Women, however, were "definitionally different from blacks." Legislators and policymakers revised this understanding in the face of feminist lobbying and the large number of complaints and lawsuits. White ethnics continued to plead for their inclusion with no success. Mary Frances Berry, a member of the U.S. Commission on Civil Rights, told the head of the Polish American Congress in the early 1980s that he must rebut the presumption that white ethnics held "white skin privileges" before she would agree to consider them disadvantaged. By the time of Berry's rebuke, most ethnic organizations had long since joined Jewish and conservative groups in filing amicus briefs in such high-profile cases as *DeFunis v. Odegaard* (1974) and *Regents of the University of California v. Bakke* (1978) in defense of colorblind constitutionalism.[29]

There remained an ad hoc quality to determining who should be a recipient of affirmative action. In its defense against Philip DiLeo's challenge to its law school admissions criteria, for example, University of Colorado administrators determined that Asian Americans, Hawaiians, and Cubans did not fit into their eligibility requirements, but Puerto Ricans did. A dean at the University of Michigan explained the importance of regional considerations in determining a school's eligibility list: "We don't consider Orientals as members of a minority, although they would be in states like California where you have large numbers living in ghetto sections." The dean added that women "aren't minorities . . . but we do make special allowances for them because they are included in the university's affirmative action agreement with the federal government." Indeed, there was a lack of consensus at the very highest levels of power. U.S. Supreme Court Justice Lewis Powell did not believe that there were compelling reasons to include Asian Americans. (Powell thought that Jews and other white ethnics were similarly situated.) At one point Nixon administration officials considered dropping Asian Americans from plans but ultimately allowed them to continue as recipients; on another occasion they forgot to include Asian Americans in revised plans but hurriedly added them at the last moment. Nixon himself was unclear as to who "belonged" in affirmative action programs: sometimes he considered white ethnics and Mexican Americans as a single group. (This was not so far-fetched: Even today, over 50% of Latinos list themselves as "white" in the federal census.) To Fordham University sociologist Ernest van den Haag writing in *National Review,* the creation of eligibility lists smacked of "unattractive arbitrariness" and "inherent capriciousness."[30]

Although it didn't address the core philosophical and constitutional arguments against affirmative action, the claim of white ethnics offered opponents another line of attack: too many people were beneficiaries of preferential programs. If programs must continue, only the economically disadvantaged should be eligible, irrespective of race, ethnicity, or gender. This meant the exclusion of the small but growing number of middle-class African Americans. "Many of the people you want me to pay back grew up in higher class backgrounds than me, often having professionals as parents," protested one unemployed academic and self-identified white man, the "son of a poorly paid postal clerk," to Jimmy Carter during his 1976 presidential campaign. To some critics, the improved economic status of African Americans in the late 1960s and early 1970s was proof that race-sensitive programs were already outdated. They pointed to news items to make their case, including a 1973 story that Harvard's admissions office had claimed that over 75 percent of their black students could no longer be categorized as "disadvantaged." New York University president James Hester concluded in his remarks to a congressional subcommittee in August 1974 that "an advantaged minority group member has the same difficulty getting in as an advantaged majority group member." The way to address inequality, it seemed, lay in paying attention to class background, not racial identity. A group of representatives from various Jewish organizations wrote to a lead official in HEW's Office of Civil Rights (OCR) and urged him to examine "such matters as family income as well as [a] more extensive evaluation of the quality of the applicant's schooling and potential educational performance."[31]

Supporters were unmoved by these calls to rethink in a wholesale manner affirmative action eligibility. To consider only working-class or poor blacks, argued the Council of Legal Educational Opportunity's Robert O'Neil, would cause "serious practical problems" in determining who was eligible. Besides, O'Neil continued, middle-class minorities continued to face the kinds of discrimination that affirmative action could best address with minimal costs. He suggested that existing plans were not the ambitious employment and wages program to address economic inequality, as envisioned by liberal unionists. Instead, affirmative action was a modest way to pull minorities into the business and professional world without disrupting the institutional workings of higher education and industry. The inclusion of middle-class African Americans would actually be cost-efficient, O'Neil reasoned, since they would not need financial assistance and "would probably assimilate more easily, and be more acceptable to white-Anglo students who are put off by street language and ghetto lifestyle."[32]

Although they returned on a regular basis to try to recast affirmative action as a colorblind program for the disadvantaged, opponents in the 1970s expended more effort trying to chip away at the number of groups covered by programs. This was a sound strategy, since affirmative action supporters themselves questioned the inclusion of certain groups. The Carnegie Council report authors, for example, noted that while Chinese Americans and Japanese Americans were "not generally educationally disadvantaged," a case could be made for recent immigrants from Asia, "especially the many Chinese coming recently from Hong Kong." Some observers criticized more sharply the capacious category of "Spanish-surnamed Americans" (later called "Hispanics"). This included not only Mexican Americans and Puerto Ricans but Cubans as well, many of whom were wealthy and seemed to some to face little or no discrimination. In a 1975 article highly critical of the "bureaucratic, legalistic muddle" of higher education affirmative action, Sheila Jackson argued in the *New York Times* that the "Spanish-surnamed" category was indefensible: it included immigrants as well as individuals whose families had long lived in the United States. Moreover, the exclusion of Sephardic Jews and Americans of Castilian descent underscored the imprecision at play. Jackson's point was that policymakers had not crafted criteria that could limit the expansion of beneficiaries. "There is no reason why the executive order could not be amended to include gays, spastics, paraplegics, persons over 50, or any number of other groups that have often been discriminated against in the labor market," she warned. Such a prospect alarmed Vernon Jordan, executive director of the National Urban League. Jordan charged that "the new minorities" were poaching scarce employment and educational benefits that rightfully belonged to African Americans. "The establishment is striving to accommodate the needs of new minorities at the expense of blacks," he told a gathering. "Unless blacks return to the spotlight of social change in America . . . all of us will lose out."[33]

Within affirmative action policy circles, many supporters considered women, especially white women, as having the weakest claim for inclusion. The reasons varied: they were too numerous, were too highly educated and skilled, or could not claim a racial or ethnic experience of discriminatory treatment. "From a practical point of view, white women don't need any protection—they can protect themselves," EEOC Commissioner Colston Lewis informed television viewers on *CBS Evening News* in April 1976. Sheila Johnson in the *New York Times* acknowledged that feminists were largely responsible for the existence of most higher education affirmative action programs, but those programs were "chiefly of benefit to women rather than minorities." The *Chronicle of Higher Education* reported that some black leaders felt that advocates for gender equality were "unfairly getting the lion's share of attention from federal investigators and college administrators." Feminists pushed back, protesting that the EEOC and the OCR were not addressing gender inequality with the same seriousness as racial inequality. The antagonism toward women was discernable on campuses, according to U.S. Civil Rights Commissioner Maurice Mitchell:

> The black and Chicano communities in my university campus have taken off vigorously and aggressively against the women's rights proponents, arguing that in fact the white women are offering themselves to beleaguered institutions as a low cost, highly acceptable substitute for the solution of serious racial problems in which minority people are out to great suffering and are deprived of their rights. . . . [I]t's become almost impossible for us to hold a civil meeting on the subject of an affirmative action program if the white women on that committee are present.

While some of this reaction could be chalked up to sexist attitudes (one black graduate student explained that "women are going to reap most of the benefits; after all, they're the ones sleeping with the men"), it also points to the gap in the 1970s between the broad acceptance of the rights revolution and lack of agreement on which social injustices and economic inequality deserved to be remedied.[34]

Affirmative action opponents offered similar reasons for excluding women. One California faculty member characterized middle-class American women as "the most privileged group of people on the history of this planet." Paul Seabury informed *Commentary* readers that the OCR's J. Stanley Pottinger and the "middle-range bureaucrats" who worked under him "scent sexism more easily than racism." When the American Jewish Congress leaders met with the heads of Harvard, Columbia, Dartmouth, Princeton, Wellesley, and a number of public universities in 1973, they reported that "the issue of merit is not nearly as serious with respect to women." Familial and individual choices, not structural or discriminatory behavior, explained the low numbers of women in certain academic programs, especially science and business, as well as the low percentage of female tenured faculty. "A large number of very capable women choose to raise a family and are not ready to devote the tremendous effort needed to become first-rate academics," concluded a member of CUNY's chemical engineering department.[35]

Thomas Sowell, conservative economist and rising star of the New Right, offered the most substantial explanation for why women did not need affirmative action programs. Echoing other critics, Sowell asserted that women "are not another 'minority' either statistically or culturally." They had not, he insisted, been excluded from higher education or discriminated against. In fact, Sowell reported that women had "higher mental test scores" than male PhDs and came from more affluent backgrounds. What then accounted for their lagging salaries and status? Sowell's key argument was that women made career and marriage choices that placed them on a different trajectory than men. "The overwhelming factor here is marriage," he told White House officials in 1975. He acknowledged that female academics earned less than male academics—their salaries in 1970 stood at 83 percent of that of a comparable male, 84 percent in 1973—but this figure only revealed how affirmative action had failed to deliver equality for women. The important thing to keep in mind, he insisted, was that women made marriage and parenthood high priorities and these hampered their employment status. Sowell offered statistics from a National Science Foundation survey that showed that the salaries for female faculty who never married were 104 percent those of male counterparts at top-rated institutions and just over 101 percent at other institutions. Policymakers, he concluded, were confusing women's fully informed choices with sex discrimination.[36]

If efforts to winnow the number of recipients seemed a distraction from core arguments against affirmative action, it helped to create the "reverse discrimination victim" who bore the emotional and financial costs of undeserving beneficiaries. These victims, the argument went, suffered from unfavorable work assignments, missed promotions, failed college and university applications, and underwent job furloughs. Such accounts of their experiences gave an immediate and tangible sense of affirmative action's effects that was missing from the dry and legalistic pleading of supporters and opponents. "Because one is a member of . . . achieving groups, should he or she as an individual be penalized?" asked Nathan Glazer. Some affirmative action supporters were sympathetic to this line of reasoning. "There is enormous frustration . . . you help the very rich and the very poor. They are in the middle," Father Theodore Hesburgh, president of Notre Dame University and chairman of the U.S. Commission on Civil Rights acknowledged in 1972. "They can't go to Notre Dame or Duke. They feel set upon and they feel no one cares about them." Former U.S. Department of Justice official Nathan Lewin rejected the view that opponents were "reactionary and crypto-racist" and acknowledged a "disquieting sameness to the groups that were being asked to bear the burden." These were "the Irish, the Poles, and the Italians who . . . were being kept out of jobs so their employers could carry out their affirmative action obligations." The excluded—"often themselves more victims than victimizers"—paid the price for employer discrimination. "A fair program," Lewin proposed, "would have required the employer to hire both black and white even if he needed only one."[37]

Few affirmative action proponents shared Lewin's perspective. They rejected the "reverse discrimination victim" argument, viewing it as a distraction from the task of securing equal opportunity or even as a disingenuous effort to destroy what little progress had been achieved for racial and gender equality. EEOC chairman John Powell considered such complaints as "insignificant" and "reverse discrimination" stories a "myth." Theodore St. Antoine, dean of the University of Michigan Law School, reckoned that "it is unfortunate that some well-qualified whites may be rejected, but then I also remember that they did not suffer slavery for 200 years." *New York Times* columnist Tom Wicker called higher education affirmative action "simple, justice long overdue" and reminded readers of the long history of excluding minority men and women of all ages. "It cannot reasonably be said that white males now are being shut out in anything remotely resembling the same manner or approaching the same numbers," he wrote.[38]

The growing number of "reverse discrimination" complaints from college and university campuses did not impress them either. Pottinger thought them "greatly overblown" and argued that department search committees used them to avoid delivering difficult news to job candidates: "Instead of having the fortitude to be direct about the man's capability, the employer sometimes indicates that HEW has established quotas and offered us as a convenient excuse." Some defenders charged that the number of complaints were few. "The critics of affirmative action frequently simply document each other," the editors of the monthly newsletter of the American Association for Affirmative Action (AAAA) wrote in 1976. "The net effect is that the same 'horror stories' are quoted and requoted until the general public is led to believe that institutions and the OCR are engaging in wide-spread illegal action." AAAA members were a group of higher education administrators and academics who organized themselves in 1975 to counter the effects of CANI. They acknowledged that it was "simplistic to deny that critics have no evidence on which to base their claims" but insisted that these incidents had occurred early in the history of higher education affirmative action. Bernice Sandler, one of the chief strategists for women's inclusion, reported that "our project has been unable to locate a single instance where a lesser qualified woman has been hired in preference to a better qualified male." Sandler concluded that it was "no longer an important issue." Washington, D.C., lawyer and liberal spokesperson Joseph Rauh Jr. was the most dismissive. "Reverse discrimination" charges were "misleading spitwords used to kill a sensible remedy for past wrongs through centuries of cruel discrimination."[39]

Those supporters who did offer their sympathy made it clear that complaints of "reverse discrimination" could not obstruct efforts to overcome the historical and structural effects of racial and gender injustice. "Every policy hurts some people who do not deserve to be hurt," admitted feminist and sociologist Rose Laub Coser. Nevertheless, "some sacrifices sometimes cannot be avoided." In their *Civil Rights Digest* exchange, Howard Glickstein responded to Miro Todorovich's report of a white, male historian being forced to work as a short-order cook by noting "there probably were 1,000 blacks with college degrees or better who worked at the post office or as Pullman porters in the past." Still, Glickstein told a group of affirmative action supporters that "we cannot ignore the problem" of those who claimed to be victims. He proposed that "we may be able to develop ways to dull the sting of affirmative action" with a compensation program. Glickstein's idea did not attract support. Robert O'Neil admitted that the accumulating grievances were "altogether understandable" but that many complaints came from applicants with mediocre records. "Displacement takes place at the bottom and not the top of the class," O'Neil assured readers.[40]

These debates continued as the two sides were unable to agree on the key points relating to higher education affirmative action. There was near-unanimity among opponents that their organizations' strong lobbying operations should work to press the federal government executive branch departments and agencies to correct what they viewed as illegal practices by college and university administrators. A few opponents counseled caution, such as Bookbinder, who wrote to a colleague that, since the percentage of such complaints remained small compared to the full docket of discrimination charges and lawsuits, "we must be careful about assuming major dislocations and bars to non-minority hiring caused by affirmative action." Most officials and staff members, however, chose to focus on the rising number of complaints coming in from across the country as proof that their deep philosophical and legal opposition reflected serious opposition sentiment across the country. The strategy of Jewish organizations in the first half of the 1970s was to monitor higher education institutions' strict adherence to government guidelines and, simultaneously, to act as partisans, setting out to refashion "hard" affirmative action into "soft" affirmative action.[41]

The Politics of Anti–Affirmative Action in the Early 1970s

It was only a matter of time before higher education became a nationwide political issue. In the 1968 presidential election race between Republican Richard Nixon and Hubert Humphrey, his Democratic rival, the existence of nascent affirmative action programs did not register as an issue; by the time Nixon launched his reelection bid against George McGovern four years later, however, government policymakers and higher education administrators had well-established programs. Nixon's exploitation of "hot button" socioeconomic issues such as crime, busing, and affirmative action helped to focus the electorate, but color-blind liberals sought a less partisan tone than the one set by the president when he charged that his challenger would bring "abortion, amnesty, and acid" to the White House. American Jewish Committee president Philip Hoffman, chose the most direct means in August 1972 when he publicized an open letter to both candidates and called on them to "reject categorically the use of quotas and proportional representation." It was a clever and simple strategy: the organization's leaders hoped to bypass Nixon's calculations and to avoid what promised to be a long and arduous lobbying campaign to reform affirmative action. The general public, he thought, would rally against both parties' support for "hard" affirmative action. The release of the "Hoffman letter" (as it became known) "triggered a major news story," one American Jewish Committee staff member bragged. As the race heated up, the *New York Times* reported that "Republican and Democratic campaign officials believe that quotas may become a major issue." "We felt certain that here was an opportunity to get both presidential candidates to issue a statement on it, in a sense to put them on the spot," Gold explained two months after the election. "If we could get a statement opposing quotas from both presidential candidates, we would then de-institutionalize the concept of quotas which was becoming institutionalized in society."[42]

Jewish leaders paid particular attention to McGovern's response. Most considered themselves staunch liberals. They watched, however, with growing worry as deep social and cultural fissures threatened the Democratic Party's viability. First came the abandonment of southern whites for the Republican Party, then the surprising success of southern segregationist George Wallace in urban precincts in 1964 and 1968. After the tumultuous 1968 election, McGovern became chairman of the newly formed "Commission on Party Structure and

Delegate Selection" and was identified with its wide range of reforms, including the requirement that women, minorities, and young people serve as Democratic Party delegates in proportion to their share of the rank and file. At the July 1972 Democratic convention, a caucus of Jewish delegates "became concerned" about a report that McGovern had pledged 10 percent of federal appointments to African Americans, a report his staff denied. On the campaign trail, McGovern told audiences of white ethnics that affirmative action was unfair, but he then seemed to promise appointments based on consideration of one's ethnic background. "You've got to remember that never have we had a Polish American on the U.S. Supreme Court. Never have we had an Italo-American on the Supreme Court. We've never had a Greek American," he reminded them. Thus, it was with some skepticism that affirmative action opponents read his reply to the Hoffman letter that "I share the concerns you have expressed and reject the quota system as detrimental to American society." When McGovern appeared before New York's Board of Rabbis, the group's sole question was about his stand on quotas. His response could not have satisfied them: according to a news report, although McGovern was "not for rigid quotas" he nevertheless "did not retract the statement he had made . . . promising minority groups representation in his Administration on the basis of their percentage in the population."[43]

Where McGovern came under considerable scrutiny, Nixon seemed to get off scot-free. The president, who began his first term by approving the implementation of the Philadelphia Plan, now pivoted away from public support for affirmative action. At the 1972 Republican Convention, Nixon spoke in favor of meritocracy and, with the general election under way, signed an order prohibiting the use of quotas in hiring minorities in companies holding federal contracts. His masterful strategizing on nearly every issue confounded critics and helped earn him a landslide victory in which Nixon received 60.7 percent of the popular vote and 520 electoral votes to McGovern's paltry 37.5 percent and 17 electoral votes. The results alienated many estranged Democrats further. ("I opened the doors of the Democratic Party and 20 million people walked out," McGovern quipped.) In addition, for all of Nixon's anti–affirmative action rhetoric, the affirmative action policies remained intact. "It is worth paying more attention to what the administration does than what it says," reminded the editors of *The New Republic*. "In practice, the government will continue to ask employers to hire and promote people who heretofore have been given the dullest, worst paid jobs." For the most part, Nixon continued to sanction hiring goals, federal agencies went on writing affirmative action plans, and the courts kept upholding the constitutionality of results-oriented targets in cases such as the Supreme Court's

Griggs v. Duke Power Co. (1971) decision. With the Watergate scandal dominating national news by mid-1973 and Nixon increasingly under siege, Jewish leaders found few sympathetic figures in the White House.[44]

They turned to the task of forming an anti–affirmative action coalition with college and university administrators. It was a logical move: in the early 1970s higher education institutions faced budget freezes and rising tuitions and struggled to establish HEW-approved affirmative action plans. One of their chief complaints was that the government's paperwork requirement for arriving at the plans was staggering. The executive director of Oregon's Independent Colleges Association characterized it as "physically and financially impossible": "It seems to blithely assume that all of our institutions have the staff of either a major corporation or a multi-university." Even the heads of large universities criticized what they viewed as a policy suited for the industrial sector and not higher education. It would be costly in administrative terms and would upset the smooth process of admissions, hiring, and promotions. Robben W. Fleming, president of the University of Michigan, characterized HEW guidelines as a "confusing hodgepodge." He told a congressional hearing in 1974 that "the practice of treating colleges and universities as though they were business firms ignores long-standing differences and practices which have contributed to the growth and development of a strong system of higher education in this country." As Columbia University officials learned the hard way in 1971, failure to comply with government affirmative action guidelines would mean an end to all federal research funds. "There was no prior warning. There was no notice of hearing or right of appeal, no clear indication in fact of the manner in which we had failed in compliance," fumed Columbia's president, William J. McGill.[45]

The coalition never materialized, largely because higher education administrators were not generally opposed to affirmative action, at least not on ethical or constitutional grounds. At first Jewish leaders were encouraged by invitations to weigh in on college and university plans. This happened in October 1972 when officials at the University of Vermont asked the American Jewish Committee to offer a critique of their proposal that "if a department contains ten or fewer faculty with no women or minorities, the next vacancy should be filled by a woman or minority." American Jewish Committee leaders informed the university promptly that this constituted a blatant quota scheme. (It is not known if Vermont administrators accepted the advice.) It became clear, however, that what administrators objected to were bureaucratic demands and threats to their autonomy. Michigan's Fleming, for example, supported the use of numerical goals for admissions (students, he reasoned, "will be here for a relatively short period of time") but not for faculty appointments ("You are hiring people whom you hope will be with you for a long time. . . . You want the very best people you can find."). Fleming and his peers treated Jewish organizations more as weapons than as allies in their struggle with HEW over turf. Howard Squadron of the American Jewish Congress reported to his organization's executive committee in 1973 on a four-hour meeting he attended with several college and university heads: "They insisted that they were practical people who saw there was a need for change and they indicated that they did not intend to be hung up on the concept of merit." Squadron added that several of those in attendance "urged AJ-Congress to help get HEW out of their hair. . . . HEW guidelines were unhelpful . . . and HEW could not effectively second guess the colleges."[46]

For a short time it seemed as if the AAUP might be a more suitable partner. There was considerable opposition to affirmative action among the AAUP membership. "At any university, my colleagues are breaking their necks looking for candidates who do not exist," complained a New York delegate at the organization's 1972 meeting. "And, frankly, I'm scared stiff. The whole academic profession is scared stiff." Those in attendance adopted a resolution endorsing "energetic and systematic attempts" at bringing white women and minority men and women into faculty ranks but cautioned that such steps "should not be construed as a policy of 'reverse discrimination.'" Critics within the ranks argued that the AAUP did not push back sufficiently against the practice of requiring employees to provide their racial and gender identities. In addition, they let pass HEW's demand that preferential hiring goals be set at departmental levels instead of institutionwide, and, more alarming, the suggestion that search committees forgo requiring that candidates earn a doctorate for faculty positions. AAUP member and SUNY Albany mathematics professor Malcom Sherman insisted that "comparatively few faculty were enthusiastic supporters of the affirmative action programs," but the administration's "bullying tactics" had silenced critics.[47]

It was difficult finding dependable allies. Opponents espousing colorblind liberalism were wary of becoming associated with the more conservative position of CANI. "The Sidney Hook group in New York . . . is too extremist but probably somewhat useful," cautioned Bookbinder to a colleague. When CANI asked the American Jewish Committee to participate in a "National Conference on Non-Discrimination in Education and Employment" in May 1973, the head of the legal division, Samuel Rabinove, turned down the invitation. "The reason for this decision essentially is that AJC is deeply committed to the principle of Affirmative Action to rectify the consequences of past discrimination," he wrote CANI's Miro Todorovich. "Since it is our belief that others who will be participating . . . do not share our strong institutional commitment in this regard, we feel that our participation would be inadvisable." Rabinove's letter underscored the challenge for liberals: they must develop effective strategies for countering "hard" affirmative action while crafting a position that would keep them at arm's length from colorblind conservatives.[48]

In the end, six Jewish organizations joined together to lobby the federal government. In August 1972 the organizations—the American Jewish Congress, the American Jewish Committee, the Anti-Defamation League, the Jewish Labor Committee, Jewish War Veterans, and Agudath Israel of America—sent Pottinger at the OCR a list with thirty-three examples of "reverse discrimination" that they claimed had occurred on campuses. Some of the schools on the list, such as Stanford University and the University of Illinois, were premier research institutions; others were liberal arts colleges, including Oberlin College and Connecticut College; still others were state-run institutions such as Fresno State College and SUNY Old Westbury. These examples, promised Samet of the American Jewish Committee to the organization's area directors, were "merely the tip of the iceberg." They followed up in December 1972, April 1973, and July 1973 with dozens of additional complaints. As they made clear in the cover letter they sent to Pottinger in December 1972, they expected results. "As an initial step," the undersigned wrote, Pottinger must "investigate the facts in these complaints. We presume that early appropriate remedial actions will be taken by all concerned including the presidents of colleges and universities and their administrative officials responsible for affirmative action problems."[49]

Although they provided few details or corroboration for many of their charges, some of their examples did seem to be documented examples of "quota" policies. One complaint concerning a failed job applicant at Florida State University's history department contained the minutes of a faculty meeting in which the department chair noted, "We are under the gun to hire a black." At the University of California at Irvine, a search committee member distributed a notice to other colleges and universities about five open positions earmarked for African American, Hispanic, and Native American candidates. "The history department is anxious to fill one of these minority positions," he announced. Some job notices called for only minority students to apply (for instance, Indiana University). The head of the Center for Human Relations at the University of Massachusetts notified three applicants that "our quotas for non-minority students had been filled by two people who are already here and underway in their programs."[50]

OCR officials were slow to respond to each set of complaints. When they finally did reply, they did not address many of them and hurriedly dismissed others. "I am able to provide you with substantive responses to a number of the items set forth in your transmittal," wrote Pottinger's assistant, Samuel Solomon, five months after the Jewish group lodged their initial complaints. Solomon, however, covered only thirteen of the thirty-three complaints ("The remaining allegations will require further examination which is currently under-way"). In some cases he reported that the conflict had been "amicably adjusted," as in Prince George's Community College in Maryland; in others, the institution in question did not receive federal contracts or financial assistance and thus did not fall under OCR jurisdiction, like at St. Mary's College in Moraga, California. Solomon informed the Jewish groups that the gathering of racial and ethnic data they criticized at some colleges and universities was, in fact, legitimate. "This Office cannot begin to operate an effective Title VII compliance program with-out reasonably accurate data of this kind," he insisted. Solomon explained the missing replies as a result, as he put it in April 1973, of "limited documentary material made available in connections with the charges."[51]

Solomon acknowledged a few cases where higher education administrators and faculty search committee members had violated HEW guidelines. These were isolated occurrences, he assured them, due to small errors. They were not systematic flaws in the government's affirmative action program. He agreed, for example, that Shippensburg State College, the College of Wooster, and Auburn University had made "ill-advised" decisions to direct job advertisements at af-firmative action recipients exclusively. Administrators at these schools "gave as-surances that these efforts would henceforth be made on a nondiscriminatory basis." With another complaint, Solomon acknowledged that the chairman of New Mexico State University's economics department had "a misunderstanding of affirmative action requirements" when he rejected a number of job candi-dates from the University of California at Los Angeles, on the grounds that they were not minorities. When Solomon reviewed a notice from a Sacramento State University department that referred to a goal of recruiting women and minori-ties "until they comprise the same proportion of our faculty as they do the gen-eral population," he admitted that this "was not in keeping with affirmative ac-tion guidelines." He promised that department chairs and administrators there would "familiarize themselves" with the guidelines "so as to preclude further misunderstandings of this nature."[52]

Jewish leaders were "shocked and dismayed" by the OCR officials' handling of their complaints. Solomon's responses "distressed" them, for he had ignored or "dismissed cursorily" so many of them. They insisted that he had not examined carefully enough the wording of the affirmative action guidelines. In the case of the University of Michigan, for example, the government's warning against establishing "unnecessarily high standards of qualification" would undermine an institution's reputation. "On what basis is a standard of qualification to be considered 'unnecessarily' high and who determines if for any particular department?" they wondered. Even when Solomon found fault with a school, as he did with Sonoma State College, he "merely admonished" its administrators. This particular institution, they insisted, "should be subjected to a total compliance review by the HEW, and forced to show that all minority people and women hired or promoted during the last two years were the best qualified candidates." They rejected Solomon's point that they had not provided sufficient documentation in many cases: "We believe that complainants should not be asked to do the Federal Government's job of investigating complaints." Where Jewish leaders expected a thorough reconsideration of higher education affirmative action, they received instead minor corrections to a policy whose shape and character remained unchanged.[53]

Opponents had little to show for their lobbying efforts. Part of the reason for this had to do with their uncertainty about what should constitute affirmative action. Most liberal critics did not want it eliminated entirely, but there was a wide range of views within opposition ranks on the validity of numerical goals, personal identity data collection, and the scope of "soft" affirmative action initiatives. They remained optimistic, however, that they would win over executive branch policymakers. They could point, for example, to Robert Hampton, chairman of the U.S. Commission on Civil Service, who in 1972 informed Bookbinder, "We share your concern that affirmative action programs and the concept of numerical goals and timetables not be distorted into de facto quota systems." Even Stephen Horn—the acting chairman of the U.S. Commission on Civil Rights, replacing Hesburgh—characterized higher education programs as "the numbers game" and "a financial burden of no small consequence" on colleges and universities.[54]

Although their influence on HEW officials seems meager, liberal opponents viewed the department's revised higher education guidelines, issued in October 1972, as a victory. These new rules distinguished between goals and quotas, prohibiting the latter. They mandated as well that affirmative action recipients gain employment through vacancies and not by bumping those already in staff and faculty positions. Naomi Levine, executive director of the American Jewish Congress, was pleased. "You will note that most of our suggestions were accepted," she bragged to executive committee members. In fact, the guidelines were fuzzy in places. The new guidelines did not, as did the original guidelines, mention whether institutions should advertise their desire that minorities and women apply. "Reverse discrimination" complaints continued to arrive at Jewish organizations headquarters. Nevertheless, federal policymakers continued to consult with their critics. One year after the release of the revised guidelines—and after the submission of four sets of complaints—the American Jewish Committee's Alfred Moses reported to Bookbinder that an OCR official had encouraged the organization to continue to bring "positive examples of the right kind of affirmative action which he can use in a forthcoming guideline memorandum to the field."[55]

HEW policymakers in the first half of the 1970s considered Jewish leaders a kind of "loyal opposition" within the affirmative action alliance. "What about the Jewish groups?" U.S. Attorney General Elliot Richardson asked the OCR's Pottinger on the eve of the release of the revised guidelines. When Pottinger informed him that he was waiting to hear back from Bookbinder, the attorney general insisted that "the more thoughtful people in that community" would realize that the guidelines were "impossible to attack": "They can't do that without [undermining] . . . all the other things they stand for." This gave Jewish leaders a certain degree of influence as well, especially in the Leadership Conference on Civil Rights, where they, along with labor unionists, stymied resolutions in support of "hard" affirmative action. They found a few allies in the civil rights establishment such as NAACP executive secretary Roy Wilkins, who called hiring and admissions programs "self-defeating nonsense." American Jewish Committee staff members even met with NOW officers. They reported that, despite a "knock-down dragout, almost a shouting match," its president, Aileen Hernandez, a former EEOC commissioner, "was not as nearly as vituperative, much more willing to consider the validity of what we were talking about." Above all, they comforted themselves in the belief that most African Americans, in the words of Philip Perlmutter, reporting from Boston, "do not worry about it." Perlmutter insisted that minorities "want to get a job, they want to be up-graded, want to end discrimination and racism. So do we." The challenge for colorblind liberals was to articulate a compelling anti–affirmative action position and, simultaneously, to draw liberals to focus on other causes.[56]

"We have started a full fledged national discussion of the subject," wrote Bookbinder in September 1972. "Whatever else may finally emerge, we have helped to create a new climate that surrounds the administration of affirmative action programs." There was no doubt that this opposition provided the intellectual and organizational drive against higher education affirmative action in its early years. From its position within liberal circles, Jewish groups attempted to thwart the growing power of the "new liberalism." They provided significant resources to influence the way the federal government and higher education institutions crafted policies. As much as Jewish leaders emphasized principled opposition, they nurtured as well a nuanced approach to securing equal opportunity that sought shared goals more than divisiveness. That was their intent, since they saw their differences with affirmative action supporters as temporary in nature, more of a misunderstanding to correct than a fatal flaw in post–civil rights liberalism. With the rising number of "reverse discrimination" lawsuits in the early 1970s, however, this more subtle approach would give way to an adversarial tone and contribute to the growing power of colorblind conservatism.[57]

CHAPTER FOUR

"Treat Him as a Decent American!"

DeFunis v. Odegaard (1974) and Colorblindness in the Courtroom

When Marco DeFunis opened a letter from the University of Washington one spring day in 1971 and read that, for the second consecutive year, he had not been admitted to its law school, he was crushed. The twenty-three-year-old magna cum laude graduate's sole professional goal was to become a lawyer. "My decision to study law has not been a recent and hasty one," DeFunis had confided to the admissions committee a year earlier. His reason for wanting to be a lawyer—to "make a contribution to society"—may have been unoriginal, but his determination to get into law school was evident. With his second application, he believed his improved qualifications would make him irresistible: he retook the Law School Admissions Test (LSAT) and scored in the top 7 percent, enrolled in the university's graduate political science program, was admitted to the Phi Beta Kappa honor society, and met with law students and the associate dean to advance his application. He shared these developments with the admissions committee, chiding them that his initial rejection "not only shocked me, but it also shocked my friends and contemporaries who knew my abilities." DeFunis assured the committee of his qualifications: "It is my greatest desire to go to the UofW Law School and if I am accepted, I have confidence that I will measure up to all the requirements of doing first rate law school work." Instead, the law school informed an indignant DeFunis that they had accepted 200 applicants and had placed his name in the bottom quartile of a waiting list of 155 applicants. He immediately appealed their decision.[1]

DeFunis's plea that the law school reconsider his status began the first significant legal challenge to affirmative action, one that would work its way to the U.S. Supreme Court in 1974 as *DeFunis v. Odegaard*. It started when DeFunis hired Josef Diamond, a local lawyer, with a referral from a fraternity brother who was a junior member of Diamond's law firm. DeFunis grew desperate when the admissions committee met, upon Diamond's request, and was unyielding. His mother even wrote the committee, begging its members to "please review his case again and treat him as a decent American!" DeFunis soon fixed on what he believed was the reason for his failed application: he learned that, while he had been rejected, thirty-six minority students with lower LSAT scores and undergraduate grade point averages had been admitted for the fall semester. In August 1971 he sued the university and, one month later, a superior court judge decided in his favor, ordering his immediate enrollment in law school. The Washington State Supreme Court reversed the lower court in March 1973. In April 1974, the U.S. Supreme Court took up DeFunis's appeal and, in a 5–4 vote, determined that since he was nearly finished with his legal studies, the case was "moot." *De-Funis* became largely forgotten, hidden in the shadows of the better-known 1978 *Bakke* decision that dealt with the constitutionality of a medical school admissions program.[2]

The forgotten status of *DeFunis* is unfortunate. This case served as a signature moment in the struggle over equality that shaped the second half of the twentieth century. As the first "reverse discrimination" lawsuit heard by the high court, it became one of a handful of judicial decisions and federal laws that framed the debates over notions of opportunity, merit, and fairness that continue today. A wide range of the American public understood the case's importance at the time. This "rather celebrated case," as Supreme Court Justice Harry A. Blackmun characterized it, attracted the attention of over fifty organizations and individuals who submitted two dozen amicus briefs. *DeFunis,* announced the American Jewish Committee's Hyman Bookbinder in 1973, "is considered as serious as the 1954 [*Brown*] decision." Affirmative action opponents did not consider the case an abstract matter or an isolated cause: it was intricately linked with debates in higher education over the value of grades, the increase in demand for professional education, cutbacks in federal financial aid support, the receding of the civil rights movement, and the always volatile state of race and gender relations. "The case is wrapped in diverse and sometimes unrelated issues that have been gaining attention since the beginning of this decade," noted a *New York Times* journalist.[3]

In a period of economic slowdown, pinched opportunities for doctoral graduates, and sharply increased competition for professional school admissions, affirmative action advocates faced a critical challenge with *DeFunis.* The "reverse discrimination" protests, complaints, and lawsuits came from academics, neoconservatives, and members of ethnic and religious organizations. Above all, it came from American Jews who were alarmed by new hiring and admissions plans. Their opposition was formidable, but they were not united in their reasons for opposing race- and gender-sensitive plans or in the alternatives to affirmative action they proposed. Some opponents were frustrated liberals who saw themselves as qualified supporters of affirmative action and backed mild, or "soft," affirmative action; they advocated a "colorblind liberalism." Other opponents were part of the ascending New Right and represented what historians Thomas Sugrue, Matthew Lassiter, Kevin Kruse, and others have called the new "colorblind conservatism" that emerged in the 1970s. They championed meritocracy and rejected government programs meant to address structural inequality. Affirmative action opponents of both types were galled by the real or threatened use of statistics, proportionality, and quotas in affirmative action plans. Their protests had been bubbling up for the previous half-decade in faculty lounges, meetings with government officials and politicians, and association headquarters across the country—but with little success.

Even before the courtroom became the key point of articulation between local activism and national efforts against affirmative action, those American Jews who viewed themselves as colorblind liberals were frustrated in their efforts to compromise with former allies already at odds over support for Israel, Black Power, urban crime, and community control of schools. Until *DeFunis* they had been at the forefront of lobbying efforts to limit affirmative action to the "soft" variety of remedial programs and aggressive recruitment efforts. They still advocated a large role for the federal government in addressing racial and gender inequality and did not accept the argument of conservatives that laws against discrimination would suffice. But a legal trial places strictures on dialogue: the courtroom is inherently structured around confrontation and the staking out clear differences with opponents. "There was an almost emotional quality in the toll [*DeFunis*] . . . exacted on former allies." It was, to use journalist Nina Totenberg's word, "painful." For American Jews and African Americans, the case "brought to the surface usually repressed feelings of racism and anti-Semitism." As colorblind conservatism gained traction in the courtroom, colorblind liberals scrambled to recover their place in the ongoing struggle over the shape and character of the rights revolution.[4]

Marco DeFunis himself became an archetypal symbol of "reverse discrimination protests. This quiet middle-class university graduate replaced the hardhat trade unionists emblematic of the late 1960s and early 1970s protests. When Supreme Court Justice Potter Stewart asked Josef Diamond at oral arguments, "What kind of American is he?" Diamond fumbled for an answer. "He comes from Jewish parents, I didn't know [it] at the time we brought this action. . . . He's [from] a middle family, his father, I think, is a furniture salesman." DeFunis was the "everyman," without a pronounced ethnic, religious, class, or gender identity. Little about him personally, in fact, exists in the public record, only a single photograph and a few quotations in the press. Unlike the working-class opponents to affirmative action, he did not riot or conspire against the law, and he showed no troubling signs of racism. DeFunis was ambitious but meritorious. To his supporters he was a victim of affirmative action. But many Americans—including some U.S. Supreme Court justices—could not yet decide. The *DeFunis* case illustrates the limited effectiveness of colorblind liberals in shaping the direction of affirmative action by the mid-1970s.[5]

The Struggle over Affirmative Action on Campus

The affirmative action program that Marco DeFunis sought to invalidate was a hybrid product of liberalism and campus unrest forged in the crucible of American higher education in the 1960s. For Marco DeFunis and his law school peers, these decisions and laws came into being as they moved into adulthood, helping to determine their education, careers, and life experiences. Most were born in the late 1940s as the Supreme Court began to strike down segregated public transportation and racially restrictive housing covenants. In a pair of decisions handed down on the same day in June 1950, the justices rejected segregated graduate school lecture halls and laboratories and whites-only public graduate school education programs. Then, just as they were beginning elementary school, the Supreme Court ruled in the 1954 *Brown v. Board of Education* case that segregated educational facilities were inherently unequal and unconstitutional. The future law students were in their teenage years and able to enter the paid workforce when Congress passed the Civil Rights Act of 1964, which banned, among other things, discrimination on the basis of race, color, creed, and sex in employment.

As this cohort of students completed their undergraduate studies, the federal courts were sanctioning newly developed programs meant to address what affirmative action supporters viewed as deep structural inequalities in the workplace and schools. Proponents moved to remedy understood injustices with new hiring, training, promotion, and admissions programs that modified, or even replaced, standard practices. Significant changes began transforming the nation's campuses. Just as the introduction of mass aptitude testing and the elimination of quotas that had kept Jews and Catholics off Ivy League campuses ushered in a new meritocratic order in the fifteen years following the end of World War

II, higher education administrators and policymakers, beginning in the mid-1960s, were reshaping the nation's campuses with special summer courses and financial aid programs for minorities. They followed with the introduction of new admissions criteria and faculty recruitment of minority men and women of all races.[6]

As with other private and public colleges and universities across the country, the University of Washington embraced affirmative action slowly at first, with modest initiatives by administrators and sympathetic faculty members who, in a period of booming enrollments and budgets, were concerned with persistent educational underachievement by minorities. Their focus early in the decade was mostly to publicize, in the language of the day, the "underutilization of manpower." They introduced into the organization- and meritocratic-worshipping midcentury university system a smattering of new recruitment, precollegiate preparation, tutoring, and financial aid programs for the "socially disadvantaged." By mid-decade university leaders were buffeted by far-reaching demands for greater student voice in governance, new curricula, and greater diversity in the student body. To civil rights activists, feminists, and federal policymakers, the affirmative action measures in place seemed inadequate. They urged greater changes in how universities admitted students and hired and promoted new faculty members. Few at the helm at these institutions responded in a manner that seemed speedy or effective.

Charles Odegaard, University of Washington president during this period, satisfied at least some of his critics. He was a graduate of Dartmouth College and had received a PhD in medieval history from Harvard University. Before coming to the University of Washington in 1958, Odegaard had served with distinction as dean of the College of Literature, Science, and the Arts at the University of Michigan. In his five years there, the college's budget doubled, the faculty increased in number from 522 to 797, and many departments and programs rose to national prominence. His colleagues in Ann Arbor were sorry to see him leave. "As Michigan mourned the loss of its able dean, Washington rejoiced," *Time* reported. Once in Seattle he set about turning a middle-level state school into a prestigious Northwest university with a rising national reputation. Under his leadership the university's enrollment more than doubled from 16,000 to 34,000 students, its graduate schools' reputations grew significantly, the operating budget shot up from around $37 million to nearly $400 million, and he oversaw the construction of thirty-five new buildings. He handled unrest by siding with the students occasionally, as in September 1967 when he refused to allow

Seattle police to come on campus and arrest the counterculture youth, including many students, who had congregated there. He explained his position as one of defending the independence and integrity of the modern university.[7]

During his fifteen years in the presidency, Odegaard moved university policy from one that forbade overt discrimination to one of support for affirmative action. Odegaard's change in perspective was remarkable. Soon after he arrived, he issued a memorandum ordering that positions be filled "solely on the basis of merit of the applicants without regard to race, creed, or color." As the decade passed, Odegaard came to believe, as he told the superior court judge at trial in 1971, that "something more than a sanitized, mechanical system is required to solve this problem in finding the true potential of individuals." By 1967 the university had adopted a "more discretionary admission policy." It took a showdown with the Black Student Union and leaders of the faculty senate in 1968, however, for Odegaard to acknowledge that minority student recruitment was "clearly inadequate." As for his negotiations with the students, Odegaard conceded that "I find it difficult not to agree with this impatience." The president told a gathering of students later that year that whites "must expect to walk that extra mile to make up for the past imposition of whites on blacks." They must do so, he went on, "not in charity . . . but in justice, in justice to right the scales among mankind." Affirmative action, he argued, would benefit white students as well: a more diverse student body would enrich their education. Society, in turn, would become more equitable and peaceful with improved race relations.[8]

Although they shared Odegaard's lofty rationale, the authors of the law school's affirmative action program justified their efforts on more concrete grounds: there was a pressing need for more minority lawyers to serve minority communities. The problem was national in scope—while there was one lawyer for every 637 Americans, there was only one black lawyer for every seven thousand blacks—but it was especially alarming in Washington, which had a total of twenty African American lawyers, five Native American lawyers, and not a single Mexican American lawyer in a state with over seventy thousand Mexican Americans. The university had graduated 3,812 law students since 1901, of whom twelve were black. As one of two law schools in the state (the Jesuit-run Gonzaga University being the other), its administrators were determined to do better. "We are trying to bring people from traditionally excluded groups into the mainstream of legal activities as one way to overcome 200 years of discrimination," proclaimed law school dean Richard Roddis at the 1971 trial.[9]

As with law schools across the country, the University of Washington faculty embraced "soft" affirmative action initiatives before moving on to adjust admissions criteria and introduce numerical goals. The defining moment in law school affirmative action came in a series of meetings with leading educators called by the U.S. Office of Economic Opportunity in 1967 and 1968 to discuss the shortage of African American lawyers. Participants established the Council of Legal Education Opportunity (CLEO), a program under the sponsorship of the Association of American Law Schools, the American Bar Association, the National Bar Association, and the Law School Admissions Test Council. CLEO's plan was modest: to hold summer institutes (Harvard Law School and other schools had already done this) and to provide financial assistance to graduates of the institutes who had been admitted to law school. For its first summer institutes in 1968, it enrolled 160 students; the number climbed to 444 the next year. CLEO's real significance was in getting law school faculty, administrators, and government officials to agree on the need for affirmative action. Once established, CLEO's objective—to increase significantly the number of minority law school graduates—necessitated pushing beyond preparatory services and into a serious reconsideration of admissions criteria. By the time the University of Washington held a CLEO institute in 1970, its law school administrators, responding to Odegaard's mandate, had recently introduced a separate assessment of minority applicants.[10]

The admissions committee considered black, Hispanic, and Native American applicants in a separate vetting process that placed less overall weight on grades and aptitude test scores. At trial, Dean Roddis defended the new method: "Part of the reason for separately evaluating the minority students is the feeling that due to educational and cultural disadvantage that may have characterized . . . the people from these groups you simply cannot assess their qualifications on the basis of the grades and the LSAT score." Roddis argued that being "qualified" meant only that an applicant possessed the likelihood or probability of completing law school. Although he admitted that "we do take . . . some minority students who at least, viewed as a group, have a less such likelihood [of graduating] than the majority student group taken as a whole," Roddis insisted that "we do not go down to the point of taking people that we think are unqualified." The criterion was necessarily subjective and fluid. "In the sense that all such standards are relative and involve comparisons of the applications presented, we have no definitive standards," observed Richard Kummert, law professor and chairman of the admissions committee.[11]

What then guided the members in their deliberations? According to University of Texas law professor and CLEO member Millard Rudd, who testified on the university's behalf, the LSAT score and the cumulative grade point average, while "very useful," were "no substitute for human judgment and evaluation." Admissions committee members must consider how minority applicants might make a "very special kind of contribution to the community" upon graduation. Like Roddis and the other Washington law faculty, Rudd steadfastly maintained that applicants admitted under affirmative action plans were qualified: "It is just in most or many schools . . . many of them will not win the race for seats." Despite Roddis's contention that "we have resisted the temptation . . . of establishing fixed quotas," the law school seemed to have an unofficial goal of minorities constituting around 10 percent of the incoming class.[12]

The *DeFunis* case revealed to general view the complex and contingent nature of university admissions for the first time. Even without an affirmative action mandate, admissions committee members faced the daunting task of choosing an incoming law school class from a large applicant pool. They considered strict quantifiable elements in applicants' files alongside other, more subjective material, such as recommendation letters and campus, work, and community experience. The committee, which included six faculty members and three law students, was charged with selecting highly qualified students but also with helping to fulfill the school's mission to raise its national profile. This was to be done by culling a diverse incoming class, many of whom should come from other parts of the country. The sheer amount of paperwork was impressive: applications to the University of Washington Law School had risen sharply of late, from 618 in 1967 to 1,601 in 1971. Out of this large group they would eventually pick 293 first-year students. The committee was guided in their work by using the "predicted first year average," or PFYA, as a benchmark for making their decisions. The PFYA was a numerical score determined by an applicant's grade point average in their junior and senior undergraduate years, their LSAT score, and a writing test score. A large number of the PFYA scores were exceedingly close. Taking a "triage" approach, they divided the applicants into three groups according to their PFYA, separating out those with a PFYA above 77.0 into a separate group. This cohort was almost certain to be accepted into the law school. The chairman of the admissions committee took over responsibility to review the third group, those with PFYA below 74.5. Very few of these applicants were accepted.[13]

The second group, those nonminority applicants whose scores fell in the 74.5 to 76.99 range, received most of the committee's attention. Each committee member took responsibility to review approximately seventy-five of these applications, paying careful attention to the array of submitted materials beyond the PFYA. In preparation for a final committee meeting, they placed these applicants into one of three groups: they recommended ten for admission, twenty to be put on the waiting list, and the remainder to be denied admittance. When they met, members compared each of the three lists with a roster of the applicants in strict PFYA order irrespective of the individual members' recommendations. There followed an open-ended discussion of the process and selections with members prepared to defend their choices.[14]

Placed alongside this large group of applicants, Marco DeFunis was impressive but not outstanding: with a PFYA of 76.23, he fell into the second group. His grade point average was 3.71—in the upper, but not top, range of applicants—but he had taken the LSAT three times and his average score was only 582, which put him in the 80th percentile. Committee members read decidedly mixed endorsements of DeFunis in his letters of support. "This guy is a person I'd refer to as the 'planner,'" wrote the university's associate dean of arts and sciences. "I admire him his persistence but there seems to be the slight tendency of not caring upon whom he might step on in the process." Two political scientists on campus wrote on his behalf as well, one of whom rated him in the "highest ten percent" in all categories, except for two where he had "no basis for judgment." The other faculty member, however, assigned DeFunis to some lower ranges, explaining that "it is perhaps because he has had to work full time and has not . . . really been able to fully involve himself in graduate work. . . . [H]e assures me that he will not have to work next year." The admissions committee kept their deliberations confidential, so it is impossible to know their composite view of DeFunis. A law student member of the committee, under cross-examination by Josef Diamond in superior court, hinted at why they did not admit DeFunis: she found the associate dean's letter, while "not as strong as derogatory" perhaps, still "negative" overall. So too his LSAT scores: he had taken the exam three times, achieving an average score that was "not as high as one might hope for."[15]

DeFunis struggled, without success, to explain the weaker aspects of his application. He pled for special consideration on the grounds that he was ill the first time he took the LSAT (he provided the court with a doctor's note); as for his second mediocre showing, a lawyer from Diamond's firm wrote the committee, DeFunis was "quite probably . . . tense from having taken such a poor examination the first time." Committee members were unmoved, informing him that they "found no reason to adjust his ranking." After their decisions, there was an appeal in the summer, then it moved promptly to trial. His application, they explained, was "below the group we accepted without special attributes being present." At the superior court trial, Roddis was less definite, admitting that DeFunis was "qualified . . . in an absolute sense I think he is qualified." Acknowledging the more open-ended and subjective nature of the admission's process, Roddis spoke of the wide range of considerations they faced and the fine shades of differences among applicants. "It may not be so much that there was something negative against him as much as in some of these other situations there were more affirmative factors that led to the decision in favor of other applicants," he explained.[16]

Interestingly, DeFunis began his legal action in August 1971 not in opposition to affirmative action but to demand an alternative admissions preference, that of a resident of the state of Washington. The initial complaint Josef Diamond submitted to the superior court did not even mention race-based admissions: it noted only "the failure on the part of the defendants to admit said plaintiff to Law School is unjust discrimination in favor of nonresidents, non taxpayers, and students who do not have the qualifications and credentials possessed by said plaintiff." Diamond included DeFunis's wife, Lucia, in the lawsuit since the couple would have to move out of the Seattle area for him to attend another law school, and she would lose her position as a dental technician. He listed DeFunis's parents as well: "They are justified in requesting and requiring that after having paid for and supported the University of Washington for more than 50 years . . . their fully qualified, capable and competent son . . . [should] be admitted to the University of Washington Law School." This was to be a case not just of a wronged applicant but also of an aggrieved family that would have to bear financial and emotional costs due to the admissions committee's decision. From a constitutional law perspective, Diamond presented a surprisingly thin case. He asked the court to order the school to enroll his client immediately and to pay court costs, damages totaling $50,000, and "such other and further relief that may be just and equitable." Law school administrators and were puzzled by the case. "The theory of the action is not entirely clear in all respects," Roddis confessed to his colleagues. Nevertheless, university counsel scrambled to prepare for the trial scheduled to begin a month later and to provide DeFunis's legal team with their request for admissions committee files.[17]

DeFunis's case came together when his lawyers discovered how the affirmative action policy worked, including the weight placed on applicant racial identity and DeFunis's own ranking. With the admissions committee files in hand, Diamond transformed the case from one about residential preference to one challenging racial preference. His questioning of university officials and committee members at trial was meant to undermine confidence in the whole admissions process: he had them read aloud the grade point averages, test scores, supporting materials, and committee members' handwritten notes of accepted minority applicants whose credentials were weaker than those of his client. The university countered with their detailed explanation of the difficulty of an open-ended process. They reminded the court that, besides the 36 minorities admitted with lower PFYAs than DeFunis, they had admitted 22 military veterans and 16 non-minority applicants with lower PFYAs and had denied 29 applicants with PFYAs higher than DeFunis entry to law school. They pointed out that, even without an affirmative action plan, DeFunis most likely would not have been admitted.[18]

Superior Court Judge Lloyd Shorett's decision on September 22, 1971, delivered a blow to the school's affirmative action program on sweeping constitutional grounds. DeFunis, Judge Shorett ruled, "had not been accorded the equal protection of the law guaranteed by the Fourteenth Amendment." After the *Brown* decision, Shorett told those gathered to hear his oral decision, the amendment "could no longer be stretched to accommodate the needs of any race. Policies of discrimination will inevitably lead to reprisals. . . . [T]he only safe rule is to treat all races alike." He ordered that DeFunis be enrolled immediately in the school's entering class and that the university pay his legal fees and court costs. "This case is of a type that will, and indeed should be, reviewed very quickly by the Supreme Court of the United States," Shorett predicted.[19]

"DeFunis did not expect to win," *Time* reported, "but to his surprise—and the University's—Seattle Court Judge Lloyd Shorett has just ordered his admission." In victory DeFunis revealed that he was "overjoyed," but he arrived on a campus where affirmative action had considerable support. "It is easy to sympathize with Marco DeFunis," wrote the school newspaper editors, but "even easier to sympathize with minority students, who through no fault of their own, fail to receive the quality of pre-collegiate education someone like DeFunis gets." President Odegaard dismissed Shorett's decision as "erroneous" and promised that the university would appeal. "It's imperative that we win," insisted the cochairman of the university's Minority Law School Association. DeFunis found few allies at the University of Washington. The rabbi in the campus ministry office supported his position, but there was no organized backing for DeFunis. Sociology professor Pierre van den Berghe criticized the university's affirmative action policy, warning that "we are now admitting to the university a number of minority students who realistically, have virtually no chance of successfully completing their studies." Minority students demanded, unsuccessfully, that administrators discipline van den Berghe. The case began to take its toll on DeFunis. On the first day of classes, a second-year law student called him a "George Wallace racist," a friend recalled later. DeFunis recounted, through his lawyers, incidents in the law school library when groups of black students pointed him out, called him a "bigot," or left en masse. Asked if he was sorry that he had filed the lawsuit, the reticent DeFunis replied, "That's my secret."[20]

The superior court trial brought into sharp relief the divide over affirmative action, which deepened as it drew increasing national attention when the case went to the Washington State Supreme Court. As they entered their appeal, the university administration's confidence was shaken. One law professor suggested abandoning the case in the hopes that they could defend their program through an expected lawsuit by a woman applicant they had rejected whose credentials were weaker than those of DeFunis. The legal team, headed by state attorney general Slade Gorton and senior assistant attorney general James Wilson, must have been relieved when Washington's high court reversed Shorett's ruling by a 7–2 margin in March 1973. In his majority opinion, Justice Marshall A. Neill found the affirmative action plan to be entirely constitutional:

> *Brown* did not hold that all racial classifications are *per se* unconstitutional; rather, it held that invidious racial classifications—i.e., those that stigmatize a racial group with the stamp of inferiority—are unconstitutional. . . . [T]he 'preference' minority admissions policy . . . is clearly not a form of invidious discrimination. The goal of this policy is not to separate the races, but to bring them together.

Neill accepted the rationale for, and the details of, the school's admissions policies. He noted that assessing professional school applications posed "complex problem[s], and require a sensitive balancing of diverse factors." The process, he went on, "need not become a game of numbers . . . [it] should remain sensitive and flexible, with room for informed judgment in interpreting mechanical indicators." By his reckoning, the school had not established a racial quota; rather, they sought a "reasonable representation."[21]

Perhaps the only solace DeFunis, his family, and lawyers could draw from the reversal was the scathing denunciations of the admissions plan from the two dissenting justices, Robert T. Hunter and Frank Hale. To Hunter, DeFunis's failure to gain admittance was an "arbitrary and capricious action, flaunting the guarantees of the equal protection provisions to all citizens." Hale found the school's criteria "vague, loose, and whimsical." He condemned the presence of students on the committee, the weight members placed on applicants' community and political activism, and the "sweeping and unsupported assumption" that all minority applicants were disadvantaged. He was careful to distinguish between university-based affirmative action and school busing, where "the benefit to one would not be at the expense of another." Hale found the university's plan neither modest nor reasonable: "Racial bigotry, prejudice and intolerance will never be ended by exalting the political rights of one group or class over that of another. The circle of inequality cannot be broken by shifting the inequalities from one man to his neighbor." Buoyed as he might have been by these opinions, Diamond faced an immediate concern for his client in the wake of the university's victory: the law school would not commit to allowing DeFunis (by then near the end of second year of study) to complete his degree. A campus reporter noted that administrators "do not wish to give the impression that all students have to do is sue if they don't get admitted under the usual channels." Diamond's task now was to secure a U.S. Supreme Court order that would keep his client in school. He then hoped to convince the court to hear the case and rule in their favor.[22]

The Supreme Court Takes Up "Reverse Discrimination"

The odds of the justices agreeing to take up *DeFunis* were slim. Of the thousands of requests to the court for the 1974 term, the justices agreed to accept only 10 percent of the cases, and fewer still actually made it to the oral arguments stage of trial. The challenge for DeFunis's lawyers was to convince the court to hear a "reverse discrimination" case in a period marked by major legal changes in the understandings of gender and racial equality. By the time of Chief Justice Earl Warren's departure in 1969, rights-based constitutionalism had become a core feature of American democracy. In his place came Chief Justice Warren Burger and then Justice Harry A. Blackmun the next year, both nominated by President Richard Nixon. They joined already-sitting justices William O. Douglas, William Brennan, Thurgood Marshall, John Marshall Harlan, Byron White, Potter Stewart, and Hugo Black in tackling thorny issues such as the death penalty, welfare rights, and abortion.[23]

Despite conservatives' expectations of a change in direction, however, the early Burger Court did not undo legal liberalism. Two unanimous decisions in 1971, in fact, suggested the justices' willingness to consider the deep workings of privilege and exclusion. In *Swann v. Charlotte-Mecklenburg Board of Education,* the high court issued its broadest desegregation ruling to date, mandating that schools must "achieve the greatest possible degree of actual desegregation" and endorsing race-conscious busing. The court held in *Griggs v. Duke Power* that a utility company's requirement of an intelligence test as a condition of employment violated Title VII of the Civil Rights Act of 1964 because it had a disparate impact on African American job applicants. With this decision, the court seemed to be signaling its sympathy with the underlying rationale for affirmative action programs that were now well established in the workplace and higher educa-tion.[24]

Would the court reconsider at least some of its reasoning and conclusions so soon after the *Swann* and *Griggs* decisions? In 1971 they passed on a case from an Arizona lower court about an aggrieved white man whom the state's bar associa-tion had refused admission (he failed the bar examination—just barely—three times) while admitting a black applicant who had received similar marginal fail-ing grades. The court's composition, however, had changed since then: in addi-tion to Burger and Blackmun, Nixon's earlier choices, Lewis Powell and William Rehnquist, took seats on the bench in 1972. The Virginia-born and -educated Powell had never served as a judge. He rose through the legal community first as a successful private practice attorney and head of Richmond's school board, then as a member of the state's school board (he was chairman in the late 1960s). As head of the Richmond board, Powell did not defy the Supreme Court's *Brown* ruling, but he moved the district toward desegregation at a glacial pace. When he was president of the American Bar Association, he wrote a report for the U.S. Chamber of Commerce in which he called for countermobilization against pub-lic interest lawyers. Justice Rehnquist's conservative credentials were even more solid: as a law clerk for U.S. Supreme Court Justice Robert H. Jackson, he wrote a memorandum arguing against court-ordered school desegregation. As a pri-vate lawyer in Arizona in the 1960s, he served as a legal advisor to Senator Barry Goldwater's 1964 presidential campaign and opposed a school desegregation plan for Phoenix's public schools. Diamond could glimpse the possibility that a more conservative Supreme Court would create a legal trajectory friendly to their position. As the justices considered the petition for certiorari in early June 1973, Justice Douglas, serving as the court's circuit judge, ordered that DeFunis be al-lowed to continue in law school, thus allowing him to begin his third and final year of law school.[25]

Although our knowledge of the justices' deliberations at this stage of the law-suit is thin, at least some of their law clerks urged them to avoid the case. It was, wrote Pierce O'Donnell, Justice Byron White's clerk, "a veritable can of worms." O'Donnell acknowledged that "it is difficult to deny that the issues raised are not of transcendent importance in a constitutional and societal sense," but, he went on, the case was "full of legal questions of first impression and replete with ramifications for related areas, many of which I suspect are as yet unfore-seen." Lewis Powell's clerks warned him away from the case as well. Jack Owens, one of Powell's clerks, argued that the case was moot since DeFunis would soon graduate. In addition, he thought that an appeal was unwarranted since "no state stuatute [*sic*] is directly involved." He wrote Powell: "I would dismiss and deny. The court should not throw itself into this thicket until it has to—when a case is going the other way makes it up here."[26]

The appellants framed their arguments in broad constitutional terms; the respondent university did so in narrow and technical ones. To DeFunis's legal team, the Washington court's decision was a disaster: "If the principles established in the opinion remain law, none of the liberties guaranteed by the Declaration of Rights in our Constitution are safe against the needs of the state whenever a majority of the court can be convinced of the state's needs." This case was timely, they suggested, since it had received "national attention. It has been commented on editorially throughout the country and has been publicized in numerous national publications." Washington's attorney general (and future U.S. senator) Slade Gorton argued that the state supreme court's judgment "rests on adequate nonfederal grounds" and that the issues needed no further consideration. If the Supreme Court were to accept jurisdiction, Gorton asserted that it should be limited to one question: "May the law school . . . constitutionally take into account, as one element in selecting from among qualified applicants . . . the races of applicants in pursuit of a state policy to mitigate gross underrepresentation of certain minorities in the law school and in the membership of the bar?" He warned that the court's reversal of the Washington court's decision "will endanger all affirmative action programs throughout the nation and across the entire spectrum of activities in which they are employed."[27]

Both sides addressed the new question of whether DeFunis's continuation in law school made the case moot. It was not moot, Gorton maintained, since, if the justices dismissed DeFunis's appeal or affirmed the Washington decision, DeFunis would be required to reapply to law school to complete his course of study. Gorton infused the case with greater significance than he had in his motion for dismissal, noting that it "raises important constitutional questions and . . . the action complained of here will be repeated" if the court were to follow the mootness doctrine. One of Diamond's colleagues, Lyle Iverson, wrote a brief, telling the court he understood the risk of the law school terminating DeFunis's legal studies. "The condition sought to be protected is still very much present, namely, his continued enrollment." It was an unusual occasion of agreement between the two sides. "There is a real issue involving rights which DeFunis is entitled to call upon the courts to protect," insisted Iverson. "This case is not moot."[28]

The court agreed, at least for the moment. It granted the certiorari petition on November 19, 1973. Both sides began to prepare their opening briefs and oral arguments, which were scheduled for early 1974. This would be a different kind of trial than that of the State of Washington Supreme Court: not only would there be the glare of national media, but the rules governing the filing of briefs, proceedings, and the significance of rendered opinions would reshape the history of affirmative action decisively. This was to be more than a case about Marco DeFunis. Now the leaders of labor, civic, business, education, and religious organizations were eager to participate in a case that might touch the lives of their organizations' members professionally, politically, and personally.[29]

Filing Amicus Briefs: The National Debate over Affirmative Action

The filing of amicus briefs in *DeFunis*, a process that attracted over three dozen universities, unions, individuals, and organizations, illustrates the keen interest a wide segment of Americans were taking in the debate over affirmative action. Although scholars disagree on the level of its direct influence on judicial decisionmaking, the amicus brief has been a formidable tool of partisan advocacy since the late twentieth century. The acceptance of testimony from "friends of the court" reveals the Supreme Court's tacit recognition that most matters have vast social, political, and economic ramifications far beyond the interests of the immediate parties. Liberal interest groups such as the National Association for the Advancement of Colored People and the American Civil Liberties Union had used them with success during the Warren Court; by the 1970s, conservatives began to submit them in appreciable numbers as well. Their greater use in the last forty years has been remarkable: in two mid-1960s landmark decisions, one establishing privacy as a constitutional right in a ruling dealing with Connecticut's statute prohibiting the sale of contraceptives (*Griswold v. Connecticut*) and the other broadening the rights of criminal suspects (*Miranda v. Arizona*), only three organizations submitted briefs in each case. In *Roe v. Wade* (1973), which resulted in the majority of justices granting women the constitutional right to abortion, nine organizations participated as "amicus" of the Supreme Court. One year later, the court received three times as many briefs in *DeFunis*. They came from organizations as diverse as the National Organization for Women's Legal Defense and Education Fund, the United Automobile Workers, the Association of American Law Schools, and the Joint Civic Committee of Italian Americans.[30]

Opponents assembled a wide range of legal and policy approaches against

affirmative action that cut across political and ideological lines. The AFL-CIO executive committee, dominated by union leaders from the skilled trades, weighed
in, as they had since affirmative action's inception, against race-conscious programs. Higher education was not a core concern of labor leaders. Still, they argued that rebuffed white students—whose anger was "not irrational"—would
contribute to the already serious problem of "backlash." Economic goals (especially full employment) remained a central focus of organized labor, and unqualified lawyers were every bit as damaging to the nation's economic health
as substandard welders. The trying economic circumstances of the 1970s, they
argued, "are not times that allow the prodigal waste of resources." Industrial,
government, and service sector unions led by "labor liberals," however, offered
their support for the university's plan. Where more conservative-led unions resisted affirmative action on the grounds that it was a threat to familial and ethnic recruitment and an attack on collective bargaining practices, labor liberals
accommodated many of these new mandates as compatible with their goal of
workplace equality. In their amicus brief, for example, the American Federation
of State, County, and Municipal Employees union argued that the Washington
program was acceptable since it gave "a limited preference to *qualified* minority applicants." Where the AFL-CIO condemned quotas, AFSCME's lawyers insisted that "the facts in *DeFunis* do not look like a 'quota.' "[31]

DeFunis received most of his amicus support from four Jewish-American
organizations: the Jewish Rights Council, the American Jewish Congress, the
Anti-Defamation League of B'nai B'rith (ADL), and the American Jewish Committee. American Jews had taken immense interest in affirmative action since
its first appearance in public elementary and secondary schools and higher education in the late 1960s. Marco DeFunis's plight—his educational achievements,
his Jewish identity, the law school's consideration of applicants' race—resonated
with many who had already concluded that educators and policymakers had
charted a disastrous course. The case laid bare the fraying of postwar American
liberalism, as many American Jews insisted on the continuing importance of
colorblind policies. "Jews have deserted the old civil rights coalition," wrote Nina
Totenberg, "because they see the DeFunis case as a matter of quotas, and quotas
are anathema to Jews because they have been used for so many centuries to keep
Jews out of universities." At a Columbia University Law School symposium in
early 1974, NAACP counsel Jack Greenberg observed that Jewish groups' support for DeFunis was "causing a rift between us . . . and doing a wrong. They are
doing a disservice to their constituents and to the country." The ADL's Arnold
Forster was unrepentant: "Hitler's actions against the Jews caused a rift too. If

this is the price of friendship not to abandon principles but to fight for them, then we yield to the former."[32]

Of the four briefs, the ADL's was the most widely discussed for its forceful denunciation of affirmative action in scrupulous terms. Its authors, Alexander Bickel and Philip Kurland, were intellectual heavyweights in constitutional law scholarship. Kurland was a law professor at the University of Chicago and a consultant to the Senate Judiciary Committee at the time of Watergate. He was one of twelve legal scholars who concluded that the transcripts of conversations recorded by Richard Nixon contained material that would support an impeachment charge against the president. Bickel, who taught at Yale Law School, was the better known of the two. He was, wrote one affirmative action supporter at the time, "the intellectual leader of the reverse-discrimination movement." He exemplified what legal historian Laura Kalman calls the "meritocratic mindset" of the group of brilliant Jewish law professors appointed to academic positions in the late 1950s. At first glance Bickel had impeccable liberal credentials. A graduate of City University of New York and Harvard Law School, he was a supporter of the *Brown* decision, opposed U.S. involvement in the Vietnam War, and backed Eugene McCarthy, and then Robert Kennedy, in their bids for the 1968 Democratic presidential nomination. By the early 1970s Bickel's sympathies had shifted rightward. This transition came partly in reaction to Yale's new grading scheme, student activist demands for a permanent professorship earmarked for an African American candidate, and the faculty's April 1970 decision to support a student strike protesting the murder trials of Bobby Seale and other Black Panthers. Bickel denounced "our current revolutionist . . . [who] offered us hate." He warned against the "dictatorship of the self-righteous." Bickel championed, as he put it in *The Morality of Consent,* published in 1975 shortly after his death, the "dispassionate, informed, disinterested judgment" of the academic.[33]

Bickel's intellectual journey was more complicated than a simple move from liberalism to conservatism. He served as a clerk for Supreme Court Justice Felix Frankfurter in the 1952 term and came to embrace the justice's belief in the judiciary creating a "reserve" in which courts held back some rulings in order to build their prestige for major cases. It was Frankfurter, in his support for the *Brown* decision, who proposed the circumspect "all deliberate speed" language in the subsequent desegregation order. Bickel echoed Frankfurter's argument that the court should exercise caution and restraint, avoiding constitutional decisions whenever possible (Bickel called this general outlook the "passive virtues"). *Brown* was valid for him because racial equality was a fundamental constitutional value, but he attacked the Warren Court's for "activism" that undercut the workings of ordinary politics. As Thomas Keck notes in his study of conservative judicial activism, Bickel and Kurland were somewhat inconsistent in their advocacy of both judicial restraint and the position that the court should rule against the choices of public university administrators. "In the face of this tension, constitutional conservatives might well have chosen to adhere to the doctrine of restraint," suggests Keck, "but their color-blind principles trumped this long-standing commitment."[34]

Their ADL brief, a forceful interpretation of the Fourteenth Amendment, contained no trace of hesitancy or awareness of this inconsistency. "If the Constitution prohibits exclusion of blacks and other minorities on racial grounds," they reminded the justices, "it cannot permit the exclusion of whites on racial grounds." In a much-cited passage, Bickel and Kurland indicted the university for the wayward course affirmative action had taken the nation from the goal of racial equality: "For at least a generation the lesson of the great decisions of this Court and the lesson of contemporary history have been the same: discrimination on the basis of race is illegal, immoral, unconstitutional, inherently wrong and destructive of democratic society. Now this is to be unlearned and we are told that this is not a matter of fundamental principle but only a matter of whose ox is gored." *DeFunis* was making clear how sharp the double-edged discourse of rights could be, just ten years after the passage of landmark civil rights legislation.[35]

The decision of other American Jews to back DeFunis was a difficult one that gave them little ability to pursue the colorblind liberal goal of forging a middle course that had, until this case, dominated the opposition to higher education affirmative action. The American Jewish Committee leadership's handling of this case, for example, reveals a conflicted group of liberals who found little appeal in Bickel and Kurland's approach. They were wary of the law school's race-conscious admissions program but alarmed by the possibility of Jewish organizations severing their ties with the civil rights community. The organization's officers and staff had come to regret the loose coalition they formed early in the decade with other Jewish groups to lobby the federal government policymakers and to pressure Richard Nixon and his Democratic opponent George McGovern on their affirmative action stances in the 1972 presidential election. The ADL brief, argued Hyman Bookbinder, was "shrill, obsessive." He urged the American Jewish Committee's executive vice president, Bert Gold, to "let them go their way." They struggled to show their continuing alliance with civil rights advocates by publicizing their shared position on affirmative action with such veterans for racial equality as Roy Wilkins and Bayard Rustin.[36]

At its December 1973 meeting, the American Jewish Committee Board of Governors decided, reluctantly, to file a brief in the case but not along the same lines as the ADL brief. The minutes of the meeting reveal that most in attendance considered their support for DeFunis necessary. "It would be a disaster if this case were lost by DeFunis because 'quotas' then would become totally acceptable in principle and practice," warned American Jewish Committee legal committee chairman Robert Pelz. Still, they hoped that their brief would be read as much for its support for affirmative action as for its condemnation of the law school's plan. One speaker at the meeting "felt we should try to get the Supreme Court to take a position which will not discourage the kind of situation which is intended to make it possible for minorities to get special attention." They would submit their brief in the hope that, as the American Jewish Committee's Alfred Moses put it, it might "color the decision and force the Justices to write something more than a simplistic decision as, for example, one that under the Fourteenth Amendment this is a clear case of discrimination."[37]

It offered a sparser brief than that of the ADL, one that questioned the rationale of law school affirmative action (for instance, why would minority lawyers serve minority communities better?) and the results of new admissions programs (why did a significantly lower percentage of black law graduates pass the bar examination than white graduates?). They concluded that the affirmative action, as currently constituted, was "an unwise practice." Individual merit, Samuel Rabinove, the American Jewish Committee's legal director and primary author of the brief, contended, "must be the crucial determinant . . . rather than artificially imposed proportional representation based on racial or ethnic extraction." Policymakers should focus on creating better elementary and secondary schools and pushing for "soft" affirmative action measures such as CLEO institutes and increased financial aid. Shortly after the Supreme Court's *DeFunis* ruling, Rabinove insisted that, while the ADL had been too harsh, they had focused on "a number of constructive 'affirmative action' alternatives to the University of Washington Law School approach." He bragged as well that "several forceful and influential black spokesmen . . . were in philosophical accord with the AJCommittee position."[38]

But not every member agreed with the American Jewish Committee's official stance. Behind the facade of unity created by the amicus brief, in fact, American Jews were conflicted in their thinking about affirmative action. In DeFunis's hometown of Seattle, the American Jewish Committee's chapter, local leader Carl Koch remembered in a 1987 interview, was "kind of a divided house. There was a lot of people . . . who really felt that affirmative action should have been on the side the American Jewish Committee was on." When staff member Seymour Samet visited Seattle in December 1971 to participate in a chapter roundtable of "minorities, merit, and higher education," he discovered that a good many members wished to file a brief on the university's side. Back in New York, Samet promised to give their proposal "serious consideration" but warned that he had "deep reservations" about such a legal intervention. A year and a half later, Samuel Rabinove reported that the Seattle chapter was "sharply divided" over the case; a "bare majority" of the executive board had voted not to file a brief. "Our Seattle people had mixed feelings about the relative equities of the case, as well as concern over possible adverse community relations consequences in the event of American Jewish Committee's involvement in it," he wrote.[39]

However much they differed with each other on the appropriateness of "soft" affirmative action, they were united in their defense of meritocracy. One self-identified Russian Jew, writing to the University of Washington, warned against making the U.S. a country of "mediocre people." To an Everett, Washington, resident, the law school's plan was a "national disgrace." "The standards in any profession must be maintained regardless of persons," he wrote the law school's Dean Roddis. The editors of the *Wall Street Journal* claimed that adherence to merit was "more in harmony with traditions of justice." DeFunis's supporters sometimes exaggerated his qualifications and portrayed minority applicants as hopelessly unqualified. "It was clear that the standard of 'qualification' that the law school applied to minority applicants was minimal," insisted Larry Lavinsky, chairman of the ADL's National Legal Committee. The university had created a "new double standard," announced columnist Nicholas von Hoffman. This now meant that "a black only has to be half as good" as a white applicant. Some opponents presented a clearly inaccurate understanding of the facts of the case. Rabbi Theodore Lewis from Brooklyn told his congregation that DeFunis was denied his alienable [*sic*] right" to pursue a legal career and that the school had administered "a special [aptitude] test" to minority applicants.[40]

The authors of the amicus briefs in support of DeFunis argued that a close connection existed between meritocracy and constitutional principles. For the Jewish Rights Council, the merit system was "extremely important for the preservation of our American way of life." In their ADL brief, Alexander Bickel and Philip Kurland explained that the goal of merit-based admissions and hiring policies "has just begun to be met." To abandon it now, they wrote, would result in "loss of efficiency and injustice." Bickel, Kurland, and others had tapped into a promising vein of argument. As Nicholas Lemann points out in his history of meritocracy in modern America, *DeFunis* was "psychologically quite different" for lawyers from the *Griggs* case: "Every member of the Supreme Court had done brilliantly well in law school. The idea of a legal meritocracy . . . animated the story of each of their lives. . . . [T]he argument that law schools shouldn't choose among applicants on the basis of their transcripts and test scores . . . was not an easy one to make at the Supreme Court."[41]

This shared understanding among American Jews, however, was stretched to the breaking point in the two Jewish organizations that supported the university, the Union of American Hebrew Congregations (UAHC) and the National Council of Jewish Women (NCJW). The UAHC and the NCJW joined sixteen other liberal groups in an amicus brief submitted by Joseph Rauh Jr. of the Americans for Democratic Action and Marian Wright Edelman of the Children's Defense Fund. The UAHC and the NCJW members were enraged that their officers had signed on to a brief that argued that the law school's admissions policy was "eminently reasonable." The UAHC, the major synagogue organization for Reform Judaism in the United States, was at the forefront of preaching social activism through the movement of prophetic Judaism in the 1950s. By the mid-1960s there emerged a conservative reaction on the part of some of the membership to urban crime, riots, the rise of Black Power, and differences with the civil rights community over support for Israel. With *DeFunis*, reform rabbis from around the country denounced their leadership for being "Jewish Uncle Toms" or "the American version of the despised and ludicrous East European Court Jew" and for "bleeding heart liberalism at best . . . self-hatred at worst." The Beth Israel Congregation in Jackson, Mississippi, decided to withhold its voluntary contributions to the UAHC's Commission on Social Action in protest. Rabbi Gunter Hirschberg, president of the New York Association of Reform Rabbis, argued against the law school plan from the position of self-interest: "I protest the issue on the grounds that a Jewish organization should not go against a Jew." A Cincinnati member acknowledged this same perspective in his opposition (DeFunis was "also a minority student") but stated his opposition on the grounds that he was "inclined to be interested in [the] promotion of people on the basis of merit." Polling data verified the divisions within the UAHC as the group's New York membership opposed the brief by a 60–8 margin (with two abstentions), while the Chicago Association of Reform Rabbis voted to commend the leadership for its "courage and sensitivity."[42]

Dissent rocked the NCJW as individuals and chapters across the country broke with the national office over the case as well. A flood of letters arrived in the New York headquarters, most of them criticizing the leadership. One member was "utterly dismayed" and "more than a little appalled and outraged," another was "disgusted," and still another—a twenty-year member from California —found the NCJW stand "personally frightening and abhorrent." All of them resigned from the NCJW. "As a woman, as a Jew, and as a lawyer," wrote a New York City member, "I find your position incompatible with my principals [*sic*] and those which I thought Council was supporting." The animosity of some letter writers underscored the deteriorating relations between American Jews and African Americans. "Since you are so biased in favor of others, may your children bring you as sons and daughters-in-law, the blacks whose rights you favor over those of the Jew," wrote a Randallstown, Maryland, woman. This bitterness did not come only from the rank and file: Jakob Petuchowski, a faculty member at the United Hebrew College, fumed to the NCJW president that "the blacks, whom you are trying to aid by your action, will ultimately be as grateful to you as they have been to the Jews who have aided their cause in the earlier decades of this century." Such protests were not confined to individuals, as chapters in such places as Cleveland; East Nassau, New York; Bedford, Massachusetts; and northern New Jersey assailed the organization's position. The president of the Philadelphia chapter reported that a local rabbi was denouncing the NCJW from the bimah and on the radio. "We are again in the process of losing members," she disclosed.[43]

In decrying the amicus brief, NCJW members made dark predictions about the legal and economic status of American Jews if affirmative action were to survive the Supreme Court challenge. "Just keep supporting quota policies," wrote several women in a letter to NCJW president Eleanor Marvin signed "Concerned Jewish Women," "and you will quota Jewish competent students right out of schools, jobs, and political rights!!" Even worse, suggested a man writing to "My dear ladies" at NCJW headquarters, the organization was "inviting an Armageddon for the Jewish community." Many folded the recent development of affirmative action into a history of persecution against Jews. A forty-year NCJW veteran from the Detroit chapter thought the organization's chief concern should be advancing opportunities for American Jews: "History has proven that no one really cares about Jews except other Jews. As members of a minority I believe that we have prior obligations to help ourselves." One Santa Monica member, reminding the leadership that "we Jews have always been the victim," pleaded with them to "make a profound effort to help our fellow Jew!" Other members, however, insisted that their opposition was not a matter of self-interest. The head of the Rabbinical Council of America told Marvin that "there may be potential Einsteins, Salks, Sabins, and Brandeises whose services to humanity may be lost because of your position." Two Flushing, New York, women felt that, by supporting the University of Washington's position, the NCJW would "ensure minority groups a job or place in school without regard to their education or job qualifications." In effect, the organization would "only serve to polarize ethnic groups in this country."[44]

NCJW leaders maintained that their position was principled and that the procedure for deciding to file the amicus brief was valid. "If DeFunis was NOT Jewish, simply white, would the Jewish community be up in arms?" wondered national affairs director Eli Fox. Eleanor Marvin acknowledged that the case had drawn attention to the "sensitivity to the suggestion of a quota system"; nevertheless, the affirmative action plan they were defending was "designed to counterbalance the cumulative efforts of discrimination suffered by racial and ethnic groups for uncounted generations." The NCJW must rise above narrow concerns, Marvin went on: "We have a moral obligation to continue this struggle in the communities of this nation and throughout the world." The decision to file a brief, she assured members, "was taken after full and extended deliberation," and, as she reminded the dissident head of the New York state chapter, "a public statement by a section of its National's stand is just not acceptable."[45]

American Jews offered differing explanations for the divisions within their organizations' ranks. The president of the NCJW's Chicago chapter hypothesized that the "fragmentation and in-fighting" over the case was rooted in the exodus of American Jews from the nation's cities to its suburbs. This "tragic isolation" kept many Jewish suburbanites from building alliances across racial and religious lines. One staff member with the Institute for Jewish Policy and Planning Research reckoned that the NCJW's pro–affirmative action stance was due to the fact that gender-sensitive hiring and admissions programs would "promote the interests of Jewish women." Other observers noted the importance of marital status in determining a person's stance on affirmative action. This manifested itself in telling ways, such as when the husband of a NCJW member in Florida responded, instead of his wife, to a routine request to pay her annual dues. The man was upset with the NCJW position on the case. Marco DeFunis, he wrote, was a "brilliant white Jewish student not accepted because minority applicants had to be given preferential treatment"—but he supported "the larger purpose of your organization and so I am paying the dues—but under protest." In a series of interviews conducted in the late 1970s, Jewish women spoke of the frequent tugs in different directions. "In this organization, members feel more Jewish than feminist. And most of our women are volunteers, they're not working women," one woman said of her organization. Still another woman claimed that she did not share other American Jews' "gut reaction" against programs with numerical goals or quotas. "Maybe it's because I always saw myself excluded as a woman, not necessarily as a Jew," she admitted. One thing was clear: Jewish feminists were furious with Jewish organizations opposing affirmative action. In a 1973 speech to the Democratic Women's Club in Washington, D.C., Congresswoman Bella Abzug reminded "her brothers" that "in attacking affirmative action programs in higher education . . . they are talking about and speaking for Jewish *men* and not for Jewish women."[46]

While DeFunis's legal team articulated to the court a claim of discrimination based on equal protection and the value of meritocracy, the university and its supporters were insisting that their program was addressing a structural inequality that had deep historical roots. Moreover, it did not violate the Constitution, wrote James Wilson in a brief to the court: "All law classifies and all law which classifies or discriminates invidiously offends the Equal Protection Clause of the Fourteenth Amendment." Since, as the authors of the NOW Legal Defense and Education Fund and the National Education Association argued, "the plain fact is that our Constitution has never been 'colorblind' is the sense used by the Petitioners," the opposition had failed to comprehend the necessary route to equality: "No one could in good faith claim that that process, or that the effects of the discrimination allowed in this country for the 335 years preceding *Brown* have been eradicated. As a result this Court has recognized that a neutral or color-blind policy—while of course desirable in the long-run—is not neutral at all when established on the background of past discrimination." The law school's defenders dismissed the notion that there should be a more targeted, race-blind way to identify the "truly" disadvantaged (a "practical impossibility," argued the Lawyers' Committee for Civil Rights under Law) or that the current method involved quotas (if true, admitted Rauh and Edelman, "this would be a difficult case"). Overall, they maintained that the admissions plan did not eliminate merit as a criterion in admissions. It simply was not the only criterion. Far from being victims, white men stood to benefit from the greater diversity in law schools. "Increasing the diversity of a student body of lively, intelligent and interesting students," suggested Archibald Cox in his brief for Harvard College, "greatly improves the quality of their education." Opponents would challenge this cornerstone to the case for affirmative action for the next thirty years.[47]

With the Supreme Court's acceptance of the case, government policymakers became interested in the case's outcome, as it would determine their future dealings with higher education institutions and interest groups. HEW's executive assistant recommended to the head of the higher education division of the Office of Civil Rights that they postpone a meeting with the American Jewish Committee until the autumn. The *DeFunis* decision, he argued, "may give us a good indication of where we stand with affirmative action generally." HEW Secretary Caspar Weinberger delayed his meeting with the ADL's Arnold Forster on the same grounds. "Valuable guidance for the Department regarding admissions and the affirmative action concept is expected from the U.S. Supreme Court when it decides the DeFunis case," he wrote.[48]

The Supreme Court Weighs In on Affirmative Action

By the time of oral arguments before the Supreme Court on February 26, 1974, the case had aroused considerable attention. The high court, observed journalist Anthony Lewis, faced "tough intellectual issues." Hyman Bookbinder reported to the American Jewish Committee's national office that the staff member assigned to attend the event could not even get into the Supreme Court building because of the crowd. "The interest in the case is escalating from day to day. . . . The lines had started forming early in the day!" wrote Bookbinder. A group of Harvard undergraduates took an overnight bus to Washington, D.C., and lined up at 4:30 a.m. to be assured of getting seats. The courtroom proceedings were deceptively simple: lawyers from both sides had approximately a half hour each to present the outline of their arguments and answer the justices' questions.[49]

In his opening statement to the court, Josef Diamond set out, in a simple, almost folksy narrative, to present his client as an innocent and childlike American who had been wronged by affirmative action. He reviewed for the justices how DeFunis ("Marco," as Diamond called him) had worked hard and yet been denied admission to law school. Diamond told of how he met with the Board of Regents ("Took the parents with us. I don't think we took the boy."), but they would not intervene in the matter. The lawsuit, he argued, was about more than DeFunis's career ambition: he made his argument on behalf of a colorblind society. "We didn't know what his religion was, nor his race, nor whether he belonged to a so-called minority group," Diamond insisted. "We didn't think it mattered . . . whether he was black or red or white." Although Diamond agreed that the PFYA alone was not an adequate basis for making admissions decisions, "to us it wasn't possible that all those being admitted were better qualified than DeFunis."[50]

It was a stripped-down argument, meant to appeal to a basic sense of fairness. In both style and substance, however, Diamond's presentation was weak. It may have had to do with inexperience: although he was a well-known lawyer (and parking lot mogul) in Seattle, this was Diamond's first and only high-profile case. At one point he appeared to interrupt Justice Marshall, who was posing a question. "Please apologize to Justice Marshall for me," he wrote Justice Brennan a few days later. "I was pressed for time and may have been a little discourteous." Diamond's appearance was a disappointment to Philip Kurland, who reported to an ailing Bickel (who died later in the year), "If we are dependent upon the advocacy of Diamond, we have lost." Diamond did not mention the Equal Protection Clause, the specific workings of the law school's admissions policy, or the historical claims of other ethnic and religious groups for inclusion in these special programs. Before the Supreme Court justices, the details of the many amicus briefs seemed curiously unimportant to the lawyer's strategy. Diamond's message was simple: "If DeFunis had been black, he would have been in. He was kept out because he was white. The only reason he was kept out. No other reason."[51]

Diamond faced his sharpest questions not from the court's most liberal members such as William Brennan or Thurgood Marshall but from Harry Blackmun, who grilled him on his premise that the highest qualified must always be admitted first. Blackmun, who had recently written the majority opinion in *Roe v. Wade*, considered his nine years as resident counsel for the Mayo Clinic in the 1950s formative in his judicial outlook, which stressed the need to balance competing values. "Let me get away from the racial aspect a little bit," Blackmun began. "Let's speak of our sister profession of medicine, with which I have had a little familiarity in the past." Did Diamond consider it valid, the justice wanted to know, for medical schools to admit applicants who desired to practice in remote areas, even though their credentials might be less impressive than that of other applicants? "Not at that level," Diamond replied, maintaining that a "soft" affirmative action program was "good, valid, and I'm all for it," but "it should be based not on race, it should be based on the disadvantaged, the underprivileged, the under cultured." Blackmun persisted: "My question was an attempt to get away from race, it was an attempt to focus on the need of a community, not on the qualifications particularly of the applicant." Diamond, however, refused to be drawn into the view that admissions committees should consider anything other than the individual applicant's merit. "I'm not ready to subscribe to the theory that minority clients are looking for minority lawyers or doctors," he told Blackmun. "I think they are looking for the best qualified doctors and lawyers."[52]

Now it was Slade Gorton's turn, for the defense. The Dartmouth College and Columbia University Law School graduate's task at oral arguments was more difficult: the attorney general for the state of Washington had to defend a skeptical court of the validity of a race-conscious admissions policy and establish at the same time the continued importance of applicants' qualifications as demonstrated, at least in part, through testing. Just as Diamond had focused on the value of a race-blind society, Gorton suggested that the law school's policy was reasonable and in line with recent Supreme Court thinking on race. "The University of Washington Law School has selected its limited number of students from a large pool of clearly qualified candidates," he explained. "The considerations employed in the difficult but necessary choice between applicants have included, among several other factors than the race of the those applicants." Gorton referred to Chief Justice Burger's holding for the entire court in *Swann* in insisting that "integration, the end of segregation, was a more important goal" than the unfortunate consequence that some applicants might not gain admittance. He reminded the justices that school authorities traditionally held broad powers to formulate and implement educational policy. They had done so in *Swann* "in order to prepare students to live in a pluralistic society." That same goal of diversity should also apply to the law school.[53]

The conservative members of the court pressed Gorton to explain in more detail the rationale for the law school's affirmative action plan. If the state of Washington had a minority population of only 2.2 percent, asked Burger, would it not follow that the law school's minority population need not exceed 2.2 percent? Gorton responded that it was not a matter of quotas, or even proportional representation. They should seek more minority students since the University of Washington was a national law school and sought a diverse student body that reflected the nation's population. More importantly, he went on, it needed more minority students ("a sufficient variety") so that "the outlook of the white students as well as of the minority students would be more understanding."[54]

Justice Rehnquist mused who exactly was "qualified" in the law school admission committee's thinking. "When you say 'qualified,'" he asked Gorton, "really by the time you've diluted that phrase as much as you have in your approach to admissions, it doesn't mean a whole lot, does it?" Gorton stumbled, maintaining that minority students with PFYA lower than DeFunis were "qualified to do law school work, and were determined by the law school Admissions Committee to be ready and able. . . . They would contribute more given the nature of the whole class, first to the law school . . . and more to the bar." He returned to the subject in response to Burger's question on whether there was "any sort of generalized study to determine whether grades had a direct correlation with success and effectiveness in the practice of law?" Gorton admitted that the university had not conducted such a study, but he referred to the amicus briefs that demonstrated that "both grades in college . . . together with the law school admissions test do not make such predictions." The PFYA, he told the court, could "predict nothing about the contribution you will make to the law school, how much income you will make in the bar, what kind of legal career you will set." He summarized the university's position: "We have a duty to pick people who will serve their nation, their society. We have a duty to see to it that the effects of an exclusionary policy ... will be ended, not only in our school but in our society as a whole."[55]

The oral arguments over, the justices met in conference to continue their deliberations. They focused on Chief Justice Burger's contention that the case was moot. Few members of the court supported this position with vigor. Lewis Powell hesitated before voting this way. He was concerned with the effect of such a decision on the court's reputation. "The case has attracted national interest," he wrote Burger, "and it is predictable that the Supreme Court ... will be criticized for taking a course of action which will be viewed by many as a means of avoiding a truly 'sticky wicket.'" Before he agreed to join Burger, Harry Blackmun's inclination had been to affirm the Washington Supreme Court's decision. He did so, however, "with some discomforts as to [the] implications." Blackmun supported the university's goal of increasing the number of minority professionals (thus passing the "rational basis" test) but acknowledged the power of the opposition's arguments. In particular, he mentioned the Bickel-Kurland ADL brief and the concern about the possibility of increased discrimination against American Jews. Blackmun sympathized with the whites who would suffer from the effects of affirmative action, and he worried that affirmative action recipients would be "demeaned" and "burdened with the need for success." He concluded: "There is an element of unfairness in that the applicant with a superior record may ... find himself left out and another with an inferior record admitted."[56]

In his dissent Justice Brennan waved aside the mootness argument as an example of "devices for sidestepping resolution of difficult cases." He asserted that, although several weeks remained in DeFunis's final law school semester, "any number of unexpected events ... might prevent his graduation." The case before the court, Brennan wrote, had been fully litigated and was "ripe for decision." By disposing of the case as moot, Brennan continued, "the Court clearly disserves the public interest.... Few constitutional questions in recent history have stirred as much debate, and they will not disappear."[57]

The most widely discussed opinion was Justice Douglas's far-ranging dissent, which addressed the importance of merit, the need to account for cultural and social disadvantages, and the colorblind principle. It is difficult to identify Douglas's exact motivation for producing such a lengthy, and often personal, document. It seems that the elderly and ailing justice wanted to make his final mark on the high court's thinking. "I might not be around next time the issue comes up," he told a law clerk. He was moved, as well, by the willingness of many of his fellow justices to subscribe to the "mootness" solution. First Amendment journalist Nat Hentoff recalled meeting Douglas for the first time in a Manhattan dentist office soon after the ruling. "He was so angry," Hentoff remembered, "that he forcefully unburdened himself on the argument in his *DeFunis* dissent."[58]

Of all the justices, Douglas seemed the most eager to grapple with the complex issues the case presented. In the earlier case involving the white applicant refused admittance to the Arizona bar, he had been the only justice to recommend that the court hear the case. Douglas was deeply sympathetic with the civil rights movement, but he identified with Marco DeFunis's plight as well. In his study of the case published a year later, CLEO's Robert O'Neil chronicled Douglas's humble youth in Washington. The future justice attended Whitman College in Washington and not a more prestigious institution because only Whitman offered him a scholarship; when he left for Columbia University Law School, he traveled part of the way on a freight car, alongside sheep. "In a real sense Marco DeFunis . . . *was* William O. Douglas, many years earlier, waiting on tables and carrying two other jobs in Walla Walla stores to put himself through school and support his widowed mother," wrote O'Neil. His past did not automatically lead him to back DeFunis fully: Douglas drew explicitly on his Washington roots in giving support for some aspects of affirmative action when, in his dissenting opinion, he noted that "coming as I do from Indian country in Washington," he discovered how Native American culture "offered competitive attitudes towards life, fellow man, and nature." Perhaps, he seemed to be saying, aptitude tests were inadequate in the assessment process.[59]

Douglas may have been eager to weigh in on affirmative action, but he did not know whether to support the University of Washington plan. He drafted eleven versions of his dissent, shifting back and forth between support for race-blind admissions and arguing that student applications must account for cultural bias. "In India they have . . . a preservation of so many seats for the untouchables. Are we promoting them [i.e., quotas] here?" he asked Slade Gorton during oral arguments. When Gorton denied that the law school adhered to a quota plan, Douglas changed the subject: "When I was teaching law many years ago, I discovered to my astonishment that these . . . so-called tests had built-in racial bias. Is there any finding in this record as to your test?" Gorton replied that there was no finding in the record "because neither party wished even to bring that subject up." Douglas persisted, telling Gorton that "I couldn't find out how they did it, but it was [a] very subtle, built-in system to see that certain minorities didn't get into the school."[60]

Douglas agonized over how to respond to these issues. In his drafts he recommended, among other things, a race-neutral lottery to fill at least some of the admissions slots, the establishment of fixed quotas for minorities, and a total ban on any consideration of applicants' race. In his official opinion, Douglas seemed at first to come down on DeFunis's side: "A DeFunis who is white is entitled to no advantage by reason of that fact; nor is he subject to any disability, no matter his race, he has a constitutional right to have his application considered on its individual merits in a racially neutral manner." And yet, Douglas went on to endorse the law school's "separate processing" of minority applicants: "I think a separate classification of these applicants is warranted, lest race be a subtle force in eliminating minority members because of cultural differences." He urged that the LSAT be abolished and replaced with a new, "highly subjective" aptitude examination to obtain from each applicant "the measure of cultural background, perception, ability to analyze and his or her relation to groups." Douglas noted that he could not conclude that the law school admissions procedure violated the Equal Protection Clause. He argued that the Washington Supreme Court judgment be vacated and the case be remanded for a new trial.[61]

Because of our limited access to the records of the court's deliberations, we can only guess at why the chief justice was able to convince four other justices to share his mootness perspective. In certain fundamental ways, all Supreme Court decisions are strategic; this one seemed particularly motivated by a wish to stave off an unpredictable ruling for which many justices were not prepared. Burger seemed resigned to accept the mootness decision as merely a delay tactic. He wrote Lewis Powell, "The critics who would condemn us for a decision in favor of *DeFunis* will doubtless be exorcized by a mootness holding. It all depends on which student 'is being gored.'" Blackmun was more optimistic, hoping to sidestep a volatile issue that might go away. "I have some feeling that the passage of the years may lessen the crisis," he wrote. "Right now racial criteria are sensitive. In one respect the present case is a backlash to *Brown*."[62]

Where Douglas seemed to absorb every perspective on affirmative action, the chief justice's majority opinion, delivered on April 23, 1974, was sparse and technical in tone and content. The five-justice majority of Burger, Rehnquist, Powell, Blackmun, and Potter Stewart employed a boilerplate explanation of mootness. Burger asserted that, because DeFunis was near the end of his final semester, "the Court cannot, consistent with the limitations of Article III of the Constitution, consider the substantive constitutional issues tendered by the parties."

The case sputtered to a conclusion in December 1974 when the Washington Supreme Court refused to reconstitute *DeFunis* as a class action lawsuit.[63]

The Legal Limbo of the Mid-1970s

As prepared as they were for the court's mootness finding, all sides were disappointed by the result. Slade Gorton complained about having been "marched up the hill and down the hill by the same court." Josef Diamond claimed that the justices had "ducked" the issues. The press editorialized the decision as a "copout," "an acrobatic feat of issue-ducking," and an "avoidance of its responsibility." Conservative columnist Smith Hempstone insisted that the issues were "clear cut." And yet, "with an agility reminiscent of Fred Astaire in his heyday," the court's members had shirked their duty. No social or legal good, these observers all seemed to be saying, could come from allowing the affirmative action questions to continue incubating.[64]

A surprising number of commentators, however, registered relief at the court's action. "Few recent decisions of the United States Supreme Court have so stirred national debate as the so-called 'non-decision' in *DeFunis v. Odegaard*," observed the ADL's Larry Lavinsky. Many in the old civil rights coalition welcomed this as an opportunity to reconsider the vexing issues away from the spotlight of litigation. In its editorial, the *New York Times* acknowledged that "at first glance" it appeared that the court had "merely run away" from making a necessary decision. Far from being a copout, however, "the Court's implicit message to the universities is to work at better procedures for the protection of the rights of all applicants." It called for rights that were "at once nondiscriminatory and humane than to rely on rigid administrative procedures that invite court-ordered management of the academic community." *The New Republic*'s Nathan Lewin suggested that "the worst thing that could have happened would have been for the Court to have [decided DeFunis] . . . since neither side has really addressed itself to the other's legitimate grievance." Louis H. Pollak, a law professor who assisted the NAACP with its brief, acknowledged that the case "wound up with a whimper," but he remained "persuaded that the whimper was the right disposition." The American Jewish Committee's president, Elmer L. Winter, was relieved by the mootness ruling as well. It was "imperative for all groups directly or indirectly involved to search for new ways to resolve the critical issues raised by the suit." The American Jewish Committee's goal, according to Winter, was not victory in the case; it was the "advancement of human rights."[65]

Of all the court's writings on *DeFunis*, Justice Douglas's opinion received the most attention for its capacious understanding of the conflicting values at play. The *Washington Post* lauded it for offering "a great deal of enlightenment." Journalist Iver Peterson noted in the *New York Times* that it was "being closely studied." And yet, most commentary focused as much on the "ambivalence and ambiguity," in the words of the ADL's Larry Lavinsky, as on its "eloquence and insight." Both supporters and opponents took a particularly pessimistic reading of the effect Douglas's dissent would have, even if they believed that he had weighed in on their side. "What Justice Douglas overlooks, perhaps deliberately," wrote Fred M. Hechingber, a member of the *New York Times* editorial board, in the *Saturday Review*, "is the fact that administrative convenience has historically dominated for too many, if not most, institutional arrangements in education." The *Washington Post*'s Nicholas von Hoffman considered Douglas's opinion a "wise and clever decision, which doesn't stand a chance of eventual acceptance." The justice's call for applicants to be considered as individuals, wrote von Hoffman, was "an impossibility among a people who feed their stomachs billions of pre-cooked mass-produced Big Macs."[66]

Affirmative action supporters were especially dejected. "The suspicion, based on Justice Douglas's assertion and on deep popular belief in the country at large, that the Constitution is color-blind," noted Peterson, "may push graduate schools closer to an abandonment of policies that give preference to race just at a time when such racial preferences are becoming unnecessary anyway, according to some professional school administrators." Those who developed, administered, and actively promoted affirmative action offered anecdotal evidence of a crisis. Charles Odegaard, by then retired as university president, told a friend of his travels to medical schools across the country. He found admissions officers "generally aware of the DeFunis case and fearful of a ruling against special consideration for minorities." Odegaard recounted how, "in some cases," faculty members "pull[ed] back" from extending to minorities "special consideration." Just two months after the ruling, James Wilson acknowledged in a speech to the National Association of College and University Attorneys that "the easy advice we could give our institutional clients would be to stay to the 'hard criteria' in making admissions decisions and thereby avoid lawsuits." The impact of *DeFunis*, observed Marilyn Gittell, Brooklyn College associate provost and affirmative action officer, "has been to reinforce the retreat and retrenchment." The NOW Task Force on Compliance reported in mid-1970s that "*all* affirmative action programs are being dismantled, starting with those in institutions of higher education." Harvard University administrator Walter J. Leonard was glum: "It seems to me that too many people are now ready to declare the trip over, when the first leg of the journey has not yet been completed."[67]

In the months after the ruling, colorblind liberals in the American Jewish Committee sought an acceptable approach to affirmative action within their own ranks. Some proposals attempted to nudge the organization closer to support for recognition of race in admissions decisions. Roger Meltzer from the Philadelphia chapter, for example, contacted the national officers to tell them how the Temple University Law School assessed "special category" students: the admissions committee first considered LSAT scores and grades and then added points to applicants' files for a variety of reasons, including minority group status. "On the surface it seems to be fair," Meltzer insisted. "After all, grade point averages are *not* infallible predictors of success and LSAT scores are probably cultural-bound." American Jewish Committee leaders, however, were unable to agree on the fundamental issue of the place of race in such decisions. Bookbinder reported to Samet in May 1974 about a two-hour meeting—"one of the finest we've ever had"—on racial preferences. "But on moving us forward on substances," he wrote, "I cannot report very much more wisdom or insight that we can muster among ourselves."[68]

Although a long-term consensus eluded them, American Jewish Committee leaders sought, in the short term, "to lower the Jewish profile on the whole issue," as Bookbinder noted in his report. To that end, they did not assist Richard Harroch, a failed applicant to the Boalt Law School at the University of California at Berkeley, in his threatened lawsuit. Harroch's background and credentials were similar to those of DeFunis: he was Jewish, his grades were impressive but not stunning (he scored 654 on the LSAT and had a junior-senior GPA of 3.95), and he was a Phi Beta Kappa member. "It is very disheartening to find that after four years of hard work in college, someone with lower qualifications was admitted ahead of me, solely because of my race," Harroch wrote the head of an American Jewish Committee chapter in California. The organization's leaders would not intervene. Referring to the "agonizing and soul-searching and bitterness over *DeFunis*," legal committee chairman Samuel Rabinove decided that he was "by no means 'gung ho' about starting a lawsuit here." He argued that "if we could accomplish something other than through litigation, such a course would indeed be preferable."[69]

American Jewish leaders worked to heal bruised relations with the civil rights community, but with little success. "If . . . we continue the sniping at each other . . . then I can safely predict an erosion of gains already achieved, the development of social calluses on this nation's commitments to justice and a resort to a right wing populism that will endanger us all," warned Samet in a letter to the NAACP's Roger Wilkins. The solution was to get the federal government to modify their guidelines for higher education affirmative action. In May 1974 the representatives of the American Jewish Committee, the American Jewish Congress, the ADL, the Puerto Rican Legal Defense and Education Fund, the National Urban League, and the NAACP sent HEW Secretary Weinberger a joint letter requesting new "nondiscriminatory guidelines" that would clarify "how educational institutions can best develop appropriate tools for special efforts to recruit persons from previously excluded groups." The signatories and their organizations held differing views on affirmative action, and they had failed in their previous attempts to arrive at conciliation with HEW—or each other. Yet, in the wake of *DeFunis,* they told Weinberger they "wish[ed] to avoid polarization."[70]

The harsh reaction they received did not bode well for a reconciliation of colorblind liberalism and racial liberalism. African American columnist William Raspberry characterized the "recent kiss-and-make-up efforts" as merely "a concession on the part of black leaders." Joseph Rauh Jr. was furious, telling his ally Marian Wright Edelman that the civil rights leaders had "pulled a monumental blooper." Rauh and Edelman sent Weinberger their own letter, "in support of guidelines providing preferences for minorities and women's groups which have been discriminated against over the years." Wilkins acknowledged Rauh and Edelman's concern; he justified his signature on the letter in light of Justice Douglas's "indication that he will not support preferential treatment based on race alone." Civil rights leaders, he maintained, should salvage affirmative action with criteria that included "other characteristics such as poverty, lack of educational opportunities, etc." At the same time Wilkins wrote the American Jewish Committee's Bert Gold to tell him that the NAACP "reserves the right to oppose guidelines . . . which might commit us wholly and completely against our basic position."[71]

Black and Jewish leaders' positions proved intractable. Bookbinder took the lead in defending the six-party letter, reminding the influential Raspberry in a letter to the *Washington Post* that opposition to "rigid quotas" did not mean opposition to affirmative action. "Just as I would resist any allegation that when Raspberry opposes busing he is really opposing integration," he noted. Jacob Petuchowski of the United Hebrew College took aim at the UAHC for its *DeFunis* brief even after the case was over and urged his friends and colleagues not to donate to the annual Reform Jewish Appeal. By the end of 1974, the American

Jewish Committee's Roger Meltzer reported that the issue of goals and timetables was still "the major problem" in conciliation efforts with civil rights leaders. Meltzer noted that the American Jewish Committee's national position was
"considerably vague" and that his Philadelphia chapter's perspective was "more
hardline, viewing them as potential shortcuts to de facto quota arrangements."
For all of the work in patching up differences, American Jewish Committee leaders had little to show. "Maybe the best we can hope for here is an agreement to
disagree," he concluded.[72]

The trajectory of the struggle over higher education affirmative action continued to pass through courtrooms in the mid-1970s as litigants challenged not
just admissions but a host of recently developed race-conscious measures for
students and faculty. When a white law student sued the Georgetown University
Law Center, alleging that the financial program developed in 1972 that set aside
60 percent of scholarship funds for "minority" and "disadvantaged" students
was discriminatory, federal district Judge Oliver Gasch sided with the plaintiff.
Such programs, he noted, are "not permissible when it allocates a scarce re-
source . . . in favor of one race to the detriment of others." In another case, the
usually confidential practice of hiring faculty members came under scrutiny at
Virginia Commonwealth University. James Albert Cramer, an applicant for a position in the sociology and anthropology department, sued after he discovered
that the search committee divided the 385 applicants into three categories: one
for "females," a second for "minority males," and a third for "white males." The
committee interviewed only women applicants for the position. Federal Judge
D. Dortch Warriner decided the case for Cramer, writing, "There will never be
sex or racial peace until the idea of sex or racial discrimination is dead and bur-
ied."[73]

The most notable efforts against affirmative action came from applicants who
had been refused admission to medical school programs. Martin Alevy, a magna
cum laude graduate of Brooklyn College who scored in the 99th percentile on
his medical school aptitude examination, filed suit in New York court after he
failed to win a place in the entering class at the Downstate Medical Center in
1974. The Kings County judge supported the center, ruling that the school was
not required to adopt a "predetermined robot-like mathematical formula" in admissions. It was not a clear-cut victory, however: the state appeals court upheld
the decision but cautioned that preferential treatment must satisfy a substantial
state interest that could not be obtained by other methods. The judge noted that
Alevy had established that the center had practiced "reverse discrimination" but
that he had "failed to establish a prima facie case of discrimination . . . in that he

failed to show his own right to relief, even if the entire minority program were eliminated."[74]

Fierce competition for professional school places and academic positions continued to motivate rejected applicants to challenge affirmative action. Three white teenage men were more successful than Alevy in their class action lawsuit against the City University of New York for denying them admission to a new accelerated medical program for undergraduates. At a federal court trial—with the support of local chapters of Italian and Jewish American organizations—the litigants' lawyers demonstrated the "increasingly arbitrary" criteria the admissions committee was using to select its students. The chairman of the admissions committee, noted presiding judge Marvin Frankel, "was overcome by a feeling of shame for having traded one human being for another on the basis of race." In his opinion Frankel emphasized that applicants in different racial groups were never compared to each other and that black and Hispanic community leaders had pressured administrators to earmark half of the incoming seats for minorities. Despite the chancellor's vow that no quota system existed, minorities did indeed occupy half the seats of the incoming class.[75]

Many Americans in the mid-1970s could not seem to make up their minds about affirmative action. To be sure, there were staunch supporters of and those decidedly hostile to affirmative action. Even with the rise of colorblind conservatism, however, there were those who opposed only some aspects of affirmative action; much like Justice Douglas, they found themselves pulled in different directions. *DeFunis* succeeded in concentrating the nation's attention on race- and gender-sensitive programs, but it revealed, as well, the uneven nature of the opposition, especially the persistence of colorblind liberals in seeking a middle ground. Strictly speaking, the case resolved nothing. But it supplied conservatives with new energy and a new strategy. Preferential treatment, goals, timetables, and quotas: the lexicon of affirmative action was being contested at that very moment at a new medical school at the University of California at Davis. The administration there had admitted to a quota in a trial involving a man named Allan Bakke, and his case would soon come before the U.S. Supreme Court.

The only clear winner in *DeFunis* was Marco DeFunis. After graduating from the University of Washington Law School in 1974, DeFunis passed the state bar examination and went on to build a successful practice as a personal injury lawyer. *Washington Law and Politics* named him a "super lawyer" in 2001. The issues his lawsuit publicized, however, continued to rankle activists and legal scholars. "The Supreme Court has skirted the issue for now, but it had no power to declare a moratorium on the controversy," the *Philadelphia Inquirer* reminded readers. The federal government, especially HEW, did not provide the necessary guidance either. "It has been almost *two years* since the *DeFunis* decision," Bookbinder wrote a Ford administration official in March 1976. "Patience is wearing out I feel compelled to report." With the rising number of lawsuits, most observers believed that the Supreme Court would revisit the subject soon. "Obviously, there will have to be a clear, definitive decision . . . before very long," predicted CLEO's Robert O'Neil. "College and universities are trying to do the best they can in the current limbo, but guidance from the courts is badly needed and will continue to be sought."[76]

The University of Washington returned to the sights of "reverse discrimination" protesters in the 1990s. Three white applicants denied admission to the law school—two women and one man—sued the university in 1997 to challenge its race-sensitive policy. In language recalling DeFunis's grievance more than two decades earlier, plaintiff Katuria Smith complained that the law school's decision was "unfair": "Schools should not determine admission standards based on race." Even DeFunis, who had not spoken publicly about his own case since the Supreme Court's ruling, weighed in by calling for "public scrutiny of the admissions process at all state-supported schools. The public has a right to know what's going on." For all the similarities in the two cases, the organizations involved were significantly different. Gone were the liberal groups who had backed DeFunis: they had switched their stance on affirmative action or offered only muted opposition. The conservative Center for Individual Rights assisted Smith and the other two plaintiffs with legal resources. Although the Ninth Circuit Court of Appeals upheld the law school's admissions criteria in 1998, opponents tasted victory that same year when voters approved "Initiative 200," a referendum barring race- and gender-based preferences in public institutions. The University of Washington subsequently suspended its affirmative action program.[77]

The opinion and commentary surrounding the many of the cases in recent decades have focused on *Bakke,* but the legal lineage originated with *DeFunis.* For all its significance in the mid-1970s, however, the case and Marco DeFunis himself were strangely absent from the press. When he died in January 2002 of a heart attack while running on the indoor track of the local Jewish community center, only the Seattle daily newspaper and the University of Washington student newspaper carried his obituary. At the time of his death, DeFunis's son was completing his last semester at Cornell University Law School.[78]

Americans remained locked in the seemingly perpetual struggle over the competing goals of diversity and meritocracy, of providing opportunity and assuring students fair consideration as individuals. The motivations of affirmative action opponents are a mix of principle, politics, and parochialism whose shape and character have varied over time. For higher education in particular, so much seems at stake for young adults (and their families) as they choose professions, apply to graduate and professional schools, and aspire to succeed. As the history of *DeFunis* demonstrates, opponents swore allegiance to equality, but they did not always agree among themselves about whether sufficient opportunity existed that would make even "soft" affirmative action unnecessary. As the arguments of colorblind conservatism came into wider circulation, colorblind liberals persisted in seeking compromise. When Justice Harry Blackmun was asked in a 1995 interview to reflect on his *DeFunis* memorandum twenty years after the decision, he expressed frustration that the struggle over affirmative action had continued. "I had hoped at the time . . . that we would mature enough and grow enough so that this discrimination which made affirmative action necessary would be cured," he said. Unfortunately, Blackmun continued, "with the political swings, it's proved otherwise, and people are always looking out for themselves, and it's been disappointing to me that it keeps cropping up."[79]

CHAPTER FIVE

"Do Whites Have Rights?"

White Detroit Policemen and the "Reverse Discrimination" Protests of the 1970s

By the time federal judge Ralph Freeman announced his decision from the bench on an affirmative action matter in the Detroit Police Department on May 9, 1975, the crowd of white protesters outside had swelled to over a thousand people. In the large, marbled U.S. District Courthouse on the downtown's West Lafayette Avenue, Freeman ordered that the traditional "last hired, first fired" seniority principle be modified so that those police officers recently hired under the city's new affirmative action plan would retain their positions in the face of massive layoffs. As Freeman delivered his ruling, the line of Detroit Police Officers Association (DPOA) members, their families and friends, city council members and union sympathizers from as far away as Buffalo and Chicago blanketed the streets surrounding the courthouse. They held signs that read "Detroit Is an Un-Equal Employment Opportunity Employer," "Uphold Our Contract," "Do Whites Have Rights?" and "Real Affirmative Action: Fire the Mayor." This last sign referred to Coleman A. Young, the city's black mayor and author of the much-hated affirmative action plan.[1]

Freeman's decision was not well received. Protesters, many of whom now stood to lose their jobs, moved to block the streets, shouting "You police the city" and "Talk about rights; we've got no rights." The *NBC Evening News* informed its viewers that "some of the officers had been drinking; all had spent several hours out in the hot sun." A fight broke out between several off-duty white officers and an off-duty black policeman, with guns drawn. "We're gonna kill you, you . . . niggers!" one man screamed. As the black police officer left for the hospital with a broken nose, a group of enraged policemen struck a local television cameraman over the head and knocked him to the ground.[2]

Reaction to what some Detroiters called a "police riot" underscored not only the deep divide over claims for racial and gender equality but also the largely unacknowledged tensions between labor union members and liberals over seniority in a period marked by economic recession and divergent interests. Mayor Young denounced the protests as a "drunken brawl," and the police chief characterized the attack on the black officer as "clearly racial." Detroit residents, beset by a spiraling crime rate, lived in a city where law enforcement was, as one journalist put it in the wake of the courthouse demonstration, "in deep trouble." The leaders of the police officers' union, led by its president Ron Sexton, dismissed the violence as a small skirmish divorced from the demonstration and its objective. They sought to frame the conflict around the defense of labor's rights, an important appeal in this heavily unionized city. "Our problem, our cause, our efforts that day were for seniority rights and nothing else. . . . We are not white, we are not black. The DPOA is all blue," they proclaimed. Their legal challenges to affirmative action would continue for the next twenty years.[3]

This history is part of the larger story of the struggle over equal employment opportunity dating back to at least the 1940s. It was given significant legal life by the federal government with the passage of Title VII of the Civil Rights Act of 1964, which banned employment discrimination on the basis of race, color, creed, and sex. In searching for ways to address structural inequality in the workplace, the EEOC, a product of Title VII, served as midwife for affirmative action. By the late 1960s, private employers and the government had begun to establish various kinds of affirmative action programs, many aimed at the building trades unions. So too did higher education institutions and the government develop plans for the nation's colleges and universities. These pitted colorblind liberals against affirmative action supporters who backed race- and gender-sensitive admissions, hiring, and promotion initiatives. The two types of opposition rarely joined forces. Colorblind liberals had little sympathy with conservative labor unionists, often denouncing them for their attempts to thwart efforts to bring minority men and women of all races to worksites for the first time. While colorblind liberals engaged in an opposition aimed primarily at restoring what they viewed as a meritocratic higher education system, labor union opponents worked to restore a well-established—and heavily labor-influenced—industrial relations system and to avoid litigation that was crippling to their coffers and negotiating strength.

The most far-ranging and sophisticated "reverse discrimination" blue-collar protests came in the mid-1970s in response to efforts by the Civil Rights Division of the U.S. Department of Justice to open up jobs in city, county, and state agencies, especially in police and fire departments. Detroit's white policemen's protest is a particularly suitable lens with which to view anti–affirmative action campaigns across the country since, as a large industrial city dominated by racial discord, Detroit was broadly representative of other city governments that faced "reverse discrimination" lawsuits in the period. The anger and despair of white men as they defended their economic status in the face of affirmative action registered with a growing segment of the public worried about their own economic status.[4]

As with the earlier blue collar opposition to affirmative action, it's tempting to dismiss the policemen's colorblind notions of merit and seniority as a thinly veiled defense of inequality. Race and gender ideology served as the backdrop to this resistance, but so too did the policemen's embrace of professionalism, public safety, and the liberal tradition of equal rights. There was an important difference in these new opposition efforts: where conservative trade unionists made their case against affirmative action on the grounds that it would destroy traditional labor control over apprenticeships and hiring halls, Detroit's police officers—along with police officers and firefighters across the country—maintained that the use of established, quantifiable measurements such as aptitude examinations and years of service were a superior means of hiring and promotion. As they moved toward a deeper understanding and a better articulation of their grievances, they crafted a set of arguments that served as a powerful counterweight to pro–affirmative action arguments at the level of national policymaking.[5]

There is yet another layer of significance to this history: the cross-racial and gender alliances white policemen formed in defense of the seniority system with "labor liberals," many of whom were at the forefront of civil rights and feminist-driven change within their own labor organizations. The dispute over where one's rights as a unionist ended and those as an affirmative action recipient began made the opposition campaign in the highly contingent years of affirmative action a complex one. Although labor liberals did not oppose affirmative action in matters of hiring and addressing discriminatory seniority systems, there were limits to their embrace of the rights revolution. Where affirmative action supporters held that seniority contract clauses, in the words of the *New York Times,* "often operate to rebuild walls of exclusion against those who wait overlong to get in—a disproportionate number of them women and minorities," labor liberals insisted that bona fide seniority systems were paramount to securing workers' economic status. The lawsuits over seniority rights in Detroit and elsewhere gave labor unionists a measure of success in influencing the shape of affirmative action policies that had eluded them in the late 1960s.[6]

"The Liberals Have the Power Now": The Politics of Police Affirmative Action

In no employment sector were the range and intensity of protests for and against affirmative action in the 1970s more remarkable than in the urban police force. Young minority men and women as well as white women, empowered by the rising expectations of social protest movements, newly elected black mayors, and the 1972 amendment to Title VII that extended discrimination bans to state and local governments, challenged police employment practices. In New York City, Chicago, Minneapolis, New Orleans, San Francisco, and other cities, they filed lawsuits on size and height requirements for new recruits, on the content of entrance and promotion examinations, and on patrol assignments. They demanded to be hired in greater numbers. The U.S. Department of Justice also contributed to this effort by taking fifty-one city, county, and state governments to court, mostly to demand changes in their police and fire departments. Their gains were impressive: in 1972 there were only seven women in the United States assigned to patrol work; by 1974 there were nine hundred on patrol, and women made up 4 percent of the total police force in the country. Advocates for affirmative action on the basis of race could claim even more success. In Chicago, for example, the percentage of blacks on the force climbed from 13 percent in 1962 to over 20 percent by the late 1970s. During the same period, the figure for Washington, D.C., went from 13 percent to 42 percent and in San Francisco, from 2 percent to 20 percent. In the 1970–1990 period blacks accounted for 41 percent of all new police hires nationwide. By the end of the 1980s, 130 U.S. cities had black police chiefs, including New York City, Chicago, Baltimore, Philadelphia, and Houston.[7]

Many police departments, however, remained stubbornly white, male preserves as veteran officers demonstrated unambiguous opposition to affirmative action. Police work had been a traditionally working-class occupation, one that required little education but provided social recognition and relative employment security. White policemen took pride in welcoming family members, friends, and coethnics to the force. There was another, more important factor at play in their opposition that divided them from the earlier protests of skilled tradesmen to affirmative action: the professionalization of law enforcement in the decades following World War II. This process accelerated in the 1960s and had begun to transform the hiring and promotions process away from the older use of these social networks to one based on merit, seniority, and formal assessment that veteran officers asserted was transparent. Police officers and state troopers in

Ohio, Wisconsin, Kentucky, New York, and other states defended this system by challenging in court the qualifications of affirmative action recruits. They argued that there were clear and empirical grounds for hiring and promoting officers and that affirmative action upset this just and orderly system.[8]

In Detroit, white policemen engaged in sustained protests that grabbed the local and national media's attention for their intensity and violence. Detroit was one of the many large industrial cities beset by staggering urban woes. Its population was divided along racial lines over the purpose and quality of the police force. In the two decades following the end of World War II, Detroit's industrial base steadily weakened as manufacturers shifted production facilities to the suburbs; between 1948 and 1967 the city lost nearly 130,000 manufacturing jobs and another 195,000 positions—mostly manufacturing—in the twenty years after that period. Whites soon followed the exodus of jobs, as new freeways reshaped the city's social geography and retail shifted from downtown to suburban malls. In their wake, the city government faced an eroded tax base, declining social services, and increased crime. By the 1960s, notes historian Jon Teaford, older central cities, such as Detroit, were "still alive but hardly vital."[9]

The city's residents offered differing explanations for its downward trajectory. For many conservative whites, the devastating 1967 riot confirmed their belief that the city's decline was due to the effect of a growing black population on the mounting crime rate and drop in housing values. For Detroit's African Americans, the riot was yet another indication of the effects of economic inequality, the failure of urban renewal, and the need for significant reform of a police department with few black officers and a long history of abuse toward black citizens. The Detroit branch of the NAACP received hundreds of complaints of the abuse of black residents at the hands of the police. "This kind of conduct . . . of the police operates effectively to keep the Negro in a segregated, second-class position," the organization's executive secretary Arthur Johnson told a U.S. Commission on Civil Rights hearing in 1960. In the wake of the riot, a group of local political, business, labor, and religious leaders came together at the invitation of Jerome Cavanaugh, the city's liberal white mayor, and formed New Detroit, Inc., to help rebuild the city. The police department, noted businessman and New Detroit board member Stanley Winkleman, "needs to be taken apart and put together again."[10]

Detroit's white policemen interpreted attempts to increase the percentages of African American men and women officers on the force (which stood at 18.6% and 2.15%, respectively, in the early 1970s) as well as the opening of more kinds of police work to women as challenges to their besieged occupation. Like police officers elsewhere, they had been alarmed in the 1960s as their behavior came under scrutiny in the light of demands for racial justice and individual rights. Buffeted by calls for reform and greater attention to the rights of suspects, police officers saw themselves, as one social psychologist put it, as "lonely and unappreciated guardians of law and order." Their economic status declined as well: the average pay for a patrolman nationally was 33 percent less than what they needed to sustain a family of four in moderate circumstances in a large city. Rank-and-file officers in Detroit took action in the mid-1960s by transforming the DPOA into a bona fide union. City officials balked at their demands, treating the unionists with considerable condescension, but DPOA members persisted and, with the backing of unions such as the United Automobile Workers, the Teamsters, and the Hotel and Restaurant Employees Union, claimed victory in 1968 when a citizens' committee, appointed to arbitrate the impasse, awarded the DPOA a pay increase.[11]

White policemen expressed their indignation with liberalism generally and affirmative action specifically in dramatic, often eloquent, fashion by portraying themselves as an oppressed group. They were part of what Ronald Formisano in his study of antibusing activism in Boston during the period calls "reactionary populism." Hamstrung by economic recession and alienated from the Democratic Party for its embrace of racial, gender, and cultural priorities at odds with their worldview, these white residents objected to new government programs, but their protest was, in Formisano's words, "cramped by limited horizons." White policemen, ignoring the role of moderate Republicans such as those in the Nixon administration in the development of affirmative action, believed it to be wholly a liberal creation. "I still like Richard Nixon," mused one officer. "He got rid of the Black Panthers, and was the first man to have the guts to tell the forced bussing people off." To DPOA members, liberals had reordered society on the basis of a misguided notion that they must pay the price for past discrimination while middle-class suburbanites evaded the consequences of such plans. White policemen valued order, security, and respect; to them, affirmative action struck at the heart of this ethos and exemplified the worst aspects of liberalism. "The whole context has shifted from the gun-toting thugs and outsiders being the villains, to the uniformed police officers, a symbol of law and order being the villain," one officer complained. Some white police officers seemed resigned ("I'm just a peon in this big drama") while others resolved to oppose affirmative action. "The liberals have the power now, and I'm not a liberal," admitted one officer in December 1974. "But I'm going to fight my way through this trying period."[12]

Detroit policemen's "reverse discrimination" protests became a touchstone for white discontent in the mid-1970s. Affirmative action was not the only liberal issue with which opponents contended but, in a city rapidly emptying of whites, it unified white police, fire, and other municipal workers who had to remain in the city due to a residency requirement. The police, more than any other group, were visible reminders of law and order. Their work knew no boundaries: they could be found patrolling the streets, eating in restaurants, directing traffic, and answering calls for assistance of all kinds. Police officers had many friends, relatives, and neighbors. In effect, the DPOA became the de facto political organization for white Detroiters who, for the most part, had retreated by the early 1970s to neighborhoods of modest two- and three-bedroom houses in the northeast and northwest corners of the city. As police did in Los Angeles, Minneapolis, and other cities, the DPOA served as a quasi-official campaign organization for their endorsed candidates. They were responsible in large measure for Roman Gribbs's election to run the city in 1969. After backing a white candidate, former police commissioner John Nichols, in his failed run against Coleman Young in 1973, they worked unsuccessfully thereafter to defeat Young in his three reelection bids.[13]

In the years leading up to Young's election, the number of minority men and women of all races in the police and fire departments bumped up, but workplace conflict remained commonplace. In July 1972, for example, the police leadership reported to city officials two incidents in different precincts in which arguments between white and black officers developed into a fight with guns drawn. That same year five women police officers filed a complaint with the Michigan Civil Rights Commission alleging a violation of unequal pay laws. They claimed that, as patrol officers, they performed the same tasks as men who held the rank and pay scale of sergeants. Police Commissioner John Nichols was not sympathetic: "It would appear that some members of our Women's Section are interested in having the best of *two worlds*—that which they can obtain as women in the traditional role, as well as that which they may obtain as individuals involved in the liberation movement."[14]

In a city where half the population was black, the 1973 mayoral race that brought Young into office as the city's first black mayor firmed up resistance to the growing political power of African Americans. The centerpiece of Young's campaign was a plan to dismantle a controversial police anticrime unit responsible for a large number of black suspects' deaths known as STRESS ("Stop the Robberies, Enjoy Safe Streets"). White policemen were even more alarmed at his promise to bring greater civilian oversight of the police department, enforce a residential requirement for city employees, and, most significantly, introduce an affirmative action plan that would push the figure of black officers from around 20 percent of the total force to 50 percent by the end of his first term in 1977. His narrow win underscored the extent of Detroit's racial divide: he received 92 percent of the black vote, while 91 percent of white voters backed John Nichols. Although Young did not play a role in a lawsuit filed by a group of women applicants to the force, he welcomed Judge Ralph Freeman's decision in May 1974 directing the police department to open all police positions to female applicants and to hire one qualified female applicant for every male applicant until further ordered.[15]

Young was unmoved by criticism of affirmative action. Of those at the helm of large U.S. cities at the time, Detroit's mayor encountered perhaps the most crippling urban woes: high unemployment, a nation-leading homicide figure (801 in 1974), and staggering white flight (there were 891,000 white residents in 1969; there were only 543,000 in 1976). In the economic realm, Young faced the near-impossible task of bringing large-scale investment into a decimated city, settling for largely ineffectual downtown office building projects, new stadium construction, and, at the end of his tenure in office, casino gambling. Busing city children to the suburbs was not a solution either, since the Supreme Court in the 1974 *Milliken v. Bradley* decision ruled that the city provided no proof that outlying municipalities were responsible for the city schools' racial composition or Detroit's residential racial segregation. The decision was, according to historian James Patterson, "pivotal in the history of postwar race relations," since it frustrated efforts to overturn de facto segregation. With an overwhelmingly black public school population, the mayor decided not to pursue busing within the city. He was left with police affirmative action as his single significant reform plan. Young told the *New York Times* that the city's future well-being depended on it: "We're not going to turn this city around, and have a united city, until we deal with the Police Department."[16]

The mayor defended his program vigorously, pointing to the long history of police harassment and violence against black citizens. He emphasized the important role of minorities and women officers in improving community-police relations. He claimed, for example, that women on patrol made sense because "there is a far less likelihood of police brutality and, consequently, of an explosive incident." In his memoir *Hard Stuff*, published in 1994 shortly after he left office, Young recalled his reaction to his opponents' charge that affirmative action was really "reverse discrimination": "My attitude was, You're damn right—the only way to arrest discrimination is to reverse it." He was not troubled by the strict numerical goals he set, explaining them as an appropriate remedy for the historically unfair treatment minorities had experienced. "If quotas are the only way to keep white folks honest, let there be quotas," he contended. In his first six months in office, the mayor disbanded STRESS, announced the establishment of fifty-five "mini-stations" (an experiment in community policing), and appointed three African Americans and one white citizen to the new police commission created as a result of the city charter approved on election day. And, as he promised, Young issued Executive Order No. 2, mandating that police personnel introduce recruitment and hiring policies so that minorities would fill one-half the Detroit Police Department ranks.[17]

"Unfair, Undemocratic, and Just Plain Dictatorial": White Policemen against Affirmative Action

In an immediate and personal sense, white policemen experienced the arrival of new recruits to the station houses and patrol cars across the city in 1974 as a loss of occupational identity and a threat to their safety. They filled the pages of *Tuebor*, the DPOA's newspaper, with news reports, gossip, and satire about affirmative action developments in the police department. Women coming on to the job for the first time were "women libbers," "gals," and "lovelies." Policemen questioned their physical abilities to serve on patrol. One *Tuebor* writer wondered: "I can just imagine one of our male-type officers getting into a beef on the street and his female partner hitting the thug with her purse. Will they spread out their leave days or just take them at that certain time of the month?" The typical woman police officer, another columnist asserted, was underweight and weak, someone who "lost their last three family trouble fights to a squirrel, a hobby horse, and someone's 11-year-old brother." The consequences of having a woman as police partner, he concluded, were serious: "Breaking someone in on the job is one thing but when there is a chance of breaking your bones in the bargain, that is another thing entirely." Veteran policemen saw the streets as a dangerous place, unsuitable for women. "Our society is bad enough," pleaded one officer. "Why must we turn over to our sick society the last of our goodness left—our women?"[18]

The very presence of women police officers challenged the masculine culture of police work, one marked by long hours, close working arrangements, coarse language, and endless talk of sports. Its contributors expressed disdain for the counterculture and sexual liberation (homosexual men were "fags," "sissies," and "funny boys"). They treated close working arrangements, especially the physical presence of women in the previously male-dominated precinct houses, as sexually charged. "How are you going to change your clothes with your lockers being on the main floor?" asked one policeman. "It could be very interesting. Some of the men will try and promise to close their eyes when they walk by."[19]

The source of the men's resistance to women officers came from home as well as their work culture. Research on the seldom-studied relationship between policemen and their spouses indicates that policemen's wives wielded significant influence over their husbands. They did not welcome policewomen on the job either. A sociological survey of patrolmen in Detroit and Oakland, California, at the time found that a large number of recruits quit because of their spouses' objections to working hours, changing shifts, and other job characteristics. In the early 1960s one state's police commission forced applicants to submit written permission slips from their wives before they became sworn officers. New York City policemen's wives formed their own association to protest the introduction of women on patrol. In addition to giving organizational form to their jealousies, it was, writes Andrew Darien in his study of the city's police department, an expression of "city wide anxiety about women patrol officers' assault upon masculinity and homosocial bonding." It is clear that Detroit policemen believed that affirmative action for women made their jobs more difficult; it may have also strained family life.[20]

White policemen were more circumspect in their commentary on the race of the new recruits, reflecting perhaps the social proscription on overt discussion of racial characteristics. Most columnists' discussions of race came in the form of ridiculing life in a city under black political leadership. As late as the mid-1960s, however, one white policeman, identified only as "Bob," offered his frank assessment of African Americans to a sociologist conducting field interviews in Detroit's predominantly black Tenth Precinct: "They're not like us. They spend a lot on themselves for cars, clothes, liquor, and living it up. They spend almost nothing on their kids." The officer explained the scarcity of blacks on the force as a result of the police command firing them, "because they don't make good officers, and not enough have come in." A decade later, *Tuebor* writers rarely referred to racial characteristics, and then only in terms of local crime stories, as in October 1975 when an officer killed a black man who had pointed a gun at his partner. The shot from the officer's revolver "sent Mr. Citizen to the big BBQ in the sky."[21]

Although there is plentiful evidence of resistance to gender-based affirmative action, the most visible "reverse discrimination" protests focused on race-based remedies to inequality. Women, it seems, did not challenge the white policemen the way that African Americans did. Two policemen writing in the March 1975 edition of *Tuebor* hinted at divisions within the ranks of women officers by distinguishing between the "women libbers" patrol officers and the older women on the force assigned to the Women's Division, whom they likened to "the ladies we choose for wives and girlfriends, [who] want to be respected for being different." The ties between black and white women officers may have been weak as well. Unlike women in industrial unions who frequently joined together to battle gender inequality in organizations such as the Coalition of Labor Union Women (CLUW), there is no evidence that women police rookies in Detroit ever formed cross-racial feminist coalitions. One scholar, writing on the status of black women in U.S. police departments reported that there was "little unity among women." White policemen faced significant challenges from feminists in the courtroom but little organizational or political opposition at the department and municipal level, thus freeing them to focus their resources on defeating the local black leadership and civil rights organizations. In a city long characterized by racial tension, black women officers most likely found support in organizations such as the Guardians of Michigan, a group formed in 1963 as a volunteer service organization for black Detroit police officers and Wayne County sheriff deputies. The Guardians were fierce critics of the DPOA: they picketed the union's headquarters, worked closely with the city administration in promoting affirmative action, and backed the mayor's collective bargaining positions against the police union, even announcing on occasion its members' intention to stay at work in the event of a strike. For this they earned the scorn of white policemen, who denounced them as "Coleman Young's children."[22]

DPOA leaders built their case against affirmative action in the media around the arguments that the city's plan was flawed in design and that it violated the rights of white men. The police unionists insisted that Young's short timetable for bringing underrepresented groups into the force had resulted in inadequate screening of applicants. "I found that to be alarming," Ron Mestdagh, a retired police officer, remembered in a 2004 interview. "We were getting people with records and there were felonies on them and high misdemeanors and we were getting their records expunged and bringing them in to the department." The local press joined DPOA members in pointing out that the police department was approving applicants with criminal records and low test scores. Like many police departments across the country, the Detroit Police Department had revised what equal employment officers, judges, and activists denounced as discriminatory criteria in assessing those interested in joining the force. They eliminated such steps as interviewing applicants' neighbors, background checks on family mem-

bers, and investigating matters of "personal morality." White policemen denounced "Mickey Mouse hiring practices" whereby the city recruited by "go[ing]
out on the street and grab[bing] as many turkeys as you can." An editorial in
the April 1975 *Tuebor* decried the new, less intensive procedures for processing
applications; a cartoon showing black men, with large afros and wild dress, walk-
ing out of Michigan's state penitentiary in Jackson and signing on to the force
accompanied the editorial.[23]

In an environment of uncertainty and distrust over what constituted equal
employment opportunity, information about affirmative action was, as Jonathan
Rieder puts it in his history of "white backlash" in Brooklyn's Canarsie neighborhood, "an amalgam of fantasy, truth and rumor." Detroit's white policemen often shared information of questionable validity on the department's application
process. "I hear that they took some men from the department who met with . . .
the colored applicants and told them the answers to the examination questions
and still a lot of them failed," reported one patrolman in the mid-1960s on an
early effort to bring more minority officers on to the force. With the introduction
of Young's affirmative action plan, *Tuebor's* columnists churned out stories that
seemed far-fetched. In December 1974, for example, two DPOA members reported that the department had sent a letter to Detroit General Hospital directed
to "a group of low I.Q. girls" encouraging them to apply to the force. It was not
clear whether the women were staff members or patients, but the officers believed it portended worse things to come: "Soon, the Department will have to go
to our mental hospitals to get prospective police officers, as they will be the only
ones crazy enough to join." Other DPOA claims were more grounded in evidence. The *Detroit News* backed the unionists' assertions that some new recruits
had troubling backgrounds when it revealed that the department had sworn in
"a great number" of officers who had reading skills below the sixth-grade level.
Several recruits had served prison time for drug-related charges, the police had
arrested another for writing bad checks, and four rookies faced charges for
shooting their spouses. The daily newspaper characterized this record as a "very
dangerous matter."[24]

Scholars have noted the importance of morality, masculinity, and race in
working-class white men's understanding of their place in the labor force. This
explanation was central to explaining the "hardhat" rebellion of skilled trades and
construction workers in the late 1960s. It remained important in the 1970s as
police officers and firefighters developed their case against affirmative action. Although morality and masculine boundaries shored up their occupational pride,
Detroit's white policemen insisted that, in this "era of negative professionalism,"

as one of them put it, race and gender considerations played no part in their critique. They portrayed themselves as defenders of a race- and gender-neutral employment system. For white policemen, the cumulative effect of affirmative action hiring was denigration of their profession and deterioration in morale. New recruitment efforts were, as one officer put it, "a personal affront." Sociologist Nicholas Alex discovered similar sentiments expressed by the white New York policemen he interviewed in the mid-1970s. Those officers spoke of "declining standards" and complained that the city accepted the "dregs of humanity." The typical new recruit, announced one policeman, "is not a peer by any sense of the word."[25]

William Hart, the chief of police, dismissed the complaints about the quality of recruits as "racism and sour grapes," but the DPOA continued its attack on affirmative action, seeking to make the case that Young and the city's black leadership were as unqualified to run the city as their recruits were to police its increasingly dangerous streets. They charged the mayor with being a corrupt political boss who was not interested in true equality. White policemen compared Young to Cleveland Mayor Carl Stokes, the first African American elected to head a major city; his troubled administration was marked by a scandal involving charges of police examination cheating and favoritism. "The kingdom of Cleveland fell into the hands of thieves and all types of fiends," wrote one officer. Just like Stokes, "Old King Coleman . . . would like to think of us as his royal subjects." Philip Tannian, the white police chief during Young's first two years in office before the mayor fired him, was a "half-wit," "Elmer Fudd," and a "puppet" for adhering closely to the mayor's affirmative action plans. Liberal judges, especially black judges, were subjected to ridicule for coddling criminals. The DPOA dubbed the city's main courthouse "the Barnum and Bailey Hall of Justice." One police officer denounced civil rights activist and judge George Crockett for presiding over the "Revolving Door Division of the Otis Elevator Company" and enabling "the scum he unleashes on society to virtually fly out the door of the Frank Murphy [Courthouse] Releasing Station." Affirmative action was "un-American," "government bungling," and "unfair, undemocratic, and just plain dictatorial." Federal judges who approved of affirmative action were "dumb affirmative action people" and "anarchists who have no regard for the law." Judges drew their understanding of police work, as one DPOA columnist suggested, exclusively from television shows.[26]

Echoing the charge made across the country by white urbanites encountering busing, affirmative action, and other equality programs, they dismissed liberals as "outsiders," many of whom were upper-class suburbanites who would not have to live with the consequences of their rulings. And, they predicted, the consequences would be dire: liberal politicians and judges had made the city uninhabitable. "Why don't people wise up to these liberals? They are giving us Homicide City," one officer pleaded. Columnists urged readers to "stand like a good soldier and fight for your rights." They characterized the crisis as an issue of citizenship. "We are . . . citizens, too, and should deserve the rights of other citizens," reminded one officer in April 1975. White policemen felt trapped: they struggled to build their union in the face of city opposition; they attempted to move out of Detroit but could not, due to the residency requirement; and they believed that affirmative action would threaten their jobs and lead to increased crime in a dangerous city.[27]

Affirmative Action on the Streets and in the Courtroom

White policemen had little direct say over whom the police department hired as rookie officers, but they did have legal recourse to challenge new promotion and layoff policies. As they drafted their litigation, DPOA leaders refined their claims against the city to emphasize the race-neutral character of merit, qualifications, and seniority. Their formal opposition to affirmative action began with a lawsuit filed in 1974 that called into question the department's new policy for promotion to sergeant. For police officers, attaining the rank of sergeant meant greater pay and prestige and the possibility of moving further up the chain of command. The promotions procedure to become sergeant in Detroit, as elsewhere, was a complicated one involving, among other things, a written exam, a professional ratings assessment by one's supervisors, and a seniority weighting. Critics argued that the eligibility register, or roster system, was discriminatory. They pointed out that the exams were culturally biased, that white supervisors manipulated the professional ratings for friends, and that the seniority requirements closed off opportunities to the department's newest members. Although the proportion of African Americans in supervisory positions increased somewhat in the years immediately preceding Young's arrival at the city's helm, the new mayor could still point to persistent inequality: in 1972, 90 percent of Detroit's black police officers were at the lowest rank of patrolman, while only 70 percent of white police officers held that position.[28]

Young moved quickly to remedy what he viewed as an untenable situation. The first sign of his change to the system came in spring 1974 when Police Commissioner Philip Tannian reversed the longstanding practice of promoting patrol officers to sergeants in strict adherence to the eligibility register. Tannian chose black candidates for advancement who were lower down on the register than some white officers. The department's new policy of promoting equal numbers of black and white officers led, in effect, to the creation of separate promotion lists. In some promotion rounds, the numerical disparity of the rankings of those white and black officers promoted seemed dramatic, as in March 1975, when the lowest-ranking white male who moved up held the 79th spot, while the lowest-ranking black male was positioned at the 494th place. White policemen faced further bad news: police personnel administrators announced plans to revamp the entire promotions systems. Among other things, they would institute an "oral board" examination to test officers' views on a variety of issues including race relations and urban policing.[29]

The DPOA leadership rejected the new procedure as discriminatory to white men and detrimental to police effectiveness, since the "best qualified" would be left behind. They charged that Young had abandoned an orderly promotions system for a dishonest one, premised on dispensing political favors. "Let's call it 'forced promotion' instead of affirmative action. Affirmative action is too nice a word," suggested one officer. A heavy dose of cynicism ran through much of their commentary: "I've got a new slogan for Mayor Young to hire more minorities: Sign up today as a police officer. Tomorrow you'll be a sergeant and next week a lieutenant." For those black officers promoted to sergeant, another policeman claimed to be "sorry," since "all Detroiters must think these officers are really stupid when the only requirement for promotion is black skin." The DPOA leadership agreed to support white officers passed over for promotion with the union's legal resources; they obtained a court order temporarily banning the promotions, but the Michigan Court of Appeals lifted the injunction in late June 1974. As an extension of the women police officers' affirmative action case, District Court Judge Ralph Freeman ordered the department in July to include at least five women in each of the next three promotion classes and four women in the fourth class as an immediate solution to the underrepresentation of women in the supervisory ranks. When the Detroit Board of Police Commissioners formally approved the race-based plan that same month, the police unionists filed a federal lawsuit. The Lieutenants and Sergeants Association (LSA), a union representing first-line supervisors, launched its own challenge in court to the new system.[30]

In their depositions and court testimony, police unionists and their lawyers emphasized the chaotic and unprofessional nature of affirmative action. The new oral board examinations were a "subterfuge" that served to "screen out the unluckies, not the incompetent." DPOA president Dave Watroba told the court that the oral examination was poorly designed and dominated by management personnel from outside Detroit. It was not, he said, a "rationally neutral employment practice." Union attorney Sheldon Adler characterized the mayor's argument that the racial composition of the police force should be roughly that of the city's general population as "pure and simple stupidity": "It is rape of the community because it does not give the community what they paid for and that is the best qualified."[31]

They focused on the importance of the written examination score in promotion decisions, arguing that it was a clear and objective standard for advancement. "The present list was drawn up as a result of merit and competition," one police attorney told the *Detroit News*. "Men have studied long hours to qualify on that list. . . . Now it appears the department is going back to the spoils system." In court, the union offered the testimony of individual officers as proof that the city was bypassing highly qualified candidates. One policeman came forward to tell how he was rejected for sergeant although he held a PhD in criminal justice; another testified that he was passed over even though he had an undergraduate degree in police administration, had graduated first in his police academy class, held four commendations and one unit citation, and ranked high on two promotions lists. The DPOA called on Dr. Erick Beckman, a member of Michigan State University's criminal justice department and a former police officer, to explain the importance of "qualifications": "The purpose of the police department is to provide a certain service. I think that service is best provided by selecting individuals who are best able to provide that service. That means individuals who have certain credentials, properly trained, properly supervised, appropriate attitudes. That is how you get the best police department, not by . . . a numerical breakdown on the basis of race." Unfortunately, DPOA counsel Walter Nussbaum noted, "many of the best qualified persons in the Department were sacrificed to the racist objectives of the Mayor and his political appointees."[32]

Their argument, and the language in which it was framed, echoed "reverse discrimination" complaints made by other white men in such places as Atlanta, Louisville, Pittsburgh, and Kansas City, Missouri. At the center of their case lay the charge that affirmative action was illegal since it violated white policemen's individual rights. Or, as the white policemen's lawyers put it in the plaintiff's brief: "The logical and specific result [of the city's plan] was the invasion of Constitutionally and statutorily protected rights of Caucasians." They emphatically rejected responsibility for the historical effects of racism and gender inequality, pointing instead to the need to protect individual rights irrespective of one's race or gender. "Maybe I should go to some other country where Affirmative

Action would work for me," complained one officer. "Maybe 300 years from now my ancestors will be able to say, 'You owe me!' What a laugh." In arguing for employment policies that ignored race or gender, white policemen claimed the language of Title VII as their own. Like colorblind liberals and conservatives, police unionists insisted that they were adhering most closely to the goal of "equal employment," not liberal judges or policymakers.[33]

To DPOA members, the city plan made a mockery of "true" civil rights. Disgruntled policemen took their complaints to Douglas Fraser, United Automobile Workers vice president and chairman of the city's police commission, who defended the mayor's affirmative action plan as "much needed." Patrolman Mitchell Skazalski, who identified himself as "a damn good cop," told Fraser he was "extremely upset" with the new policies since he was a college graduate and had scored well on the examination yet department officials had passed him by for promotion. "How am I expected to relate to this individual who is now my superior when, I have been proven more qualified than he, and [he] has kept me from increasing my income by 25%, while he has increased his at my expense," Skazalski wrote. Another policeman characterized the new system as "simply unfair": "I was raised in a home atmosphere that taught me that hard work and integrity would be rewarded, but I am beginning to wonder." His effort to do well on the sergeant's examination depended on family sacrifice, since "my wife spent many hours keeping our children quiet so I could study."[34]

The delay, or denial, of promotion had long-term consequences for pay and pension levels. Ron Mestdagh recalled how he "studied my ass off" but was not promoted until his third attempt, while black applicants with lower scores won their promotions earlier: "A lot of times as a white officer you would be commanded by a black sergeant and knew full well that he had not performed as well on the test or [promotions] process as you did, [but that] he had your stripes." Mestdagh, who came on the police force in 1968, took "very personally" the residency requirement as well. He lived in the city's far east side in a white neighborhood known locally as "Copper Canyon" and watched as his white neighbors moved to the suburbs while he remained in a house that steadily lost its value. Mestdagh worked at extra jobs to help pay his children's Catholic school tuition so they would not have to attend Detroit's failing public schools. "I thought my rights were being violated," he said.[35]

This embrace of individual rights sat alongside an older worldview of scarcity and a corresponding belief that one's job was "property," to be handed down to one's family, neighbors, or coethnics. *Tuebor* columnists took pleasure in announcing relatives of veteran police officers coming on to the job for the first time. Whether they opposed busing in Boston, the introduction of skill trades training programs for minorities in Philadelphia, or police affirmative action in Detroit, the convictions of those caught up in "white backlash" were the same: the amount of goods and services was finite, and they had to hold on to "their share." They perceived African Americans as getting more than what rightfully belonged to them. "These quotas and Philadelphia plans make us angry," one unemployed construction worker in Canarsie explained. Echoing labor leaders' calls for full employment, this worker recommended "creat[ing] plans to help both sides. Create jobs, but don't take from one to give to the other and create bitterness." The two asymmetrical perspectives—individual merit guiding hiring and promotion decisions, and jobs or trades being distributed along collective lines—were difficult to reconcile, but at least one Detroit policeman tried in his monthly column in November 1974: affirmative action, he claimed, "means that a white officer's son, brother, nephew, etc. has NO chance of getting on the job even though he may have a degree or be more qualified than everyone else."[36]

In response to police unionists' charges, city attorneys offered an "operational needs" defense of the new promotion plan that focused on the necessity for a diverse workforce to lower crime rates and improve police-community relations. "The Police Department must be representative of the community. . . . If the city is to survive the police must have the trust of the community," argued James Andany, chief counsel for the city. In his deposition, Young reminded the court that all of the officers were eligible for promotion by having passed the written exam. Young was unimpressed with the practice of ranking candidates according to their marks on the exam: "I do not consider seriatim eligibility on a roster as sacrosanct. . . . A black police officer who is 95 [slots down on the register] can be much more successful in performing his duties than a white police officer who is 5." When the DPOA attorney asked the mayor for proof of this, Young snapped, "I'm not talking about a study, I'm talking about what happens in life." Police unionists may have considered the mayor's concession on the absence of empirical evidence for this important claim a victory of sorts, but he dashed their hopes that he would reconsider. In fact, Young claimed that his plan did not go far enough. "It will take 40-damn years to produce a Department that has an equal number of Black sergeants and white sergeants. . . . I think we ought to be going something like 80–20 [percent]."[37]

Another crisis, one that tested the reach of affirmative action, engulfed the entire city in 1975. The local labor federation allied itself with the DPOA when recent police recruits, facing layoffs as a result of a severe budget shortfall, went to court to modify the seniority principle of "last hired, first fired" in order to preserve their recent employment gains. In April, when Young announced an $8 million cut to the police budget, Chief Tannian drew up plans to furlough 825 officers and demote 35 lieutenants and 260 sergeants, all on the basis of strict seniority. With the mayor's tacit approval, two black officers' organizations, the Guardians of Michigan and the "Concerned Police Officers for Equal Justice," convinced federal district judge Damon Keith, a black jurist, to enjoin the city temporarily from laying off or demoting some three hundred black officers. City negotiators told DPOA leaders that personnel cuts would only be canceled if the union agreed to contract concessions.[38]

This crisis united liberal and conservative unionists as the debate over seniority and affirmative action that raged in Detroit and across the country revealed a significant fault line dividing liberal unionists and other liberals during the economic recession of the mid-1970s. The challenges made to seniority after the passage of Title VII had resulted in modifications to certain procedures for counting years of service and granting "retroactive" seniority to specific classes of victims of discrimination. It had not overturned the "last hired, first fired" precept. Unionists might disagree about the exact form it should take in specific work settings, but they were steadfast in their loyalty to seniority. In Detroit, Young faced stiff resistance, even from his erstwhile supporters, who embraced affirmative action in hiring but were committed as well to seniority as a race- and gender-neutral principle to be defended with vigor. Fraser broke publicly with Young over the contentious issue. He rejected the layoff scheme, arguing that seniority was a "right that is earned and should not be tampered with." Fraser faced unrest within his own union, the UAW, over the issue. His administrative assistant, Tony Connole, told him of a meeting with Detroit's UAW Local 942 president Claude Dukes: "He has a couple of nephews on the force and was concerned that seniority would not be followed." More alarming was Dukes's warning that "people in his plant were very disturbed over the precedent that might be set by this kind of court decision." In the local press Young responded to union detractors, reminding them that he had been a "union man most of my life" but that seniority rights were "not that sacred, not bigger than the U.S. Constitution's guarantee of civil rights."[39]

The DPOA leadership appealed to unionists in a full-page advertisement in the *Detroit News*. They characterized the "last hired, first fired" practice as "the cornerstone and lifeblood of unions" and warned readers that the denial of seniority "could happen to you and your family." Twenty-year-old officer Gil Kohls rejected the idea that union members were motivated by self-interest: "I didn't mind the layoffs so much when they were done according to seniority. But now, what's to protect the older guys from losing their jobs?" Some DPOA backers argued that Young was responsible for souring race relations by challenging traditional seniority practices. "Mayor Young wants to disregard seniority and keep only his black friends working at the Police Department," wrote one man from the working-class suburb of Warren. "All union men in Detroit should walk off their jobs if Young carries out his plans." Most supporters who sent letters to the daily newspaper made their argument in racially-neutral terms: "The recent Federal Court order on Detroit police officers is a threat to every union in this country," "The time has come for all union members in the area to support Detroit police officers in their struggle for survival. If the officers' union is destroyed, other unions will meet the same fate," and "Enough is enough. . . . If the state's labor unions stand for [this] . . . they are spineless."⁴⁰

This wide-ranging support of liberal unionists across race and gender lines for both seniority and affirmative action highlights the clash of two systems, or languages, of "rights" in the post–civil rights era. The improved relationship in the mid-1970s between the DPOA and the Metropolitan Detroit AFL-CIO, the local labor federation dominated by industrial unions, came about as they sought to protect the "security" of seniority even while disagreeing sharply over other aspects of affirmative action. Detroit area liberal labor leaders had kept the DPOA at arm's length in the past: they routinely complained of police racism and joined with the NAACP, the ACLU, and other organizations in the 1960s to urge the establishment of a citizen's review board to oversee the police department. But they were wary as well of the Young administration and organizations they considered dominated by middle-class leaders such as the National Urban League, criticizing their labor relations record with municipal unions. In the midst of the furor over layoffs, Metropolitan Detroit AFL-CIO president Tom Turner, a black unionist, appeared before a DPOA membership meeting to tell them of his support. "On the question of seniority, the AFL-CIO is colorblind," announced Turner. "That is the official position of the AFL-CIO. The DPOA could use the AFL-CIO as an ally when it is attacked." At the national level, organizations such as the CLUW and the Coalition of Black Trade Unionists were offering their own strong support for the "last hired, first fired" principle. Although the police union never affiliated with the labor federation, Turner considered them "our trade union neighbors" and supported their collective bargaining demands with the city in the 1970s and 1980s.⁴¹

The appeal to union principles, however, did not heal the rift in the police ranks. There is only scant evidence of cross-gender, and none of cross-racial, support for maintaining the seniority system. A *Tuebor* columnist congratulated one female officer in the Sixteenth Precinct for turning down an assignment since she "would rather not take a job from a more senior, fellow DPOA member." When another woman police officer refused to be moved up the promotion list and accept assignment to sergeant's school, she made public her letter to command stating that she opposed affirmative action and was willing to wait her "proper turn"; a black patrolman took her place. Despite DPOA attempts to rally minority officers to the cause of seniority, no black officers in a department polarized along racial lines would commit publicly to such a principle. And yet there is evidence that black police officers valued seniority. Wayne State University psychologist John Teahan, for example, found in his study of black and white Detroit recruits in the early 1970s that both groups ranked "family security"—the bedrock on which seniority had been built—as their most important occupational goal. Black officers listed "equality" as their second most important goal.[42]

What was already a hard-fought struggle between white policemen and the mayor now ballooned into a split across the city. Technically, Judge Ralph Freeman's order, the one that sparked the courthouse violence in May 1975, did not revoke seniority rights: the 275 officers, who could remain on the job while the city proceeded with the layoffs of veteran white officers, were paid with federal government money distributed through the Comprehensive Education and Training Act (CETA) and, therefore, Freeman argued, were not on the same police force. White policemen dismissed the judge's reasoning as disingenuous and another example of liberalism gone awry. In the midst of these crises, some officers resigned from the force and sought law enforcement positions elsewhere (especially in the Sun Belt and northern Michigan); others stayed and continued to resist affirmative action. "Things are getting tense and sometimes ugly in this recession-rocked city as summer nears. . . . This city is steadily becoming a worse place to be," observed a *New York Times* reporter in a story on the police demonstration.[43]

Over the course of the next two years, continued city-DPOA conflict tested the limits of civic order. In a deal brokered by Judge Damon Keith, the DPOA membership avoided the impending layoffs in June 1975 by agreeing to contract concessions. These givebacks, white officers held, were yet another sign of a liberal city government demanding that others shoulder the burden for its ineptitude. Later that summer, during two days of violence, arson, and looting along the city's Livernois Avenue brought on by the fatal shooting of a local black man by a white bar owner, Young and his police commanders faced off against the DPOA once again. Police unionists criticized the mayor's onsite management of the police deployment as well as his order limiting officers' use of force in response to the unrest as still more examples of poor leadership. They were equally incensed by the absence of women officers on riot patrol, which, they argued, proved the inferiority of the new recruits. Young asserted that the DPOA membership was on the verge of outright revolt: as an example, he claimed that three white policemen had sped by him on Livernois Avenue and tossed a smoke bomb under a police cruiser parked next to him. When Young announced a second set of layoffs the following June, a large number of white policemen reported themselves sick in a "blue flu" protest in reaction to a new lawsuit filed to save the jobs of junior black officers. The city administration faced the unpleasant choice of potentially insubordinate officers on patrol or insufficient officers to police its streets.[44]

By the late 1970s, the courtroom became the dominant forum for police disputes, as it had been for higher education affirmative action opponents. This was a reflection both of the growing sense of the futility of grassroots white protests in a city firmly in the hands of black political leaders and of the DPOA's commitment to a costly and lengthy legal process that, nevertheless, held out the promise that judicial rulings would ultimately deliver justice. Nevertheless, police unionists continued to mobilize against Young in the political arena, albeit with increasingly disappointing results. In the absence of a viable white candidate in the 1977 mayoral race, the DPOA were reduced to backing Young's main opponent, black city councilman Ernest Browne. He lost badly to the mayor, who called Browne "the first black White Hope." Some white Detroiters sought alternatives to living under Young's rule. Residents in the overwhelmingly white northwest section of Detroit (roughly, the Sixteenth Precinct) launched a short-lived campaign to secede from the city. Many whites did what their former neighbors had been doing for two decades and left for the suburbs. By 1980 blacks made up over 70 percent of the city's population; by 1990 that figure would be close to 80 percent.[45]

The composition of the police force reflected this decades-old transformation of Detroit to that of a "black" city. African American men and women claimed a growing share of the DPOA membership, with affirmative action boosting the percentage of blacks on the police force from 18.7 percent of the total force in 1974 to 35.6 percent in 1978 (black women made up 9 percent of the force and white women made up 4.4 percent). For the first time, a black policeman was elected to a union leadership position and sat on the board of directors beginning in 1976. Although they continued to pour resources into affirmative action legal challenges, DPOA leaders attempted to soften the union's image and portray the mayor as the source of strife. The rank and file elected a white officer, thirty-one-year-old David Watroba, as president in 1978 after a campaign in which Watroba formed a biracial advisory board of police officers. In victory, Watroba warned Young to "change his style": "He can't play the racial political game with us now, because the cracks he makes about the police won't be aimed at just white officers any more." By the time of the 1986 DPOA election, nonwhites, by a slight margin, outnumbered white police officers for the first time. Nevertheless, union members elected another white policeman, Thomas Schneider, to head the DPOA, a position he held for many years.[46]

To the relief of white policemen—and the labor movement—a series of appellate court and Supreme Court decisions, beginning in the mid-1970s, ruled that affirmative action could not be expanded at the expense of seniority rights. The first significant Supreme Court decision came in 1976 when the court, in *Franks v. Bowman Transportation,* ordered that measures could be taken to provide a "rightful place" remedy (that is, retroactive seniority to the date of discrimination) for specific victims of unequal treatment with traditional seniority arrangements generally left intact. The next year, in *Teamsters v. U.S.,* the court was even more forceful in its support for seniority: "An otherwise neutral, legitimate seniority system does not become unlawful under Title VII simply because it may perpetuate pre-[Civil Rights] Act discrimination." During the police layoff controversy in 1976, the Sixth U.S. Circuit Court of Appeals in Cincinnati gave the DPOA a legal victory on the seniority issue, declaring that the jobs of police officers hired with CETA funds were not exempt from layoff. In the face of a rise in gang-related violence and the mayor's success in negotiating additional CETA money, city officials recalled all furloughed officers before a layoff controversy arose once again.[47]

When Detroit laid off more than a thousand police officers in 1979 and early 1980, it did so according to strict seniority, reducing the proportion of black officers below the rank of sergeant from 39 percent of the force in 1978 to 28 percent in 1983. Despite Supreme Court decisions, the Detroit NAACP chapter took up the cause of the recently laid-off officers, arguing in a case they filed that the constitutional protections embedded in the city's affirmative action plan superseded seniority rights secured through collective bargaining. To the delight of the backers of *NAACP v. DPOA,* U.S. District Court Judge Horace Gilmore ruled in the plaintiffs' favor in February 1984. As Gilmore proceeded to craft his remedy, however, the Supreme Court handed down yet another decision in June 1984, this one involving affirmative action, seniority, and layoffs in the Memphis Fire Department. Once again, the court upheld vested rights in a bona fide seniority system over the demands of a municipal affirmative action plan (*Firefighters Local 1784 v. Stotts*). Since neither the union nor nonwhite workers were parties to the consent decree that established the plan, the justices reasoned that they could not be seen as agreeing to give up seniority rights. The *Stotts* ruling, DPOA president Watroba proclaimed, "proves . . . that we did nothing wrong by sticking to the seniority system in layoffs."[48]

The DPOA was able to check the reach of police affirmative action, but they did not prevail in their challenge to the centerpiece of the city's plan, its promotion policy. Even in a period of supposed liberal dominance of federal employment policy and law, however, the DPOA found allies sitting on the bench, especially U.S. District Court Judge Fred Kaess, who ruled in the police union's favor in February 1978. Kaess, a conservative jurist nominated to the court by President Dwight D. Eisenhower in 1960, rebuffed the city's "operational needs" argument, noting the absence of firm evidence to support claims that local crime rates dropped with increased diversity on the police force; overall, he downplayed the lingering effects of inequality and claimed instead that the city's policies were "profoundly at odds with the traditions of individual merit and race neutrality, concepts implicit in the Constitution and of fundamental importance to all races." Kaess's critics denounced his decision, calling it, in the words of the director of the city's department of human rights, "a drastic setback to minorities and women in their struggle for equality of opportunity in employment and education."[49]

The city appealed. It won a favorable ruling from the Sixth Circuit Court of Appeals in October 1979 on the grounds that Kaess had erred in his analysis of the city's "operational needs" argument and had overlooked "the continuing effect of the pre-1973 exclusionary practices," which the three-judge panel found compelling. Although they remanded the case for further consideration of constitutional issues as well as determination of a date for ending the program, affirmative action supporters celebrated their victory, which the Supreme Court confirmed in 1981 when it rejected their petition for a writ of certiorari and refused to hear the case. The police unionists pushed on, challenging aspects of the plan for the next fifteen years. Meanwhile, Mayor Young reached his long-sought goal in the late 1980s, when black officers at all ranks made up approximately one-half of the police force.[50]

The clearest judicial support for Detroit's affirmative action plan came a few months before the Appeals Court decision in 1979, with Judge Damon Keith's ruling in U.S. District Court against the LSA in its separate challenge to the promotion plan. Keith, who returned to the district court bench from his recently secured appeals court seat in order to hear the case, found the mayor's plan "reasonable" and "morally just and necessary." The African American judge's background and legal reasoning were in stark contrast to that of Kaess: Keith was a graduate of Howard University Law School in the late 1940s and active in the Democratic Party. He was a member of the Michigan Civil Rights Commission before his appointment to the federal bench by President Johnson in 1967. In his 1973 decision involving the local utility company, Detroit Edison, he ordered that it fill specific vacancies on the ratio of three black applicants for every two white applicants until black employees constituted 25 percent of the workforce; he ruled as well that it must promote one black supervisor or foreman for every white promoted. In addition, he was the author of the Appeals Court decision against the white Memphis firefighters that the Supreme Court later overturned. "Black judges must take every opportunity to fashion the law in a manner that reflects the 300 year history of discrimination our people have suffered in this land," Keith wrote in a 1983 law review article.[51]

Where Kaess rejected remedies that considered race, Keith delved into the "sad and sorry record" of police department discrimination and concluded that just such a remedy was necessary. At the end of the trial, which lasted 55 days and produced over 6,300 pages of transcripts and 230 exhibits introduced as evidence, Keith gave little weight to the union lawyers' argument that promoting the highest-ranking officers on the eligibility roster would result in more qualified supervisors. He reasoned that the written exam's value was dubious enough to allow for the promotion of candidates out of sequence; they had all "passed" the exam by achieving a certain score and, therefore, were all equally qualified in this regard. While allowing that there did not exist explicit evidence to justify the "operational needs" defense, Keith accepted as adequate proof the recent drop in violence against police officers as well as the insistence of police and city leaders that a diverse police force was necessary.[52]

The decision came as a blow, but not as a surprise, to the LSA leadership. "We knew going into that case that we weren't going to win," J. Preston Oade Jr., the union's attorney, recalled in 2008. "Judge Keith wasn't going to override affirmative action in the City of Detroit. It wasn't going to happen." Oade contended that the obvious reason was his sympathy for affirmative action programs as well as his friendship with Young ("They came up together"). Still, for Oade, a high school dropout with a lackluster law school record, the case provided vital on-the-job legal training (he was still in law school when the case began). The law firm for which he worked, which represented several high-profile union clients, including Jimmy Hoffa's Teamster local, put the newly minted attorney in charge of the case. Oade remembered that the "most compelling evidence" the LSA legal team offered was modeled on the landmark 1954 *Brown v. Board of Education* decision in which the NAACP offered expert testimony on the psychological toll of discrimination on African American children. In this same way, the psychologist who testified for the LSA concluded that the effects of the police department's affirmative action plan was "emotionally devastating" for white officers.[53]

Keith's decision epitomized liberal judicial thinking on affirmative action. He focused on the historical forces at play in structuring the workplace hierarchy and embraced the notion of "distributive justice," concluding that new hiring and promotion practices must compensate for past injustices. Although he acknowledged that the plaintiffs' position had "facial appeal," Keith firmly rejected it: "In a perfect world, plaintiffs would be correct. The world has been far from perfect for blacks, however. It has been especially far from perfect for blacks in the Department and blacks who applied to the Department." Decisions about promotion were based on several factors, including public policy and safety concerns. Besides, he noted, "no one has a right to be promoted." Affirmative action, he concluded, "was required to undo the present effects of years of systemic discrimination." To give added force to his ruling, Keith made the city plan a court order in 1980 to help stave off "continuing efforts to undermine affirmative action" from "reverse discrimination" lawsuits.[54]

"Reverse discrimination" protests continued to influence politics and workplace relations in far-ranging ways even with the declining significance of the labor liberals. In the political realm, their significance shifted from local politics to the national politics of an ascending conservatism marked by Ronald Reagan's election to the presidency in 1980. The Reagan administration identified the elimination of affirmative action as one of its chief goals. It drew from the rhetoric of those plaintiffs in the 1970s, such as the DPOA members, in emphasizing the importance of individual rights, merit, and qualifications as the ideal criteria for hiring, promotion, and university admissions decisions. William Bradford Reynolds, assistant attorney general for civil rights, supported by Edwin Meese III, White House counselor and, after February 1985, the attorney general, led the drive. Reynolds argued that affirmative action plans with numerical goals were "racial preferences" and were "morally wrong." He singled out the Detroit Police Department in December 1983 for "us[ing] discrimination to cure discrimination" and submitted a brief to the Supreme Court asserting that the plan was unconstitutional. When the court refused to reconsider the case, the

U.S. Commission on Civil Rights, under the direction of Clarence Pendleton, denounced Detroit's promotion plan for what Pendleton considered its overly broad remedies: "'Simple justice' is not served . . . by preferring non victims of an employer's discrimination over innocent third parties solely on account of their race." White police officers received the news with disappointment as well. One Georgia policeman wrote to Justice Harry Blackmun as "one of the several hundred thousand white male police officers across the country that was profoundly shocked" by the high court's action. Calling the Detroit plan an "insidious policy [that] affects the very soul of this great nation," he asked Blackmun, "Have you no feeling for what is inherently wrong?"[55]

Detroit's white policemen eventually enjoyed their own legal victory, but only after Young's plan had ended and only on technical grounds relating to the duration of the plan, not its overall validity. In March 1993 the Appeals Court ruled that the department had continued affirmative action promotion longer than necessary (it ended in May 1989) and that the plan was not sufficiently tailored to satisfy Fourteenth Amendment equal protection guarantees. The judges remanded the case to district court to determine if any relief to white policemen was necessary. The district court judge announced a settlement between the city and the officers the following year, ordering that the plaintiffs receive additional retirement benefits, provided they had remained on the force for the entire period of dispute and had never been promoted to sergeant. In addition, the city agreed to pay some of the DPOA's and individual plaintiffs' legal fees. As the veteran policemen, many approaching retirement, listened to the judge, however, they learned that, although the court understood them to have suffered a "real and unfortunate injury" due to affirmative action, it was "reasonable for some persons innocent of wrong doing to bear some burden in order to correct the harsh effects of a grievous wrong of constitutional dimensions and enhance the public safety by improved law enforcement." It was essentially the same message that affirmative action supporters had delivered to them in the 1970s.[56]

The resentment of affirmative action opponents endured over the course of the two-decade life of the city's plan, underscoring the deep divide along race and gender lines in many of the nation's workplaces. Most of the participants viewed the struggle as one involving race, not gender. Ron Mestdagh, for example, did not remember any acrimony over the hiring of women into formerly male-defined police jobs. "It worked out well. . . . They were eminently qualified." Preston Oade Jr. argued that "it's different when it's framed in terms of gender." Oade went on to observe that he had "never seen an affirmative action program for women that pits women against men. I'm not aware of a single case where any public organization gives a merit exam and then splits it into two lists, one for men and one for women." The lower visibility of conflict between men and women officers was especially true in Detroit, where longstanding racial animosity defined politics and employment. If the level of opposition to gender-based affirmative action did not seem as high as that for race-based programs, male police officers nevertheless viewed women officers' abilities as inferior to their own. A 1982 study of the Oakland, California, police force revealed that over 70 percent of the men questioned either "disagreed" or "disagreed strongly" with the statement, "Women are capable of performing the patrol functions as well as men." This treatment often carried over into police unions and organizations, including the National Black Police Association, where women members complained of marginalization.[57]

Despite the evidence of improved relations among police officers in departments across the country, white policemen remained angry at what they perceived to be the fundamental unfairness of affirmative action. "To this day I am still very, very bitter about the whole thing because they moved the goal post on us . . . through nothing I did—but they penalized me for it," Ron Mestdagh maintained in 2004 as he recalled the financial setback he experienced. Because of the delay in promotion, he retired as a sergeant and not a lieutenant. "It really demoralizes people to go the full route to seek a promotion, taking the tests, placing high on the list and then being passed over," noted one white Detroit policeman. "How many times is it fair to pass one person over? . . . [Affirmative action] tends to lessen the focus on competence and put it on the question of race." Even after police affirmative action ended, the DPOA leadership and its white members continued to battle with city politicians over longstanding grievances rooted in their resistance to the rule of black politicians. When, in 1999, the state's legislature passed a law invalidating the much-hated residency requirement, over 20 percent of the city's police officers fled to the suburbs in the following year alone.[58]

Although the emotions of the crisis had cooled considerably, few of those involved had changed their minds. Preston Oade Jr. summarized the case as "race pitted against merit. That's a very unfortunate combination isn't it?" In the years following the Detroit police cases, Oade went to work for the Mountain States Legal Foundation, a conservative public-interest law firm. There, he won a case before the Supreme Court in *Wygant v. Jackson Board of Education* (1986) involving seniority and teachers' layoffs. From his successful legal position in a Denver law firm, he insisted in a 2008 interview that he was not particularly conservative ("I'm a lawyer, I have a client to represent") or opposed to affirmative action (his law firm "actively recruits minority lawyers and mentors minority lawyers"). Still, Oade embraced colorblind meritocracy even at this late date. "The whole American dream and the core value of America . . . is being judged on merit," he concluded.[59]

As a labor liberal, the UAW's Douglas Fraser maintained his qualified support for police affirmative action. A few years before his death in 2008, Fraser reflected on the rationale for the city's plan. "When you think back to the composition of the police and look at it today, I don't think the old Police Department could survive," Fraser said. "You couldn't have had a basically all white police department. I don't think they could police effectively." He understood the resentment of the white officers: "Some of my friends say, 'It doesn't hurt anybody.' Like hell it doesn't. Somebody gets hurt. My view is you have to make up for past sins. . . . Unfortunately, somebody has to pay—innocent people." True to his union principles, however, he insisted that labor liberals were correct in joining with the DPOA in defense of seniority. "I would take that position today," Douglas noted.[60]

In his nationally syndicated column in 1979, black journalist Carl Rowan wrote that the Detroit police lawsuits were "infinitely more important than either . . . *Bakke* or *Weber* . . . because they go to the heart of issues like law and order, of the staffing of police and fire departments in our increasingly black cities." Rowan might have made even wider claims for the significance of these "reverse discrimination" protests. They gave rise to a counterlanguage of "rights," deployed first by these white policemen and then by conservative politicians, commentators, and lawyers in a full-fledged challenge to affirmative action. The Detroit protests reveal the role of "qualified" affirmative action backers such as unionists in Detroit and elsewhere, whose position in defense of seniority reminds historians to look in a more nuanced way at what constituted "liberal" and "conservative" stances in the 1970s. Their legacy is less visible because the Supreme Court's intervention preserved seniority systems; the potential for a full-scale split between liberal unionists and other liberals did not materialize. And yet, they too affected affirmative action programs by limiting their reach to hiring and promotion policies, not termination decisions. Just as white policemen demonstrated in a dramatic manner the level of resistance to affirmative action, liberal unionists complicate our history of affirmative action through their embrace of some aspects of the city's plan and rejection of others. They do not fit easily in our understanding of the history of affirmative action. The interplay of race, gender, and class identities was complex. In Detroit, "whiteness" and "gender interests" had the power to divide and unite workers and residents in surprising ways as they struggled over the meaning of rights and equality.[61]

The Detroit cases came at a time when the meaning of affirmative action and its opposition remained contested. As the growing use of litigation in the mid-1970s shifted the momentum of affirmative action opposition toward colorblind conservatism, colorblind liberals who had, until that point, worked with policymakers and in court to modify higher education affirmative action turned in a concentrated way to the political process. Their objectives were fixed on maintaining an alliance with civil rights allies and, at the same time, becoming standard bearers for race and gender justice in the post–civil rights era. Labor liberals aimed as well to shift the political focus away from the rights revolution and to full employment and labor law reform as a way of addressing the collective rights of American workers. Both agendas would be a daunting task in a period characterized by stalled liberalism, a sour economy, and a growing conservative movement.

CHAPTER SIX

"The Fight for True Nondiscrimination"

The Politics of Anti–Affirmative Action in the 1970s

In the mid-1970s, the future of affirmative action was in doubt as the nation's attention focused for the first time in a sustained way on the preferential policies that had been in place for nearly a decade. The number of articles in newspapers and periodicals on the topic increased steadily. In 1976 *U.S. News and World Report* became the first national news magazine to place a story on affirmative action opposition on its cover when it ran the piece "Reverse Discrimination: Has It Gone Too Far?" That same year the producers of *All in The Family,* one of the most popular and politically charged television situation comedies of the decade, dedicated an episode to the subject. In this particular story it is not Archie Bunker, the bigoted patriarch of a Queens, New York, working-class family, who complains about affirmative action: rather, it is his son-in-law, Michael Stivic, a New Left activist and graduate student. "Mike" struggles to come to terms with the loss of a coveted fellowship to an African American candidate. "I understand why [he] . . . got the job. That's the way things are today," he tells the university dean delivering the disappointing news. When the dean explains the need for affirmative action and asks him, "How do you think the scales of justice have been balanced for the blacks?" a clearly conflicted Mike replies, "Lousy, but they shouldn't be balanced against anybody." It is left to Archie to capture the changed political commitments of the period. "It turns out you're the guy against the coloreds. I never was," he crows.[1]

Although scores of race- and gender-sensitive hiring, admission, and promotion plans had taken root in the nation's workplaces and on its campuses, their legitimacy hung in the balance as the number of "reverse discrimination" complaints and lawsuits continued to climb. In its first "reverse discrimination" case, the U.S. Supreme Court in 1974 ruled in *DeFunis v. Odegaard* that, since the plaintiff's studies were nearly completed, his legal challenge to the University of Washington Law School was moot. It would first rule on the constitutionality of higher education affirmative action in *Regents of the University of California v. Bakke* in 1978.

But the judicial branch did deal with blue-collar affirmative action in the interim. A series of federal court decisions, culminating in the high court's *Franks v. Bowman Transportation* decision in 1976, prohibited affirmative action in lay-offs if it violated bona fide seniority systems. These were not total defeats, but alarmed supporters sought clear judicial approval of the rationale behind affirmative action. When it came to seniority, they argued that, in the face of the deep economic recession then under way, the viability of program objectives depended on widening the scope of affirmative action to include procedures for firing as well as hiring employees. Unionists of all stripes, including those "labor liberals" supportive of most affirmative action, unsurprisingly rejected this view.

As the struggle over retaining the "last hired, first fired" principle continued in the courts, a number of studies appeared that concluded that higher education affirmative action programs were poorly designed, enforced in an uneven manner, and delivered disappointing results. "The general feeling among many women's leaders, affirmative action officers, and some administrators is that affirmative action is not working," reported the *Chronicle of Higher Education*. To many observers, the chief culprit was the U.S. Department of Health, Education, and Welfare (HEW), which oversaw college and university affirmative action programs. Although hundreds of the thirteen hundred higher education institutions had their own homegrown plans, the federal government required all of them to obtain approval. By December 1975, however, HEW's Office of Civil Rights (OCR) had given its imprimatur to only thirty-one plans. Few colleges and universities were able to meet their stated numerical goals, but none experienced the promised withdrawal of federal funds for failing to do so.[2]

In general, HEW had a dismal record of rooting out discrimination on campus: by the end of 1974 it had not resolved even one of the 616 equal employment discrimination complaints it received between 1971 and 1974. The most devastating indictment of government efforts came from the Carnegie Council on Policy Studies in Higher Education. Its members, led by the chairman, former University of California chancellor Clark Kerr, proclaimed that "few federal programs are now so near self-destruction. Seldom has such a good cause spawned such a badly developed series of mechanisms."[3]

The data on how far affirmative action recipients progressed were not encouraging either. Although their share of professional and graduate student populations increased noticeably (in law and medical schools, for example, women went from single digits to around 25 percent), they had only minor success in securing tenured faculty positions. "The question of who is to get hired, promoted and placed on tenure is still the critical issue in affirmative action," a *New York Times* journalist wrote. "It is greatly complicated by the sagging economy and enrollment slow-down in higher education, which have meant less faculty turnover and fewer positions available." Higher education administrators disliked the expense and challenge to their autonomy. They balked at the government's demand for increased representation of women and minorities at the individual departmental level. When embattled OCR director Peter Holmes resigned in late 1975, he admitted that there was "a widespread feeling that the process has become very burdensome and I wonder if it is yielding the intended results." Beyond the disappointing increase in faculty positions, women academics in particular reported continuing discriminatory treatment. The most obvious forms of mistreatment began to fade, but "the minutiae of sexism," as Mary P. Rowe of the Massachusetts Institute of Technology put it, remained acute. "Invisibility, harassment and sexist psychiatric problems affect women in educational institutions in many ways."[4]

Affirmative action supporters were glum. "The five-year history of affirmative action in American universities can only be characterized as a wholesale retreat. Its opponents have been substantial," said a disappointed Marilyn Gittell of Brooklyn College. Howard Glickstein, former general counsel of the U.S. Commission on Civil Rights, blamed the "reverse discrimination" protestors. USCCR Commissioner Mary Frances Berry zeroed in on the poorly trained OCR compliance officers, who "would not know what an affirmative action plan with a high probability of success looks like." As well, the editors of the American Association for Affirmative Action (AAAA) found anti–affirmative action bias in publications such as the *New York Review of Books*, the *Chronicle of Higher Education*, and the *AAUP Bulletin*. Despite the troubled status of admissions and hiring programs, supporters mobilized through organizations such as the AAAA and the Committee for Affirmative Action in Universities whose board members included Arthur Schlesinger Jr., John Rawls, Irving Howe, and Alfred Kazin.[5]

The prospects of an opposition victory, however, were very much in doubt. There was no certainty that the Supreme Court would rule against affirmative action, and there was no trend toward canceling programs. Opponents argued that these programs were, as a *National Review* writer put it, the product of "a few middle-ranking officials in the Department of Labor and HEW and their offshoots," but this ignored the considerable support for affirmative action. Bernard Davis, a Harvard Medical School faculty member, found this out when he wrote an article for the *New England Journal of Medicine* in 1976 charging that the school's affirmative action program had resulted in lowered academic standards. Protesters picketed outside Davis's office, and a crowd of four hundred people gathered in the center of campus to denounce his comments, as did the Association of American Medical Colleges and the National Medical Association in print. Although many affirmative action opponents' criticisms of HEW echoed those of supporters (Princeton economist Richard Lester slammed it for being understaffed and having a high turnover rate), they focused as well on a principled rejection of programs. Sidney Hook, a prominent philosopher and affirmative action opponent, wrote to Kerr to complain that the Carnegie Council's report, despite its negative assessment, backed affirmative action. "There is a fundamental incoherence in your Council's recommendations that reflects a desire to reconcile incompatibles," Hook lectured Kerr.[6]

Opponents seized on the faltering state of affirmative action and moved aggressively to get Congress and President Gerald Ford to eliminate programs. The anti–affirmative action ranks, however, were divided among labor liberals, colorblind liberals, and colorblind conservatives. Each approached the matter differently. Labor leaders' attention remained fixed on preserving seniority systems. This was an issue about which other opponents remained indifferent (some even backed affirmative action in blue-collar jobs). Jewish American organizations continued to champion colorblind liberalism. They looked to sympathetic Democrats in Congress to strip numerical goals and quotas from college plans but simultaneously urged the expansion of "soft" affirmative action programs. Where exactly to draw the line between the two kinds of programs eluded them: some Jewish leaders accepted the use of numerical goals on a limited basis, while others rejected them firmly. Their strength already diluted by a lack of allies, colorblind liberals and their congressional allies failed to influence a legislative body increasingly influenced by the "new" liberalism inspired by the rights revolution as well as the ascending New Right political movement. As the influence of colorblind liberalism waned in the mid-1970s, colorblind conservatives grew. They worked through the Committee on Academic Non-Discrimination and Integrity (CANI), an organization of disaffected liberals, neoconservatives, and conservatives, to nurture their relationships with sympathetic members of the Ford White House staff.

For all their efforts, by the eve of the *Bakke* decision, "reverse discrimination" protests had produced few results. This poor showing was rooted as much in the lack of support from national politicians as in their weak cohesion and differing views on what constituted equality. Even CANI failed to win over the moderate Gerald Ford, whose brand of cautious politics made him hesitant to thwart existing affirmative action programs. As the first generation of affirmative action opposition fizzled, colorblind conservatives took their place by applying potent rhetoric and disciplined focus on merit and competence. Throughout the previous decade, they had raised their electoral and ideological visibility with an appeal to cultural conservatism, support for a reinvigorated Cold War stance, and anticrime and -tax rhetoric. By the late 1970s, conservative foundations and New Right politicians drew on CANI's contributions and launched fresh challenges to affirmative action.

Opposing Affirmative Action from within the Democratic Party

The Democratic Party in the 1970s was a fragmented party. Although the steady departure of southern whites to the Republican Party lessened rancor over civil rights, white voters in the urban north lashed out at the party's new social and cultural commitments. When Democratic Party reforms in the wake of the 1968 presidential defeat of Hubert Humphrey reduced significantly the influence of white urban politicians and union leaders, some constituents switched their allegiance as well or began splitting their votes. Despite the electoral boost Democratic candidates received in the wake of the Watergate scandal, there was little coherence or internal party discipline. With the backlash against liberalism well under way, old-line Democrats in Congress watched in confusion as younger party leaders embraced moderate, and even conservative, economic policies alongside support for busing, abortion rights, and affirmative action. These newly elected Democrats included Colorado's Gary Hart, an environmentalist and manager of George McGovern's 1972 presidential campaign; in addition, there was Paul Tsongas from Massachusetts, a Peace Corps alumnus, as well as Harold Ford, Tennessee's first black congressman. Some of these politicians would help form the Democratic Leadership Council in the mid-1980s. (Civil rights activist Jesse Jackson dubbed the group "Democrats for the Leisure Class.") Long-serving Oregon representative Edith Green recalled in 1975, "For years I participated in the great national struggle against . . . both discrimination on the basis of race and discrimination on the basis of sex." Green, a member of John Kennedy's Presidential Commission on the Status of Women and a co-author of Title IX, a landmark law mandating educational equity, denounced "quotas represent[ing] the crudest form of mindless inequality." She went on: "I find it hard to understand the reasoning that now leads well-intentioned people, in simplistic zeal, to institute reverse quotas. Do they believe one injustice deserves another?"[7]

James O'Hara was the most prominent critic in Congress of higher education affirmative action. O'Hara was a stalwart liberal: he had championed organized labor's causes and civil rights legislation and was a strong supporter of Lyndon Johnson's Great Society programs. Raised in Detroit and educated at a Jesuit high school in the city, he received his undergraduate and law degrees from the University of Michigan; O'Hara served as a combat paratrooper in World War II and then practiced law before his election to represent Michigan's "thumb region" (the Lake Huron area north of Detroit) in 1959. From his post as chairman of the House Subcommittee on Postsecondary Education, O'Hara intervened on a regular basis with HEW officials on behalf of feminists fighting sex discrimination at the University of Michigan. He was equally active, however, in assisting administrators at Michigan State University, the University of Notre Dame, and other institutions concerned about the suffocating government demands for student racial, ethnic, and gender data and compliance with the approved process for affirmative action plans. Many of these administrators did not oppose affirmative action, just the specific compliance details, but O'Hara took a principled stand. When Congressman Jim Wright wrote to him in December 1974 on behalf of Texas Christian University's chancellor to grumble about paperwork requirements ("almost literally a truckload"), O'Hara's sharp response went beyond responding to the perceived bureaucratic burden: "Race and sex are simply none of the government's damned business—nor are they the business of any employer."[8]

O'Hara convened the largest and most public forum on higher education affirmative action to date when he held ten days of hearings in August and September 1974. Although affirmative action supporters appeared before the subcommittee, the congressman designed the event so that the opponents could make their case. The president of the American Federation of Teachers, Albert Shanker, urged lawmakers to reject race- and gender-sensitive programs in favor of labor's goal of full employment; Miro Todorovich, executive director of CANI, portrayed HEW guidelines and college and university programs as an attack on meritocracy and individual rights; and Stanley Dacher of New York's Jewish Community Council argued that affirmative action penalized young people who were not responsible for past discrimination. All of those who appeared in opposition, whether they were colorblind liberals or conservatives (and even Shanker as the sole voice of organized labor) offered moral and practical (few made legal) objections. At the same time, O'Hara was not afraid to criticize opponents who testified, as when Todorovich mentioned that he did not oppose numerical goals or quotas, O'Hara snapped, "You are trying to demonstrate that you aren't a bunch of sexists and racists . . . by saying, 'Well maybe it is OK for the construction trade.' If I were you I would be a little careful on that." This "fashionable method" of higher education opposition was still on his mind two months later, when, in a speech to the American Council on Education, he said that he "did not accept the argument that what is good enough for the tool crib is not good enough for the faculty club." O'Hara's colorblind liberalism was pure. "I cling to the old-fashioned belief . . . that there are no such things as group rights," he told his audience.[9]

Affirmative action opponents lauded O'Hara, treating him as their official spokesman. "Courageous and farsighted," "Most impressed," and "an eloquent, thoughtful and democratic a statement of the basic proposition . . . as I have ever read" went a few of the congratulatory letters. Harvard's Bernard Davis cheered his "forthright analysis of the problem of discrimination." In *Measure,* a magazine sponsored by the University Centers for Rational Alternatives (a group closely allied with CANI), the editors wrote that they were relieved that "there has finally been a fair public airing of arguments on all sides. . . . The sophistry that goals are not quotas has, for once, been held up to the light of public scrutiny." Shanker gave the Democratic lawmaker "a round of applause" and credited him for HEW's decision to issue revised affirmative action guidelines in December 1974, which seemed to many opponents to curb "hard" affirmative action. The labor leader hoped that "now that the government seems to have straightened itself out on the question of quotas, the Democratic Party will soon do likewise." O'Hara embraced this leadership role: in a letter to Naomi Levine of the American Jewish Congress, he acknowledged "making speeches and writing letters for some time now trying to express my concerns over . . . illegal efforts . . . to pervert the Constitutional and legal mandates that we should disregard race, color, sex, national origin, etc."[10]

In the aftermath of the well-publicized hearings, O'Hara began to field "reverse discrimination" complaints. One frustrated historian confessed that he was plunged into "bitterness, degradation, and a sense of alienation" when the head of a search committee informed him that he would not be hired, since the job must go to an affirmative action recipient. Another failed applicant wrote "in regard to what I fell [*sic*] is a case of discrimination for a young white male." He explained that he had been waiting for over three years for the phone company to hire him as a permanent employee only to find that "they *have* to hire black males and girls first." O'Hara replied with sympathy, explaining, "You have been caught in the middle of two of the most divisive issues facing our nation." The first issue was affirmative action; the second, he argued, was "the disaster that has resulted from the economic policies of the Nixon-Ford Administration." He admitted to being "a little disturbed" by a woman's story of her son's inability to get admitted to medical school, commenting: "I think the law is being violated. I would like to know more about whether or not your son has run into any quota systems and where." Affirmative action supporters began to contact O'Hara as well to persuade him of the validity of "hard" affirmative action. Mary Gray, head of "Committee IV" of the American Association of University Professors, for example, requested a meeting to present the case for numerical goals in hiring and admissions. O'Hara agreed to meet but warned that he was "kind of nervous about the kind of 'enforcement' which assumes universal guilt and demands the suspected institution demonstrate its purity by achieving a predetermined racial or sex mix in its staff or enrollment."[11]

The challenge for O'Hara and like-minded legislators was to parlay the positive reactions to the hearings into legislative results. "The fight for true nondiscrimination may have won a battle, but the combat is far from over," *Measure*'s editors wrote. Until then their efforts had been small and unsuccessful. In late 1969 Democratic and Republican lawmakers attempted a last-minute maneuver to stop the Nixon administration's affirmative action plan for skilled trades and construction workers, known as the Philadelphia Plan. They tried to give the comptroller general (at the time, Elmer Staats, who was opposed to affirmative action) effective veto power over such measures. Nixon's congressional allies, however, forced opponents to back down with the threat of a Christmas legislative session. Their next chance came with the Equal Employment Opportunity Act of 1972. The focus of most of the negotiating over the bill lay in determining whether the U.S. Equal Employment Opportunity Commission (EEOC) should be given cease-and-desist powers to enforce Title VII of the Civil Rights Act of 1964's ban on employment discrimination. Conservative Democratic senator Sam Ervin attempted to inject a provision that would ban affirmative action plans containing numerical goals. It was a ham-handed, confusing amendment that Ervin had drawn up quickly, and it went down to defeat, 44 votes to 22. Still, with about one-third of the U.S. Senate absent for the deliberations and vote, it was not a clear rebuke of "reverse discrimination" sentiment in Congress. Nevertheless, the growing number of executive orders, court decisions, and consent decrees frustrated legislators' abilities to thwart affirmative action. In the early 1970s they pursued a modest strategy of direct contact with HEW officials to object to higher education guidelines and enforcement procedures.[12]

Prospects for legislative intervention increased significantly by mid-decade. The resignation of Richard Nixon and the 1974 congressional elections scrambled the national political landscape and gave opponents cause for optimism. So too did interest in the *DeFunis* case and the growing "reverse discrimination" protests in police and fire departments, which were made more intense by mounting unemployment. The most promising anti–affirmative action initiative came in the form of an amendment to the Public Health Service Act dealing with medical school admissions that came up for a vote in the House of Representatives in 1975: "No person shall, on the basis of race, color, national origin, or sex, be excluded from or admitted to participation in, denied or provided the benefits of, or be subjected to discrimination under any program organized under this part." Its sponsors, Henry Waxman and James Scheuer, were liberal Democrats. Waxman, after serving several terms in the California Assembly, was a newly elected congressman. New York's Scheuer was the better known of the two. Having made his mark as a successful real estate developer, he entered Congress as a reformer in 1964 and championed the Great Society's "Head Start" education program for children, consumer, and reproductive rights and opposition to U.S. involvement in the Vietnam War.[13]

The Scheuer-Waxman Amendment, as it was known, was a touchstone for opponents left uncertain of how to proceed in the wake of *DeFunis*. Their biggest support came from the leaders of Jewish American organizations. Arnold Forster, general counsel of the Anti-Defamation League of B'nai B'rith, sent his "heartiest congratulations" for attempting to deal with "the scariest problem afflicting our medical school. . . . Our investigative files are overflowing with documentation on this sorry situation." Just as they had been doing since the late 1960s, however, they sought to balance their opposition with an appreciation of the need for some kind of affirmative action. Will Maslow of the American Jewish Congress liked the amendment but wrote that "we ought to state specifically that the amendment is not intended to bar any legitimate affirmative action program." Naomi Levine thought this alternative program might be "an admissions criteria [*sic*] which consider cultural, economic, or educational disadvantage rather than race in determining an individual applicant's potential."[14]

The two Democratic lawmakers' bill drew the ire of affirmative action supporters, who argued that it would cripple the struggle for equality. USCCR members wrote that the Scheuer-Waxman Amendment perpetuates "the historic exclusion of members of racial minority groups and women from the more advanced and highly paid health professions." Sumner Rosen, a board member of the Health Manpower Development Corporation, worried that it would "limit severely if not totally bar any serious efforts by medical, dental, or other professional schools to recruit minority group members." Scheuer rejected Rosen's charge that he was at the forefront of "a retreat which is taking on alarming momentum": he emphasized his support for "soft" affirmative action while insisting that "when two people compete for a position the only criteria that can fulfill that fundamental right of equal opportunity is that their objective merit alone will determine the results." Scheuer's relationship with fellow liberals grew tense. "I cannot believe the Jim Scheuer I know will . . . want to throw his weight against more Black doctors and greater medical care for Blacks who many white doctors are too busy to help," wrote an angry Joseph Rauh Jr., a well-known liberal and Washington, D.C., lawyer. Scheuer replied, "Discrimination is immoral and unconstitutional, and discrimination in the future is unacceptable as a remedy for discrimination in the past." He took offense at Rauh's attack: "I defer to no one in my commitment to equal opportunity." The toll on personal relationships was evident in Rauh's followup letter, in which he claimed that Scheuer's response revealed "your deep guilt feelings" and that, after speaking to the New York legislator's wife at a fundraising dinner, "I got the distinct impression that you are not even carrying your home on this issue."[15]

The amendment failed by an 18 to 10 vote in the full House Interstate and Foreign Commerce Committee. There were several reasons for its defeat, including the USCCR's public campaign against it. In addition, despite presenting a neutral stance in public, HEW officials lobbied moderate Republican congressmen to oppose the measure, which about half of them did. With the White House in Republican hands and Democratic legislators divided over affirmative action, colorblind liberals in Congress struggled, unsuccessfully, to push their cause into the law books. Their ranks were weakened considerably with the departure of Edith Green in 1974 and James O'Hara in 1976. There was another reason for their disappointing showing: colorblind liberals still could not agree among themselves about the acceptable limits of affirmative action. In 1973, for example, New York representative Ed Koch proposed legislation to amend Title VII to clamp down on programs with numerical goals or quotas. Samuel Rabinove of the American Jewish Committee thought that Koch's short-lived legislation merited "serious consideration," while Hyman Bookbinder, the American Jewish Committee's chief lobbyist, called it "a very bad idea" and argued that "Title VII now says everything we need to support our anti–reverse discrimination posture." These internal differences had made consensus on legislation and lobbying executive branch officials elusive, as the appearance of higher education affirmative action and continued to plague organizations throughout the 1970s.[16]

Conservative lawmakers offered surprisingly little legislation on the matter. The exception was New York's junior senator, James Buckley, the brother of writer and conservative power broker William F. Buckley Jr. The one-term senator recalled in a book of his political musings published in 1975 his shock at learning from letters by "reverse discrimination" victims how affirmative action worked: "A *quota* system? Surely there must have been a mistake. Quota systems were things out of the dark ages of the American past, when only a specified number of Jews would be allowed into medical schools or a certain percentage of Catholics hired at a given institution." These hiring and admissions plans were "wrong from the point of view of civil liberties, wrong from the point of view of academic freedom, wrong from the point of view of elementary justice." In March 1976 he introduced a bill, along with eight Republican cosponsors. (Republican Jack Kemp proposed a similar measure in the House at the same time.) The new law would prohibit "quotas, or goals or objectives designed to establish quotas, or programs designed to expand applicant pools and participation regarding the statistical composition of any entity of a Federal contractor or grantee." Buckley's bill even proscribed the employers, unions, and higher education institutions from collecting data on individual's race, color, religion, national origin, or gender. This proposal, more far-reaching than anything Democratic critics had offered, did not come up for a vote in the Senate committee to which it was assigned, the Committee on Labor and Public Welfare.[17]

Buckley's bill was a sign of the New Right's growing interest in affirmative action. It was a colorblind conservative perspective. Where most Jewish American leaders and Democratic politicians acknowledged continuing inequality, Buckley rejected the view that it was serious or that government should involve itself much in eradicating it with large programs. "Certain groups, notably black Americans, suffer from the effects of generations of paternalism and dependency," he allowed. The result was that they were "handicapped by a deficiency of certain traditions and skills and self-confidence." Buckley's solution was modest in scope: the federal government should employ a "targeted approach" with equity financing (not outright loans, he insisted) to bolster black-owned enterprises. The goal was to "help individuals acquire the experience to become competitive." For Buckley it came down to fighting dysfunctional individuals and families and communities through black entrepreneurism, not challenging structural barriers to equality.[18]

Growing Conservative Opposition in the Federal Executive Branch

The short-lived promise of a congressional solution did not distract affirmative action opponents from continuing to press HEW to change its course. In the early years of higher education affirmative action, Jewish organizations led the way, first by holding low-key meetings with government officials and then with the stepped-up demand that HEW respond to the dozens of "reverse discrimination" complaints they had forwarded from student and faculty "victims." Jewish leaders raised the opposition's visibility considerably in 1972 when they made a public request that the two main candidates for the U.S. presidency, Richard Nixon and George McGovern, announce their positions on affirmative action. By the time of the *DeFunis* decision, however, these organizations' officers and staff members had stepped back from the front lines for fear that their liberal objectives were suffering irreparable damage due to this focus on a single issue.

A changing of the guard was under way, as CANI became the new public face of anti–affirmative action. Its leaders emphasized the value of colorblind meritocracy and spoke little of "soft" affirmative action. They were primed to do battle with higher education affirmative action. Until then CANI had served mostly as a forum for disgruntled scholars, but with the rising tide of anger within the academic community, they mobilized their members to influence admissions and hiring criteria. Although they participated in litigation—CANI attempted to file an amicus brief in *DeFunis,* but the Supreme Court rejected it—and were in contact with legislators, including O'Hara, the leadership dedicated its resources to leveraging members of the executive branch. This was no easy task: for all of his machinations, Nixon never rejected affirmative action. Indeed, key administration figures were divided over how to come down in *DeFunis.* In the end, Nixon decided that no government brief would be submitted. "The affirmative action programs as we know them today were formulated and implemented during the Nixon years," observed Todorovich and CANI chairman Sidney Hook. "When the outcry against reverse discrimination and other malpractices was raised, the Nixon administration, embroiled in its struggle for sheer survival, refused to do anything to ameliorate the situation."[19]

They were especially disdainful of HEW's OCR and, unlike Jewish organizations, did not deal directly with its policymakers. Groups such as the American Jewish Committee interpreted OCR director Peter Holmes's December 1974 memorandum as an improvement in its insistence that higher education systems could not earmark certain positions for affirmative action recipients or that programs could not result in a "dilution of standards." CANI leaders, however, were not mollified by Holmes's directive. There was much with which they disagreed, but the sticking point remained the government's distinction between "quotas" and "goals." The latter, Holmes insisted, "are good faith estimates of the expected numerical result. . . . They are not rigid and inflexible quotas which must be met." But the OCR's flawed dealings with colleges and universities continued to plague it. In June 1975 they were caught unprepared to process the rush of institutions submitting their affirmative action plans, so, as a short-term solution, they approved temporary plans for schools in danger of losing federal contracts due to noncompliance.[20]

CANI's most promising ally in the executive branch was Caspar Weinberger, who served as HEW secretary from 1973 to 1975. Weinberger, who held a number of cabinet positions ending with a term as secretary of defense in the Reagan administration, made his displeasure with "hard" affirmative action clear on a regular basis. "The colleges weren't happy about this, and I wasn't either," he recalled in his memoir. "If a fair and broad search for qualified candidates . . . degenerated into fear that a college's federal funds would be endangered if it did not fill a specific number of vacancies with black or Asian or women appointees (or some other specific group), then we would achieve only quotas and reverse discrimination." Shortly after becoming secretary of HEW, he told a congressional hearing that he was against "any kind of mechanistic statistical approach to ending discrimination in employment." When Gerald Ford came to the Oval Office, Weinberger briefed the new president on the "great difficulty" in distinguishing between goals and quotas and the "unnecessary and basically ineffective and terribly burdensome requirements" of higher education affirmative action. He made common cause with a coalition of six major Jewish organizations as well, assuring them that he "share[d] your concern about abuses in affirmative action programs" and promising to push for a full investigation of their complaints. When HEW staff members were slow in responding, he acknowledged that there was "no excuse for the delay of ten months."[21]

Yet Weinberger did not—could not—simply cancel higher education programs. Although the OCR was part of HEW, the actual authority for the programs was shared among a number of departments and agencies, including the Labor Department. The key elements were a series of executive orders signed by Lyndon Johnson and Richard Nixon mandating affirmative action with goals and timetables. Weinberger was stuck in the middle, maintaining an unofficial alliance with affirmative action opponents and prodding Ford to rethink the very existence of higher education affirmative action. He avoided open dissent. In an April 1975 response to a letter from Sidney Hook, Weinberger acknowledged that he "agree[d] wholeheartedly with most of [your] points." Still, he defended the existing guidelines, insisting that "what is required is not the hiring of any group nor the employment of an unqualified person, but only a broader search and a wider pool from which to choose qualified people." He sent Ford a memorandum three months later, however, in which he referred to the guidelines as "unduly burdensome, counterproductive and incompatible with the realities of academic employment." Weinberger complained that the labor secretary, John Dunlop, did not "sufficiently appreciate the need for expeditious action on the matter" and begged Ford for his "specific review of this matter" due to "the exceptional circumstance which surround the current controversy."[22]

What CANI needed was an influential White House insider, and they found this in Robert Goldwin, a special consultant to the president. He came to the administration with impressive credentials: after earning his doctorate in political science at the University of Chicago, Goldwin held a Guggenheim Fellowship and several academic positions, including a deanship at St. John's College in Annapolis, Maryland. Before arriving in Washington, D.C., he served as an adviser to Donald Rumsfeld, who was the U.S. Ambassador to NATO and then became Ford's defense secretary. Goldwin was a student of conservative political philosopher Leo Strauss, and he brought Strauss's deep suspicion of modern liberalism and what he saw as excessive enthusiasm for equality to "seminars" he offered the president. He invited Irving Kristol, Gertrude Himmelfarb, Thomas Sowell, and other conservative scholars to participate in these events. When Ford left office, Goldwin became a resident scholar at the American Enterprise Institute, a conservative think tank, where he wrote extensively on American politics. "Few individuals had as much influence on the thinking of conservative policy makers," Rumsfeld wrote at the time of Goldwin's death in 2010. Goldwin "was the Ford administration's one-man think tank, its intellectual compass, and bridge to a new conservatism."[23]

Goldwin played an invaluable role as the conduit for the anti–affirmative action position, as when he invited Sowell, a conservative economist, to share his negative findings with those at the highest level of government. Goldwin took on the task of representing their legislative interests as well: when Todorovich informed him of the Scheuer-Waxman Amendment's fate, Goldwin requested that he "let me know of any legislation on this subject pending before Congress, especially before a vote occurs." He used his direct access to Ford to remind him, following the president's meeting with Jewish leaders, that "the source of the 'quota' problem is not to be found in legislation"; rather, Goldwin wrote, they came from Revised Order No. 4. "Quotas are quotas and discrimination is discrimination. They should have no place in our laws or regulations." Thanks to Goldwin, administration advisors and officials heard CANI's steady drumbeat of "reverse discrimination" charges. In January 1976, for example, Todorovich notified Goldwin that HEW seemed to approve of the University of South Carolina's philosophy department requiring applicants to provide their name on the supposedly anonymous equal employment opportunity data form. Ford's advisor, in turn, sent this information to a number of administration figures including White House Domestic Council member Richard "Dick" Parsons, domestic affairs assistant James Cannon, and Labor Secretary John Dunlop along with a note that "reverse discrimination in hiring in order to meet mandated 'numerical goals' is quite apparent."[24]

But affirmative action supporters checked Goldwin's and CANI's efforts with their own lobbying and litigation strategy. Feminists in organizations such as the National Organization for Women (NOW) and the Women's Equity Action League were responsible in large measure for the establishment of higher education admission and hiring programs. In the early 1970s, their members had filed hundreds of discrimination complaints, which brought federal officials to the first substantial higher education guidelines. Supporters kept up the pressure on the OCR. Describing proposed guidelines in 1972 as "water[ing] down the concept of goals so much as to make it virtually meaningless," a group of civil rights leaders, including the Urban League's Vernon Jordan, the NAACP's Roy Wilkins, and antipoverty activist Marian Wright Edelman, told the OCR's Pottinger that the "politically timed and motivated" revision would destroy compliance efforts. Wilkins wrote Weinberger again to complain that HEW's December 1974 guidelines made a "mockery of the concept of affirmative action." Women academics weighed in as well. The officers of the Association of Women in Science wrote Ford to remind him that "goals are flexible and affirmative in intent, not discriminating and restrictive." A representative from the "Sociologists for Women in Society" urged the president to "ignore the charges of 'reverse racism/discrimination.'" There was nothing wrong, she argued, with the government "*insuring* that a proportionate amount of women and minorities are guaranteed academic positions for which they are qualified." Ford's assistant to the Domestic Council, Roger Semerad, assured her of the president's commit-

ment to affirmative action. He reminded her, however, that "standards and criteria for employment may not be applied inconsistently on the basis of race or sex
or deny equality of opportunity."[25]

The affirmative action supporters' biggest impact on HEW came in November 1974 with a lawsuit meant to force the government to make colleges and universities comply with Labor Department regulations. "Up until approximately
nine months ago, HEW attempted to apply DOL regulations to higher education
employment with a great deal of flexibility," Weinberger and Dunlop reported to
presidential assistant James Cannon in late June 1975. They acknowledged that
"the prospects of plaintiffs successfully litigating the case were quite good." The
cabinet secretaries concluded that "under the circumstances, HEW made the
only reasonable decision that it could, i.e., enforce fully the DOL regulations." It
was a setback for Weinberger, who confided that he was exploring "the possibility of changing the DOL regulations, at least to the extent that they applied to
academic employment."[26]

CANI leaders, sensing perhaps that their influence was slipping, pushed
White House officials hard for a meeting with Ford. The time seemed right:
the O'Hara hearings had publicized the "reverse discrimination" cause, the poor
economy had heightened anxiety over competition for employment, and the
OCR's December 1974 revised guidelines, known as the "Holmes Memorandum," had failed to satisfy critics. "Help us maintain the freedom, quality, and
decency of the academy. It is late in the day. Our plea is urgent and sincere," four
members wrote Ford in early December. When, a few days later, philosophy professor Paul Kurtz's request for a meeting was refused—Ford had a "scheduling
conflict"—Todorovich turned to Robert Goldwin. CANI members, he explained
to Goldwin, "feel that we have done more than our share of gradual, step-by-step
visitation of intermediate officials and have learned that the question of a com-
plexity transcending a particular official or department." Goldwin went to work
on CANI's behalf. He wrote Roger Semerad to ask him to arrange a meeting
between Ford and CANI members (who, he promised, were "first rate"). "Their
position is that the Holmes memorandum was an excellent forward step but
some problems still exist," Goldwin explained.[27]

CANI leaders had their long-sought meeting in late February 1975, but they
met with an assortment of presidential aides and cabinet officials, not President Ford or the HEW and labor secretaries. Still, it was an important occasion
in the history of the fight against affirmative action. For the first time, a group
of dedicated anti–affirmative action advocates gathered in the White House to
lobby federal officials. According to the notes they prepared for the meeting, they

reviewed for the Ford administration representatives the "heavy-handed, costly and wasteful intervention by the federal bureaucracy into the hiring procedures of universities." Holmes's recent memorandum, in which he retained the use of numerical goals and timetables, was "essentially a defense of the *status quo*." The government, they contended, was "able to justify the nondiscriminatory nature of goals and timetables only by a rationale which destroys any reason for their existence." In practice, the difference between goals and quotas for them was minimal. "If hiring by race and sex is wrong, then good faith efforts to do it are also wrong," CANI members concluded. They went into the meeting arguing that their organization represented the major anti–affirmative action critics. These opponents, "many of whom have long and distinguished records as fighters for equality and proponents of civil rights," included James O'Hara and Edith Green. "We feel we are at a watershed," CANI leaders proclaimed in their statement.[28]

Much to their dismay, however, the meeting did not result in changes to higher education affirmative action policies. The post-meeting analysis among the government's participants reveals how little CANI's arguments moved them. Roger Semerad offered the strongest endorsement of the aggrieved academics, but he merely called for more study. "In my opinion a number of ideas, points of view, and misconceptions surfaced at this meeting which can only be dealt with by further clarification and communications," he offered weakly. Semerad did push the CANI agenda along somewhat by noting that "if the [CANI] suggestions have merit we should also examine what actions might be taken to accomplish the objectives inherent in these recommendations." Other respondents were less enthusiastic. Virginia Trotter, an assistant secretary at HEW, agreed that "goals and timetables leave much to be desired" but pointed out a problem with the proposal made at the meeting that higher education institutions might be allowed to create their own "hearing boards" to deal with equal employment opportunity policies and complaints. This would not work, she noted, since the same discriminatory practices under review "might also be prevalent in the attitudes of those represented on the appellate board." Trotter also took a swipe at the notion that a wider pool of affirmative action applicants, not a program of hiring goals and timetables, was a better policy. "This assumption has long been with us, and I think we need more substantial data," she cautioned.[29]

The OCR's Peter Holmes offered the most detailed comments. He rejected outright CANI's contention that colleges and universities should not collect applicants' personal identity data (this was "central to any civil rights enforcement program") and its demand to eliminate hiring goals ("goals, of course, are not quotas"). Still, it was a thoughtful, if not supportive, take on CANI's positions. He acknowledged that some academic departments often sought out minority men or women of all races merely to satisfy government compliance. The way to correct this, Holmes wrote, was to make search committee members document their hiring process more carefully and "explain why his or her department did not achieve its affirmative action goals." He suggested that goals created on a department-by-department basis might not be the best method of meeting affirmative action objectives. Instead, "we should ask colleges and universities to do a more general type of 'utilization analysis' and establish a single campus-wide goals and timetable." This would be an important reform but would not satisfy CANI members. As to ending race- and gender-sensitive programs, Holmes noted that he "share[d] the concern of many of our critics," but the government's guidelines should be reformed, not eliminated. "An effort to eliminate them (or tamper with them in any way) would be viewed as a massive civil rights retreat," he concluded.[30]

Despite being rebuffed, CANI leaders persevered in their lobbying of the Ford administration. Goldwin continued to serve as their key White House contact. Todorovich warned him in March 1975 that the EEOC's "next great push" would be "the establishment of stringent, rigid and even impossible criteria for 'validating' job standards." This would be "disastrous" for higher education and might result in the "abandonment of the Ph.D. or publication of scholarly work." They sounded the general alarm about the ill effects of higher education preferences. Sidney Hook, along with Yale law professor Eugene Rostow and three other CANI members, informed *New York Times* readers, "We have daily evidence that numerical goals cause less qualified persons to be chosen. . . . Progress in eliminating unfair discrimination would be well served by outlawing all numerical goals." Goldwin sent their letter to Roger Semerad with a note: "It states the criticism of affirmative action enforcement most briefly and focuses on the issue of numerical goals or quotas. I think that should be the target. How does our follow-up stand on this subject?" Weinberger kept on the issue as well, suggesting to Ford that "the most helpful and best way to remove discrimination is to require a broader and comprehensive recruiting process but *not* to require either goals that must be met or quotas."[31]

Other administration members offered encouragement but little else. "Please do not assume that because no progress is evident to you," Semerad assured Todorovich, "that we have not . . . moved forward in the Administration's review of our affirmative action." L. William Seidman, an assistant to Ford on economic policy, added this postscript to a letter to Paul Kurtz acknowledging some news clippings on affirmative action: "Keep pushing—you are on the right and fair course." Ford himself appeared to ponder the issue without resolving it. In March he responded to a lengthy memo from James Cannon about the "considerable difficulty" of higher education regulations and to Weinberger's efforts to work with John Dunlop on an "appropriate and mutually acceptable course of action" with the scrawled reply that "I have read this and obviously some decisions have to be made." The next month Semerad reported to Goldwin that Ford was "aware of the situation and is anxious that it be resolved." Ford would only take action, however, "if the Secretaries cannot reach an agreement." As for CANI, Semerad promised Todorovich that he would "let you know as soon as I have something new to report."[32]

In the end the news was not good: the OCR's April 1976 guidelines were a clear endorsement of "hard" affirmative action. Policymakers included boilerplate language on the illegality of quotas, but the guidelines went further than previous ones in mandating numerical goals and in encouraging higher education institutions to move beyond considering standard evidence of merit. "It is particularly appropriate to broaden the criteria where the educational development of an applicant has been hindered or restricted by severe economic deprivation or racial discrimination," they held. "In such cases, admission may be warranted on the basis of relative promise even where all applicants who are admitted may not have the highest academic indices." This was exactly the approach at issue in the *DeFunis* case. By 1976 even higher education administrators who remained critical of HEW enforcement mechanisms were falling in line behind OCR guidelines. The records of the "Federal Advisory Committee for Higher Education," a group whose members included administrators from major universities, HEW and Labor Department officials, and NOW and Urban League (but not CANI) representatives, reported that they were "not opposed to goals . . . but rather [were] focusing on inconsistencies in their application and misperceptions by compliance officers and universities."[33]

Gerald Ford's position on affirmative action policy is central to this history. Some historians argue that Nixon's successor avoided decisive action as a self-serving route to winning the 1976 presidential election. His was, writes Mary Frances Berry, "a holding action presidency. . . . The president did not see his role as initiating government action or even reacting to anything, unless absolutely necessary." In his history of affirmative action, Terry Anderson moves quickly over the Ford years when "affirmative action took a back seat, while enforcement stumbled along." Ford certainly perfected the art of stalling affirmative action opponents. When he finally met with CANI members at a followup meeting in

September 1975, his Domestic Affairs assistant James Cannon advised him not to state his position. Rather, Cannon told the president to speak in general terms about the need to oppose discrimination and ask the group, "How best can we achieve this objective?" At the meeting's conclusion, Ford was to request that the cabinet members present explore the issue further and present their positions at the next regular cabinet meeting.[34]

Although Ford appeared evasive or indifferent, he moved quietly to settle conflict such as the "reverse seniority" debate. It was a difficult task in an administration whose members harbored divergent views on equal employment policy. "The issue is pretty hot. There is no consensus because opinion is well defined around the table," one White House staff member wrote. When the EEOC proposed guidelines to modify the "last hired, first fired" practice, only the USCCR backed them. The other relevant bodies joined together on the "Coordinating Council on Equal Employment"—the U.S. Civil Service Commission, the Labor Department, and the Justice Department (not to mention labor unions and the Chamber of Commerce)—opposed the EEOC. Richard Parsons told the EEOC's acting chair Ethel Bent Walsh that "delaying the vote on the proposed guideline pending a meeting with the Coordinating Council was a good idea." Walsh agreed, although Parsons noted in a letter to Cannon that "I don't believe the EEOC is in much of a mood to compromise." The commission abandoned its efforts as appellate court decisions signaled the futility of challenging bona fide seniority systems. Political calculations played an important role in the way Ford's advisors dealt with the EEOC. In January 1976, for example, the president's associate counsel, Bobbie Greene Kilberg, wrote White House counsel Philip Buchen to discourage the president from naming an undistinguished business leader with no equal opportunity experience then under consideration as EEOC chairman. She did so on the grounds that the appointment would "yield the President no political points." Greene went on to characterize the EEOC as "unreasonable on the seniority issue and on a number of other workplace concerns." She pushed instead for "a moderate to conservative trade unionist (female if possible) [who] could make a real difference in the EEOC's perception of the seniority issue."[35]

Hidden among these political maneuvers was Ford's support for affirmative action. He avoided difficult decisions, and he was careful to criticize any policy language that smacked of quotas, but he believed in race- and gender-sensitive programs. Although the public record is admittedly thin on the matter, the moderate Republican spoke in 1975 of how "a much wider range of employment opportunities can be opened." The next year Ford offered a mixed endorsement: "The President believes the concept of affirmative action is a moral and political imperative at the Federal level. However, the President is convinced that the use of inflexible, mechanical means of achieving equality of opportunity—such as quotas—is inappropriate," according to a memo produced by the Ford administration. Yet, neither Ford nor the members of his administration canceled affirmative action programs. In fact, when, in the midst of the economic recession, Chrysler Corporation requested "leeway to grant a suspension of the [affirmative action] regulations for a period of several months or so" due to "an altogether unnatural situation for compliance reviews," the White House rejected their plea on the grounds that the company had not made "a sufficient case for granting an exemption from the legal requirements."[36]

Just as Jewish organizations failed to win government officials over to colorblind liberalism in the early 1970s, CANI could not bring the Ford administration to embrace colorblind conservatism either. As the Republican Party tacked rightward in the coming years, Ford's pro–affirmative action sympathies emerged more clearly. In the late 1990s he penned a guest editorial in the *New York Times* in support of the undergraduate and law school race-conscious admissions programs at the University of Michigan then facing a legal challenge. The Supreme Court heard the cases in 2003. Working with James Cannon, the former president brought together two dozen prominent retired military officers to sign an amicus brief in support of the Michigan programs. It was, writes journalist and legal analyst Jeffrey Toobin, a "quiet and powerful legacy for the university and the country." In retrospect, CANI members faced long odds in bringing policymakers and a majority of politicians to accept their vision of an idealized meritocracy.[37]

"Reverse Discrimination" Litigation and Presidential Politics in the Mid-1970s

By the time Ford left office in January 1977 after his defeat to Jimmy Carter, affirmative action opponents had shifted their attention back to the courtroom as a result of the *Bakke* case. Many of the issues Marco DeFunis and his supporters had raised a few years earlier reappeared in Allan Bakke's lawsuit against the University of California at Davis School of Medicine (UCD). There was one aspect to UCD's admissions criteria absent from the one DeFunis experienced at the University of Washington Law School: its admissions committee set aside 16 percent, or eight of its fifty first-year places, for affirmative action recipients. Bakke's lawyer built their case around challenging this quota system. It began when Bakke applied to UCD in 1973 and 1974. The committee rejected him both times while it accepted "special applicants" with lower test scores and marks. The California trial court judge found that the university had employed an illegal quota system, but he did not order Bakke's admission since it was not clear that he would have been offered a place were it not for the affirmative action program. On appeal, the California Supreme Court held that the medical school's program had violated the Equal Protection Clause and ordered Bakke's admission to UCD. By the time of oral arguments before the U.S. Supreme Court in October 1977, dozens of organizations and individuals had filed amicus briefs in support of both sides. Labor liberals, colorblind liberals, and colorblind conservatives rallied to Bakke's cause. These included the American Federation of Teachers, CANI, various Jewish American and white ethnic organizations, and Congressman Henry Waxman. Marco DeFunis wrote the brief for the "Young Americans for Freedom."[38]

Just as with *DeFunis,* the *Bakke* case revealed significant divisions within many of these organizations. The members of the board of trustees at Columbia University were split over approving their institution's brief in support of UCD; it only passed when the university's general counsel shepherded a compromise version to a vote. Although the American Association of University Professors had backed affirmative action since the early 1970s, dissenters threatened to derail efforts to lodge their amicus brief. Jewish organization leaders continued to search for consensus with little progress. Two groups, the National Council of Jewish Women and the Social Action Commission of the Union of American Hebrew Congregations, had backed the university in *DeFunis,* a move for which both organizations' leaders received harsh rebukes, some of which were accompanied by resignations. They chose not to weigh in formally on *Bakke.* A spokesman for the Social Action Commission explained their decision as a result of the "irreconcilable differences among our constituency over the case, and in view of the degree in which attitudes have frozen since the *DeFunis* case." Prominent Jewish American affirmative action supporters were livid. Joseph Rauh Jr. charged them with creating a "topsy-turvy world" in which liberal Jews had abandoned the cause of equality.[39]

As for labor liberals, the growing influence of feminists and civil rights activists in the labor movement had shifted an increasing number of unions in the last half of the 1970s to support "hard" affirmative action. *Bakke* served as a kind of transitional case in this process for the American Federation of Labor–Congress of Industrial Organizations (AFL-CIO): the labor federation rejected considerations of race or gender as criteria for hiring or promotion. It was a position conservative skilled trades and construction unions shared, along with police and fire unions and industrial and service sector unions usually identified with civil rights and liberal causes. As they had in *DeFunis,* the AFL-CIO executive council filed an amicus brief in support of the rejected white, male applicant. Federation officers, however, were themselves moving into the pro–affirmative action column. When the court ruled in 1978 that UCD's earmarking of medical school admissions was illegal but that race sensitive programs were, generally, acceptable, they endorsed the conclusion. "We favor aggressive, positive efforts to integrate, instead of mere passive agreement not to discriminate," the labor leaders wrote. Although the AFL-CIO still rejected "quotas or unfair preferential treatment," they backed "recruiting, hiring, counseling, training, upgrading and promoting minorities and women." Evidence of their changed position emerged the following year in *United Steelworkers v. Weber.* In that case, the federation supported the union defendant and not Brian Weber, an aluminum plant worker in Louisiana who sued his union over its plan to select apprentices using racial proportionality.[40]

Winn Newman, chief counsel for the International Union of Electrical Workers (and then the American Federation of State, County, and Municipal Employees), and assistant counsel Carol Wilson told the U.S. Civil Rights Commission in 1981 that unions could play a central role in battling inequality if only government would let them. Union-style affirmative action, they explained, "relies on basic trade union principles such as plant-wide seniority and job posting and bidding to achieve maximum equal employment opportunity." Although the union joined other unions and labor groups in providing amicus support for affirmative action lawsuits, Newman maintained that the IUE program did not "rely on such controversial terms as 'goal,' 'quotas,' and 'preferential treatment,' which are anathema to the industrial relations world."[41]

Labor liberals, however, were more concerned with salvaging seniority systems and securing labor law reform and full employment than in promoting affirmative action. Even its strongest union supporters saw it as a limited tool in bringing about economic security and workplace justice. As they looked out over a workforce battered by recession and eight years of Republican control of the White House, labor leaders sought assistance from Jimmy Carter. They were soon disappointed with the new president and with Congress. Unionists lost every key legislative battle, including the crucial one for labor law reform. The bill before legislators called for expedited recognition elections and stronger penalties for employers violating labor law. The House of Representatives approved the measure, but it stalled in a Senate filibuster in 1979. Carter, never really a labor favorite, hardly lifted a finger on their behalf. (When he might have contacted wavering senators on the evening before a crucial vote, the president went bowling in the White House instead.) His passions were deregulation, government reorganization, and improving international human rights. When Douglas Fraser, United Automobile Workers president and well-known labor liberal, resigned in disgust from the president's "Labor-Management Group" in 1978, he denounced what he characterized as employers' vicious multimillion-dollar campaign against labor law reform. Douglas charged that they were engaged in "a one-sided class war." "The Republican Party remains controlled by and the Democratic Party heavily influenced by business interests," he wrote.[42]

Carter's decision to submit an amicus brief in support of UCD's program was deeply dispiriting to colorblind liberals. The Georgia Democrat voiced his approval for affirmative action as early as 1974 in a speech to the Equal Employment Opportunity Council that sounded strikingly similar to Lyndon Johnson's foundational address on the subject to Howard University graduates a decade earlier. "Complete equity or equality is not enough because there must be . . . a commitment to compensatory opportunities," Carter proclaimed. "We could not tell our black citizens and our female citizens. . . . 'Okay, you have been feeling the adverse effect of legal and illegal discrimination for generations; now we'll treat you exactly as we do our white men.'" He caused a furor during the primaries when he announced to the press that these groups "should have not only equal employment, but should also have compensatory opportunity." One consultant warned Carter adviser Stuart Eizenstat that the candidate should avoid "red flag or code words" such as "quotas" that "serve to exacerbate the festering wounds." For the rest of the presidential campaign, Carter avoided the topic of affirmative action.[43]

Higher education critics offered prompt and predictable denunciations of the candidate's "compensatory" comment. A public policy professor at the University of Michigan thought Carter "seriously naïve," adding, "you have recently lost the vote I might have given you in tomorrow's primary." Carter's comment, wrote another, "was a real boner—one of those decisions that may win the nomination but lose the election." One Stanford University faculty member vowed, "I shall not only not vote for you but campaign against you." The problem with the candidate's position, explained yet another, was his notion of "collective guilt": "a most dangerous idea to play around with; and of undoing the wrongs of the past there is no end." Some letter writers attacked the decision to focus on hiring instead of increasing the pool of qualified affirmative action recipients. The setting of numerical goals was a "ridiculous situation" since the number of eligible minority men and women of all races for many positions was "utterly inadequate." "Quotas" and "compensatory education," explained an English professor from the University of Pennsylvania, would "destroy the academic integrity of our institutions, and expose our students to bogus learning." And, of course, there were letters that contrasted race- and gender-conscious policies against the heroic struggles for equality. "Reverse discrimination constitutes not only a perversion of the civil rights legislation of the 1960s," explained one man, "but also an inequitable application of those franchises guaranteed every citizen under the Constitution."[44]

President Carter disappointed civil rights advocates and feminists as well. He lobbied for passage of the Equal Rights Amendment but favored some restrictions on abortion. In 1979 Carter dismissed former Democratic congresswoman Bella Abzug from the National Committee for Women, which, in turn, prompted the resignation of twenty-six of the forty committee members. Carter and Abzug had locked horns over the importance of gender issues in his administration. He supported an amendment to the Public Works Employment Act that required at least 10 percent of federal contract dollars to go to qualified minority businesses, what were called "set-asides." Carter was motivated, claims Mary Frances Berry, "not necessarily as a matter of racial justice but as a political calculation." As an example of his detachment from civil rights issues, Berry notes that the USCCR worked hard to secure a meeting with the president that he ended after only fifteen minutes. Carter rounded out his presidential tenure by offering a feeble urban policy, widely criticized as inadequate, to deal with the woes of the nation's cities.[45]

Nevertheless, the beleaguered Democrat maintained his support for affirmative action. His approach to the *Bakke* case, however, was, in historian Terry Anderson's words, "cautious and somewhat confusing." As interest in the case mounted following the Supreme Court's granting of certiorari in February 1977, Carter struggled publicly to find a coherent position. "I hate to endorse the proposition of quotas for minority groups, for women or for anyone else," he confessed to a journalist. Two members of his administration charged with producing the amicus brief, Solicitor General Wade McCree Jr. and Assistant Attorney General Drew Days, came in for harsh criticism when a leaked draft of theirs offered only lukewarm endorsement of higher education affirmative action and sharp criticism of UCD's plan. EEOC chairwoman Eleanor Holmes Norton warned that "by filling such a brief, we ourselves will be acting . . . to set back the national effort to achieve equality. It would be better that the government did not file at all." The Congressional Black Caucus as well as the NAACP, the Urban League, the National Council of Negro Women, and other organizations telephoned and sent telegrams to the White House. In the end Carter took the advice of two of his closest aides, Stuart Eizenstat and Bob Lipshutz, to replace the "too dispassionate" draft with a strong endorsement of affirmative action. They would avoid the vexing "quota" issue by arguing that the court remand the case to a lower court to determine whether in fact a quota existed. To highlight the administration's commitment, Attorney General Griffin Bell and not, as was the practice, the Solicitor General signed the seventy-four-page brief. The government delivered it in October 1977, less than two weeks before the justices heard oral arguments.[46]

Jimmy Carter may have been wary of UCD's brand of affirmative action, but he never seemed to consider opponents' arguments seriously. Where the Ford administration was sprinkled with colorblind conservatives, CANI leaders had no contacts in the Carter administration. Colorblind liberals within the Democratic Party voiced their displeasure with the White House's stance on *Bakke* from outside the White House but gained no political traction. The associate executive director of the American Jewish Congress "regret[ted]" the president's support for "hard" affirmative action. Shanker warned that "once you institute preferential treatment along racial lines, you are again opening the door to discrimination along the same lines." Shanker wrote to Vice President Walter Mondale both to remind him of the union's support for "soft" affirmative action and to argue that UCD's plan would "inevitably deny individual rights." Mondale, perhaps trying to lessen the tension, noted that "the government's brief took the position that the issue of the constitutionality of quotas is not properly before the court given the inadequate trial record." He observed that the government "recognized that programs using rigid racial quotas are exclusionary and therefore unconstitutional." Still, he insisted that affirmative action was "a way to overcome the effects of prior discrimination."[47]

It was a half-hearted attempt to win over colorblind liberals. For their part, Carter and Mondale pulled their punches on whether the UCD plan mandated quotas and highlighted the shared commitment to address racial and gender inequality. As had been the case since affirmative action's inception, there were colorblind liberals who did support limited use of numerical goals in search of corrective justice. Most refused to cross this line, however fuzzy it seemed at times, as even "soft" affirmative action tested the meritocratic system they championed. This powerful but scattered opposition could not strike the right political chord in a decade in which postwar liberalism was slowly hemorrhaging. Their legislative and executive branch lobbying in the years leading up to *Bakke* had failed to dislodge affirmative action programs, which proved durable even in the face of criticism and considerable unpopularity.

Bakke and the Emergence of Colorblind Conservatism

The *Bakke* case belongs to the second, more familiar, chapter in the history of affirmative action, one defined almost exclusively by colorblind conservatives. The decision handed down in June 1978 was not a complete victory for either side. In Justice Lewis Powell's controlling decision for a divided court, he concluded that UCD's special admissions program had denied Allan Bakke's constitutional rights as contained in the Fourteenth Amendment's Equal Protection Clause. Powell affirmed, however, the rights of colleges and universities to undertake good-faith efforts to diversify their campuses. Although dissatisfied with the mixed outcome, an ascending New Right saw the value in supporting lawsuits such as Bakke's for the stark choices these legal actions offered public officials. They believed that there was a good chance that the increasingly conservative court might tip the vote against affirmative action. In the decade following *Bakke,* conservative foundations provided substantial backing to "reverse discrimination" litigants. The old strategy of labor union and Jewish civic group leaders seeking to reform affirmative action through better public policies and legislation gave way to court-centered and state-wide referendum campaigns of organizations such as the Center for Equal Opportunity, the Center for Individual Rights, and the Independent Women's Forum. Even CANI's efforts seemed unproductive and unrealistic to this new generation of anti–affirmative action activists. "I think they saw these various problems as passing, as anomalous, as something that could be reasoned out of by good arguments than as things that are more structural and sociological," explained Stephen Balch, longtime head of the National Association of Scholars, an academic association dedicated to opposing multiculturalism and affirmative action.[48]

The Pacific Legal Foundation was the first conservative public interest law firm to become engaged in affirmative action litigation. Roy Green, a businessman who headed the California Chamber of Commerce's "Welfare Program Department," and Ronald Zumbrum, a member of California governor Ronald Reagan's welfare reform task force, founded the PLF in 1973. The purpose of the organization, the authors of the PLF's annual report wrote, was "to be a 'friend in court' for the taxpaying citizen, the businessman, the farmer." According to the admiring writer of a 1976 *Barron's* article, the well-funded foundation was "staffed by a clutch of brilliant lawyers" and had "a skein of smashing legal victories" to its credit, against what the magazine described as "the rampage of environmentalists" and "clever poverty lawyers." Some of these early courtroom victories included opposing the U.S. Forest Service's brush land control service in California, forcing the U.S. Environmental Protection Agency to use DDT (a controversial synthetic pesticide) to control moth infestation in the Pacific Northwest, bringing about tighter controls on welfare eligibility in Illinois, and challenging a court ruling on the constitutionality of excluding pregnancy from disability coverage. The PLF's special passion was in fighting land use regulations. It did so in order to preserve "freedom of choice, the concept of private property and freedom of movement."[49]

The foundation soon turned its attention to countering affirmative action on the grounds that it was an "unnecessary and destructive intrusion of federal control into American higher education." By the time of *Bakke,* the PLF had won over 80 percent of the more than 150 legal proceedings in which it was involved, and its fifteen fulltime lawyers, based in Sacramento, worked with offices in San Diego, Seattle, and Washington, D.C. "Government regulations fixing various types of 'quotas' on business, agriculture, industry and education are beginning to create undreamed of problems for those entities and a majority of Americans," the authors of a PLF report warned in 1977. The language they used in denouncing affirmative action was remarkably similar to that employed by colorblind liberals, but it was larded with an antigovernment rhetoric that was absent from earlier opposition efforts.[50]

The message of affirmative action opponents became more consistent and less complicated in the late 1970s. Conservatives at the helm of opposition efforts rejected the liberal and unionist willingness to weigh competing interests and principles; in their place they presented a moral clarity that burnished their public credentials. "It is degrading, not uplifting, to acquire a position in life by virtue of skin color," declared conservative scholar Abigail Thernstrom in 1977. Thernstrom turned the burden of responsibility for racism on affirmative action supporters who argued that Justice Powell's diversity rationale benefited white students as well as black students. "It is an odd point. 'Blacks will educate whites in the reality of social diversity.' But have not blacks served white needs long enough?" While failing to eliminate race- and gender-conscious programs, concludes political scientist Ira Katznelson, "they . . . succeeded in occupying the high ground of color-blind equality." Even opponents' harshest critics acknowledged the powerful effect of this approach. The battle over higher education affirmative action in the 1970s, writes Nancy MacLean, "tutored the right in what had eluded its standard-bearers throughout the glory years of the civil rights movement: a morally and politically legitimate language for continued racial and gender exclusion." Where opponents early in the decade sought reconciliation with affirmative action supporters, there was intractability to the division in the decades following *Bakke*. Colorblind conservatives pressed their case in the courtroom, the political arena, and the media. "Reverse discrimination" became central to the rising fortunes of the New Right and to the familiar struggle that continues to rage today.[51]

Conclusion

In March 2008 Barack Obama delivered what commentators at the time identified as a signature speech on the nation's race relations. It was a critical point
in his campaign for the Democratic Party's nomination for the U.S. presidency.
The address, at Philadelphia's National Constitutional Center, came amid controversy over the then-Senator's relationship with his former pastor, Reverend
Jeremiah Wright. Obama's task was to answer widespread charges that he shared
what many viewed as Wright's racially divisive and unpatriotic positions. The
candidate, however, provided much more than a rebuttal to those who would tie
him to the minister. He insisted as well on recognizing, as Obama put it, "the
complexities of race in this country that we've never really worked through, a
part of our union that we have yet to perfect."[1]

There was just one reference to affirmative action—that some thought his can-
didacy "an exercise in affirmative action"—but Obama spoke to the core issues
surrounding race- and gender-sensitive hiring and admissions programs. While
giving his implicit approval to these programs, he warned that "white resentments" were "grounded in legitimate concerns." In a televised debate a month
later, the candidate addressed affirmative action directly. Obama endorsed it "as
a means of overcoming both historic and potentially current discrimination."
He denounced, however, "the quota system" and wondered if his daughters, who
had "a pretty good deal," should not be eligible for such programs.[2]

Obama's comments, which came more than four decades after affirmative action began, reflected the complex, often contradictory, position many Americans
took on these hiring, promotion, and admissions programs. As I have emphasized in this book, for the first ten years of its history, unionists and liberals led
the opposition. Some labor leaders closed ranks in defense of a skilled trades
and construction union system that protected white male privilege. They resisted
equal employment opportunity and even resorted to violence on occasion. Other

union opponents had a different response: they accepted affirmative action, often grudgingly, and tried to accommodate its programs to existing industrial relations practices. These "labor liberals" never attached priority to affirmative action in bringing about workplace equality, focusing instead on full employment and labor law reform. In the mid-1970s they clashed with civil rights activists, feminists, and policymakers over efforts to undo the time-honored seniority principle of "last hired, first fired" during the severe recession. The conflict over seniority put labor liberals in alliance with unionists who had resisted affirmative action in general. These tense, occasionally violent confrontations in workplaces as well as the mounting litigation tested the alliance of labor liberals with civil rights advocates and feminists.

At the same time that unionists were staving off this fundamental change to the seniority system, liberal opponents to affirmative action were promoting colorblind meritocracy in colleges and universities. Jewish American organizations took the lead in lobbying government officials to abandon policies they argued not only violated individual rights but might also revive quotas like the ones that kept racial and religious minorities out of the nation's most prestigious institutions through the mid-twentieth century. "Colorblind liberals" attempted to check this opposition with support for strong antidiscrimination enforcement. They backed "soft" affirmative action in the areas of recruitment, remedial education, and increased financial assistance for recipients. Some opponents even agreed that numerical goals were acceptable on a short-term basis.

For this first generation of opponents, it was a messy balancing act of honoring frequently contradictory commitments. In the end, they fell short. Most Jewish organizations committed their divided memberships to back Marco DeFunis's lawsuit against the University of Washington Law School challenging its preferential program. The case made its way to the U.S. Supreme Court, where, in its first "reverse discrimination" case, the justices ruled in 1974 that, since DeFunis was nearly finished with his studies, the case was moot. The efforts of colorblind liberals did not bear fruit in the legislative or executive branches either: U.S. presidents Richard Nixon, Gerald Ford, and Jimmy Carter offered at least adequate support for affirmative action policies, and colorblind liberals were not able to pass their legislation in a divided Congress. What seemed at the time like vulnerable policies, however, proved durable in the face of an opposition that lacked consensus on key issues and could not gain political traction.

By the late 1970s, the better-known second generation was engaging in the "adversarial legalism" that has come to define affirmative action opposition. As conservative foundations came forward in support of an increasing number of "reverse discrimination" litigants, the halting colorblind liberal approach gave way to sharply defined arguments framed for courtroom proceedings. This position was distinctive in its positing of colorblindness and meritocracy as inviolable, its rejection of policies that addressed the historical nature of discrimination, and its greatly reduced role for government in assuring workplace equality. These views enjoyed particular support within the federal government in the 1980s during Ronald Reagan's presidency. Led by Attorney General Edwin Meese and William Bradford Reynolds, head of the Justice Department's Civil Rights Division, affirmative action foes tried to get Reagan to issue an executive order ending programs in the government and with federal contractors. Not surprisingly, liberal activists denounced the effort. So too did business leaders, especially those from large corporations that had already folded the goal of a diverse workforce into their corporate cultures. Key Republicans, some of whom served in the administration and backed preferential policies for political and principled reasons, did not approve either. The combined force of this opposition thwarted the effort to dismantle affirmative action programs.[3]

Conservatives attempted to undercut affirmative action in other ways. They secured the appointment of conservatives to head federal policy and enforcement bodies. Two of the most important figures in the Reagan administration were Clarence Thomas, U.S. Equal Employment Opportunity Commission chairman, and Clarence Pendleton Jr., U.S. Commission on Civil Rights chairman. From their positions of power, these two black conservatives oversaw reductions in staff and a mounting discrimination complaint backlog. When it came to litigation, they threw the weight of their respective commissions behind "reverse discrimination" lawsuits. This strategy fit in well with the concurrent growth in the number of conservative federal judges on the bench. Among the more than 370 judges Reagan appointed over the course of his two presidential terms, affirmative action foe Antonin Scalia came to serve on the Supreme Court, and Nixon-appointee conservative William Rehnquist moved from serving as associate justice to chief justice in 1986.[4]

The considerable number of "reverse discrimination" cases in the thirty years since *Bakke* have come to dominate conservative opposition. Those filing numerous state and federal court cases have attacked nearly every aspect of affirmative action programs. The Supreme Court heard nearly two dozen such cases. Some dealt with blue-collar work (*Steelworkers v. Weber*, 1979; *Sheet Metal Workers v. EEOC*, 1986) and union seniority provisions (*Firefighters Local #1784 v. Stotts*, 1984; *Wygant v. Jackson Board of Education*, 1986; *Firefighters v. Cleveland*, 1986; *U.S. v. Paradise*, 1987). Other cases before the court challenged the Public

Works Employment Act of 1977, which mandated that a certain percentage of federal contract dollars be earmarked for minority-owned businesses (*Fullilove v. Klutznick*, 1980; *City of Richmond v. J. A. Croson Co.*, 1989). In these cases the plaintiffs' lawyers argued that the equal protection component of the Fifth Amendment's Due Process Clause as well as Title VII of the Civil Rights Act of 1964 prohibited "set-aside" schemes. Although most "reverse discrimination" cases dealt with race-sensitive programs, the justices addressed gender-sensitive programs in their 1987 decision involving a California municipal government's promotions scheme (*Johnson v. Transportation, Santa Clara County*).[5]

With the exception of union seniority challenges, the court for the most part ruled in favor of affirmative action plans. That began to change in the late 1980s. According to political scientist Thomas Keck, a "new style of conservative activism" emerged, one that saw conservative justices abandoning the notion of judicial restraint for a pronounced tendency to second-guess social programs, even if it meant unelected judges would be imposing their decisions on elected officials. In *Wards Cove Packing Co. v. Atonio* (1989), the justices ruled by a 5–4 margin that employees had the burden of proving the discriminatory effects of employment practices. This was a significant break with the court's 1971 ruling in *Griggs v. Duke Power Co.* in which the justices held that statistical racial disparity in the workforce was proof of discrimination. Affirmative action supporters faced two other defeats: white workers who were affected by a consent decree could challenge its legality even if they had not taken part in the original litigation (*Martin v. Wilks*, 1989), and minorities who claimed they worked under a discriminatory seniority system had only three hundred days from the plan's effective date to file a lawsuit (*Lorance v. AT&T*, 1989).[6]

As the ideological composition of the Rehnquist Court continued to shift rightward, affirmative action came under renewed scrutiny. In 1990 they ruled in *Metro Broadcasting, Inc. v. Federal Communications* that the government's promotion of preference plans to increase minority ownership of the airwaves was legal. Five years later, and with Clarence Thomas recently seated on the bench, the court turned against affirmative action in *Adarand Construction, Inc. v. Pena*, holding that racial classification could survive strict scrutiny only if the government could provide evidence of a compelling state interest and if the policy in place was sufficiently narrow to compensate for specific instances of discrimination.[7]

Although they succeeded in circumscribing some programs, opponents did not defeat affirmative action in the courts either. Their best opportunity after *Bakke* came with a pair of cases decided in 2003 involving undergraduate and law school admissions at the University of Michigan. In *Gratz v. Bollinger* the majority of the Supreme Court justices decided that the university's practice of awarding automatic bonus points to underrepresented minorities seeking undergraduate admissions was not narrowly tailored to meet the diversity interest set forth by Justice Lewis Powell in *Bakke.* They reached the opposite conclusion, however, in the law school case, *Grutter v. Bollinger.* In her majority decision, Justice Sandra Day O'Connor explained that the school's policy of "individualized, holistic" review of all applications did not unduly harm nonminorities. Unlike the undergraduate point system, the use of race in law admissions was based on achieving the compelling state interest of a diverse student body. "Unlike the program at issue in *Gratz v. Bollinger,* the law school awards no mechanical, predetermined diversity 'bonuses' based on race or ethnicity," O'Connor noted.[8]

The dissenting justices rejected her reasoning. Chief Justice Rehnquist accepted the "limited circumstances" under which drawing racial distinctions was permissible, but he found Michigan's positing of a "critical mass" goal of minority students to be "a naked effort to achieve racial balancing." Justices Scalia and Thomas were absolute in their rejection of affirmative action. Scalia labeled the school's program "unconstitutional"; Thomas denounced the law school's assertion that their admissions criteria delivered "educational benefits" as merely "classroom aesthetics" that violated the principle of equality embedded in the Declaration of Independence and the Fourteenth Amendment's Equal Protection Clause.[9]

Despite fresh legal challenges, the affirmative action debate has calcified since the 1970s. There is a remarkable similarity between the ethical and legal claims from both sides in the recent past and those made as far back as 1974 in *DeFunis v. Odegaard.* In their much-discussed 1997 book *America in Black and White,* Harvard professors Stephan and Abigail Thernstrom summed up the case for colorblind meritocracy by linking the origins of affirmative action to continuing troubled race relations. "As two authors for whom the 1960s were formative years, we remain committed to race-neutral policies," they wrote. This was not simply because such policies were "morally right": "In a society already deeply divided along lines of race, we see divisive race-conscious programs as dangerous." Just as Jewish American leaders had warned decades earlier, the Thernstroms sounded the alarm against "elaborate statistical data on the racial composition of the population." They argued that the growth of the black middle class was a result of economic growth and not preferential hiring or admissions programs.[10]

The charges against affirmative action in the first decade of the new century continued along these lines. They included the well-worn claim that preferential programs created victims both white and black. "It is hard to hold my family accountable for hundreds of years of anything in this country. Yet, because of my genes . . . I do not have equal opportunity," one Butler University faculty member and self-described "second generation" American wrote to the *Chronicle of Higher Education*. Terrence Pell, head of the Center for Individual Rights, warned in 2008 that, as a result of affirmative action, "people are losing jobs, and their kids are not getting into colleges, and they want to know why." Pell and others rejected the imprimatur Justice Powell gave "diversity" in *Bakke*. Yale Law School's Peter Schuck denounced diversity policies as "a feel-good policy for white elites" that missed its mark in addressing the truly disadvantaged. The responsibility of affirmative action recipients to deliver on the promise of campus diversity, Schuck insisted, was unfair to these students, and it ran counter to the best interests of higher education. "Americans . . . value diversity only when it is achieved in ways that are consistent with deeply held moral values like merit," he concluded. Taking another angle, some critics have argued that, although they seemed to benefit from preference programs, minority students would suffer due to academic failure and face growing white resentment. University of Texas law professor Lino Graglia chimed in that "a policy based on the assumption that black students cannot be expected to meet requirements applicable to others . . . cannot be the long-term solution for achieving racial equality."[11]

As always, the central claim of opponents was the superiority of colorblind meritocracy. "Meritocracy is a good thing, it is a productive thing, it is a fair thing. . . . If you don't have meritocracy you have group claims settled by political muscle," maintained Stephen Balch, longtime director of the National Association of Scholars (NAS) in a 2009 interview. Balch's organization, a self-described "association of academics working to foster intellectual freedom and to sustain the tradition of reasoned scholarship and civil debate," came together in the mid-1980s in the wake of the demise of the Committee on Academic Non-Discrimination and Integrity. Like its predecessor, NAS fought against "trivialized curricula," "ideological litmus tests in faculty hiring," and affirmative action (a policy marked by "tortuous law, academic hair-splitting, racial spoils, and psychological intimidation"). Its membership consists largely of conservatives and disaffected liberals (including the Thernstroms) who advocate a return to the higher education system of the 1950s and early 1960s. This was a time, in Balch's words, when "people did their work . . . in a methodologically rigorous way and in a disinterested way."[12]

Although they have come up short in the courtroom, colorblind conservatives have succeeded in fashioning compelling ethical and legal claims for their position. Where affirmative action supporters have focused on policymaking (and defending these policies in court), opponents have honed a clear narrative that portrays the introduction of preferential policies as breaking with civil rights advancements of the 1950s and 1960s. There are two parts to this narrative. First, as a legal matter, they argue that the law prohibits numerical goals and quotas. They cite as proof the language contained in the Fourteenth Amendment's Equal Protection Clause and the Civil Rights Act of 1964 that an individual's race, color, creed, and gender are immaterial in assessing their qualifications for employment, promotion, or admission. To do otherwise would be to open the sores of racism, sexism, and religious discrimination so recently healed. Second, opponents insist that affirmative action is un-American and undemocratic because unelected policymakers and judges cheat individuals and society from reaping the benefits of talent and hard work with unfair schemes that the voters would never endorse.[13]

It is a forceful and direct message that affirmative action supporters have not countered in an equally compelling manner. "The theory under which affirmative action is justified is often not articulated," admits Jack Greenberg, the former director-counsel of the National Association for the Advancement of Colored People's Legal Defense Fund. Part of the problem is that supporters have been hobbled by a lack of consensus over which groups should be eligible for affirmative action consideration; there has always been an ad hoc quality to the process of determining eligibility. Although activists and policymakers have generally closed ranks in defense of affirmative action, proponents worry that fewer resources will be available to address the deep currents of racism that have affected African Americans. In the 1970s some civil rights leaders lashed out against gender-sensitive programs on the grounds that undeserving white women benefited from programs designed for minorities. This opposition faded as opinion polls revealed that public support improved if programs included women.[14]

More recently, skeptics have started to question whether recent immigrants have legitimate reasons for inclusion. As historian Nancy MacLean writes, "The new Americans benefitted from resources originally intended for those historic victims of unequal U.S. citizenship." Nevertheless, supporters have attempted to maintain a broad coalition in defense of affirmative action and insist at the same time that the diversity rationale not obscure the strong moral claims of African Americans to its benefits. "Racism in the United States continues to be defined by a dichotomy not between black and white, but between black and nonblack," observes a group of sociologists, political scientists, and legal scholars in a volume defending affirmative action.[15]

Opponents have generally sidestepped this issue. Their scorn for multiculturalism does not distract from adherence to the colorblind principle irrespective of the recipient group. Instead, they have fixed on Asian Americans' "model minority" status as proof of meritocracy's value. It is difficult to gauge the level of Asian American support for affirmative action in the early years, given the lack of polling data and the mostly top-down manner in which policymakers included them. Several Asian American organizations did provide amicus support for university defendants in *DeFunis* and *Bakke*. By the 1980s, however, this support seemed to wane, as some states such as California considered them a "non protected" class. In the late 1990s, several Chinese American families successfully sued Lowell High School, a selective San Francisco magnet school, for rejecting their children in order to meet affirmative action admissions goals. Not all Asian Americans, however, opposed preferences. Around the same time, for example, Asian Americans joined black and Latino students in a lawsuit charging that the admissions policies put in place at the University of California at Berkeley, after the state's voters forbade affirmative action, were unjust to minorities.[16]

Asian American organizations have been divided on the issue. The Asian American Legal Foundation joined other opponents in campaigning against affirmative action, while the Asian American Justice Center threw its weight behind race- and gender-sensitive programs. The issue is made more complicated by the fact that, according to a 2008 study, Asian American students, rather than white students, are the most disadvantaged by elite institutions' consideration of ethnicity and race. Affirmative action opponents have seized on such data to make their case. "What is held against them? Their hard work, their intelligence, their diligence, their creativity—that is held against them," proclaimed one affirmative action opponent at a forum on higher education admissions. In language similar to that offered in the 1960s and 1970s about Jewish American success, this critic urged that "what is good for Asian Americans today can be good for African Americans ten years from now, or who knows who else."[17]

In recent years, colorblind conservatives have pointed to a string of anti–affirmative action referendum victories in California, Washington, Nebraska, and Michigan as proof of the correctness of their position. Fifty-eight percent of Michigan voters in 2006 approved a ban on preferences in university admissions, state hiring practices, and contracts, thus negating the effects of the Supreme Court's *Grutter* ruling. Affirmative action, commented one state resident, "is something that was needed in the past. But America on the whole has gone beyond that." Ron Edwards, a black talk show host in the Detroit area, backed the measure as well, arguing that those who receive special consideration will end up doubting their own abilities. "If you want to hurt a racist, succeed," he explained. The force behind most of the referenda, including Michigan's, was Ward Connerly, a black Californian, a regent for that state's university system, and the founder of the American Civil Rights Institute. "At last, we can hope to see each other as individuals rather than categories," Connerly wrote.[18]

As important as those referenda are, they do not provide a full picture of the American public's view of affirmative action. For Ann Selzer, a pollster who studied the Michigan referendum, voters' views were "personal and complicated. Even within a single person, you can see division and uncertainty." Polling data over the decades bear out Selzer's observation. Although a clear majority of Americans reject affirmative action when pollsters define it in a strong manner, an equally large number back it when asked about general approaches to equal opportunity. Much depends on the wording of the question. In May 2009, for example, only 31 percent of those polled by the Pew Research Center agreed that "we should make every effort to improve the position of blacks and minorities, even if it means giving them preferential treatment." The Pew results indicate a continuing racial divide in opinion, with just 22 percent of whites agreeing with this statement but 58 percent of blacks and 53 percent of Hispanics agreeing. When asked, however, if they favored "affirmative action programs to help blacks, women and other minorities to get better paying jobs and education," fully 70 percent of those polled responded positively. The Pew data, as well as other polling results, revealed a public filled with ambivalence. Even minorities' support for affirmative action is not overwhelming. White voters seem to reject preferences but acknowledge to pollsters the seriousness of persistent discrimination and inequality.[19]

Public opinion poll results underscore the continuing significance of the approach of labor liberalism and colorblind liberalism that was so dominant in the 1960s and 1970s. Still, the political force of these two perspectives is barely perceptible today. This is true especially for labor liberalism. Even as union leaders embraced affirmative action in the 1970s, the labor movement was entering a long period of decline from which it has yet to emerge. The causes of this decline are many and in some cases predate the 1970s: they included sophisticated corporate antiunion campaigns, lackadaisical organizing efforts, globalization, and a labor industrial system tilted in favor of employers. If labor liberals fit somewhat uncomfortably in the post–World War II political order, it fared even worse at the hands of Reagan Republicans and the neoliberal-driven presidential administrations of Jimmy Carter and Bill Clinton. The percentage of private sector employees who belong to a union today is in the single digits. As for affirmative action, historian Nelson Lichtenstein points out that it "rectified but a slice of the social and economic conditions that have made work and life less than satisfactory for so many minority Americans." Like many labor supporters, he calls for a commitment to "traditional labor liberal goals" including full employment, labor reform laws, and "genuine occupational opportunities available at all reaches of the job hierarchy."[20]

One criticism is that affirmative action is as misdirected as it is insufficient. As far back as the 1960s, liberal opponents argued that preference programs should serve the disadvantaged irrespective of race or gender. This is a view that some affirmative action supporters endorse, however weakly. (Barack Obama did so in noting his daughters' affluent upbringing.) William Julius Wilson's argument in his 1987 book, *The Truly Disadvantaged,* gave added weight to the view that most blacks, along with poor whites and others, face daunting challenges that hiring and admissions programs focused on middle-class minorities do not address. In his books and essays over the past fifteen years, Michael Lind has argued that the "radical center" consisting of the nation's middle-class and working-class majority should push back against the "mushy middle" of professional and elite Americans whose brand of identity politics and moderate economic conservatism has served so few well. Affirmative action, scholar and critic Walter Benn Michaels contends, "is a kind of collective bribe rich people pay themselves for ignoring economic inequality." These critiques recall the arguments of the liberals and labor leaders analyzed in this book who resisted the emerging policies of the day.[21]

There is yet another thread of affirmative action opposition, one that avoids the shopworn debates over race and quotas by focusing on the processes colleges and universities employ in assessing applicants. Strictly speaking, it is not about race- or gender-based preferences at all; rather, it is an indictment of legacy preferences, athletic scholarships, and special consideration for donors' children and "faculty brats." In books with titles like *The Price of Admission, Creating a Class,* and *The Gatekeepers,* these authors decry the clutter of money and other factors in admissions decisionmaking and urge higher education institutions to embrace a "need-blind" approach in selecting their incoming classes. In their analysis of how privilege works, they argue that affirmative action is a means of preserving these practices by distracting the public with race-based preferences. Some of these authors endorse a colorblind meritocracy as the most precise and just way to award jobs and admissions. Other commentators have observed that the surge in immigration to the United States since the mid-1960s and the rise in multiculturalism have created a new generation of successful "ethnics" who, through marriages with members of members of other groups, have made race-based claims to suffering from discrimination less common. Thinking back to the publication of his book *Postethnic America* nearly fifteen years earlier, historian David Hollinger saw Obama's achievements in 2008 as proof that affirmative action may no longer be necessary: "Today we seem closer to engaging inequalities that are too often understood in ethnoracial rather than economic terms."[22]

Where conservatives have remained unmoved from their set position, earlier foes have continued to balance competing claims for justice. Perhaps the most dramatic example of this is Nathan Glazer, author of the widely read 1975 book *Affirmative Discrimination.* Where Glazer once led the charge against higher education affirmative action, he came to support the University of Michigan's admissions programs in the late 1990s. This former champion of colorblind meritocracy claimed that "the reality is that strict adherence to this principle would result in few African Americans getting jobs, admissions, and contracts." Affirmative action supporters were startled by Glazer's move—one called it "half-hearted and replete with reactionary innuendo." So too were former allies, including neoconservative Irving Kristol, who wrote Glazer to inform him that his new argument was "very persuasive—though not to me!" Still, even Kristol admitted that he was "relaxed about the use of affirmative action in certain settings," including police departments and higher education. "But the less of it, the better, to my mind. . . . Affirmative action leads to racial polarization—or at least encourages such a tendency."[23]

The fight over affirmative action continues to be marked by charges and countercharges of racism and sexism. This is clear from the modest but steady number of discrimination complaints male workers and white workers file with the Equal Employment Opportunity Commission every year (about 10 percent of the total for race and 18 percent for sex discrimination). In the 1960s, stark, often violent, forms of segregation throughout the United States still defined the everyday experience of racial and ethnic minorities. Women of all races felt the sting of gender inequality that limited the kinds of work they could do as well as the conditions and pay under which they labored. In education they faced significant limitations, as the male-defined professional and academic worlds assigned them a marginal place. If opponents were alarmed by how emerging affirmative action policies violated their sense of colorblindness and fairness, supporters embraced them as necessary tools to deal with racial and gender inequality.[24]

This was not lost on colorblind liberals. Writing to a colleague in 1978, Naomi Levine of the American Jewish Congress noted that she "promised that our staff would try to come up with a formula that would achieve the objective of ending the exclusion of minority groups" without using numerical goals or quotas. Levine confessed that "we have not developed such a formula and I am not sure that it is possible to do so. But I am sure that we have an obligation to try. . . . [W]e have to show the black community that we have not deserted them on an issue which they view as the litmus test of support." Those coming of age today have not experienced a world of work and school marked by the kinds of overt discrimination, still fresh when Levine wrote, that gave rise to affirmative action policies, but they do live in an age of deepening economic inequality with new obstacles to equality.[25]

"Our fondness for stark dichotomies has led us to transform practically all the difficult political issues we face into questions of constitutional law," writes James Kloppenberg in *The Virtues of Liberalism*. It was this "politics of false choices," as Kloppenberg calls it, that both informed this first generation of opponents and limited the effectiveness of their response to affirmative action. Compared to the civil rights movement, this is a history lacking in heroes and drama. It is a story of policymaking, litigation, and lobbying; its actors went about weighing competing moral claims in a climate informed as much by parochial concerns as by high principles. Over four decades later and despite periodic calls for placing an "expiration date" on affirmative action programs, preferential policies seem to be fixtures in our courts, college and university admissions offices, and personnel departments in government and in the private sector. Affirmative action has become as much a proxy for the politics of race and gender as it is a set of group and individual claims for justice. With constitutional principles and the economic well-being of Americans in the balance, the unimagined solution to the affirmative action struggle seems as elusive today as it did in 1965, when Lyndon Johnson challenged his listeners to "fulfill the fair expectations of man."[26]

Introduction

1. "Negative Action," *Wall Street Journal*, August 23, 1965.

2. "Negative Action"; Lyndon B. Johnson, "To Fulfill These Rights" (June 4, 1965), *Public Papers of the Presidents of the United States: Lyndon B. Johnson, 1965* (Washington, DC: GPO, 1966), 3:635; and Charles Abrams, foreword, in Robert L. Carter et al., *Equality* (New York: Pantheon Books, 1965), vii.

3. *Regents of the University of California v. Bakke,* 438 U.S. 265 (1978).

4. Barbara Lindmann Schlei and Paul Grossman, *Employment Discrimination Law* (1976; repr. Chicago: American Bar Association, 1983), 775.

5. George Lipsitz, *The Possessive Investment in Whiteness: How White People Profit from Identity Politics* (Philadelphia: Temple University Press, 2006), 5, 16.

6. Charlotte Steeh and Maria Krysan, "The Polls—Trends: Affirmative Action and the Public, 1970–1995," *Public Opinion Quarterly* 60 (1996): 128–29, 132–34.

7. John Sibley Butler, "Affirmative Action in the Military," *Annals of the American Academy of Political and Social Science* 523 (September 1992): 196–206; Charles Moskos, "Affirmative Action: The Army's Success," *Washington Post*, March 15, 1995; Bootie Cosgrove-Mather, "Race Quotas Divide Military, Bush: President and the U.S. Army at Odds over Affirmative Action," *CBS Evening News*, June 6, 2003, www.cbsnews.com/stories/2003/06/06/eve ningnews/main557442.shtml; John Kaplan, "Equal Justice in an Unequal World: Equality for the Negro—The Problem of Special Treatment," *Northwestern University Law Review* 61:3 (July–August 1966): 384; and Barbara A. Perry, *The Michigan Affirmative Action Cases* (Lawrence: University Press of Kansas, 2007), 29.

8. John D. Skrentny, "Policy-Elite Perceptions and Social Movement Success: Understanding Variations in Group Inclusion in Affirmative Action," *American Journal of Sociology* 111:6 (May 2006): 1762–1815; and Derrick Bell, "Love's Labor Lost? Why Racial Fairness Is a Threat to Many White Americans," in *Who's Qualified?* ed. Susan Sturm and Lani Guinier (Boston: Beacon Press, 2001), 46.

9. Alan Brinkley, *The End of Reform: New Deal Liberalism in Recession and War* (New York: Knopf, 1995), 226, 257, 268–69.

10. Typescript, "Comments on Senator Lister Hill's Criticism of Civil Rights Bill," AFL-

CIO Legal Department, January 31, 1964, box 9, folder 13, AFL-CIO Department of Legislation Collection, George Meany Memorial Archives, Silver Spring, Maryland.

The historical literature on the labor movement's role in civil rights legislation is large. See, for example, Nelson Lichtenstein, *The Most Dangerous Man in Detroit: Walter Reuther and the Fate of American Labor* (New York: Basic, 1995); and Chen, *Fifth Freedom*.

11. Gunnar Myrdal, *An American Dilemma: The Negro Problem and Modern Democracy* (New York: Harper and Row, 1944), 1021, 1023.

12. David Carroll Cochran, *The Color of Freedom: Race and Contemporary American Liberalism* (Albany: SUNY Press, 1999), 18, 22, 27–28; and Thomas J. Sugrue, "The Tangled Roots of Affirmative Action," *American Behavioral Scientist* 41 (April 1998): 886–87.

13. T. H. Marshall, *Class, Citizenship, and Social Development: Essays by T. H. Marshall,* ed. Seymour Martin Lipset (Garden City, NY: Doubleday, 1962), 102.

14. Jack Greenberg, "Race Relations and Group Interests in the Law," *Rutgers Law Review* 13 (Spring 1959): 503; Marshall and Hill quoted in Moreno, *From Direct Action to Affirmative Action*, 82–83.

15. George Kelley, "Rights, Not Ratios," *America* 109 (October 12, 1963): 424; "Liberalism and the Negro: A Round-Table Discussion," *Commentary* 37 (March 1964): 26; and memorandum, "Attack by the 'Coordinating Committee for Fundamental American Freedom' upon Kennedy Civil Rights Bill," December 6, 1963, Container 84, Part I, Leadership Conference on Civil Rights Papers, Library of Congress, Washington, D.C.

16. *DeFunis v. Odegaard*, 416 U.S. 312 (1974).

17. Jeffrey M. Berry, *The New Liberalism: The Rising Power of Citizen Groups* (Washington, DC: Brookings Institution Press, 2000), 34, 43, 48–49, 59. On the Democratic Party after 1968, see John B. Judis and Ruy Teixeira, *The Emerging Democratic Majority* (New York: Scribner, 2004); and Bruce Miroff, *The Liberals' Moment: The McGovern Insurgency and the Identity Crisis of the Democratic Party* (Lawrence: University Press of Kansas, 2007).

18. The reasons for the delay in conservative legalism is discussed by Johnathan O'Neill, *Originalism in American Law and Politics: A Constitutional History* (Baltimore: Johns Hopkins University Press, 2005); Steven M. Teles, *The Rise of the Conservative Legal Movement: The Battle for Control of the Law* (Princeton: Princeton University Press, 2008); Mark Tushnet, "The Warren Court as History: An Interpretation," in *The Warren Court in Historical and Political Perspective,* ed. Mark Tushnet (Charlottesville: University Press of Virginia, 1993); and Thomas M. Keck, *The Most Activist Supreme Court in History: The Road to Modern Judicial Conservatism* (Chicago: University of Chicago Press, 2004). On colorblind conservatism, see Matthew D. Lassiter, *The Silent Majority: Suburban Politics in the Sunbelt South* (Princeton: Princeton University Press, 2006); Kevin Kruse, *White Flight: Atlanta and the Making of Modern Conservatism* (Princeton: Princeton University Press, 2005); Joseph Crespino, *In Search of Another Country: Mississippi and the Conservative Counterrevolution* (Princeton: Princeton University Press, 2007); Christopher Bonastia, *Knocking on the Door: The Federal Government's Attempt to Desegregate the Suburbs* (Princeton: Princeton University Press, 2006); and Michael K. Brown et al., *Whitewashing Race: The Myth of a Color-Blind Society* (Berkeley: University of California Press, 2003).

19. Michel Rosenfeld, *Affirmative Action and Justice: A Philosophical and Constitutional Inquiry* (New Haven: Yale University Press, 1991), 2.

Chapter 1. "The Best 'Affirmative Action Program' Is Creating Jobs for Everyone"

1. Harold McKinney to Don Slaiman, March 5, 1964, box 16, folder 15; Don Slaiman to Boris Shishkin, January 23, 1962, Hal Leyshan to Don Slaiman, January 2, 1966, box 16, folder 48; clipping, Robert M. Lewin, "Integration Swings to Upbeat as Musicians Unions Merge," *Chicago Daily News*, January 12, 1966, box 16, folder 48, all in American Federation of Labor–Congress of Industrial Organizations, Department of Civil Rights: Discrimination Case Files, 1947–1984 Collection, George Meany Memorial Archives, Silver Spring, Maryland [hereafter, AFL-CIO Case Files Collection].

2. MacLean, *Freedom Is Not Enough*, 90; Banks, " 'Last Bastion,' " 20; and "Title VII of the Civil Rights Act of 1964 and Minority Group Entry into the Building Trade Unions," *University of Chicago Law Review* 37:2 (Winter 1970): 330.

3. Paul Frymer, *Black and Blue: African Americans, the Labor Movement, and the Decline of the Democratic Party* (Princeton: Princeton University Press, 2008), 6, 15–16, 72; and Jean T. McKelvey, "Sex and the Single Arbitrator," *Industrial and Labor Relations Review* 24 (April 1971): 353.

4. Pamphlet, *A Common Goal—Equal Opportunity*, AFL-CIO Publication No. 80 (March 1966), box 8, folder 22, American Federation of Labor–Congress of Industrial Organizations, Department of Legislation Collection, George Meany Memorial Archives, Silver Spring, Maryland [hereafter, AFL-CIO Legislation Collection]; handwritten notes, "Meeting with Drew Days," n.a. [William Pollard], May 23, 1977, box 28, folder 50, American Federation of Labor–Congress of Civil Rights, George Meany Memorial Archives, Silver Spring, Maryland [hereafter, AFL-CIO Civil Rights Collection].

5. Kevin Boyle, *The UAW and the Heyday of American Liberalism, 1945–1968* (Ithaca: Cornell University Press, 1995), esp. 161–205; Lichtenstein, *State of the Union*, 191–211; and MacLean, *Freedom Is Not Enough*, 65.

6. Deslippe, *"Rights, Not Roses,"* 114–45; Cobble, *Other Women's Movement*, 145–205; Gabin, *Feminism in the Labor Movement*, 188–228; and Herbert Hill, "Black Workers, Organized Labor, and Title VII of the 1964 Civil Rights Act: Legislative History and Litigation Record," in *Race in America: The Struggle for Equality*, ed. Herbert Hill and James E. Jones Jr. (Madison: University of Wisconsin Press, 1993), 313.

7. Lichtenstein, *State of the Union*, 206.

8. Testimony of Herbert Hill, *Hearings, "Ad Hoc" Committee on Federal Contract Compliance*, December 5, 1968, U.S. House of Representatives, Washington, D.C. (typescript in author's possession); F. Ray Marshall and Vernon M. Briggs, *The Negro and Apprenticeship* (Baltimore: Johns Hopkins University Press, 1967), 113–19; and Banks, " 'The Last Bastion,' " 43.

9. Typescript, U.S. Department of Labor, "Action Taken by Local Building Trades to Provide Equal Employment Opportunity," n.d. [1963], box 17, folder 10, AFL-CIO Legislation Collection; Frymer, *Black and Blue*, 36; and Joseph A. Loftus, "Unions Lagging on Integration," *New York Times*, June 1, 1963.

10. Frymer, *Black and Blue*, 54–57, 62–63; Lichtenstein, *Most Dangerous Man in Detroit*, 370, 374–75, 380; and Hinshaw, *Steel and Steelworkers*, 203, 207.

11. Graham, *Civil Rights Era*, 27–28, 35, 40; Chen, *Fifth Freedom*, 210, 218; Deslippe, *"Rights, Not Roses,"* 60–66, 116–24; and Frymer, *Black and Blue*, 41.

12. Banks, *"'The Last Bastion'"* 48–50; Sugrue, *Sweet Land of Liberty*, 273; Moreno, *From Direct Action to Affirmative Action*, 30, 32, 55, 186, 201; *Hughes v. Superior Court* 339 U.S. 460 (1950); and Stacy Kinlock Sewell, "Contracting Racial Equality: Affirmative Action Policy and Practice in the United States, 1945–1970" (PhD diss., Rutgers University, 1994), 98–100, 106–7.

13. Whitney Young, "Domestic Marshall Plan," *New York Times Magazine*, October 6, 1963; Anderson, *Pursuit of Happiness*, 77; editorial, "Right Goal, Wrong Method," *New York Times*, July 23, 1963; Theodore Kuperman, letter to editor, *New York Times*, July 18, 1963; Sewell, "Contracting Racial Equality," 197; and Banks, *"'The Last Bastion'"* 51.

14. Sugrue, *Sweet Land of Liberty*, 267–70; Moreno, *From Direct Action to Affirmative Action*, 201–7; Herman Belz, *Equality Transformed: A Quarter-Century of Affirmative Action* (New Brunswick, NJ: Transaction, 1991), 18–20; Graham, *Civil Rights Era*, 28, 35, 40–43; and Sewell, "Contracting Racial Equality," 145–51.

15. Edward T. Chase, "Quotas for Negroes," *Commonweal* 79 (January 17, 1964): 453; and Robert L. Carter chapter, in Carter et al., *Equality*, 26–27, 132.

16. Typescript, "Affirmative Action Commitment under Executive Orders 10925 and 1114," January 1964, box 23, folder: Reedy, EEOC/2, George E. Reedy Files, Lyndon B. Johnson Presidential Papers, Lyndon Baines Johnson Library, Austin, Texas; and Chen, *Fifth Freedom*, 214–16.

17. Executive Order 11246, 30 FR 12319 (September 28, 1965); Executive Order 11375, 32 FR 14303 (October 17, 1967); Sewell, "Contracting Racial Equality," 173; and Belz, *Equality Transformed*, 32.

18. Gareth Davies, *From Opportunity to Entitlement: The Transformation and Decline of Great Society Liberalism* (Lawrence: University Press of Kansas, 1996), 66–67; Office of Policy Planning and Research, *The Negro Family: The Case for National Action* (Washington, DC: U.S. Department of Labor, 1965), 3; Daryl Michael Scott, *Contempt and Pity: Social Policy and the Image of the Damaged Black Psyche, 1880–1996* (Chapel Hill: University of North Carolina Press, 1997), 153–55; and typescript, Speech by Anthony Rachal Jr. to Middle Tennessee Federal Executive Council Seminar, November 11, 1968, container 85, folder: Commission on Civil Rights, Leadership Conference on Civil Rights Papers / Series I, Library of Congress, Washington, D.C. [hereafter, LCCR / Part I Papers].

19. Sugrue, *Sweet Land of Liberty*, 271; Mary Francis Berry, *And Justice for All: The United States Commission on Civil Rights and the Continuing Struggle for Freedom in America* (New York: Knopf, 2009), 115, 117–19, 139–40, 161; and transcript, Minutes, Executive Session, November 1, 1968, box 1, U.S. Commission on Civil Rights Meeting Minutes Records (RG 453), National Archives, College Park, Maryland.

20. Belz, *Equality Transformed*, 28; Moreno, *From Direct Action to Affirmative Action*, 230; and Graham, *Civil Rights Era*, 249.

21. Graham, *Civil Rights Era*, 195; and Alfred W. Blumrosen, "Quotas, Common Sense, and Law in Labor Relations: Three Dimensions of Equal Opportunity," *Rutgers Law Review* 27 (1974): 676.

22. Graham, *Civil Rights Era*, 244–45; Sonia Pressman Fuentes, interview by Dennis

Deslippe, Potomac, Maryland, November 23, 1993, Walter Reuther Archives, Wayne State University, Detroit; Sonia Pressman Fuentes, "The Law against Sex Discrimination in Employment and Its Relationship to Statistics," *American Statistician* 26:2 (April 1973): 18.

23. Alfred W. Blumrosen, "Strangers in Paradise: *Griggs v. Duke Power Co.* and the Concept of Employer Discrimination," in *Equal Employment Opportunity: Labor Market Discrimination and Public Policy*, ed. Paul Burstein (New York: De Gruyter, 1994), 106; Konrad Mark Hamilton, "From Equal Employment to Affirmative Action: A History of the Equal Employment Opportunity Commission" (PhD diss., Stanford University, 1998), 140–42, 149–60; Clifford Alexander Jr. to Henry Fowler, April 12, 1968, box 7, folder: Office Files, Henry McPherson / EEOC, White House Central Files / Aides File: Harry McPherson, Lyndon B. Johnson Presidential Papers, Lyndon Baines Johnson Library, Austin, Texas.

24. Belz, *Equality Transformed*, 32; Sugrue, *Sweet Land of Liberty*, 363; Proceedings, *Fifty-Fourth Convention of the Building and Construction Trades Department, AFL-CIO* (Bal Harbour, Florida, 1967), 55–56; Graham, *Civil Rights Era*, 290; and Anderson, *Pursuit of Happiness*, 108–9.

25. Anderson, *Pursuit of Happiness*, 120; and Frymer, *Black and Blue*, 37–38.

26. George P. Shultz, "Priorities in Policy and Research for Industrial Relations," *Proceedings of the Industrial Relations Research Association: Annual Winter Meeting 21* (1969), 3, 5; Graham, *Civil Rights Era*, 342; Robert H. Zieger, *For Jobs and Freedom: Race and Labor in America since 1865* (Lexington: University Press of Kentucky, 2010), 187; typescript, "Statement of the NAACP on 'The New York Plan' for Employment of Minorities in the Building Trades," April 1, 1970, box 27, folder: Minority Hiring Plans, 1969–1972, Roy Wilkins Papers, Library of Congress, Washington, D.C. [hereafter, Wilkins Papers].

27. Herrich Roth to Richard Nixon, December 23, 1969, Reel 20, "Civil Rights during the Nixon Administration 1969–1974, Part 1: The White House Central Files," microfilm (Frederick, MD: University Publications of America, 1989) [hereafter, Nixon Civil Rights Microfilm Collection].

28. Doris Gibson to Galen Martin, October 11, 1966, box 28, folder 29; Joseph Doherty to Donald Slaiman, October 18, 1967, box 28, folder 31; and Viola May Kanatz to Donald Slaiman, November 2, 1966, box 28, folder 31, AFL-CIO Civil Rights Collection.

29. C. J. Haggerty to Willard Wirtz, February 1, 1968, box 28, folder 47; Willard Wirtz to C. J. Haggerty, February 2, 1968, box 28, folder 47; Robert Belton to William Pollard, February 14, 1967, box 28, folder 15, all in AFL-CIO Civil Rights Collection; and typescript, "Statement of the NAACP on 'The New York Plan' for Employment of Minorities in the Building Trades," April 1, 1970, box 27, folder: Minority Hiring Plans, 1969–72, Wilkins Papers.

30. Transcript, "Labor News Conference," July 8, 1969, box 41, folder 40, AFL-CIO Legislation Collection; Benjamin W. Wolkinson, "The Effectiveness of EEOC Policy in the Construction Industry," *Proceedings of the Twenty-Fifth Anniversary Meeting: Industrial Relations Board Association, December 28–29, 1972* (1973), 365–66; and pamphlet, Bayard Rustin, *Conflict or Coalition? The Civil Rights Struggle and the Trade Union Movement Today* (1969), box 41, folder 41, AFL-CIO Legislation Collection.

31. Irwin Dubinsky, "Trade Union Discrimination in the Pittsburgh Construction Industry," *Urban Affairs Quarterly* 6:3 (March 1971): 302; Charles Kelly, letter to editor, *New*

York Times, August 8, 1963; and typescript, George Meany, "Labor and the Philadelphia Plan," January 12, 1970, box 6, folder 20, AFL-CIO Legislation Collection.

32. Typescript, George Meany, "Labor and the Philadelphia Plan," January 12, 1970, box 6, folder 20, AFL-CIO Legislation Collection; memorandum, Louis Sherman to C. J. Haggerty, July 1, 1968, box 28, folder 50, AFL-CIO Civil Rights Collection; Gary Armstrong to Richard Nixon, June 25, 1970, Reel 20, Nixon Civil Rights Microfilm Collection; and Marcus Loftis to Hobart Rowan, January 19, 1970, box 41, folder 41, AFL-CIO Legislation Collection.

33. Lichtenstein, *State of the Union*, 228–29; Joshua B. Freeman, *Working-Class New York: Life and Labor since World War II* (New York: New Press, 2001), 234, 237; Richard Lemon, *The Troubled American* (New York: Simon and Schuster, 1969), 34–40; and E. E. LeMasters, *Blue-Collar Aristocrats: Life-Styles at a Working-Class Tavern* (Madison: University of Wisconsin Press, 1975), 33, 189.

34. Gus Tyler, "White Workers / Blue Mood," in *The World of the Blue-Collar Worker*, ed. Irving Howe (New York: Quadrangle Books, 1972), 207; Andrew Levison, *The Working-Class Majority* (New York: Coward, McCann and Geoghegan, 1974), 153; and typescript, Remarks by John Lyons, AFL-CIO Equal Opportunity Conference, Washington, D.C., May 28, 1969, box 28, folder 48, AFL-CIO Civil Rights Collection.

35. Miroff, *Liberals' Moment*, 185–86, 189; and Levison, *Working-Class Majority*, 235.

36. Lipsitz, *Possessive Investment in Whiteness*, 41; MacLean, *Freedom Is Not Enough*, 92–93; Anderson, *Pursuit of Happiness*, 121; transcript, Press Conference: William H. Brown III, August 29, 1969, box A10, folder: Equal Employment Opportunity / 1, Arthur F. Burns Papers, 1969–78, White House Series, 1969–70, Gerald R. Ford Presidential Library, Ann Arbor, Michigan; and typescript, Speech: Robert Georgine, Washington, D.C., June 7, 1975, box 1, folder 4, American Federation of State, County, and Municipal Employees Program Development Records, Walter P. Reuther Library, Wayne State University, Detroit [hereafter, AFSCME Program Records].

37. Graham, *Civil Rights Era*, 335–40; and Belz, *Equality Transformed*, 37.

38. Memorandum, Louis Sherman to C. J. Haggerty, July 1, 1968, box 28, folder 50, AFL-CIO Civil Rights Collection; *Asbestos Workers, Local 53 v. Vogler*, 407 F.2d 1047 (5th Cir., 1969); *Patterson v. Newspaper and Mail Deliverers Union*, 384 F. Supp. 585 (S.D. N.Y., 1974); *Dobbins v. IBEW, Local 212*, 292 F. Supp. 413 (S.D. Ohio, 1968); *United States v. Plumbers and Pipefitters, Local 73*, 314 F. Supp. 160 (S.D. Ind., 1969); *United States v. Sheet Metal Workers, Local 36*, 416 F.2d 123 (8th Cir., 1969); *United States v. National Asso. Of Bridges et al.*, 315 F. Supp. 1202 (W.D. Wash, 1970); *Contractors Assoc. of Eastern Penn. v. Sec. of Labor*, 442 F.2d 159 (3rd Cir., 1971), cert. denied, 404 U.S. 854 (1971); and Frymer, *Black and Blue*, 89.

39. Graham, *Civil Rights Era*, 335; Peter Schoemann to Andrew Biemiller, January 24, 1967, box 38, folder 58, AFL-CIO Legislation Collection; Ronnie Blumenthal quoted in Equal Employment Opportunity Commission, *Making a Right a Reality: An Oral History in the Early Years of the EEOC, 1965–1972* (Washington, DC: EEOC, 1990), 20.

40. EEOC Discrimination Case No. 6-2-692, Juan Galaviz against Asbestos Workers Local 53, February 3, 1966, box 1, folder 47; Doris Gibson to Donald Slaiman, November

21, 1966, box 1, folder 48, both in AFL-CIO Case Files Collection; and William Pollard to Donald Slaiman, August 3, 1972, box 33, folder 15, AFL-CIO Civil Rights Collection.

41. Ina Boon to William Pollard, October 24, 1975, box 8, folder 59; handwritten notes: "Meeting with Black Firefighters under the Auspices of the NAACP," n.a. [William Pollard], January 28, 1976, box 8, folder 59; and handwritten notes: Meeting with St. Louis Firefighters and Community Leaders," n.a. [William Pollard], March 23, 1976, box 8, folder 58, all in AFL-CIO Case File Collection.

42. William Pollard to Donald Slaiman, January 25, 1971, box 32, folder 4; typescript, Winn Newman, "Temporary Experimental Procedural Changes," July 27, 1966; Winn Newman to Commissioner Jackson, October 3, 1966; Richard Berg to Charles Duncan, May 26, 1966, all in box 33, folder 12; William Pollard to Donald Slaiman, January 25, 1971, box 32, folder 4, all in AFL-CIO Civil Rights Collection.

43. Typescript, Lane Kirkland, Address to Jewish Labor Committee, November 28, 1972, Container 114, folder: Congressional Black Caucus / Affirmative Action, LCCR / Part I Papers; Frymer, *Black and Blue*, 93; and typescript, speech, Robert Georgine, June 7, 1975, box 1, folder 4, AFSCME Program Records.

44. Levin quoted in McKee, *Problem of Jobs,* 246; and Lichtenstein, *State of the Union,* 228–30.

45. Frymer, *Black and Blue,* 158; and typescript, "Draft of Policy Statement on Implementation of Title VII," April 20, 1966, box 28, folder 45, AFL-CIO Civil Rights Collection.

46. Kim Moody, *An Injury to All: The Decline of American Unionism* (New York: Routledge, 1988), 88; and Jefferson Cowie, "Vigorously Left, Right, and Center," in *America in the Seventies,* ed. Beth Bailey and David Farber (Lawrence: University Press of Kansas, 2004), 76.

47. Summary memorandum, "8,854 Job Discrimination Complaints Filed with EEOC in First Year," n.d. [1966], box 7, folder 8, Katherine Ellickson Collection, 1921–78, Walter Reuther Archives of Labor and Urban Affairs, Wayne State University, Detroit; Sonia Pressman Fuentes, interview by Sylvia Danovitch, Potomac, Maryland, December 27, 1990 (transcript in author's possession); Ginger Timberlake to George Meany, August 26, 1972, box 55, folder 22, AFL-CIO Legislation Collection; *Weeks v. Southern Bell,* 408 F.2d 228 (1969); and Lois Kathryn Herr, *Women, Power, and AT&T: Winning Rights in the Workplace* (Boston: Northeastern University Press, 2003), 81.

48. Lichtenstein, *Most Dangerous Man,* 375, 411; Boyle, *UAW and the Heyday,* 212–19; Gabin, *Feminism in the Labor Movement,* 214; and Marcellus Stepp, interviewed by John Barnard, Detroit, June 10, 1993, United Automobile Workers' International Executive Board Oral History Project, Walter Reuther Archives of Labor and Urban Affairs, Wayne State University, Detroit.

49. Minutes, IEB meeting, October 6, 1969, box 17, United Automobile Workers' International Executive Board Minutes Collection, Walter Reuther Archives of Labor and Urban Affairs, Wayne State University, Detroit [hereafter, UAW IEB Minutes Collection].

50. Ibid.

51. *Griggs v. Duke Power Co.,* 401 U.S. 424 (1971); Robert S. Smith, *Race, Labor, and Civil Rights: "Griggs versus Duke Power" and the Struggle for Equal Employment Opportunity*

(Baton Rouge: Louisiana State University Press, 2008); Graham, *Civil Rights Era*, 383–90; MacLean, *Freedom Is Not Enough*, 108–10; Anderson, *Pursuit of Happiness*, 128–29; and Stein, *Running Steel*, 184.

52. CLUW *News*, Winter 1975, box 13, folder 1; pamphlet, "Statement of Purpose, Structure and Guidelines, adopted by Coalition of Labor Union Women Founding Convention, March 23–24, 1974, Chicago, IL," box 1, folder 17; clipping, *Philadelphia Inquirer*, January 29, 1974, box 1, folder 5; CLUW *News*, Summer 1975, box 13, folder 1, all in Coalition of Labor Union Women Collection, Walter Reuther Archives of Labor History and Urban Affairs, Wayne State University, Detroit [hereafter, CLUW Collection].

53. Clipping, James P. Gannon, "Factory-Bias Right," *Wall Street Journal*, January 5, 1967, box 1, folder 38, AFL-CIO Civil Rights Records; and Hinshaw, *Steel and Steelworkers*, 207.

54. Jesse Merrill, interview by Merle David, Ottumwa, Iowa, September 16, 1981, Iowa Labor History Oral Project, State Historical Society of Iowa, Iowa City, Iowa; Deslippe, *"Rights, Not Roses,"* 146–65; and Hugh Brimm to E. T. Kehrer, March 9, 1966, box 24, folder 58, AFL-CIO Civil Rights Collection.

55. *Quarles V. Philip Morris, Inc.*, 279 F. Supp. 505, 516 (E.D. Va., 1968); *Papermakers, Local 189 v. U.S.*, 416 F.2d 980 (5th Cir., 1969); and *Robinson v. Lorillard Corp.*, 444 F.2d 791 (4th Cir., 1971).

56. Hinshaw, *Steel and Steelworkers*, 211–20; Stein, *Running Steel*, 170–80; Alfred W. Blumrosen, "The Law Transmission System and the Southern Jurisprudence of Employment Discrimination," in *Equal Employment Opportunity*, ed. Burstein, 235–36.

57. William B. Gould, "Black Workers inside the House of Labor," *Annals of the American Academy of Politics and Social Science* 407 (May 1973): 82; and typescript, "Summary of Seniority Civil Rights Decree: Issued by United Steelworkers of America," May 3, 1974, box 29, folder 44, AFL-CIO Civil Rights Collection.

58. Marylin Bender, "Job Discrimination, 10 Years Later," *New York Times*, November 10, 1974; Hinshaw, *Steel and Steelworkers*, 181, 216; EEOC Discrimination Charge No. 0771770957, Jack Hustace against USW Local 13, May 6, 1977, box 23, folder 115; EEOC Discrimination Charge No. 052771992, Robert Bennett against Jones and Laughlin Steel and USW Local 185, August 30, 1977, box 23, folder 127; EEOC Discrimination Charge No. 052771990, Robert Whetzel against Jones and Laughlin Steel, August 30, 1977, box 23, folder 128, all in AFL-CIO Case File Collection.

59. Ronald Ellis against South Central Bell and CWA Local 10806, October 14, 1976, box 4, folder 143; EEOC Discrimination Charge No. TNK4-0164, John Mele v. IBEW Local 52 and U.S. Department of Justice, October 12, 1973, box 6, folder 17, both in AFL-CIO Case Files Collection; and *Mele v. Dept. of Justice*, 395 F. Supp. 592 (N.J., 1975).

60. Typescript, "Resolutions: Affirmative Action," AFSCME International Convention, June 1974, box 1, folder 1, AFSCME Program Records; minutes, IEB Meeting, May 21, 1975, box 20, UAW IEB Minutes Collection; clipping, Lewis J. Carter, "Seniority and Affirmative Action," *The Builder*, n.d. [1974–75], box 2, folder 27, Coalition of Black Trade Unionists Collection, Walter P. Reuther Archives of Labor and Urban Affairs, Wayne State University, Detroit [hereafter, CBTU Collection].

61. Patterson, *Grand Expectations*, 790; editorial, "Equality and Scarcity," *New York*

Times, January 13, 1975; and Nina Totenberg, "Recession's Special Victims: Newly Hired Blacks, Women," *New York Times,* March 19, 1975.

62. Totenberg, "Recession's Special Victims"; "Who Gets the Pink Slip?" *Time,* February 3, 1975, 58; Alfred W. Blumrosen and Ruth G. Blumrosen, "The Duty to Plan for Fair Employment Revisited: Work Sharing in Hard Times," *Rutgers Law Review* 28 (1975): 1105–6; and Paul Delaney, "U.S. Weighs Rules on Job Seniority," *New York Times,* July 31, 1975.

63. Typescript, "Remarks of William Pollard before the Hungry Club Forum, Atlanta, March 10, 1976," box 31, folder 8, American Federation of Teachers President's Office, Albert Shanker Collection, Walter P. Reuther Library, Wayne State University, Detroit; Ernest Holsendolph, "Recession Layoffs and the Civil Rights of Minorities," *New York Times,* January 25, 1975; "On Seniority," *John Herling Labor Letter* (December 27, 1975), 1; clipping, Elliot Bredhoff, "Destroying Seniority Principle Won't Solve Employment Crisis," *AFL-CIO News* (November 1, 1975), box 1, folder 7, AFSCME Program Records; and William Pollard to Civil Rights Committee, December 8, 1975, box 32, CRD Collection.

64. Jerry Wurf, "Merit: A Union View," *Public Administration Review* 34:5 (September/October 1974): 433; typescript, n.a. [Winn Newman], March 27, 1975, box 156, Group 2, International Union of Electrical Workers Collection, Rutgers University Library, New Brunswick, New Jersey; memorandum, Paul Jennings and David Fitzmaurice to All Local Unions, January 10, 1975, box 1, folder 3, AFSCME Program Records; and typescript, Statement of Marc Stepp, "Ad Hoc Hearing and Strategy Session on 'Affirmative Action in Employment,'" Washington, D.C., November 11, 1975, box 1, folder 29, Marc Stepp Papers, Walter P. Reuther Library, Wayne State University, Detroit.

65. Minchin, *Hiring the Black Worker,* 112, 139, 201, 233; Deslippe, *"Rights, Not Roses,"* 189–90, 192–92; Mary Margaret Fonow, *Union Women: Forging Feminism in the United Steelworkers of America* (Minneapolis: University of Minnesota Press, 2003), 129; "CBTU Replies to Meany," *John Herling Labor Letter* (September 13, 1975), 1; testimony of Charlie Hayes, "Ad Hoc Hearing and Strategy Session on 'Affirmative Action in Employment,'" Washington D.C., November 11, 1975, and typescript, "Full Employment: Our Central Focus," March 22, 1976, both in box 2, folder 27, CBTU Collection; and "Layoffs Based on Seniority Defended by Black Leader," *Detroit News,* May 25, 1975.

66. Quoted in an unidentified press clipping, n.d. [1975], box 14, folder 11. For CLUW's official statement against violating seniority in layoffs, see CLUW *News,* Summer 1975, box 13, folder 1; Olga Madar to Jerry Parish, March 17, 1975, box 14, folder 11; Olga Madar to Karen DeCrow, May 5, 1975, box 14, folder 12, all in CLUW Collection; Catherine Conroy, interview by Elizabeth Balanoff, August 1976, Milwaukee, Wisconsin, Twentieth Century Trade Union Women: Vehicle for Social Change, Oral History Project, Institute of Labor and Industrial Relations, University of Michigan / Wayne State University, Detroit.

67. "Today's Summary and Analysis," *Daily Labor Report* No. 73 (April 15, 1975), box 12, folder: Equal Employment Opportunity Commission / 1, Philip W. Buchen Files, Gerald R. Ford Presidential Library, Ann Arbor, Michigan [hereafter, Buchen Files]; *Watkins v. Steelworkers, Local 2369 and Continental Can Co.,* 369 F. Supp. 1221 (1974), 516 F.2d 41 (1974); typescript, Brief for the Union Defendant, *Watkins v. USW Local 2369,* September 17, 1974, box 24, folder 85, Civil Rights Department Collection; and Holsendolph, "Recession Layoffs," 17.

Chapter 2. *"This Strange Madness"*

1. "Agnew Hits Open Admissions as a 'Strange Madness,'" *Chronicle of Higher Education*, February 24, 1970; and "Text of Vice-President Agnew's Criticism of Lowered Entrance Standards," *Chronicle of Higher Education*, April 20, 1970.

2. "Text of Vice-President Agnew's Criticism."

3. "Admissions Officers Say Agnew May 'Misunderstand' the Process," *Chronicle of Higher Education*, March 23, 1970; William Hamilton Jones, "Educators Respond with Anger, Surprise to Agnew's Attack on Admissions Policies," *Chronicle of Higher Education*, April 27, 1970.

4. J. R. Pole, *The Pursuit of Equality in American History*, 2d ed. (Berkeley: University of California Press, 1993), 476.

5. Historians have only recently begun to address the history of higher education affirmative action. See, for example, Anderson, *Pursuit of Fairness*, 142–46; John D. Skrentny, *The Minority Rights Revolution* (Cambridge: Harvard University Press, 2002), 166–73; Dean Kotlowski, *Nixon's Civil Rights: Politics, Principle, and Policy* (Cambridge: Harvard University Press, 2001), 116–17; and MacLean, *Freedom Is Not Enough*, 185–224.

6. Nicholas Lemann, *The Big Test: The Secret History of the American Meritocracy* (New York: Farrar, Straus, Giroux, 1999), 188.

7. Patterson, *Grand Expectations*, 68–70.

8. John R. Thelin, *A History of American Higher Education* (Baltimore: Johns Hopkins University Press, 2004), 260–316; Lemann, *Big Test*, 70, 85, 102–4, 110, 204, 208; William P. Lapiana, "Merit and Diversity: The Origins of the Law School Admissions Test," *St. Louis University Law Journal* 48 (Spring 2004): 955–89; and Christopher Jencks and David Riesman, *The Academic Revolution* (New York: Doubleday, 1968), 280–86.

9. Lemann, *Big Test*, 134–35; Susan Welch and John Gruhl, *Affirmative Action and Minority Enrollments in Medical and Law Schools* (Ann Arbor: University of Michigan, 1998), 52–53; Lapiana, "Merit and Diversity," 978; and Jencks and Riesman, *Academic Revolution*, 18–19.

10. Marcia Graham Synnott, *The Half-Opened Door: Discrimination and Admissions at Harvard, Yale, and Princeton* (New York: Houghton Mifflin, 2005), 151; Lemann, *Big Test*, 142; and President's Committee on Civil Rights, *"To Secure These Rights": The Report of the President's Committee on Civil Rights* (Washington, D.C., GPO, 1947), 68.

11. Peter Novick, *That Noble Dream: The "Objectivity Question" and the American Historical Profession* (New York: Cambridge University Press, 1988), 69n9, 174n10, 366n7, 172–73, 339.

12. Jencks and Riesman, *Academic Revolution*, 294; Ruth Rosen, *The World Split Open: How the Modern Women's Movement Changed America* (New York: Viking, 2000), 40–43; and Patterson, *Grand Expectations*, 367.

13. Rosen, *World Split Open*, 42; Jencks and Riesman, *Academic Revolution*, 294; Patterson, *Grand Expectations*, 367; Linda K. Kerber, *No Constitutional Right to Be Ladies: Women and the Obligations of Citizenship* (New York: Hill and Wang, 1998), 357n250; and Linda

Eisenmann, *Higher Education for Women in Postwar America, 1945–1965* (Baltimore: Johns Hopkins University Press, 2006), 58, 64.

14. Adam Fairclough, *Better Day Coming: Blacks and Equality, 1890–2000* (New York: Viking, 2001), 45–47, 175; Katznelson, *When Affirmative Action Was White*, 133–34; Thelin, *History of American Higher Education*, 231–32; Howard Ball, *The "Bakke" Case: Race, Education, and Affirmative Action* (Lawrence: University Press of Kansas, 2000), 3; and Christopher J. Lucas, *American Higher Education: A History*, 3d ed. (New York: Palgrave MacMillan, 2006), 261.

15. Patterson, *Grand Expectations*, 386; Welch and Gruhl, *Affirmative Action and Minority Enrollments*, 55–56; *Sweatt v. Painter*, 339 U.S. 629 (1950); *McLaurin v. Oklahoma State Regents for Higher Education*, 339 U.S. 637 (1950); and Kellis E. Parker and Betty J. Stebman, "Legal Education for Blacks," *Annals of American Academy of Politics and Social Sciences* 407 (May 1973): 145, 147.

16. Martin Luther King Jr., "Our God Is Marching On!" (1965) in *A Testament of Hope: The Essential Writings and Speeches of Martin Luther King, Jr.*, ed. James M. Washington (New York: Harper One, 1990), 229.

17. Eisenmann, *Higher Education for Women*, 98, 142, 157, 165–68, 181–209.

18. Education Policies Commission, *Higher Education in a Decade of Decision* (Washington, DC: EPC, 1957), 26–27, 33; and Rockefeller Brothers Fund, *Prospect for America: The Rockefeller Panel Reports* (New York: Doubleday, 1961), 370–73, 381.

19. Edmund W. Gordon and Doxey A. Wilkerson, *Compensatory Education for the Disadvantaged* (New York: College Entrance Examination Board, 1966), 123–33, 138–46. The Williams College plan allowed schools to select up to 10 percent of the incoming freshmen class with applicants having "a flair, a forte, a strength of character" who would not be eligible on the basis of results from standard aptitude tests.

20. Skrentny, *Minority Rights Revolution*, 166–67.

21. Gordon and Wilkerson, *Compensatory Education*, 146; James Alan McPherson, "The Black Student: A Problem of Fidelities," *Atlantic Monthly*, April 1970; and *Steward v. New York University*, 430 F. Supp 1305 (1976).

22. Skrentny, *Minority Rights Resolution*, 169; and Henry K. Beecher and Mark D. Altschule, *Medicine at Harvard: The First Three Hundred Years* (Hanover, NH: University Press of New England, 1977), 475–81.

23. Leslie W. Dunbar, *A Republic of Equals* (Ann Arbor: University of Michigan Press, 1966); Gordon and Wilkerson, *Compensatory Education*, 154; and Ernest Gellhorn, "The Law School and the Negro," *Duke Law Journal* 1968:2 (December 1968): 1091.

24. Walter Berns, "The Assault on the Universities: Then and Now," in *Reassessing the Sixties: Debating the Political and Cultural Legacy*, ed. Stephen Marcelo (New York: Norton, 1997); Skrentny, *Minority Rights Revolution*, 167; Novick, *That Noble Dream*, 475–76; and Walter Goodman, "The Return of the Quota System," *New York Times*, September 10, 1972.

25. Freeman, *Working-Class New York*, 229–33.

26. Ibid.

27. Clipping, Stephen Soloman, "A Jew and a Kenyan Clash over 'Reverse Discrimina-

tion,'" *Philadelphia Inquirer,* October 13, 1974, folder: September–December 1974, box 25, Intergroup Relations and Social Action Department Records, American Jewish Committee Archives and Record Center, New York [hereafter, AJCommittee Intergroup Records]; type-script, "Situation Statements," Wolverine Law Student Association of Wayne State University, July 13, 1970, and memorandum, Charles Joiner to All Wayne State Law School Students, August 25, 1970, box 42, folder 13, both in box 42, folder 13, William Rea Keast Collection, Walter P. Reuther Library, Wayne State University, Detroit; and clipping, "Law Protest Gets Black Readmitted," *Detroit Free Press,* September 1, 1970, box 56, folder 16, Wade H. McCree Jr. Papers, Walter P. Reuther Library, Wayne State University, Detroit.

28. Carnegie Council on Policy Studies in Higher Education, *Making Affirmative Action Work in Higher Education: An Analysis of Institutional and Federal Policies with Recommendations* (San Francisco: Jossey-Bass Publishers, 1975), 55; Graham, *Civil Rights Era,* 282; Freeman, *Working-Class New York,* 200; and Anderson, *Pursuit of Happiness,* 142.

29. Rosalind Rosenberg, "Women in the Humanities: Taking Their Place," in *The Humanities and the Dynamics of Inclusion since World War II,* ed. David A. Hollinger (Baltimore: Johns Hopkins University Press, 2006), 254–58; Carnegie Council, *Making Affirmative Action Work,* 55; Jean King and Mary Yourd to George Schultz, May 27, 1970, box 26, folder: Sex Discrimination at UM, James G. O'Hara Papers, 1958–1987, Michigan Historical Collections, Bentley Historical Library, University of Michigan, Ann Arbor, Michigan [hereafter, O'Hara Papers].

30. Lucy Komisar to Press Representatives, June 15, 1970, and Ann Scott and Lucy Komisar, *"And Justice for All": Federal Equal Employment Efforts against Sex Discrimination,* n.d. [1970], both in carton 18, folder: New Compliance for Affirmative Action, National Organization for Women Papers of Officers, 1967–82 (unprocessed addenda), Schlesinger Library, Harvard University, Cambridge, Massachusetts.

31. Bernice Sandler, "The Day WEAL Opened Pandora's Box," *Chronicle of Higher Education,* January 22, 1973; Carnegie Council, *Making Affirmative Action Work,* 97, 131; MacLean, *Freedom Is Not Enough,* 190; Bernice Resnick Sandler, interviewed by Mimi Alpervin, New York, November 18, 1985, American Jewish Women of Achievement, Dorot Jewish Division, New York Public Library, New York; and Skrentny, "Policy-Elite Perceptions," 1778–81.

32. Carol Hermstatt Shulman, *Affirmative Action: Women's Rights on Campus: ERIC Clearinghouse on Education* (Washington, DC: American Association for Higher Education, 1972), 1; and "Excerpts from U.S. Affirmative Action Guidelines," *Chronicle of Higher Education,* October 10, 1972.

33. Mitchell Bruce Pearlstein, "Selected Jewish Responses to Affirmative Action Admissions: Toward Conceptual Understanding" (PhD diss., University of Minnesota, 1980), 35–39; O'Neil, *Discriminating against Discrimination,* 7; and Peter Kihss, "Moynihan Scores Ethnic Quota Idea," *New York Times,* June 5, 1968.

34. Joshua Michael, "'If I Am Not for Myself . . .': The American Jewish Establishment in the Aftermath of the Six-Day War," *American Jewish History* 88:2 (June 2000): 262; Stuart Svonkin, *Jews against Prejudice: American Jews and the Fight for Civil Liberties* (New York: Columbia University Press, 1997), 6; and Cheryl Lynn Greenberg, *Troubling the Wa-*

ters: Black-Jewish Relations in the American Century (Princeton: Princeton University Press, 2006), 91–92, 95, 108–12, 213.

35. Martha Biondi, *To Stand and Fight: The Struggle for Civil Rights in Postwar New York City* (Cambridge: Harvard University Press, 2003), 108; Kevin M. Schultz, "Religion as Identity in Postwar America: The Last Serious Attempt to Put a Question on Religion in the United States Census," *Journal of American History* 93 (September 2006): 359–84; typescript, "Resolution: Executive Committee Resolutions, 1950–1975," American Jewish Congress Records, American Jewish Historical Society, New York [hereafter, AJCongress Records]; and typescript, "AJC Quotas and the Negro Protest Movement," November 1, 1963, Reel 5, Frame 0002, Bayard Rustin Papers [microfilm] (Bethesda, MD: University Publications of America, 1988).

36. Greenberg, *Troubling the Waters*, 227; Jerald Podair, *The Strike That Changed New York: Blacks, Whites, and the Ocean Hill–Brownsville Crisis* (New Haven: Yale University Press, 2002), 5–6, 15, 65; and Seymour Martin Lipset and Earl Raab, *Jews and the New American Scene* (Cambridge: Harvard University Press, 1995), 156.

37. Richard D. Kahlenberg, *Tough Liberal: Albert Shanker and the Battle over Schools, Unions, Race, and Democracy* (New York: Columbia University Press, 2007), 53, 61, 71, 131, 196, 218, 222; Albert Shanker to John Horwitz, September 9, 1977, box 41, folder 42, American Federation of Teachers President's Office: Albert Shanker Collection, Walter P. Reuther Library, Wayne State University, Detroit; and transcript, Albert Shanker Speech, National Press Club Luncheon, September 24, 1974, Washington, D.C., www.reuther .wayne.edu/node/3998.

38. Freeman, *Working-Class New York*, 231–32; Steven E. Frieder, "Intergroup Relations and Tensions in New York City," in *American Jewish Yearbook: 1970*, vol. 71 (New York: American Jewish Committee / Philadelphia: Jewish Publications Society of America, 1970), 221; Synnott, *Half-Opened Door*, 16; Pearlstein, "Selected Jewish Responses," 186; and Milton Himmelfarb, "Are Jews Still Liberals?" *Commentary* 43:4 (April 1967): 70, 72.

39. Pearlstein, "Selected Jewish Responses," 94, 118; and transcript, Tarrytown Horse Conference on Negro-Jewish Relations, May 25, 1969, box 45, folder: Tarrytown Conference, AJCongress Records.

40. Clipping, Sol Abramowitz, letter to the editor, *Jewish Post*, April 5, 1974, Marco DeFunis Collection, American Jewish Archives, Cincinnati [hereafter, DeFunis Collection]; "Max" to American Jewish Committee, April 19, 1974, box 25, folder: Affirmative Action, January–May 1974, AJCommittee Intergroup Records; and clipping, Jean Herschaft, "2 Jewish Groups Hear from Irate Members," *Jewish Post*, March 8, 1974, DeFunis Collection.

41. Irving Spiegel, "2 Rabbis Assail 'Quota System,'" *New York Times*, March 25, 1973; Ida Joyrich to Earl Marvin, June 17, 1974, container 16, folder: DeFunis v. Odegaard, 1973–75, National Council of Jewish Women, National Office Records: Group II, Library of Congress, Washington, D.C.; and Evelyn Avery to Norman Podhoretz, April 20, 1973, box 25, folder: Affirmative Action, 1973 and Earlier, AJCommittee Intergroup Records.

42. Jerome A. Chaines, "Affirmative Action: Jewish Ideals, Jewish Interests," in *Struggles in the Promised Land: Toward a History of Black-Jewish Relations in the United States,*

ed. Jack Satzman and Cornel West (New York: Oxford University Press, 1997), 299–361; minutes, Executive Committee Meeting, May 12, 1969, box 6, folder: Executive Committee Minutes, 1969, AJCongress Records; typescript, "Chronology of AJC Activities and Statements," September 16, 1972, box 186, folder: Quotas, September 1972, Bertram Gold Papers, American Jewish Committee Archives and Records Center, New York [hereafter, Gold Papers]; typescript, "Position Statement on Compensatory and Preferential Treatment in Education and Employment," October 24, 1969, box 25, folder: Affirmative Action 1973 and Earlier, AJCommittee Intergroup Records; and Benjamin R. Epstein, interviewed by David C. Berliner, July 5, 1973, Politics of American Jews Project, Dorot Jewish Division, New York Public Library, New York.

43. Charles Kadushin, *The American Intellectual Elite* (Boston: Little, Brown, 1974), 30–31; Avital Hadassah Bloch, "The Emergence of Neoconservatism in the United States, 1960–1972" (PhD diss., Columbia University, 1990), 4–19, 256, 269–70, 288–89, 295; Jeane Kirkpatrick, "Neo-Conservatism as a Response to the Counterculture," in *The Neo-Con Reader*, ed. Irwin Stelzer (New York: Grove Press, 2004), 235; Murray Friedman, *The Neoconservative Revolution: Jewish Intellectuals and the Shaping of Public Policy* (New York: Cambridge University Press, 2005), 100–115; and Matthew Berke, "Neoconservatism," in *A Companion of American Thought*, ed. Richard Wrightman Fox and James T. Kloppenberg (Cambridge, MA: Blackwell, 1995), 484–86.

44. Friedman, *Neoconservative Revolution*, 116, 129.

45. "Education, Crisis, Amid the Calm," *Time*, October 8, 1973, www.time.com/time .magazine/article/0,9181,907999,00.html.

46. Sidney Hook, Paul Kurtz, and Miro Todorovich, eds., *The Idea of a Modern University* (Buffalo: Prometheus Books, 1974), xiii–xiv, 18, 228, 233, 241.

47. Paul Seabury, "HEW and the Universities," *Commentary* 53:2 (February 1972): 43; John H. Bunzel, "Liberal in the Middle," in *Political Passages: Journeys of Change Through Two Decades, 1968–1988*, ed. John H. Bunzel (New York: Free Press, 1988), 148, 160; John H. Bunzel, "Affirmative Action in Higher Education: A Dilemma of Conflicting Principles," www.hoover.standford.edu/publications/epp/89/89b.html, accessed November 3, 2004; and O'Neil, *Discriminating against Discrimination*, 137.

48. "Faculty Backlash," *Newsweek*, December 4, 1972; CANI Steering Sub-Committee to "Dear Professor," n.d. [1974–75], box 181, folder 3, Sidney Hook Papers, Hoover Institution Archives, Stanford University, Stanford, California; Daniel Bell, "On Meritocracy and Equality," *Public Interest* 29 (Fall 1972): 38, 65–66; Cheryl M. Fields, "Everybody Criticized," *Chronicle of Higher Education*, September 2, 1975; Miro Todorovich to Robert Goldwin, March 19, 1975, box 5, folder: Higher Education / Affirmative Action 2, David H. Lissy Files / Domestic Council, Gerald R. Ford Presidential Library, Ann Arbor, Michigan [hereafter, Lissy Files].

49. Nathan Glazer, "From Socialism to Sociology," in *Authors of Their Own Lives: Intellectual Autobiographies by Twenty American Sociologists*, ed. Bennett M. Berger (Berkeley: University of California Press, 1990), 194–200; Nathan Glazer, "Negroes and Jews: The New Challenges to Pluralism," *Commentary* 38 (December 1964): 32; and Nathan Glazer, *Affirmative Discrimination: Ethnic Inequality and Public Policy* (New York: Basic Books, 1975), 40, 43, 68–69, 198, 219.

50. Paula England, "Neoclassical Economists' Theories of Discrimination," in *Equal Employment Opportunity*, ed. Burstein, 67–68; "New Horizons for State Snooping," *National Review*, October 17, 1964; Ralph K. Winter Jr., "Improving the Economic Status of Negroes through Laws against Discrimination: A Reply to Professor Sovern," *University of Chicago Law Review* 34:4 (Summer 1967): 854; "This Week," *National Review*, January 12, 1971; and "Black Progress and Liberal Rhetoric," *National Review*, April 27, 1973.

51. Thomas Sowell, *Black Education: Myths and Tragedies* (New York: David McKay, 1972), 38–39, 69–70, 80, 93, 113, 123; and MacLean, *Freedom Is Not Enough*, 241.

52. MacLean, *Freedom Is Not Enough*, 196, 241, 246; Friedman, *Neoconservative Revolution*, 119, 129, 131; and Alice O'Connor, "Financing the Counter-Revolution," in *Rightward Bound: Making America Conservative in the 1970s*, ed. Bruce J. Schulman and Julian E. Zelizer (Cambridge: Harvard University Press, 2008), 152–53, 158–68.

53. Press release, Institute of Human Relations, May 19, 1973, and Samuel Rabinove to Bert Gold, September 5, 1973, both in box 186, folder: Quotas–Affirmative Action, 1973, Gold Papers; Pearlstein, "Selected Jewish Responses," 124; and Walter Goldman, "The Return of the Quota System," *New York Times*, September 10, 1972.

54. Typescript, "Yearly Report on Litigation and Other Legal Proceedings, October 1972–September 1973," n.d. [September 1973], box 29, folder: CLAS, 1973, AJCongress Records; memorandum, Samuel Rabinove to National Legal Committee, February 9, 1972, box 26, folder: DeFunis Case, 1972–74, AJCommittee Intergroup Records; minutes, Commission on Equal Opportunity Meeting, January 15, 1973, box 18, folder: Commission Minutes, 1970, National Jewish Community Relations Advisory Council Records, American Jewish Historical Society, New York [hereafter, Jewish Council Records]; Paul Perlmutter to Seymour Samet, April 6, 1973, box 186, folder: Quotas–Affirmative Action, 1973, Gold Papers; and Seymour Samet to Hyman Bookbinder, March 5, 1973, box 25, folder: Affirmative Action, 1973 and Earlier, AJCommittee Intergroup Records.

55. Clipping, Stephen Solomon, "A Jew and a Kenyan Clash over 'Reverse Discrimination,'" *Philadelphia Inquirer*, October 13, 1974, box 25, folder: September–December 1974, AJCommittee Intergroup Records.

Chapter 3. *"This Issue Is Getting Hotter"*

1. Video, Public Policy Forums [American Enterprise Institute], *Affirmative Action: Answer to Discrimination, May 28, 1975*, Special Media Archives Services Division, National Archives II, College Park, Maryland [hereafter, Public Policy Forum Video (1975)].

2. Ibid.

3. Transcripts, U.S. Commission on Civil Rights Meeting, May 8, 1972, Washington, D.C., box 7, U.S. Commission on Civil Rights Meeting Minutes, 1968–1974, 1977–1979, Record Group 453, National Archives II, College Park, Maryland [hereafter, USCCR Records]; clipping, Jenkins Lloyd Jones, "Affirmative Action," *Washington Star*, September 7, 1974, box 6, folder: Affirmative Action, Patricia Lindh and Jeanne Holm Files / Public Liaison Office, Gerald R. Ford Presidential Library, Ann Arbor, Michigan [hereafter, Lindh and Holm Files]; Sheila K. Johnson, "It's Action, But Is It Affirmative?" *New York Times*, May 11, 1975.

4. Minutes, Commission on Equal Opportunity, January 15, 1973, box 18, folder: Minutes, Commission on Equal Opportunity, 1970, Jewish Council Records; typescript, "Affirmative Action and Quotas on the Local Scene," n.d. [1994], container 16, folder: DeFunis v. Odegaard / 2, National Council of Jewish Women National Office Records, Group II, Library of Congress, Washington, D.C. [hereafter, NCJW National Office Records]; and Edward R. Weidlein, "Affirmative Action Has Little Impact on Faculty Hiring, Study Shows," *Chronicle of Higher Education,* August 27, 1973.

5. *Morgan v. Hennigan,* 379 F.Supp. 463 (1974); "Excerpts from U.S. 'Affirmative Action' Guidelines," *Chronicle of Higher Education,* October 10, 1972; and Robert L. Jacobson, "'Reverse Discrimination' Seen as Danger in Faculty Hiring," *Chronicle of Higher Education,* May 5, 1972.

6. Larry M. Lavinsky, "DeFunis v. Odegaard: The 'Non-Decision' with a Message," *Columbia Law Review* 75:3 (April 1975): 523–24; Sidney Hook, "A Quota Is a Quota Is a Quota," *New York Times,* November 12, 1974; typescript, "Comments: Memorandum to College and University Presidents," January 9, 1974, box 5, folder: Higher Education–Affirmative Action / 1, Lissy Files.

7. Gertrude E. Zorsley, "The Fight over University Women," *New York Review of Books,* May 16, 1974; and Howard Glickstein and Miro Todorovich, "Discrimination in Higher Education: A Debate on Faculty Employment," *Civil Rights Digest* (Spring 1975): 7, 15, 17, 19.

8. Pearlstein, "Selected Jewish Responses," 221; typescript, "Background Memorandum on Group Interest and Individual Rights," n.d. [May 1972], box 186, folder: Quotas, January–August 1972, Gold Papers; typescript, "The Anti-Semitic Aspects of Reverse Discrimination," n.d. [1975], box 46, folder 43, Alexander Bickel Papers, Yale University Library, New Haven [hereafter, Bickel Papers]; and minutes, Executive Committee Meeting, May 12, 1969, box 6, folder: Executive Committee Minutes, 1969, AJCongress Records.

9. Minutes, Commission on Equal Opportunity Meeting, March 27, 1972, box 18, folder: Commission on Equal Opportunity Minutes, 1970, AJCRAC Records; typescript, National Jewish Community Relations Advisory Council, "Position on Affirmative Action," June 1975, box 22, folder: Miscellaneous Background Materials, 1975–78, LCCR / Part I Papers; Goodman, "Return of the Quota System"; and Chaines, "Affirmative Action," 299.

10. Minutes, "Debate on Preferential Treatment," March 16, 1972, box 6, folder: Executive Committee Meetings, 1972, AJCongress Records; and Naomi Levine to S. W. Herell, October 11, 1974, box 29, folder: CLSA & UA, 1973, AJCongress Records.

11. Typescript, "Position Statement on Compensatory and Preferential Treatment in Education and Employment," November 11, 1969, box 41, folder 41, American Federation of Labor–Congress of Industrial Organizations, Department of Legislation Records, George Meany Memorial Archives, Silver Spring, Maryland; and typescript, "Summary: Workshop on Quotas and Preferential Treatment," May 6, 1972, box 186, folder: Quotas, January–August 1972, Gold Papers.

12. Bertram Gold, interviewed by Milton Krents, November 27, 1972, American Jewish Committee Quotas Project, Dorot Jewish Division, New York Public Library, New York; Roger Meltzer to Paul Weinberg and Jules Whitman, December 4, 1974, box 25, folder: September–December 1974, AJCommittee Intergroup Records; Seymour Brief to Samuel

Rabinove, December 7, 1972, and Samuel Rabinove to Seymour Brief, December 19, 1972, both in box 186, folder: October–December 1972, Gold Papers; and minutes, Consultation Meeting, October 25, 1972, box 186, folder: October–December 1972, Gold Papers.

13. Memo, Hyman Bookbinder to Bert Gold, September 14, 1972, box 186, folder: Quotas, September 1972; summary notes, Staff Coordinating Committee, August 29, 1972, box 186, folder: Quotas, January–August 1972; Hyman Bookbinder to Seymour Samet, January 24, 1972, box 186, folder: Quotas, January–August 1972, all in Gold Papers; and David Andelman, "A.J.C. Moves to Back Off from Opposition to Quotas," *New York Times,* September 1, 1972.

14. Seymour Brief to Hyman Bookbinder, June 11, 1974, box 25, folder: June–August 1974, AJCommittee Intergroup Records; Hyman Bookbinder to Samuel Samet, January 8, 1973, box 186, folder: Quotas–Affirmative Action, 1972, Gold Papers; Philip Hoffman, letter to editor, *New York Times,* September 16, 1972; and Philip Hoffman to John Morsel, April 11, 1973, box 186, folder: Quotas–Affirmative Action, 1973, Gold Papers.

15. Typescript, "Resolution on Inquiries," February 12, 1973, and minutes, Executive Committee Meeting, February 12, 1973, both in box 6, folder: Executive Committee Minutes, 1973, AJCongress Records; Irving Spiegel, "Jewish Congress Asks HEW to Destroy Ethnic Questionnaire," *New York Times,* August 2, 1976; Louis Weiser to Gerald Ford, July 15, 1976, box 5, folder: Higher Education–Affirmative Action (5), Lissy Files; and "Racial Survey Is Halted in Coast School District," *New York Times,* October 20, 1976.

16. Mordeca Jane Pollack, "On Academic Quotas," *New York Times,* March 4, 1975; and Carnegie Council, *Making Affirmative Action Work,* 10.

17. Bell, "On Meritocracy and Equality," 37; Sam Rabinove to Seymour Samet, April 15, 1974, box 25, folder: Affirmative Action, January–May 1974, AJCommittee Intergroup Records; Richard Gambino, "The Ethnic Revolution and Public Policy," in *The Idea of a Modern University,* ed. Sidney Hook, Paul Kurtz, and Miro Todorovich (Buffalo: Prometheus Books, 1974), 223.

18. Glickstein and Todorovich, "Discrimination in Higher Education," 14–15; typescript, "Affirmative Action and Quotas on the Local Scene," n.d. [1974], container 16, folder: DeFunis v. Odegaard / 2, NCJW National Office Records; Ray Marshall, "Black Workers in the Unions," in *The World of the Blue-Collar Worker,* ed. Irving Howe (New York: Quadrangle Books, 1972), 260; and Bert Gold to Elmer Winter, n.d. [1977], box 30, folder: Quotas, Goals, Timetables, 1977, Domestic Affairs and Legal Department Records, American Jewish Committee Library, New York.

19. Michael Harrington, *The Other America: Poverty in the United States* (New York: Macmillan, 1962), 18; Mario D. Fantini and Gerald Weinstein, *The Disadvantaged: Challenge to Education* (New York: Harper Row, 1968), 5; Gordon and Wilkerson, *Compensatory Education,* 1–2, 138; and Christopher Jencks and David Riesman, *The Academic Revolution* (New York: Doubleday, 1968), 143, 147.

20. Micaela di Leonardo, *The Varieties of Ethnic Experience: Kinship, Class, and Gender among California Italian-Americans* (Ithaca: Cornell University Press, 1984), 130; Schulman, *The Seventies,* 80–84; Matthew Frye Jacobsen, *Roots Too: White Ethnic Revival in Post–Civil Rights America* (Cambridge: Harvard University Press, 2006), 7, 8–9; Jonathan Rieder, *Canarsie: The Jews and Italians of Brooklyn against Liberalism* (Cambridge: Harvard

University Press, 1985), 118; and Dennis Deslippe, "'We Must Bring Together a New Coalition': The Challenge of Working-Class White Ethnics to Color-Blind Conservatism in the 1970s," *International Labor and Working-Class History* 74 (Fall 2008): 149–52.

21. Barbara Mikulski, "Who Speaks for Ethnic America?" *New York Times,* September 28, 1970; Nathan Glazer, *Affirmative Discrimination: Ethnic Inequality and Public Policy* (New York: Basic Books, 1975), 233n6; Francis X. Clives, "20 Other Italian Groups Meet with State Rights Chief in Complaints of Bias," *New York Times,* June 26, 1971; Diane Henry, "A Survey of Italian-Americans Finds Government Is Ignoring Their Needs," *New York Times,* February 6, 1975; Skrentny, "Policy-Elite Perceptions," 1785; and Andrew M. Greeley, *Why Can't They Be Like Us? America's White Ethnic Groups* (New York: E. P. Dutton, 1971), 156.

22. Walter H. Waggoner, "A White N.A.A.C.P. Set Up in Newark," *New York Times,* May 4, 1973; Richard Servo, "Italian-Americans Here Unite to Fight 'Reverse' Bias," *New York Times,* June 28, 1974; and "Racial Slurs No Longer Laughing Matter," *Italian Tribune* (Newark, NJ), April 4, 1970, Newspaper Collection, Historical Society of Pennsylvania, Philadelphia, Pennsylvania.

23. MacLean, *Freedom Is Not Enough,* 244; and Skrentny, "Policy-Elite Perceptions," 1785.

24. Skrentny, "Policy-Elite Perceptions," 1783, 1785, 1795–96, 1799; and *Federal Register* 36:250 (December 29, 1971): 25, 165.

25. Servo, "Italian-Americans Here Unite"; clipping, "Admission Demanded by Same Standards for Blacks, Indians," *St. Paul Dispatch,* May 2, 1970, box 26, folder: DeFunis Case, 1972–1974, AJCommittee Intergroup Records; *DiLeo v. University of Colorado et al.,* 196 Colo. 216 (1978); 441 U.S. 927 (1979) [cert. denied]; press release, "Coalition Report / News of Italian American Achievement," August 1975, box 30, folder: Employment, National Center for Urban Ethnic Affairs Collection, Special Collection, University of Notre Dame Library, South Bend, Indiana; Aloysius Mazewski to the President, April 7, 1980, box 1, folder: Affirmative Action 2/80–10/80, Records of the Office of the Special Assistant for Ethnic Affairs, Stephen Aiellos Subject Files, 1980–81, Jimmy Carter Presidential Library, Atlanta.

26. Samuel Rabinove to Bert Gold, February 17, 1972, box 186, folder: Quotas, January–August 1972, Gold Papers; Seymour Samet, interviewed by Milton Krents, November 22, 1973, New York, American Jewish Committee Quotas Project, Dorot Jewish Division, New York Public Library, New York; clipping, Samuel Rabinove, "Law School Minorities: What Price Admission?" *America,* April 28, 1973, box 26, folder; DeFunis Case, 1972–74, AJCommittee Intergroup Records; minutes, Commission on Equal Opportunity Meeting, March 27, 1972, box 18, folder: Commission Minutes, 1970–, AJCRAC Records; Seymour Samet to Brant Coopersmith, April 10, 1973, box 186, folder: Quotas–Affirmative Action, 1973, Gold Papers; and Ronald Sullivan, "Jews Designated as Official Minority," *New York Times,* October 27, 1975.

27. Bert Silver to William Raspberry, March 18, 1974, box 268, folder: Affirmative Action, Miscellany (February–October 1974), NCJW–National Office Records; Larry M. Lavinsky, "*DeFunis v. Odegaard:* The 'Non-Decision' with a Message," *Columbia Law Review* 75:3 (April 1975): 527; and typescript, "Background Memorandum on Group Interests and

Individual Rights," n.d. [May 1972], box 186, folder: Quotas (January–August 1976), Gold Papers.

28. Gambino, "Ethnic Revolution," 208; Glazer, *Affirmative Discrimination*, 187; and Public Policy Forum Video (1975).

29. "Guidelines on Discrimination Because of Religion or National Origins," 41 CFR 60–50, 401: 243–245 (1973); Skrentny, "Policy-Elite Perceptions," 1785–87; James G. Driscoll, " 'Reverse Discrimination' Means . . . Scram White Man," *National Observer*, July 13, 1974; Charlayne Hunter, "Job Rights Gain Called Imperiled," *New York Times*, December 1, 1975; *DeFunis v. Odegaard*, 416 U.S. 312 (1974); and *Regents of the University of California v. Bakke*, 438 U.S. 265 (1978).

30. *DiLeo v. University of Colorado et al.*, 196 Colo. 216 (1978); John Peterson, "U-M Creates Two Admissions Policies," *Detroit News*, June 26, 1973; John C. Jeffries Jr., *Justice Lewis F. Powell, Jr.* (New York: Charles Scribners Sons, 1994), 472–73; Skrentny, "Policy-Elite Perceptions," 1795; and Ernest van den Haag, "Reverse Discrimination: A Brief against It," *National Review*, April 29, 1977.

31. Lester Jackson to Jimmy Carter, May 16, 1976, box 33, folder: Correspondence "Not Sent," Sam Bleicher's Subject Files, 1976, Jimmy Carter Library, Atlanta; James D. Anderson, "Race in American Higher Education: Historical Perspectives on Current Conditions," in *The Racial Crisis in American Higher Education: Continuing Challenges for the Twenty-First Century*, ed. William A. Smith, Philip G. Altbach, and Kofi Lomotey (Albany: SUNY Press, 2002), 11; testimony of James Hester, *Hearings before the Special Subcommittee on Education of the Committee on Education and Labor, House of Representatives*, 93rd Cong., 2nd Sess., Part 2/A, August 8, 1974 (Washington, DC: GPO, 1975), 113; and Morris Sherer et al. to Samuel Soloman, March 8, 1973, box 46, folder 43, Bickel Papers.

32. O'Neil, *Discriminating against Discrimination*, 124, 151.

33. Carnegie Council, *Making Affirmative Action Work*, 25; Johnson, "It's Action, But Is It Affirmative?"; press release, National Urban League, "Jordan Charges Quota Issue Designed to Split Labor–Civil Rights Alliance," September 19, 1972, container 114, folder: Congressional Black Caucus / Affirmative Action, Leadership Conference on Civil Rights Papers / Part I, Library of Congress, Washington, D.C. [hereafter, LCCR / Part I Papers]. Some Hispanics believed that African Americans were already monopolizing government equal opportunity programs. In California, for example, several Mexican Americans filed federal lawsuits charging state-run colleges with favoring blacks over them in employment and education programs. See *Crafts v. Board of Governors of California Colleges*, Civil No. 75-337 (N.D. Cal., filed February 18, 1975).

34. Transcript, CBS Evening News, April 18, 1976, box 12, folder: EEOC (3), Buchen Files; Johnson, "It's Action, But Is It Affirmative?"; Cheryl M. Fields, "Affirmative Action, 4 Years After," *Chronicle of Higher Education*, August 5, 1974; Harold Orlans, "Affirmative Action and Higher Education," *Annals of the American Academy of Political and Social Sciences* 523 (September 1992): 151; Leta Johnson to Andrew Young, October 15, 1975, box 152, folder: 8/4/75–3/31/75, White House Central Files–Subject Files, Gerald R. Ford Presidential Library, Ann Arbor, Michigan [hereafter, White House Central Files]; and transcript, U.S. Commission on Civil Rights Meeting, Washington, D.C., December 12, 1972, box 9, USCCR Records.

35. Joseph A. King, "Affirmative Action Gone Wild," *America*, April 17, 1976; Paul Seabury, "HEW and the Universities," *Commentary* 53:2 (February 1972): 38; minutes, Executive Committee Meeting, January 8, 1973, box 6, folder: Executive Committee Minutes, 1973, American Jewish Congress Records, American Jewish Historical Society, New York [hereafter, AJCongress Records]; and Revel Shinnar to James Schever, May 5, 1975, box 26, folder: Hearings, O'Hara Papers.

36. Thomas Sowell to Robert Goldwin, August 9, 1975, box 5, folder: Higher Education—Affirmative Action (3), Lissy Files; Thomas Sowell, *Affirmative Action Reconsidered: Was it Necessary in Academia?* (Washington, DC: American Enterprise Institute, 1975), 28, 32, 36.

37. Nathan Glazer, "Leaning Over Backwards," *New York Times*, March 12, 1972; transcripts, U.S. Commission on Civil Rights Meeting, August 29, 1972, Washington, D.C., box 7, USCCR Records; and clipping, Nathan Lewin, "Which Man's Burden?" *New Republic*, May 14, 1974.

38. Bernice Sandler, "Is 'Affirmative Action' Penalizing Males?" *Chronicle of Higher Education*, May 14, 1973; John E. Peterson, "U-M Law Dean Defends 'Dual Admissions' Policy," *Detroit News*, June 28, 1973; and Tom Wicker, "The Real Reverse of Racism," *New York Times*, January 19, 1975.

39. "HEW Probing Reverse Bias in Colleges," *Washington Post*, November 22, 1972; "Goals, Quotas?" *AAAA Newsletter* 2:2 (March 15, 1976): 5 and "Reverse Discrimination," *AAAA Newsletter* 2:1 (February 1, 1976): 6, both in box 30, folder: American Association for Affirmative Action, Lindh and Holm Files; Sandler, "Is 'Affirmative Action' Penalizing Males?" 4; and typescript, Statement of Joseph Rauh, Jr., *"Ad Hoc" Hearings and Strategy Session on Affirmative Action*, November 11, 1975, box 127, folder: Employment subcommittee, LCCR / Part I Papers.

40. Rose Laub Coser, "Affirmative Action: Letter to a Worried Colleague," *Dissent* 22 (Fall 1975): 368; Glickstein and Todorovich, "Discrimination in Higher Education," 15; typescript, Statement of Howard Glickstein, *"Ad Hoc" Hearings and Strategy Session on Affirmative Action, November 11, 1975*, box 127, folder; Employment Subcommittee, LCCR / Part I Papers; O'Neil, *Discriminating against Discrimination*, 140.

41. Hyman Bookbinder to Seymour Samet, August 30, 1973, box 186, folder: Quotas—Affirmative Action, 1973, Gold Papers.

42. "Democrats: The Long Journey to Disaster," *Time*, November 20, 1972, www.time.com/time/magazine/article/0,9171,712186,00.html; Kotlowski, *Nixon's Civil Rights*, 40–42, 117; Natalie Flatow to Bert Gold, September 26, 1972, box 186, folder: Quotas, September 1972, Gold Papers; Andelman, "A.J.C. Moves"; Bertram Gold, interviewed by Milton E. Krents, New York, December 27, 1972, American Jewish Committee Quota Project, Dorot Jewish Division, New York Public Library, New York.

43. Theodore White, *The Making of the President, 1972* (New York: Atheneum Publishers, 1973), 24–33; John Herbers, "Is the Cure Worse than the Disease?" *New York Times*, September 10, 1972; and "God May Be a Democrat: But the Vote Is for Nixon," *Time*, October 30, 1972, www.time.com/time/magazine/article/0,9171,906627,00.html; and Andelman, "A.J.C. Moves to Back Off," 6.

44. Anderson, *Pursuit of Fairness*, 137; Joe McGinniss, "Second Thoughts of George

McGovern," *New York Times,* May, 6, 1973; "The Quota Controversy," *New Republic,* October 21, 1972; and Kotlowski, *Nixon's Civil Rights Politics,* 114–15.

45. Jim Sullivan to Al Ullman, September 25, 1974, box 26, folder: Hearings, O'Hara Papers; Statement of Robert W. Fleming, *Hearings before the Special Subcommittee* (1974), 94–95; William J. McGill, "The New Tensions on Campus," *Life,* October 8, 1971. HEW countered that Columbia University had failed to meet several deadlines, the first of which was set two years earlier. See John Herbers, "Columbia Warned on Hiring Policies," *New York Times,* November 5, 1971.

46. Bert Gold to Raul Hilberg, October 16, 1972, box 186, folder: Quotas, October–December 1972, Gold Papers; Statement of Robert W. Fleming, *Hearings before the Special Subcommittee* (1974), 111; minutes, Executive Committee Meeting, January 8, 1973, box 6, folder: Executive Committee Minutes, 1973, AJCongress Records; and minutes, Commission on Equal Opportunity Meeting, January 15, 1973, box 18, folder: Commission on Equal Opportunity Minutes 1970–, AJCRAC Records.

47. Robert L. Jacobson, "'Reverse Discrimination' Seen as Danger," 3; typescript, Malcom J. Sherman, "Affirmative Action and the AAUP," n.d. [December 1975], box 26, folder: Reverse Discrimination, O'Hara Papers.

48. Hyman Bookbinder to Alfred Moses, August 9, 1973, box 186, folder: Quotas / Affirmative Action, 1973, Gold Papers; and Samuel Rabinove to Miro Todorovich, May 1, 1973 and Earlier, AJCommittee Intergroup Records.

49. Typescript, "Preferential Treatment and Other Improper Procedures in Admissions and Employment at Colleges and Universities: Illustrative Instances," August 8, 1972, box 46, folder 43, Bickel Papers; memorandum, Seymour Samet to Area Directors, November 13, 1972, box 186, folder: Quotas, October–December 1972, Gold Papers; and Morris Sherer et al. to J. Stanley Pottinger, December 20, 1972, box 46, folder 43, Gold Papers.

50. Typescript, "Preferential Treatment and Other Improper Procedures in Admissions and Employment at Colleges and Universities: Illustrative Complaints (Second Compilation)," December 20, 1972; typescript, "Preferential Treatment and Other Improper Procedures in Admissions and Employment at Colleges and Universities: Illustrative Complaints (Third Compilation)," March 28, 1973; and typescript, "Preferential Treatment and Other Improper Procedures in Admissions and Employment at Colleges and Universities (Fourth Compilation)," July, 18, 1973, all in box 46, folder 43, Bickel Papers.

51. Samuel Solomon to David Brody, January 8, 1973; Samuel Solomon to David Brody, October 15, 1973; and Samuel Solomon to David Brody, April 9, 1973, all in box 46, folder 43, Bickel Papers.

52. Samuel Solomon to David Brody, March 9, 1973, and Samuel Solomon to David Brody, April 10, 1973; both in box 46, folder 43, Bickel Papers.

53. Morris Sherer et al. to Samuel Solomon, March 8, 1973, and typescript, "Analysis of Sam Solomon Letter of October 15, 1973," n.d. [October 1973], both in box 46, folder 43, Bickel Papers.

54. Robert Hampton to Hyman Bookbinder, August 30, 1972, container 114, folder: Congressional Black Caucus / Affirmative Action, LCCR / Part I Papers; and transcript, Meeting minutes, October 10, 1972, box 7, USCCR Records.

55. Memorandum, Naomi Levine to Executive Committee, October 20, 1972, box 6,

folder: Executive Committee Agenda and Memoranda, 1950–1980, AJCongress Records; and Alfred Moses to Hyman Bookbinder, August 6, 1973, box 186, folder: Quotas—Affirmative Action, 1973, Gold Papers.

56. Transcript, Telephone Conversation, October 2, 1972, box 133, folder: Telecons—October 1–5, 1972, Elliot L. Richardson Papers; Bert Gold to Gene DeBow, January 22, 1973, box 186, folder: Quotas—Affirmative Action, 1973; clipping, Roy Wilkins, "The Case against Quotas," *Washington Post*, March 3, 1973; Samet interview, AJCommittee Quotas Project; and Philip Perlmutter to Samuel Samet, April 6, 1973, all in box 186, folder: Quotas—Affirmative Action, 1973, Gold Papers.

57. Hyman Bookbinder to Bert Gold, September 14, 1972, box 186, folder: Quotas, September 1972, Gold Papers.

Chapter 4. "Treat Him as a Decent American!"

1. Application Statement, June 18, 1970, and Application Statement: Question 11, n.d. [1971], both in folder: DeFunis v. Odegaard I, box 8, Records of University of Washington Law School Dean, University of Washington Libraries, Seattle [hereafter, Law Dean Records]; and Answers to Interrogatories, n.d. [September 1971], *DeFunis versus Odegaard and the University of Washington: The Records*, vol. 1, ed. Ann Fagan Ginger (Dobbs Ferry, NY: Oceana Publisher, 1974), 21–48 [hereafter, *DeFunis Record*].

2. Mrs. Marco DeFunis to Admissions Board, May 24, 1971, box 8, folder: DeFunis v. Odegaard I, Law Dean Records; DeFunis v. Odegaard, Finding of Fact and Conclusions of Law, October 18, 1971, *DeFunis Record*, 1:121–29; *DeFunis v. Odegaard*, 82 Wn. 2d 11 (1973), 507 P .2d 1169 (1973), 416 U.S. 312 (1974); and *Regents of the University of California v. Bakke*, 438 U.S. 265 (1978).

3. Memorandum, DeFunis v. Odegaard, No. 73-235, box 186, folder: DeFunis v. Odegaard (2 of 2), Harry A. Blackmun Papers, Library of Congress, Washington, D.C. [hereafter, Blackmun Papers]; typescript, minutes, American Jewish Committee Board of Governors Meeting, December 3, 1973, box 26, folder: DeFunis Case, 1972–74, AJCommittee Intergroup Records; and Iver Peterson, "Time to Decide If Whites Are Victimized," *New York Times*, November 25, 1973.

4. Nina Totenberg, "Discriminating to End Discrimination," *New York Times*, April 14, 1974.

5. Excerpts from Oral Arguments, February 26, 1974, *DeFunis Record*, 3:1330.

6. Lemann, *Big Test*, 204–8; and Marcia Graham Synnott, *The Half-Opened Door: Discrimination at Harvard, Yale, and Princeton, 1900–1970* (Westport, CT: Greenwood Press, 1979).

7. "Wanted: Prestige," *Time*, February 24, 1958, www.time.com/time/magazine/article/0,9171,863029,00.html; Judi Hunt, "Former UW President Charles Odegaard, 88, Dies," *Seattle Post-Intelligencer*, November 17, 1999, www.seattlepi.com/local/obit171.shtml; and "Odegaard: In the Hot Seat at the UW," *Seattle Post-Intelligencer*, December 10, 1999 [www.seattlepi.com/century/cent10.shtml].

8. Memorandum, "Equal Opportunity," February 3, 1959, box 41, folder: Committee on Discrimination, 1958–59, Records of the President: Charles Odegaard, University of

Washington Libraries, Seattle [hereafter, President's Office Records]; Excerpts, Trail Transcripts, September 14, 1971, *DeFunis Record*, 1:79; and clipping, "President Odegaard Reviews Minority Recruitment Efforts," *University of Washington Daily*, October 30, 1968, box 69, folder: Minority Recruitment, 1968, President's Office Records.

9. McPherson, "Black Law Student," 93; Brief of the National Conference of Black Lawyers, n.d. [1974], *DeFunis Record*, 3:1230–31; Brief of the Lawyers' Committee for Civil Rights Under Law, *DeFunis Record*, 3:991; clipping, "Reverse Discrimination," *Time*, October 11, 1971, box 37, folder: DeFunis v. Odegaard, Vice President for Minority Affairs Records, University of Washington Libraries, Seattle [hereafter, VP Records].

10. McPherson, "Black Law Student," 92; Kellis E. Parker and Betty J. Stebman, "Legal Education for Blacks," *Annals of the American Academy of Politics and Social Science* 407 (May 1973): 148; and excerpts, trial transcripts, September 14, 1971, *DeFunis Record*, 1:58, 68, 77–8.

11. Excerpts, trial transcripts, September 14, 1971, *DeFunis Record*, 1:57, 106, 109–10.

12. Ibid., 1:16–17, 69, 109–10.

13. Answers to interrogatives, n.d. [September 1971], *DeFunis Record*, 1:24–25. The PFYA weighting was GPA (x 3.4751), LSAT (x .0159), and writing score (x .0456).

14. Ibid., 1:32–34.

15. Complaint for Mandamus, n.d. [August 1971]; Form B: Statement of Dean of Students of Comparable College Official, 1-19–70, box 8, folder: DeFunis v. Odegaard I, Law Dean Records; Form C: Statement of College Faculty Member, January 12, 1970; Form C: Statement of College Faculty Member, February 9, 1971; and excerpts, trial transcripts, September 14, 1971, all in *DeFunis Record*, 1:4, 84.

16. Craig Steinberg to Robert Hunt, June 5, 1971, box 8, folder: DeFunis v. Odegaard I, Law Dean Records; Answers to Interrogatories, n.d. [September 1971] and excerpts, trial transcripts, both in *DeFunis Record*, 1:34, 61; and O'Neil, *Discriminating against Discrimination*, 11.

17. Complaint for Mandamus Injunction and Damages, n.d. [August 1971], *DeFunis Record*, 1:4, 6, 8; and memorandum, Richard Roddis to Faculty/Staff, August 20, 1971, box 8, folder: DeFunis v. Odegaard I, Law Dean Records.

18. Excerpts, Trial Transcripts, *DeFunis Record*, 1:57.

19. Oral Decision, DeFunis v. Odegaard, September 22, 1971, *DeFunis Record*, 1:115–116.

20. Clipping, "Reverse Discrimination," *Time*, October 11, 1971,; clipping, "Student Wins Law School Entry Case," *Seattle Post-Intelligencer*, September 23, 1971; Editorial, "DeFunis Case," *University of Washington Daily*, September 29, 1971; Press Release: Statement by Charles Odegaard, University of Washing Information Services, September 24, 1971; clipping, Jim Gill, "Minority Law Students Decry DeFunis Decision," *University of Washington Daily*, n.d. [September 1971]; clipping, "UW Panel Urges No Action in Race Case," *Seattle Post-Intelligencer*, September 28, 1971, all in box 37, folder: DeFunis v. Odegaard, VP Records; David Balint, "In Memoriam: Marco DeFunis," June 21, 2006, www.balinlaw.com/serendipity/index.php?/archives/56-In-Memoriam.MarcoDeFunis.html; and Totenberg, "Discriminating to End Discrimination."

21. Arval Morris to Murray Schwartz, October 8, 1971, box 8, folder: DeFunis v. Odegaard I, Law Dean Records; *DeFunis v. Odegaard*, 82 Wn. 2d at 27, 507 P .2d at 1179.

In his concurring opinion, Justice Wright agreed with Neill's findings but noted "the desirability of more complete published standards for admission. The publication of such standards would insure not only the complete fairness of the process, but also the appearance of fairness." [Id. at 45, 507 P .2d at 1189]

22. Id. at 68, 507 P .2d at 1201; and clipping, Wanda Adams, "University Wins DeFunis Case in 7-2 Decision," *University of Washington Daily*, March 9, 1973, box 37, folder: DeFunis v. Odegaard, VP Records.

23. Lee Epstein et al., *The Supreme Court Compendium: Data, Decisions, and Developments*, 3d ed. (Washington, D.C.: Congressional Quarterly Press, 2003), 70, 228–29. They received requests to hear 2,308 paid cases and 2,348 *in forma pauperis* cases in 1974, of which they agreed to grant review of 235 and 28, respectively. Only 157 eventually received oral argument docket numbers. In 2001 the figure was 2,210 paid cases and 6,985 *in forma pauperis*; the Court accepted 82 and 6, respectively.

24. *Swann v. Charlotte-Mecklenburg*, 402 U.S. 1 (1971); *Griggs v. Duke Power*, 401 U.S. 424 (1971); and Keck, *Most Activist Supreme Court in History*, 108–9.

25. Cert. memorandum, Johnson v. Committee on Examinations, 71-1362, June 6, 1972, box 1535, folder: Cert. memoranda 71-1351 to 1462, William O. Douglas Papers, Library of Congress, Washington, D.C. [hereafter, Douglas Papers]; John C. Jeffries, *Justice Lewis F. Powell* (New York: Charles Scribner's Sons, 1994), 469; Teles, *Rise of the Conservative Movement*, 61–62; Mark Tushnet, *A Court Divided: The Rehnquist Court and the Future of Constitutional Law* (New York: W.W. Norton, 2005), 22–23, 27, 42; and Order of Douglas, as Circuit Judge, June 5, 1973, *DeFunis Record*, 1:201.

26. Pierce O'Donnell, Preliminary Memorandum, DeFunis v. Odegaard, October 19, 1973, and Jack B. Owens, Supplemental Memorandum, DeFunis v. Odegaard, October 12, 1973, both in box 162, folder: 17, Lewis F. Powell, Jr. Papers, Lewis F. Powell, Jr. Archives, Washington and Lee University Law School, Lexington, Virginia.

27. Jurisdictional Statement, or In the Alternative Petition for Certiorari, n.d. [1973] and Motion of Dismissal, n.d. [1973], both in *DeFunis Record*, 1:224–25, 261, 263, 279.

28. Appellees-Respondents' Memorandum on the Question of Mootness, October 31, 1973, and Petitioners' Memorandum on Mootness, n.d. [October 1973], both in *DeFunis Record*, 1:287, 299–302.

29. *DeFunis v. Odegaard*, 414 U.S. 1038 (November 19, 1973).

30. Gregory A. Caldeira and John R. Wright, "*Amici Curiae* before the Supreme Court: Who Participates, When, and How Much?" *Journal of Politics* 52 (August 1990): 782–806; Gregory A. Caldeira and John R. Wright, "Organized Interests and Agenda Setting in the U.S. Supreme Court," *American Political Science Review* 82 (December 1988): 1109–27; Donald R. Songer and Reginald S. Sheehan, "Interest Group Success in the Courts: *Amicus* Participation in the Supreme Court," *Political Science Research Quarterly* 46 (June 1993): 339–54; *Miranda v. Arizona* 384 U.S. 436 (1966); *Griswold v. Connecticut*, 381 U.S. 479 (1965); and *Roe v. Wade* 410 U.S. 113 (1973).

All *amici curiarum* briefs are in the Ginger volume. For a discussion of the role of the NAACP and the ACLU in filing briefs, see Lucas A. Powe, *The Warren Court and American Politics* (Cambridge: Harvard University Press, 2000), 22–23, 31, 196, 398, 431; and Kerber, *No Constitutional Right*, 169, 189–90, 194–97, 199.

31. Brief of the AFL-CIO, January 1974, *DeFunis Record*, 2:515, 522–23; and A. L. Zwerdling and Janet Kohr to Jerry Wurf, February 6, 1974, box 1, folder: 1, American Federation of State, County, and Municipal Employees Program Development Records, Walter P. Reuther Archives of Labor and Urban Affairs, Wayne State University, Detroit.

32. Totenberg, "Discriminating to End Discrimination"; clipping, Jean Herschaft, "NAACP Officials View on DeFunis Causing Rift with Blacks Accepted," *Jewish Post*, April 12, 1974, Marco DeFunis Collection, American Jewish Archives, Cincinnati [hereafter, DeFunis Collection]; Brief of the Advocate Society et al., n.d. [1974], *DeFunis Record*, 1:422.

33. Obituary, "Philip B. Kurland, 74, Scholar Who Ruled on Nixon Tapes," *New York Times*, April 18, 1999; Laura Kalman, "The Dark Ages," in *History of the Yale Law School: The Tercentennial Lectures*, ed. Anthony T. Kronman (New Haven: Yale University Press, 2004), 162, 164–67; Marilyn Gittell, "The Illusion of Affirmative Action," *Change* (October 1975): 39; and Alexander M. Bickel, *The Morality of Consent* (New Haven: Yale University Press, 1975), 140, 142. My thanks to Professor Kalman for clarifying this notion of "hoarding prestige." Personal e-mail correspondence, June 21, 2010.

34. Keck, *Most Activist Supreme Court*, 146. See also Laura Kalman, *The Strange Career of Legal Liberalism* (New Haven: Yale University Press, 1996), 29, 214–15, 225, 232–33; Powe, *Warren Court*, 43, 72, 513, 529.

35. Brief of the Anti-Defamation League of B'nai B'rith, n.d. [1974], *DeFunis Record*, 1:485.

36. Hyman Bookbinder to Bert Gold, January 25, 1974, box 25, folder: Affirmative Action: January–May 1974, AJCommittee Intergroup Records.

37. Typescript, minutes, American Jewish Committee Board of Governors' Meeting, December 3, 1973, box 26, folder: DeFunis Case, 1972–74, AJCommittee Intergroup Records.

38. Brief of the Advocate Society et al., n.d. [1974], *DeFunis Record*, 1:422–23, 435, 446; Samuel Rabinove to Arnold Gardner, May 21, 1974, box 25, folder: Affirmative Action: January–May 1974, AJCommittee Intergroup Relations. Seventy-one percent of whites passed the examination; see Brief of the Advocate Society et al., n.d. [1974], *DeFunis Record*, 1:436.

39. Transcript, Interview with Carl G. Koch, by Howard Droker, Seattle, Washington, August 19 and 28, 1981, University of Washington Libraries, p. 48, Carl G. Koch Papers, University of Washington Library Special Collections, Seattle; Seymour Samet to Peter Schnurman, December 14, 1971, box 1, folder: Membership Meeting, December 2, 1971, American Jewish Committee Seattle Chapter Records, University of Washington Library Special Collections, Seattle; Samuel Rabinove to Gene Brandzel, January 20, 1973, and memorandum, Samuel Rabinove to Area Directors, May 1, 1973, both in box 26, folder: DeFunis Case, 1972–74, AJCommittee Intergroup Records.

40. Emil Lackow to Ladies and Gentlemen, May 25, 1974, box 8, folder: DeFunis v. Odegaard IV, Law Dean Records; Walter Higgins to Richard Roddis, September 16, 1971, box 8, folder: DeFunis v. Odegaard I, Law Dean Records; "Review & Outlook: Judging Racial Quotas," *Wall Street Journal*, March 11, 1974; Lavinsky, "*DeFunis v. Odegaard*," 523; clipping, Nicholas von Hoffman, "Justice, Injustice," *Washington Post*, May 3, 1974, box 37, folder:

DeFunis v. Odegaard, VP Records; and clipping, "From the Rabbi: *Temple Topics* (Progressive Shaari Zedek Synagogue)," March 11, 1974, DeFunis Collection.

41. Brief of the Jewish Rights Council, n.d. [1974] and Brief of the Anti-Defamation League of B'Nai B'rith, n.d. [1974], both in *DeFunis Record*, 1:452–53, 251–52; and Lemann, *Big Test*, 204.

42. Brief of the National Council of Jewish Women et al., n.d. [1974], *DeFunis Record*, 3:1107; Michael E. Staub, *Torn at the Roots: The Crisis of Jewish Liberalism in Postwar America* (New York: Columbia University Press, 2002), 57, 80–82; clipping, "From the Rabbi," *Temple Topics* (Progressive Shaari Zedek Synagogue), March 11, 1974, DeFunis Collection; clipping, Wayne Dosick, Letter to Editor, *Jewish Post and Opinion*, April 1, 1974; I. B. Koller to unknown, April 16, 1974; clipping, Jean Herschaft, "NAACP Officials View on DeFunis Causing Rift with Blacks Accepted," *Jewish Post*, April 12, 1974; Herman Schottenfels to Alexander Schindler, March 1, 1974; and clipping, "2 Rabbinical Bodies Differ on DeFunis," *Jewish Post and Opinion*, April 26, 1974, all in DeFunis Collection.

43. June Slutsky to Eleanor Marvin, April 3, 1974; Myrna Broadman to Eleanor Marvin, March 26, 1974; and Nina Green to Mrs. Eleanor Marvin, April 1, 1974, all in container 16, folder: DeFunis v. Odegaard 2, NCJW National Office Records; Mrs. Sidney Gold to Ladies, January 1, 1975, folder: DeFunis v. Odegaard, 1973–75, NCJW National Office Records; Mrs. E. Miller to NCJW, March 10, 1974, Container 16, folder: DeFunis v. Odegaard 2, NCJW National Office Records; Jacob Petuchowski to Mrs. Edward Rosenthal, March 11, 1974, DeFunis Collection; Lillian Glantz to Mrs. Stanley P. Morse, April 8, 1974; Joyce Wolfberg to Eleanor Marvin, March 25, 1974; Sydell Yegelmel to Mrs. Earl Marvin, March 29, 1974, all in container 16, folder: DeFunis v. Odegaard, NCJW National Office Records; and Sonia Crane to Mrs. Earl Marvin, May 30, 1974, Container 16, folder: Defunis v. Odegaard, 1973–75, NCJW National Office Records.

44. Concerned Jewish Women to Eleanor Marvin, March 11, 1974; Natalie Morrison to Eleanor Marvin, March 24, 1974; and Jerome Greenblatt to Ladies, March 1, 1974, Container 16, folder: DeFunis v. Odegaard 2; Rose Lample to Rochelle Cantz, May 7, 1974, DeFunis v. Odegaard, 1973–75, container 16; Louis Bernstein to Eleanor Marvin, March 16, 1974, container 16, folder: DeFunis v. Odegaard 2, NCJW National Office Records; Mariann Springer and Jan Benson to Eleanor Marvin, March 13, 1974, NCJW National Office Records.

45. Clipping, "2 Jewish Groups Hear From Irate Members," *Jewish Post-Intelligencer,* March 8, 1974, DeFunis Collection; memorandum, Eleanor Marvin to Section Presidents and National Affairs Committee, February 26, 1974, box 268, folder: Affirmative Action Miscellany, National Council of Jewish Women, Washington Office Records, Library of Congress, Washington, D.C. [hereafter, NCJW Washington Collection]; and Eleanor Marvin to Barbara Leslie, May 24, 1974, Container 16, folder: DeFunis v. Odegaard, 1973–75, NCJW National Office Records.

46. Mitchell Bruce Pearlstein, "Selected Jewish Responses to Affirmative Action Admissions: Toward Conceptual Understanding" (Ph.D. diss., University of Minnesota, 1980), 120; Milton Friedman to Mrs. Nathan Primak, June 17, 1974, Container 16, folder: DeFunis v. Odegaard, 1973–75, NCJW National Office Records; Abzug quoted in MacLean, *Freedom Is Not Enough*, 212.

In the 1990s some members still listed their names in the organization's directory according to their husbands' first name and surname. Faith Rogow, *Gone to Another Meeting: The National Council of Jewish Women, 1893–1993* (Tuscaloosa: University of Alabama Press, 1993), 191–93.

47. Brief of the Respondents and Appendix, January 29, 1974; Brief of the National Organization for Women Legal Defense and Education Fund, Inc., and National Education Association, n.d. [1974]; Brief of the National Council of Jewish Women et al., n.d. [1974]; Brief of the President and Fellows of Harvard College, n.d. [1974], all in *DeFunis Record*, 2:565, 863, 3:991, 1150.

48. Samuel Solomon to Dewey Dodds, March 12, 1974, and Caspar Weinberger to Arnold Forster, March 25, 1974, both in box 26, folder: Affirmative Action, January–May 1974, AJCommittee Intergroup Records.

49. Anthony Lewis, "The Legality of Racial Quotas," *New York Times*, March 3, 1974; Hyman Bookbinder to Seymour Samet, February 26, 1974, box 26, folder: DeFunis case, 1972–74, AJCommittee Intergroup Records; and O'Neil, *Discriminating against Discrimination*, 30.

50. Excerpts from Oral Arguments in the United States Supreme Court, February 26, 1974, *DeFunis Record*, 3:1327–28, 1333.

51. *DeFunis Record*, 3:1333; Josef Diamond to William Brennan, February 28, 1974, box 327, folder 3, Series 1, William J. Brennan, Jr. Papers, Library of Congress, Washington, D.C.; and Philip Kurland to Alexander Bickel, March 18, 1974, box 46, folder 46, Bickel Papers.

52. Steven L. Wasby, "Justice Harry A. Blackmun: Transformation for 'Minnesota Twin' to Independent Voice," in *The Burger Court: Political and Judicial Profiles,* ed. Charles M. Lamb and Stephen C. Halper (Urbana: University of Illinois Press, 1991), 63; for a discussion on the importance of the Mayo Clinic experience on his thinking in the *Roe* decision, see Linda Greenhouse, *Becoming Justice Blackmun: Harry Blackmun's Supreme Court Journey* (New York: Times Books, 2006), 82–101.

53. Excerpts from Oral Arguments in the United States Supreme Court, February 26, 1974, *DeFunis Record*, 3:1335, 1339–40.

54. *DeFunis Record*, 3:1336.

55. *DeFunis Record*, 3:1337–38, 1339.

56. Lewis Powell to Chief, March 11, 1974, box 186, folder: DeFunis v. Odegaard I and memorandum, DeFunis v. Odegaard, No. 73-235, box 186, folder: DeFunis v. Odegaard (2 of 2), both in Blackmun Papers.

57. *DeFunis* 416 U.S. at 349.

58. Lemann, *Big Test,* 206; Nat Hentoff, "One by One," *Legal Times,* June 18, 2001, 62.

59. O'Neil, *Discriminating against Discrimination,* 43; Cert. memorandum, Johnson v. Committee on Examinations, 71-1362, June 6, 1972, box 1535, folder: Cert. memoranda 71–1351 to 1462, Douglas Papers; and *Johnson v. Committee on Examinations,* 407 U.S. 915 (1972).

60. Excerpts from Oral Arguments in the United States Supreme Court, February 26, 1974, *DeFunis Record*, 3:1339.

61. *DeFunis v. Odegaard,* 416 U.S. 349. See, for example, Draft Opinion No. 3; Draft

Opinion No. 4; Draft Opinion No. 6, all in box 1655, folder: DeFunis v. Odegaard / 2, Douglas Papers.

62. *DeFunis v. Odegaard*, 416 U.S. 349; Chief Justice to Justice Powell, March 14, 1974, and memorandum, DeFunis v. Odegaard, No. 73-235, folder: DeFunis v. Odegaard (2 of 2), both in folder: DeFunis v. Odegaard 1, box 186, Blackmun Papers.

63. *DeFunis v. Odegaard*, 416 U.S. at 317; and *DeFunis*, 84 Wn. 2d 617, 529 P .2d 438 (1974).

64. Clipping, "High Court Decides Not to Decide on DeFunis," *University of Washington Daily*, n.d. [April 1974], box 37, folder: DeFunis v. Odegaard, VP Records; Fred M. Hechingber, "Justice Douglas's Dissent in the DeFunis Case," *Saturday Review*, July 27, 1974; clipping, Stephen Solomon, "A Jew and a Kenyan Clash over 'Reverse Discrimination,'" *Philadelphia Inquirer*, October 13, 1974, box 25, folder: September–December 1974, AJCommittee Intergroup Records; Fletcher N. Baldwin Jr. "*DeFunis v. Odegaard*, The Supreme Court and Preferential Law School Admissions: Discretion Is Sometimes Not the Better Part of Valor," *University of Florida Law Review* 27:2 (Winter 1975): 360; and clipping, Smith Hempstone, "High Court Shirked Duty in Side-Stepping DeFunis," n.s., May 1, 1974, box 37, folder: DeFunis v. Odegaard, VP Records.

65. Lavinsky, "*DeFunis v. Odegaard*," 520; editorial, "DeFunis Non-Decision," *New York Times*, April 24, 1974; clipping, Lewin, "Which Man's Burden?"; and press release, April 23, 1974, all in box 26, folder: DeFunis Case, 1972–74, AJCommittee Intergroup Records.

66. Clipping, editorial, "The DeFunis Ruling," *Washington Post*, April 26, 1974, box 37, folder: DeFunis v. Odegaard, VP Records; Iver Peterson, "DeFunis Decision May Bring Pressure to End Race as College Admission Criterion," *New York Times*, April 30, 1974; Lavinsky, "*DeFunis v. Odegaard*," 530; Hechingber, "Justice Douglas's Dissent," 50; von Hoffman, "Justice, Injustice."

67. Peterson, "DeFunis Decision May Bring Pressure," 20; Charles Odegaard to John Bowers, February 28, 1976, and typescript, James Wilson, Speech Delivered at Fourteenth Annual Conference, National Association of College and University Attorneys, Chicago, June 27, 1974, both in box 1, folder: DeFunis v. Odegaard, Odegaard Papers; Gittell, "Illusion of Affirmative Action," 42; memorandum, NOW Task Force on Compliance to All Interested Persons, August 28, 1975, box 32, NOW Records, 1966—unprocessed, Schlesinger Library, Radcliffe Institute, Harvard University, Cambridge, Massachusetts; and Walter J. Leonard, "Affirmative Action at Harvard," *Chronicle of Higher Education*, March 31, 1975.

68. Roger Meltzer to Samuel Rabinove and Seymour Samet, October 15, 1974, box 25, folder: September–December 1974, AJCommittee Intergroup Records; and Hyman Bookbinder to Seymour Samet, May 7, 1974, box 26, folder: DeFunis Case, 1972–74, AJCommittee Intergroup Records.

69. Hyman Bookbinder to Seymour Samet, May 7, 1974, box 26, folder: DeFunis Case, 1972–74, AJCommittee Intergroup Records; Richard Harroch to [Ernest] Weiner, April 30, 1974; and Ernest Weiner to Samuel Rabinove, May 3, 1974; and Samuel Rabinove to Harry Fleischman, August 5, 1974, all box 26, folder: Harroch, 1974, AJCommittee Intergroup Records.

70. Seymour Samet to Roger Wilkins, April 25, 1974, box 26, folder: DeFunis Case,

1972–74, AJCommittee Intergroup Records; Benjamin Epstein et al. to Caspar Weinberger, May 20, 1974, box 268, folder: Affirmative Action: Miscellany, February–October 1974, NCJW Washington Collection; and memorandum, Peter Holmes to the Secretary, November 26, 1975, box 5, folder: Higher Education: Affirmative Action (1), Lissy Files.

71. Clipping, William Raspberry, "Finding a Substitute for 'Quotas,'" *Washington Post*, n.d. [June 1974]; Joseph Rauh to Marian Wright Edelman, June 6, 1974; Marian Wright Edelman and Joseph Rauh to Caspar Weinberger, June 6, 1974; Roger Wilkins to Joseph Rauh, June 4, 1974; and Roger Wilkins to Bert Gold, June 4, 1974, all in box 268, folder: Affirmative Action: Miscellany, February–October 1974, NCJW Washington Collection.

72. Clipping, Hyman Bookbinder, letter to editor, *Washington Post*, June 22, 1974, box 26, folder: DeFunis Case, 1972–74; Charles Mintz to Jakob Petuchowski, October 29, 1974, AJA Records; clipping, letter to editor, Morris Schappes, *Amsterdam News*, August 3, 1974, box 26, folder: DeFunis Case, 1972–74; and Roger Meltzer to Paul Weinberg and Jules Whitman, December 4, 1974, box 25, folder: September–December 1974, all in AJCommittee Intergroup Records.

73. *Flanagan v. Georgetown College*, 417 F. Supp. 384 (D.D.C., 1976); and *Cramer v. Virginia Commonwealth University*, 415 F. Supp 673 (E.D. Va., 1976).

74. *Alevy v. Downstate Medical Center*, 78 Misc. 2d. 1091, 359 N.Y.S. 2d 246 (1974); and *Alevy*, 39 N.Y. 2d 326, 384 N.Y.S. 2d 82 (1976).

75. Clipping, "White Says CUNY Bias Barred Him," *New York Post*, May 30, 1974, box 25, folder: Affirmative Action: January–May 1974, AJCommittee Intergroup Records; Iver Peterson, "Kibbee Denies C.C.N.Y. Medical Course Uses Minority Quotas," *New York Times*, June 20, 1974; typescript, Complaint: Class Action, Michael Scognamiglio and Robert Trotta against Board of Higher Education et al., January 20, 1975, box 29, folder: Affirmative Action, 1975, Domestic Affairs / Legal Committee, American Jewish Committee Archives and Record Center, New York; and *Hupart v. Board of Education of the City of New York*, 420 F. Supp. 1087 (S.D. N.Y., 1976).

76. Sara Jean Green, "Marco DeFunis, Student in 1971 UW Bias Suit, Dies at 52," *Seattle Times*, January 18, 2002, http://community.seattletimes.nwsource.com/archive/?date=20 020118&slug=marco18mo; clipping, Solomon, "A Jew and a Kenyan Clash"; Hyman Bookbinder to David Lissy, March 8, 1976, box 5, folder: Higher Education: Affirmative Action (4), Lissy Files; and O'Neil, *Discriminating against Discrimination*, ix.

77. J. C. Conklin, "UW Law School Sued," *UW Daily Online* March 7, 1997; Michelle Malkin, "Diversity Rhetoric Can't Hide UW's Discriminatory Policy," *Seattle Times*, March 11, 1997; *Smith v. University of Washington Law School*, 2 F. Supp. 2d 1324 (W.D. Wash., 1998), aff'd., 233 F.3d 1188 (9th Cir., 2000), cert. denied, 532 U.S. 1051 (2001); and Steven A. Holmes, "Victorious Preference Foes Look for New Battlefield," *New York Times*, November 10, 1998.

78. *Grutter v. Bollinger*, 539 U.S. 306 (2003); *Gratz v. Bollinger*, 539 U.S. 244 (2003); and Green, "Marco DeFunis, Student."

79. Interview with Harry A. Blackmun, Interviewed by Harold Hongju Kob, June 27, 1995, Washington, D.C., Justice Harry A. Blackmun Oral History Project, Supreme Court Historical Society / Federal Judicial Center, Washington, D.C.

Chapter 5. "Do Whites Have Rights?"

1. Norman Sinclair, "Big Police Walkout Called Doubtful," *Detroit News,* May 10, 1975.

2. Ibid.; Video clip, NBC Evening News, May 9, 1975, Recording No. 483111, Vanderbilt Television News Archives, Nashville, Tennessee; and William A. Stevens, "The Recession Increases Racial Tensions in Detroit," *New York Times,* May 15, 1975.

3. Charlie Cain, "Mayor Warns Police after 'Drunken Brawl,'" *Detroit News,* May 11, 1975; "Media Pours Gasoline on Match," *Tuebor,* June 1975. *Tuebor* is housed at the Walter Reuther Archives of Labor and Urban Affairs, Wayne State University, Detroit. For the decade of the 1970s, the Reuther Archives hold copies of *Tuebor* only for 1974–75. *Tuebor* means "I will defend" in Latin.

4. Norman C. Amaker, *Civil Rights and the Reagan Administration* (Washington, DC: University Press of America, 1988), 125–26; Raymond Wolter, *Right Turn: William Bradford Reynolds, the Reagan Administration, and Black Civil Rights* (New Brunswick, NJ: Rutgers University Press, 1996), 208–9; Thomas Byrne Edsall with Mary D. Edsall, *Chain Reaction: The Impact of Race, Rights, and Taxes on American Politics* (New York: Norton, 1991; 1992), 123.

5. The literature on working-class conservatism and white male workers' resistance to liberalism is large. See, for example, Jefferson Cowie, "Nixon's Class Struggle: Romancing the New Right Worker, 1969–1973," *Labor History* 43:3 (August 2002): 257–83; Kenneth D. Durr, *Behind the Backlash: White Working-Class Politics in Baltimore, 1940–1980* (Chapel Hill: University of North Carolina Press, 2003); Ronald P. Formisano, *Boston against Busing: Race, Class, and Ethnicity in the 1960s and 1970s* (Chapel Hill: University of North Carolina Press, 192); Maria Kefalas, *Working Heroes: Protecting Home, Community, and Nation in a Chicago Neighborhood* (Berkeley: University of California Press, 2003); and Freeman, *Working-Class New York.*

6. Editorial, "Equality and Scarcity," *New York Times,* January 13, 1975.

7. Catherine H. Milton, "The Future of Women in Policing," in *The Future of Policing,* vol. 9, ed. Alvin Cohn (Beverly Hills, CA: Sage, 1978), 186; Edsall with Edsall, *Chain Reaction,* 124; W. Marvin Dulaney, *Black Police in America* (Bloomington: Indiana University Press, 1996), 102, 122; James B. Jacobs and Jay Cohen, "The Impact of Racial Integration on Police," *Journal of Police Science and Administration* 6 (1978): 169, 175; Stephen Leinen, *Black Police, White Society* (New York: New York University Press, 1984), 22–23; and Andrew Hacker, *Two Nations: Black and White, Separate and Unequal* (New York: Scribner, 1992), 121.

For examples of relevant court cases, see, *Baker v. City of St. Petersburg,* 400 F. 2d 294 (5th Cir., 1968); *National Assoc. for the Advancement of Colored People v. Allen,* 340 F. Supp. 703 (1972); *Bridgeport Guardians, Inc. v. Bridgeport Civil Service Commission,* 497 F. 2d 1113 (2nd Cir., 1974); *Arnold v. Ballard,* 390 F. Supp. 723 (1975); *Afro-America Patrolmen's League v. Duck,* 538 F. 2d 328 (6th Cir., 1976); *United States v. City of Chicago,* 411 F. Supp. 218 (1976); and *Shield Club v. City of Cleveland,* 538 F. 2d 329 (6th Cir., 1976).

8. Andrew T. Darien, "Patrolling the Border: Integration and Identity in the New York City Police Department, 1941–1975" (PhD diss., New York University, 2000); Michael G. Krzewinski, "The Historical Development and Effects of Affirmative Action in the City of

Milwaukee Police" (PhD diss., University of Wisconsin–Milwaukee, 2000); John H. Mc-Namara, "Uncertainties in Police Work: The Relevance of Police Recruits' Backgrounds and Training," in *The Police: Six Sociological Essays,* ed. David J. Borda (New York: Wiley Books, 1967), 183; Nicholas Alex, *New York Cops Talk Back: A Quest for Blue Power* (New York: Wiley, 1976), 13–21; Seymour Martin Lipset, "Why Cops Hate Liberals—And Vice Versa," in *The Police Rebellion: A Quest for Blue Power,* ed. William J. Bopp (Springfield, IL: Charles C Thomas, 1971), p. 38; and Arthur Neiderhoffer, *Behind the Shield: The Police in Urban Society* (Garden City, NJ: Doubleday, 1967).

For examples of police "reverse discrimination" cases, see *Fraternal Order of Police v. City of Dayton,* 310 N.E. 2d 269 (Ohio Ct. App., 1973); *Button v. Rockefeller,* 351 N.Y.S. 2d 488 (1973); *Oburn v. Shapp,* 521 F. 2d 142 (3rd Cir., 1975); and *Reeves v. Eaves,* 411 F.Supp. 531 (N.D. Ga., 1976).

9. Sugrue, *Origins of the Urban Crisis,* 143; Fine, *Violence in the Model City,* 458; and Jon C. Teaford, *The Twentieth-Century American City: Problem, Promise, and Reality,* 2d ed. (Baltimore: Johns Hopkins University Press, 1993), 126.

10. Testimony of Arthur L. Johnson, *Hearings before the United States Commission on Civil Rights, Hearings Held in Detroit, Michigan, December 14 and 15, 1960* (Washington, DC: GPO, 1961), 307; and Patrick James Ashton, "Race, Class, and Black Politics: The Implications of the Election of a Black Mayor for the Police and Policing in Detroit" (PhD diss., Michigan State University, 1981), 240–41.

11. Pamela Irving Jackson, *Minority Group Threat, Crime, and Policing: Social Context and Social Control* (New York: Praeger, 1989), 32–33, 72–75; Dulaney, *Black Police,* 20–21, 26; Susan E. Martin, " 'Outsider Within' the Station House: The Impact of Race and Gender on Black Women Police," *Social Problems* 41 (August 1994), 338; U.S. Civil Rights Commission, *Police and the Blacks: U.S. Civil Rights Commission Hearings* (New York: Arno Press / *New York Times,* 1971), 210; typescript, staff report: Detroit Commission on Community Relations, "A Synopsis of Background, Findings, Conclusions and Recommendations of a Study of Detroit Police Departmental Personnel Selection Practices," January 15, 1962, and typescript, "The Police, Law Enforcement and the Detroit Community, Summer 1965: A Report to the People of Detroit," August 1965, both in box 1, folder 4, Tom Turner Collection, Metropolitan Detroit AFL-CIO, Walter P. Reuther Archives of Labor and Urban Affairs, Wayne State University, Detroit [hereafter, Turner Collection]; Thomas F. Pettigrew, *Racially Separate or Together?* (New York: McGraw-Hill, 1971), 9; William J. Bopp, "The Detroit Riot," in *Police Rebellion,* ed. Bopp, 162–72; and Wilbur C. Rich, *Coleman Young and Detroit Politics: From Social Activist to Power Broker* (Detroit: Wayne State University, 1989), 207–8.

12. Formisano, *Boston against Busing,* 3; Robert Olson, "Schaefer Chatter," *Tuebor,* November 1974; John L. Cooper, *The Police and the Ghetto* (Port Washington, NY: Kennikat Press, 1980), 95; John T. Barr, "Almost Suburbia," *Tuebor,* February 1975; Robert Olson, "Schaefer Chatter," *Tuebor,* June 1975; and Robert Olson, "Schaefer Chatter," *Tuebor,* December 1974.

13. Ashton, "Race, Class, and Black Politics," 268–69; Sugrue, *Origins of the Urban Crisis,* 266; and Eugene Eidenburg and Joe Rigent, "The Police and Politics," in *Police in Urban Society,* ed. Harlan Hahn (Beverly Hills, CA: Sage, 1971), 291, 296.

14. John Nichols to Common Council Members, August 10, 1972, box 5, folder: Police Department/1973 (1) and John Nichols to Nicholas Hood, June 6, 1972, box 41, folder: Police Department/1972, both in Mel Ravitz Papers, Walter P. Reuther Archives of Labor and Urban Affairs, Wayne State University, Detroit.

15. Thompson, *Whose Detroit?* 237; Ashton, "Race, Class, and Black Politics," 310–11, 319, 417–19, 426n15; Sandy McClure, "6 Officers Fired by Chief Hart," *Detroit Free Press,* July 30, 1963; Jeffrey S. Adler, "Introduction," in *African-American Mayors: Race, Politics, and the American City,* ed. David R. Colburn and Jeffrey S. Adler (Urbana: University of Illinois Press, 2001), 12; and *Schaefer v. Tannian,* 394 F. Supp. 1128 (E.D. Mich., 1974).

16. Remer Tyson, "Detroit Hangs in There: Mayor Young a Year Later," *The Nation,* March 1, 1975; Sugrue, *Origins of the Urban Crisis,* 270; Formisano, *Boston against Busing,* 12, 223; *Milliken v. Bradley,* 418 U.S. 717 (1974); Patterson, *Grand Expectations,* 734; and William Stevens, "High Goals of Detroit's Black Mayor Foiled by Recession," *New York Times,* January 22, 1975.

Funding for the Joe Louis Arena, the home of the Detroit Red Wings hockey team, came in part from a $38 million loan from the Carter administration. The arena was completed in 1980. See Thomas, *Redevelopment and Race,* 157.

17. Coleman Young and Lonnie Wheeler, *Hard Stuff: The Autobiography of Coleman Young* (New York: Viking, 1994), 210, 212–13; Rich, *Coleman Young,* 209–12; and Thompson, *Whose Detroit?* 236–39.

18. Larry Gumbrecht, "Garden Spot of the East," *Tuebor,* April 1975; Thomas Kostera, "View from the Bottom of the Barrel," *Tuebor,* November 1974; Thomas Kostera, "View from the Bottom of the Barrel," *Tuebor,* August 1975; and Larry Gumbrecht, "Garden Spot of the East," *Tuebor,* June 1975.

19. Larry Gumbrecht, "Garden Spot of the East," *Tuebor,* October 1974; Len Fritz, "Shades of Seven," *Tuebor,* July 1975; and Greg Kranich and Jim McKeague, "The Score from Four," *Tuebor,* August 1975.

20. Eva Schlesinger Buzawa, "The Role of Selected Factors upon Patrol Officers Job Satisfaction in Two Urban Police Departments" (PhD diss., Michigan State University, 1979), 53n2; Darien, "Patrolling the Border," 366; Anthony V. Bouza, *The Police Mystique: An Insider's Look at Cops, Crime, and the Criminal Justice System* (New York: Perseus Publishing, 1990), 142.

21. Albert J. Reiss, *The Police and the Public* (New Haven: Yale University Press, 1971), 36, 44–45; Mark Ostermann and Frank Dankiewicz, "Garden Spot of the East," *Tuebor,* October 1975.

22. Bill Grandon and Rick Hatlen, "2nd to None," *Tuebor,* March 1975; Martin, "'Outsider Within,'" 395; Rich, *Coleman Young,* 215; Robert Pavich, "Tannian Promotes 27 Blacks despite Police Union Protest," *Detroit News,* August 1, 1974; Tim Kiska, "Black Cop Group Reports to Young, Union Chief Says," *Detroit Free Press,* June 2, 1984; Michael Tucker, "Black Cops in Turmoil," *Detroit News,* September 14, 1980; Mike Martindale, "Marchers Picket Police Union Office," *Detroit News,* September 9, 1980; Rebecca Powers and Nolan Finley, "Young Plan to Avert Layoffs Hit," *Detroit News,* September 4, 1980; and John Tittsworth, "Black Police Group Opposes Any Strike," *Detroit News,* April 25, 1980.

Women industrial unionists united on cross-racial lines on many occasions. See

Deslippe, *"Rights, Not Roses,"* 130–34, 143, 165; Fonow, *Union Women,* 56–63, 95–103, 172; Gabin, *Feminism in the Labor Movement,* 158–59; and Cobble, *Other Women's Movement,* 43–44, 202–3, 244n96.

23. Ronald Mestdagh, interviewed by Dennis Deslippe, Madison Heights, Michigan, October 25, 2004, Detroit Police Department Affirmative Action Oral History Collection, Walter P. Reuther Archives of Labor and Urban Affairs, Wayne State University, Detroit [hereafter, Mestdagh interview]; Thomas Kostera, "Views from the Bottom of the Barrel, *Tuebor,* July 1975; and editorial, "Further Harrassment of Officers," *Tuebor,* April 1975.

24. Rieder, *Canarsie,* 111; Reiss, *Police and the Public,* 29; Siemaszko and Vitorators, "Women's Division," *Tuebor,* December 1974; Norman Sinclair, "Detroit Police Finding Addicts among Recruits," *Detroit News,* December 28, 1975; and "Police Unions Wants Review of Training," *Detroit News,* August 13, 1977.

25. Michele Lamont, *The Dignity of Working Men: Morality and the Boundaries of Race, Class, and Immigration* (Cambridge: Harvard University Press, 2000), 2–3, 51, 56–57, 66; and Andy McGregor, "Fifteenth Commandment," *Tuebor,* July 1975; and Alex, *New York Cops Talk Back,* 37.

26. Sinclair, "Detroit Police Finding Addicts"; Leonard N. Moore, *Carl B. Stokes and the Rise of Black Political Power* (Urbana: University of Illinois Press, 2002), 116–20; Don Brady and Bill Jourdain, "One Down," *Tuebor,* April 1975; Larry Gumbrecht, "Garden Spot of the East," *Tuebor,* April 1975; Ashton, "Race, Class, and Black Politics," 331–32; Larry Gumbrecht, "Garden Spot of the East," *Tuebor,* January 1975; Norman Sinclair, "Gap Stays, and Officers Oust Sexton," *Detroit News,* August 19, 1975; Dan McGinnis, "News and Views from the Inner City Blues," *Tuebor,* July 1975; Robert Olson, "Schaefer Chatter," *Tuebor,* July 1975; Thomas Kostera, "Views from the Bottom of the Barrel," *Tuebor,* August 1975; and Robert Olson, "Schaefer Chatter," *Tuebor,* September 1974.

27. Formisano, *Boston against Busing,* 172, 176, 235; John T. Barr, "Almost Suburbia," *Tuebor,* January 1975; Robert Olson, "Schaefer Chatter," *Tuebor,* June 1975; Don Brady and Bill Jourdain, "One Down," *Tuebor,* April 1975. Frank Murphy served in the 1930s and 1940s as mayor of Detroit, governor of Michigan, U.S. attorney general, and Justice of the U.S. Supreme Court. He died in 1949.

28. Typescript, Detroit Urban League, "Employment Progress of Black Officers in the Detroit Police Department," October 24, 1972, 11, Purdy Library General Collection, Wayne State University, Detroit.

29. Robert Pavich, "Tannian Defends Promotion of 27 Black Policemen," *Detroit News,* August 2, 1974; *Detroit Police Officers Assn v. Young,* 446 F. Supp. 979 (E.D. Mich., 1978). In contract negotiations, the DPOA proposed that the written examination count for 70%, performance evaluation (i.e., service ratings) 7%, seniority 20%, and veterans preference 35%; the city wanted the written examination to count for only 40%, the promotional evaluation (i.e., oral boards) 45% (the DPOA wanted it eliminated), performance evaluation 7%, college credit 3%, and veterans preference 2%. See typescript, "DPOA Promotional Demands," n.d. [November 1977] and typescript, "City of Detroit Proposals," November 21, 1977, both in DPOA v. Young Case Files 75-71376/74-71838, U.S. District Court, Eastern District of Michigan, Federal Archives Records Center, Chicago [hereafter, DPOA v. Young Case Files].

30. Robert Olson, "Schaefer Chatter," *Tuebor,* February 1975; Ed Janowicz, "Contact Eleven," *Tuebor,* November 1974; *Schaefer v. Tannian,* 10 Fair Emply. Cas. (BNA) 896 (E.D. Mich., 1974); and Ashton, "Race, Class, and Black Politics," 351–55.

31. Robert Olson, "Schaefer Chatter," *Tuebor,* December 1974, 29; transcript, Testimony of David R. Watroba, October 20, 1977, DPOA v. Young Case Files; and transcript, Closing Argument, Sheldon Adler, December 22, 1977, DPOA Case Files.

32. Robert Pavich, "Plan Designed to Promote Blacks Riles Police Union," *Detroit News,* May 24, 1974; transcript, Testimony of Bruce Balmas, October 6, 1977; transcript, Testimony of Harvey Thomas Harris, Jr., October 6, 1977; deposition, Dr. Erick Beckman, December 14, 1977; transcript, Closing Argument, Walter Nussbaum, December 22, 1977, all in DPOA v. Young Case Files.

33. *Reeves v. Eaves,* 411 F. Supp. 531 (N.D. Ga., 1976); *Commonwealth v. Flaherty,* 404 F. Supp. 1022 (W.D. Pa., 1975); *Doores v. McNamara,* 476 F. Supp. 987 (W.D. Mo., 1979); Plaintiff's Brief in Support of Findings of Fact and Conclusions of Law, December 21, 1977, DPOA v. Young Case Files; Bill Grandon and Rick Hatlen, "2nd to None!" *Tuebor,* December 1974; and Thomas J. Sugrue, "Breaking Through: The Troubled Origins of Affirmative Action in the Workplace," in *Color Lines: Affirmative Action, Immigration, and Civil Rights Options for America,* ed. John David Skrentny (Chicago: University of Chicago Press, 2001), 44–45.

34. Pavich, "Tannian Promotes 27 Blacks"; Mitchell Skazalski to Commissioner [Douglas Fraser], July 23, 1974, and Evan Marshall to Douglas Fraser, July 28, 1974, both in box 3, folder 21, Douglas Fraser: Vice-President, United Automobile Workers Collection, Walter P. Reuther Library of Labor and Urban Affairs, Wayne State University, Detroit [hereafter, Fraser Collection].

35. Mestdagh interview.

36. Formisano, *Boston against Busing,* 193; Edsall with Edsall, *Chain Reaction,* 9; Benjamin W. Wolkinson, *Blacks, Unions, and the EEOC: A Study of Administrative Futility* (Lexington, MA: Lexington Books, 1973), 13; Rieder, *Canarsie,* 118; and Bill Grandon and Rick Hatlen, "2nd to None!" *Tuebor,* November 1974.

37. "Kaess' Ruling on Black Police Preference Upset," *Detroit News,* June 23, 1977; and Deposition, Coleman A. Young, May 24, 1977, DPOA v. Young Case Files.

38. Paul Bernstein and Norman Sinclair, "A New Police Layoff Plan Vowed," *Detroit News,* May 1, 1975; and Norman Sinclair, "Fraser Backs Police on Seniority Rights," *Detroit News,* May 8, 1975.

39. Sinclair, "A New Police Layoff Plan Vowed"; Tony Cannole to Douglas Fraser, May 12, 1975, box 3, folder 18, Fraser Collection; and Don Ball, "2 Unions Offer Plans to Prevent Layoff of Detroit City Workers," *Detroit News,* May 14, 1975.

40. Sinclair, "Fraser Backs Police"; Sinclair, "A New Police Layoff Plan Vowed"; letter to editor, *Detroit News,* May 12, 1975; letter to editor, *Detroit News,* May 9, 1975; letter to editor, *Detroit News,* May 11, 1975.

41. Typescript, Statement of Tom Turner, Detroit Police Officers Association Membership Meeting, May 11, 1976, box 56, folder 27 and press release: Tom Turner, February 2, 1979, box 43, folder 8, both in Turner Collection; and Howard Warren, "Turner Says Young Flubs Labor Talks," *Detroit News,* May 10, 1979.

For Metropolitan Detroit AFL-CIO's criticism of Detroit police officers, see clipping, "Citizen's Police Board Backed by Labor Council," *Detroit Free Press*, January 20, 1961; Graten Little to Jerome Cavanaugh, December 17, 1963; Alex Fuller to Louis Miriani, October 6, 1959, all in box 1, folder 4, Turner Collection. For an example of the labor federation's complaint against civil rights organizations as employers, see Milton Tambar to Urban League, Board of Director's Office, January 12, 1972, box 17, folder 38, Turner Collection.

42. John Barr, "Almost Suburbia," *Tuebor*, October 1975; Ashton, "Race, Class, and Black Politics," 374n9; and typescript, John E. Teahan, "A Study of the Values and Attitudes of Black and White Police Officers (1972)," Department of Psychology, Wayne State University, Detroit.

43. "Idled Detroit Officers Seek Soo Police Chief Job," *Detroit News*, July 30, 1976; and William A. Stevens, "The Recession Increases Racial Tensions in Detroit," *New York Times*, May 15, 1975.

44. Paul Bernstein, "Police Accept No-Layoff Plan," *Detroit News*, June 11, 1975; Pat Murphy, "Lady Police Draw Praise and Gripes," *Detroit News*, July 31, 1975; Lou Gordon, "Was City Soft in Riot?" *Detroit News*, August 3, 1975; Young and Wheeler, *Hard Stuff*, 208; David Ashenfelter, "Police Residency Hearings Ordered," *Detroit News*, June 22, 1976; William Dunn, "1,000 Police to Be Laid-Off," *Detroit News*, June 26, 1976; and Robert Ankeny, "Black Police in Court to Block Layoff Plans," *Detroit News*, June 17, 1976.

45. William A. Clark, "Secession: Northwest Detroit Area Talks of Pullout," *Detroit News*, June 15, 1975; and Thompson, *Whose Detroit?* 273n73. The Sixteenth Precinct was 97.7% white in 1970; see typescript, "Population Characteristics for Detroit: By Precinct, 1970: Tables I & II," DPOA v. Young Case Files.

46. Buzawa, "Role of Selected Factors," 115; Sinclair, "Gap Stays, and Officers Oust Sexton"; Norman Sinclair, "Police Union Alters Style," *Detroit News*, October 11, 1978; and John Castine, "Race Splits DPOA Campaigns," *Detroit Free Press*, October 22, 1986.

47. *Franks v. Bowman Transp. Co.*, 424 U.S. 747 (1976); and *Teamsters v. United States*, 431 U.S. 324 (1977).

48. David Kushma and Sandy McClure, "1,103 Detroit Police Layoffs Ruled Illegal," *Detroit Free Press*, February 23, 1984; David Kushma and Sandy McClure, "Police Layoff Case May Cost Millions, Split Races," *Detroit Free Press*, February 24, 1984; David Kushma, Gregory Huskisson, and Jack Kresnak, "City Told to Rehire White Cops," *Detroit Free Press*, November 8, 1984; *Firefighters Local Union No. 1784 v. Stotts*, 467 U.S. 561 (1984); and David Kushma and Ron Kzwonkowski, "Young Predicts 'Grim' Impact," *Detroit Free Press*, June 13, 1984.

49. *Detroit Police Officers Ass'n. v. Young*, 446 F. Supp. 979 (E.D. Mich., 1978); Federal Judicial Historical Office, Federal Judicial Center, "Federal Judges Biographical Database: Frederick William Kaess," www.fjc.gov/history/home.nsf/judges_frm, accessed February 10, 2010; and Agnes Bryant, "Judge Kaess Strikes Down Police Department Affirmative Action," *Liberator*, March–April 1978, box 47, folder 111, Turner Collection.

50. *Detroit Police Officers Ass'n. v. Young*, 608 F. 2d 671 (6th Cir., 1979), 452 U.S. 938 (1981); and Gregory Huskisson, Christopher Cook, and Roger Chesley, "Police Promotions Costly Policy Brings Officers Closer to City, Not to Each Other," *Detroit Free Press*, January 29, 1990.

51. *Baker v. City of Detroit*, 483 F. Supp. 930 (E.D. Mich., 1979); *Stamps v. Detroit Edison Co.*, 365 F. Supp. 87 (1973); and Damon Keith, "Should Colorblindness and Representativeness Be a Part of American Justice?" *Howard Law Journal* 26:1 (1983): 6–7.

52. *Baker v. City of Detroit*, 483 F. Supp. 930 (E.D. Mich., 1979); and History of the Federal Judiciary, *Federal Judges Biographical Database: Damon Jerome Keith*, www.fjc.gov/history/home.nsf/judges_frm, February 10, 2010.

53. J. Preston Oade Jr., telephone interview with Dennis Deslippe, June 9, 2008, Detroit Police Department Affirmative Action Oral History Collection, Walter P. Reuther Archives of Labor and Urban Affairs, Wayne State University, Detroit [hereafter, Oade interview]. The Southfield, Michigan, law firm employing Oade was Lippit, Harrison, Perlove, Friedman, and Zak.

54. *Baker v. City of Detroit*, 483 F. Supp. 980, 994, 1002 (E.D. Mich., 1979); 504 F. Supp. 841 (E.D. Mich., 1980).

55. Hugh Davis Graham, "Civil Rights Policy," in *The Reagan Presidency: Pragmatic Conservatism and Its Legacies*, ed. W. Elliot Brownlee and Hugh Davis Graham (Lawrence: University Press of Kentucky, 2003), 284–85; Amaker, *Civil Rights*, 126; Wolter, *Right Turn*, 208–9; Robert Pear, "Judges Continuing to Uphold Quotas," *New York Times*, February 10, 1985; William Bradford Reynolds, "They Use Discrimination to Cure Discrimination," *New York Times*, December 11, 1983; Robert Pear, "Administration Is Hoping to Force Court to Confront Racial Quotas," *New York Times*, December 5, 1983; U.S. Commission on Civil Rights, *Statement of the U.S. Commission on Civil Rights, Concerning the Detroit Police Department's Racial Promotion Quota* (Washington, DC: USCCR, 1984); and James Rowell to Harry Blackmun, January 17, 1984, box 1008, folder 4, Blackmun Papers.

56. *Detroit Police Officers Ass'n. v. Young*, 989 F. 330 (6th Cir., 1993); Allan Lengel, "Ruling Ends Affirmative Action for Cops," *Detroit News*, March 25, 1993; and Order Approving Proposed Settlement Pursuant to Federal Rule of Civil Procedure 23(e), September 20, 1995, DPOA v. Young Case Files.

57. Mestdagh interview; Oade interview; James Langford Westbrook, "In a Pig's Eye: A Study to Examine Police Officers' Views, Attitudes, and Opinions toward Themselves, Their Own Profession, and Society at Large" (PhD diss., Golden Gate University, 1982), 40; and typescript, Proceedings of the National Black Police Association Convention, Nashville, Tennessee, October 5, 1976, box 14, folder: National Black Police Association, Records of Domestic Policy Staff, 1976–81, Robert Malson's Subject File, Jimmy Carter Presidential Library, Atlanta.

58. Leinen, *Black Police*, 40, 154; Mestdagh interview; Huskisson, Cook, and Chesley, "Police Promotions Costly"; and Suzette Hackney, "Cops Use New Rule to Move Out of Detroit," *Detroit Free Press*, July 9, 2001.

59. Oade interview; *Wygant v. Jackson Board of Education*, 476 U.S. 267 (1986).

60. Douglas Fraser, interview with Dennis Deslippe, April 25, 2005, Detroit, Michigan, Walter Reuther Archives of Labor and Urban Affairs, Wayne State University, Detroit.

61. Clipping, Carl T. Rowan, "Keith Ruling on Police More Vital Than Bakke," *Detroit News*, October 15, 1979, box 114, folder 35, Turner Collection.

Chapter 6. *"The Fight for True Nondiscrimination"*

1. Transcripts, U.S. Commission on Civil Rights Meeting, May 8, 1972, Washington, D.C., box 7, U.S. Commission on Civil Rights Meeting Minutes, 1968–1974, 1977–1979, Record Group 453, USCCR Records; cover, *U.S. News and World Report*, March 29, 1976; "Mike's Move," *All in the Family* (Season 6, Episode 129; 1976 / February 2; Norman Lear, creator).

2. Memorandum, Paul O'Neill to the President, August 7, 1975, box 1, folder: Affirmative Action, August 1975–June 1976, Richard Parsons Files, Gerald R. Ford Presidential Library, Ann Arbor, Michigan [hereafter, Parsons Files].

3. Fields, "Affirmative Action, 4 Years After"; Gene Maeroff, "Program to Spur College Hiring of Women and Minority Teachers Lags Amid Continuing Controversy," *New York Times*, December 28, 1975; and Carnegie Council, *Making Affirmative Action Work*, 10, 14.

4. John B. Parrish, "Women in Professional Training—An Update," *Monthly Labor Review*, November 1975; Alice H. Amsdem and Collette Moser, "Job Search and Affirmative Action: Supply and Mobility of Women Economists," *American Economic Review* 65:2 (May 1975): 91; Maeroff, "Program to Spur College Hiring," 25; Mary P. Rowe, "The Progress of Women in Education Institutions: The Saturn Rings Phenomenon," *Graduate and Professional Education of Women: Proceedings of the American Association of University Women Conference*, May 9–10, 1974 (Washington, DC: AAUW, 1974), 2.

5. Gittell, "Illusion of Affirmative Action"; Cheryl M. Fields, "Everybody Criticized," *Chronicle of Higher Education*, September 2, 1975; Mary Berry, "The Mythology of Equal Treatment," n.s., n.d. [1975] (in author's possession); "Affirmative Action, Higher Education, and the Press," *AAAA Newsletter*, May 15, 1976, box 30, folder: American Association for Affirmative Action, Lindh and Holm Files; Gene I. Maeroff, "New Group Backs Hiring Guidelines," *New York Times*, February 27, 1975.

6. Allan C. Ornstein, "Are Quotas Here to Stay?" *National Review*, April 26, 1974; J. W. Foster, "Race and Truth at Harvard," *New Republic*, July 17, 1976; Richard A. Lester, *Antibias Regulations of Universities: Faculty Problems and Their Solutions* (New York: McGraw Hill, 1974), 105–6; Sidney Hook to Clark Kerr, September 24, 1975, box 182, folder 15, Sidney Hook Papers, Hoover Institution Archives, Stanford University, Sanford, CA [Hook Papers].

7. Jackson quoted in James T. Patterson, *Restless Giant: The United States from Watergate to "Bush v. Gore"* (New York: Oxford University Press 2005), 190–91; Edith Green, "Fears and Fallacies: Equal Opportunities in the 1970s," *University of Michigan Business Review*, n.d. [1975], box 182, folder 5, Hook Papers; obituary, "Ex-Representative Edith Green, 77, is Dead," *New York Times*, April 23, 1987; Patterson, *Restless Giant*, 76–107; Schulman, *The Seventies*, 8, 38, 51; and Edsall with Edsall, *Chain Reaction*, 89–90, 93–95.

8. Obituary, "Ex-Representative James O'Hara, 62, Dies," *New York Times*, March 16, 1989. For examples of O'Hara's advocacy, see James O'Hara to Phyllis Evenberg, August 24, 1970, box 26, folder: Sex Discrimination at UM; James O'Hara to Jean King, July 31, 1970, box 26, folder: Sex Discrimination at UM; James O'Hara to Elliot Richardson, July 31, 1970, box 26, folder: Sex Discrimination at UM; James O'Hara to Caspar Weinberger, June 23, 1975, box 26, folder: Affirmative Action / General 2; Theodore Hesburgh to James

O'Hara, July 3, 1975, box 26, folder: Affirmative Action / General 2; and James O'Hara to Jim Wright, January 21, 1975, box 26, folder: Affirmative Action / General 3, box 26, folder: Affirmative Action / General 2, O'Hara Papers.

9. Testimony of Albert Shanker, *Hearings before the Special Subcommittee on Education of the Committee on Education and Labor, House of Representatives,* 93rd Cong., 2nd Sess., Part 2A: Civil Rights Obligations, August 8, 9, 12, 14, 15; September 17, 19, 20, 23, 25, 1974 (Washington, DC: GPO, 1975), 655; Testimony of Miro Todorovich, ibid., 478; Testimony of Stanley Dacher, ibid., 488; comments of chair, James O'Hara, ibid., 485; and "Congressman O'Hara on Nondiscrimination," *Measure* [University Centers for Rational Alternatives] 32 (November 1974): 1–2, box 26, folder: Response to O'Hara Speech, O'Hara Papers.

10. Yvonne Vandengel to James O'Hara, January 18, 1975; Steven Sample to James O'Hara, December 27, 1974; Maurice Rosenberg to James O'Hara, December 5, 1974; Bernard Davis to James O'Hara, January 13, 1975; clipping, "Affirmative Action Hearings Held," *Measure* 32 (November 1974): 4–6, all in box 26, folder: Responses to O'Hara Speech, O'Hara Papers; Albert Shanker, "Strong Voices against Ethnic Hiring," *American Teacher* 59:6 (February 1975): 4; James O'Hara to Naomi Levine, n.d. [November 1974], box 29, folder: CLSA + VA, 1973, American Jewish Congress Records, American Jewish Historical Society, New York.

11. Frederick Shaw to James O'Hara, December 31, 1974; Gary Bach to Gentlemen [EEOC], October 26, 1976; James O'Hara to Gary Bach, November 10, 1976; Grace Yee to James O'Hara, December 1, 1975; James O'Hara to Grace Lee, December 30, 1975, all in box 26, folder: Reverse Discrimination, O'Hara Papers; James O'Hara to Mary Gray, December 6, 1974, box 26, folder: Affirmative Action / General 1, O'Hara Papers.

12. "Affirmative Action Hearings Held," 6; Anderson, *Pursuit of Fairness,* 124, 134–45; and Haskell Lazere to Seymour Samet, July 18, 1972, box 186, folder: Quotas, Jan–August, 1972, Gold Papers.

13. U.S. House of Representatives, Special Subcommittee on Education of the Committee on Education and Labor, *Hearings: Legal Education Opportunities,* June 5, 1974 (Washington, DC: GPO, 1974), 6–7; and Jennifer 8. Lee, "James H. Scheuer, 13-Term New York Congressman, Is Dead at 85," *New York Times,* August 31, 2005.

14. James O'Hara to James Scheuer, June 23, 1975; Arnold Forster to James Scheuer, April 24, 1975; Will Maslow to James Scheuer, May 28, 1975; Naomi Levine to James Scheuer, April 25, 1975, all in box 26, folder: Hearings, O'Hara Papers.

For examples of academics writing in support of the amendment, see August Meier to James Scheuer, April 29, 1975; Fritz Machlup to James Scheuer, April 27, 1975; Paul Flory to James Scheuer, April 29, 1975, all in box 26, folder: Hearings, O'Hara Papers.

15. Typescript, "Statement of the U.S. Commission on Civil Rights on the Scheuer-Waxman Amendment to the Health Manpower Bill," n.d. [1975]; Summer Rosen to James Scheuer, March 18, 1975; Joseph Rauh Jr. to James Scheuer, April 16, 1975; James Scheuer to Joseph Rauh Jr., April 17, 1975; Joseph Rauh Jr. to James Scheuer, April 28, 1975, all in box 26, folder: Hearings, O'Hara Papers.

16. Miro Todorovich to Robert Goldwin, May 5, 1975, box 8, folder: HU2, White House Central Files; "Ex-Representative O'Hara Dies," 311; obituary, "Ex-Representative Green,

77, is Dead," D31; Hyman Bookbinder to Samuel Rabinove, January 29, 1973; and Samuel Rabinove to Hyman Bookbinder, January 31, 1973, both in box 25, folder: Affirmative Action, 1973 and Earlier, AJCommittee Intergroup Records.

17. James L. Buckley, *If Men Were Angels: A View from the Senate* (New York: Putnam, 1975), 235–36; James O'Hara to Robert Becker, July 23, 1976, box 26, folder: Reverse Discrimination, O'Hara Papers; MacLean, *Freedom Is Not Enough,* 231; U.S. Senate, "S. 3069:Antidiscrimination Action," introduced March 2, 1976, 94th Cong., 1975–76, http://thomas.loc.gov, accessed July 23, 2010.

18. Buckley, *If Men Were Angels,* 242–43.

19. "Motion for Leave to File Brief, February 1974, (denied: February 25, 1974)," *De-Funis Record,* 1:405; Miro Todorovich to James O'Hara, November 1, 1974, box 26, folder: Affirmative Action / General 1, O'Hara Papers; Timothy O'Neil, *"Bakke" and the Politics of Equality: Friends and Foes in the Classroom of Litigation* (Middletown, CT: Wesleyan University Press, 1985), 180–81; and Sidney Hook and Miro Todorovich, "The Tyranny of Reverse Discrimination," *Change* (Winter 1975/1976): 42.

20. "Memorandum to Colleges and Universities, December 1974," box 5, folder: Higher Education / Affirmative Action 1, Lissy Files; Carnegie Council, *Making Affirmative Action Work,* 127–29; Bernard DeLury to William Kilberg, November 7, 1975, box 5, folder: Higher Education / Affirmative Action 5, Lissy Files; Hook and Todorovich, "Tyranny of Reverse Discrimination," 42.

21. Caspar W. Weinberger, *In the Arena: A Memoir of the 20th Century* (Washington, DC: Regnery Publishing, 2001), 222–23; Eileen Shanahan, "Weinberger Sees Flaws in Quotas," *New York Times,* July 31, 1973; Caspar Weinberger to the President, March 4, 1975, box 1, folder: Affirmative Action / February–May 1975, Parsons Files; and Caspar Weinberger to Arnold Foster, March 25, 1974, box 25, folder: Affirmative Action / January–May 1974, AJ Committee Intergroup Records.

22. Caspar Weinberger to Sidney Hook, April 4, 1975, box 5, folder: Higher Education / Affirmative Action 3, Lissy Files; and memorandum, Caspar Weinberger to the President, July 2, 1975, box 1, folder: Affirmative Action / August 1975–June 1976, Parsons Files.

23. Emma Brown, "Robert A. Goldwin, 87; Political Scientist, White House Adviser," *Washington Post,* January 22, 2010; and Tevi Troy, "The Corner," *National Review Online,* January 13, 2010, http://corner.nationalreview.com.

24. Thomas Sowell to Robert Goldwin, August 9, 1975, box 5, folder: Higher Education / Affirmative Action 3, Lissy Files; Robert Goldwin to Miro Todorovich, May 8, 1975, box 8, folder: HU2-1, WH Central Files; memorandum, Robert Goldwin to the President, June 25, 1976, box 1, folder: Affirmative Action, August 1975–June 1976, Parsons Files; and memorandum, Robert Goldwin to Edward Levi et al., January 12, 1976, box 5, folder: Higher Education / Affirmative Action 4, Lissy Files.

25. Marian Wright Edelman to J. Stanley Pottinger, April 30, 1972, and Roy Wilkins to Caspar Weinberger, January 29, 1975, both in box 22, folder: Affirmative Action 1972, Joseph Rauh, Jr. Papers, Library of Congress, Washington, D.C. [hereafter, Rauh Papers]; Lynda Holmstrom to Gerald Ford, January 23, 1975, and Roger Semerad to Lynda Holmstrom, March 1, 1975, both in box 8, folder: March 1, 1975–April 14, 1975, White House

Central Files, emphasis in original; and Anna-Riitta Fuchstal to Gerald Ford, February 19, 1975, box 5, folder: Higher Education / Affirmative Action 1, Lissy Files.

26. *WEAL v. Weinberger,* Civ. No. 74-1720 (D.D.C., filed November 26, 1974); and Caspar Weinberger and John Dunlop to James Cannon, June 24, 1975, box 1, folder: Affirmative Action, June–July 1975, Parsons Files.

27. Arnold Beichman et al. to Gerald Ford, December 6, 1974; Paul Kurtz to Gerald Ford, December 9, 1974; Roger Semerad to Paul Kurtz, December 28, 1974; Miro Todorovich to Robert Goldwin, January 6, 1975; and Robert Goldwin to Roger Semerad, January 25, 1975, all in box 5, folder: Higher Education / Affirmative Action 1, Lissy Files.

28. Roger Semerad to Richard Parsons, March 6, 1975, and memorandum for CANI–Domestic Council Meeting, February 27, 1975, both in box 5, folder: Higher Education / Affirmative Action 1, Lissy Files.

29. Roger Semerad to Richard Parsons, March 6, 1975, and Virginia Trotter to Roger Semerad, n.d. [March 1975], both in box 5, folder: Higher Education / Affirmative Action 1, Lissy Files.

30. Peter Holmes to Roger Semerad, March 13, 1975, box 5, folder: Higher Education / Affirmative Action 1, Lissy Files.

31. Miro Todorovich to Robert Goldwin, March 19, 1975; clipping, Sidney Hook et al., letter to editor, *New York Times,* March 29, 1975; Robert Goldwin to Roger Semerad, April 8, 1975, all in box 5, folder: Higher Education / Affirmative Action I, Lissy Files; memorandum, Caspar Weinberger to the President, March 4, 1975, box 5, folder: Higher Education / Affirmative Action Lissy Files.

32. Roger Semerad to Miro Todorovich, April 8, 1975, box 5, folder: Higher Education / Affirmative Action 1, Lissy Files; L. William Seidman to Paul Kurtz, May 23, 1975, box 5, folder: Higher Education / Affirmative Action 3, Lissy Files; James Cannon to the President, March 10, 1975; Jeremy Jones to Jim Cannon, March 17, 1975; Roger Semerad to Robert Goldwin, April 11, 1975; and Roger Semerad to Miro Todorovich, April 4, 1975, all in box 5, folder: Higher Education / Affirmative Action 1, Lissy Files.

33. Memorandum, Martin H. Gerry, "Admissions Memorandum to College and University Presidents"; typescript, Summary of Meeting, April 28, 1976; typescript, Summary of Meeting, May 27, 1976; and Lawrence Lorber to David Lissy, July 1, 1976, all in box 5, folder: Higher Education / Affirmative Action 4, Lissy Files.

34. Berry, *And Justice for All,* 141; Anderson, *Pursuit of Fairness,* 145; memorandum, James Cannon to the President, n.d. [September 1975], box 8, folder: August 1, 1975–September 10, 1975, WH Central Files.

35. Memorandum, n.a. to Mr. Dunlop, April 24, 1975, box 6, folder: EEOC / September 1974–September 1975, Parsons Files; Lawrence Glick to Ethel Bent Walsh, April 13, 1975, and clipping, "Today's Summary and Analysis," *Daily Labor Report* No. 73 (April 15, 1975), both in box 12, folder: EEOC/1, Buchen Files; Dick Parsons to James Cannon, April 15, 1976, and Dick Parsons to James Cannon, May 6, 1975, both in box 6, folder: EEOC / September 1974–September 1975, Parsons Files; and Bobbie Greene Kilberg to Philip Buchen, January 8, 1976, box 12, folder: EEOC/3, Buchen Files.

36. Memorandum, Press Secretary to Heads of Departments and Agencies, March 6, 1975, box 152, folder: April 15, 1975–July 31, 1975, WH Central Files; typescript, "Issues:

Affirmative Action," January 22, 1976, box 6, folder: Affirmative Action, Lindh and Holm Files; John Ford to L. William Seidman, February 26, 1975, and David Hartquist to Dudley Chapman, March 6, 1975, both in box 152, folder: August 9, 1974–April 30, 1975, White House Central Files.

37. Jeffrey Toobin, "Gerald Ford's Affirmative Action," *New York Times,* December 30, 2006.

38. Ball, *"Bakke" Case,* 49–61, 80–85; MacLean, *Freedom Is Not Enough,* 221–23, 251, 315; *University of California v. Bakke,* 438 U.S. 265 (1975), 18 Cal. 3d34, 553 p. 2d1152, aff'd in part and reversed in part.

39. O'Neil, *"Bakke" and the Politics of Equality,* 137, 197; memorandum, Kenneth Tollett to AAUP *Ad Hoc* Committee on *Bakke* Case, April 22, 1977, box 2, folder: Bakke/2, Domestic Policy Staff Records: Deborah Hyatt's Subject Files, Jimmy Carter Presidential Library, Atlanta; and Joseph Rauh to Alex Ross, July 15, 1977, box 21, folder: Affirmative Action, 1977, Rauh Papers.

40. Ball, *"Bakke" Case,* 84; O'Neil, *"Bakke" and the Politics of Equality,* 291–92n5; typescript, "Statement by AFL-CIO Executive Council on 'Affirmative Action' after *Bakke* Case," August 7, 1978, box 21, folder: Affirmative Action, 1978, Rauh Papers; MacLean, *Freedom Is Not Enough,* 249–56; Stein, *Running Steel,* 186–92; and *United Steelworkers v. Weber,* 443 U.S. 193 (1979).

41. Typescript, [Winn Newman], March 27, 1975, box 156, group 2, International Union of Electrical Workers Collection, Rutgers University Library, New Brunswick, New Jersey; Winn Newman and Carol Wilson, "The Union Role in Affirmative Action," *Labor Law Journal* 32 (June 1981): 323–25, 329.

42. Gary M. Fink, "Fragile Alliance: Jimmy Carter and the American Labor Movement," in *The Presidency and Domestic Politics of Jimmy Carter,* ed. Herbert D. Rosenbaum and Alexej Ugrinsky (Westport, CT: Greenwood Press, 1994), 788–90; Andrew Battista, *The Revival of Labor Liberalism* (Urbana: University of Illinois Press, 2008), 50–51; Martin Halpern, "Jimmy Carter and the UAW: Failure of an Alliance," *Presidential Studies Quarterly* 26:3 (Summer 1996): 763; and Jefferson Cowie, " 'A One-Sided War': Rethinking Doug Fraser's 1978 Resignation from the Labor-Management Group," *Labor History* 44:3 (2003): 314.

43. Typescript, Jimmy Carter, "Speech to Equal Employment Opportunity Council," (September 16, 1974), box 3, folder: Civil Rights / July 1974–October 1976, Records of the 1976 Campaign; Stuart Eizenstat Subject Files, Jimmy Carter Presidential Library, Atlanta [hereafter, Eizenstat Files]; Charles Mohr, "Carter Says Reagan Would Be 'A Divisive Figure' for G.O.P.," *New York Times,* May 5, 1976; and David Berg to Stuart Eizenstat, June 19, 1976, box 3, folder: Civil Rights / July 1974–October 1976, Eizenstat Files.

44. Andrew Seidel to Jimmy Carter, May 17, 1976; Paul Games to Jimmy Carter, n.d. [May 1976]; Sullivan Marsden to Jimmy Carter, May 15, 1976; John Lyon to Jimmy Carter, May 17, 1976; Howard Brogan to James Carter, May 21, 1976; Roland Frye to Jimmy Carter, May 20, 1976; and Herbert Riggins to Jimmy Carter, July 7, 1976, all in box 33, folder: Correspondence / Affirmative Action and Compensatory Opportunity, Records of the 1976 Campaign: Sam Bleicher Subject Files, Jimmy Carter Presidential Library, Atlanta.

45. Hugh Davis Graham, "Civil Rights Policy in the Carter Presidency," in *The Carter Presidency: Policy Choices in the Post-New Deal Era,* ed. Gary M. Fink and Hugh Davis

Graham (Lawrence: University Press of Kentucky, 1998), 202, 205, 208, 210; and "Anger over Abzug Firing," *Time,* January 29, 1979, www.time.com/time/magazine/arti cle/0,9171,912307,00.html; Berry, *And Justice for All,* 161–63; Sugrue, *Sweet Land of Liberty,* 523.

46. Anderson, *Pursuit of Fairness,* 147; Ball, *"Bakke" Case,* 71–77; Bruce J. Kaufman and Scott Kaufman, *The Presidency of James Earl Carter, Jr.,* rev. ed. (Lawrence: University Press of Kansas, 2006); memorandum, Eleanor Holmes Norton to Jimmy Carter, September 9, 1977, and memorandum, Jody Powell to "Mr. President," September 8, 1977, box 2, folder: Bakke Case, Records of Martha (Bunny) Mitchell; Subject File, 1977–78, Jimmy Carter Presidential Library, Atlanta; "Blacks Urge Carter to Back 'Affirmative Action,'" *New York Times,* September 10, 1977; memorandum, Stu Eizenstat and Bob Lipshutz, September 6, 1977, box 2, folder: Bakke/1, Records of Domestic Policy Staff/Deborah Hyatt's Subject Files, Jimmy Carter Presidential Library, Atlanta; and Paul Delaney, "U.S. Brief to Support Minority Admissions," *New York Times,* August 24, 1977.

47. Delaney, "U.S. Brief to Support," 41; Steven V. Roberts, "Bakke Case: Many Moderates Near Consensus on College Admissions," *New York Times,* November 9, 1977; Albert Shanker to Walter Mondale, September 9, 1977, and Walter Mondale to Albert Shanker, September 28, 1977, both in box 49, folder: 6, American Federation of Teachers President's Office; Albert Shanker Papers, Walter P. Reuther Archives of Labor and Urban Affairs, Wayne State University, Detroit.

48. *University of California v. Bakke,* 438 U.S. at 265, 271; MacLean, *Freedom Is Not Enough,* 249; Teles, *Rise of the Conservative Legal Movement,* 234–37; and author's telephone interview with Stephen H. Balch, November 20, 2009 (in author's possession).

49. Dana L. Thomas, "On the Right Side: The PLF is Doing Yeoman Work," *Barron's,* February 26, 1976; and Pacific Legal Foundation, *The First Report: A Record of Achievement* (Sacramento, 1974), housed at Stanford University Law Library, Stanford, California.

50. Pacific Legal Foundation, *Third Annual Report* (Sacramento, 1975), 4; Pacific Legal Foundation, *Sixth Annual Review* (Sacramento, 1978–79), 1; "NCAA and Foundation Join in Challenging Government Quotas," *The Reporter* [PLF] 3:2 (February/March 1977): 4, all housed at Stanford University Law Library, Stanford, California.

51. Clipping, Abigail Thernstrom, "The Credentials of Color," *Times Literary Supplement,* April 1, 1977, box 1, folder: Odegaard v. DeFunis, Charles D. Odegaard Papers, University of Washington Special Collections, Seattle; MacLean, *Freedom Is Not Enough,* 224; and Katznelson, *When Affirmative Action Was White,* 150.

Conclusion

1. Transcript, Barack Obama, "A More Perfect Union," *New York Times,* March 18, 2008, www.nytimes.com/2008/03/18/us/politics/18text-obama.html.

2. Ibid.; Peter S. Canellos, "On Affirmative Action, Obama Intriguing but Vague," *Boston Globe,* April 29, 2008, www.boston.com/news/nation/articles/2008/04/29/on_affir mative_action_obama_intriguing_but_vague.

3. Robert A. Kagan, *Adversarial Legalism: The American Way of Law* (Cambridge: Harvard University Press, 2001), 51, 55; Graham, "Civil Rights Policy," 289–90; Edsall with

Edsall, *Chain Reaction*, 187, 189, 191; David L. Rose, "Twenty-Five Years Later: Where Do We Stand on Equal Employment Opportunity Law Enforcement?" in *Equal Employment Opportunity*, ed. Burstein, 50–51; and MacLean, *Freedom Is Not Enough*, 303–4, 312–13.

4. Edsall with Edsall, *Chain Reaction*, 187; MacLean, *Freedom Is Not Enough*, 312–13; Anderson, *Pursuit of Fairness*, 189–90.

5. *United Steelworkers of America v. Weber*, 443 U.S. 197 (1979); *Sheet Metal Workers v. EEOC*, 478 U.S. 421 (1986); *Firefighters Local Union #1784 v. Stotts*, 467 U.S. 561 (1984); *Firefighters v. Cleveland*, 478 U.S. 501 (1986); *Wygant v. Jackson Bd. Of Ed.*, 476 U.S. 267 (1986); *United States v. Paradise*, 480 U.S. 149 (1987); *Fullilove v. Klutznick*, 44 U.S. 448 (1980); *City of Richmond v. J. A. Croson Co.*, 448 U.S. 469 (1989); and *Johnson v. Santa Clara County*, 480 U.S. 616 (1987).

6. Keck, *Most Activist Supreme Court*, 139–42, 181–86; *Wards Cove Packing Co. v. Atonio*, 490 U.S. 642 (1989); *Martin v. Wilks*, 490 U.S. 755 (1989); and *Lorance v. AT&T Technologies*, 490 U.S. 900 (1989).

7. *Metro Broadcasting, Inc. v. Federal Communications Commission*, 497 U.S. 547 (1990); and *Adarand Construction, Inc. v. Pena*, 515 U.S. 200 (1995).

8. *Gratz v. Bollinger*, 539 U.S. 244 (2003); and *Grutter v. Bollinger*, 539 U.S. 306 (2003).

9. *Grutter v. Bollinger*, 539 U.S. 306, 346, 350 (2003).

10. Stephan and Abigail Thernstrom, *America in Black and White: One Nation, Indivisible* (New York: Simon Schuster, 1997), 17, 450–51, 540.

11. Richard McGowen, letter to editor, *Chronicle of Higher Education*, March 23, 2001. http://chronicle.com/weekly/v47/:28/28b00401.htm; Peter Schmidt, " 'Bakke' Set a New Path to Diversity for Colleges," *Chronicle of Higher Education*, June 20, 2008, chronicle. com/weekly/v54/i47/41a00103.htm; Peter H. Schuck, *Diversity in America: Keeping Government at a Safe Distance* (Cambridge: Harvard University Press, 2003), 134–35, 190; and Lino A. Graglia, "Why Racial Preferences Aren't the Answer," *Chronicle of Higher Education*, March 7, 2008.

12. Stephen H. Balch, telephone interview with Dennis Deslippe, November 20, 2009 (tape in author's possession); "Who We Are," www.nas.org/who.cfm and Ashley Thorne and Peter Wood, "Affirmative Spoils," www.nas.org/polArticles.cfm=175, both on the National Association of Scholars website.

13. Belz, *Equality Transformed*, 24, 26; and Raymond Wolters, *Right Turn: William Bradford Reynolds, the Reagan Administration, and Black Civil Rights* (New Brunswick, NJ: Transaction Publisher, 1996), 10, 172, 181.

14. Greenberg quoted in Katznelson, *When Affirmative Action Was White*, 150.

15. MacLean, *Freedom Is Not Enough*, 315; Brown et al., *Whitewashing Race*, xi.

16. Skrentny, "Policy-Elite Perceptions," 1776; MacLean, *Freedom Is Not Enough*, 226, 258–59; Teresa Chi-Ching Sun, "A Case Study of the Admission Dispute between the University of California at Berkeley and the Asian Community of California in the 1980s" (PhD diss., Seton Hall University, 1995), 14–16, 53, 59, 66–67, 73, 103; Mitchell J. Chang and Peter N. Kiong, "New Challenges of Representing Asian American Students in U.S. Higher Education," in *The Racial Crisis in American Higher Education: Continuing Challenges for the Twenty-First Century*, ed. William A. Smith, Philip G. Altbach, and Kofi Lomotey (Albany: State University of New York Press, 2002), 140, 146.

17. Peter Schmidt, "Study Challenges Assumptions about Affirmative Action Bans," *Chronicle of Higher Education*, February 8, 2008, chronicle.com/weekly/v54/i22/22a02002. htm; "Money, Merit, and Democracy at the University: An Exchange," in *Higher Education Under Fire: Politics, Economics, and the Crisis of the Humanities*, ed. Michael Berube and Cary Nelson (New York: Routledge, 1995), 181.

18. Perry, *Michigan Affirmative Action Cases*; Robert E. Pierre, "Affirmative Action Foes Seek Michigan Referendum," *Washington Post*, March 5, 2004; Dawson Bell, "Civil Rights Proposal Has Voters Conflicted," *Detroit Free Press*, October 18, 2006; and Ward Connerly, "My Fight Against Racial Preferences: A Quest Toward 'Creating Equality,'" *Chronicle of Higher Education*, March 10, 2000.

19. Bell, "Civil Rights Proposal"; "Public Backs Affirmative Action, But Not Minority Preferences," June 2, 2009, Pew Research Center Publications, http://pewresearch.org/pubs/1240/sotomayor-supreme-court-affirmative-action-minority-preferences; *Newsweek* Poll (conducted by Princeton Survey Research Associates), May 21–22, 2008 in *PollingReport.Com: Race and Ethnicity*, www.pollingreport.com/race.htm; and CNN/Opinion Research Corp. Poll, January 14–17, 2008, ibid.

20. McKee, *Problem of Jobs*, 247; and Lichtenstein, *State of the Union*, 207.

21. William J. Wilson, *The Truly Disadvantaged: The Inner City, the Underclass, and Public Policy* (Chicago: University of Chicago Press, 1987); Michael Lind, *Next American Nation: The New Nationalism and the Fourth American Revolution* (New York: Free Press, 2995); Michael Lind, "Now More Than Ever, We Need a Radical Center," *Salon*, April 20, 2010, www.salon.com/opinion/feature/2010/04/20/radical_center_revisited; and Walter Benn Michaels, *The Trouble with Diversity: How We Learned to Love Identity and Ignore Inequality* (New York: Metropolitan Books, 2006), 86.

22. Daniel Golden, *The Price of Admission: How America's Ruling Class Buys Its Way into Elite College—and Who Gets Left Outside the Gates* (New York: Three Rivers Press, 2007); Jacques Steinberg, *The Gatekeepers: Inside the Admissions Process of a Premier College* (New York: Penguin Press, 2003); Mitchell L. Stevens, *Creating a Class: College Admissions and the Education of Elites* (Cambridge: Harvard University Press, 2009); and David A. Hollinger, "Obama, Blackness, and Postethnic America," *Chronicle of Higher Education*, February 29, 2008.

23. Nathan Glazer, "In Defense of Preferences," *New Republic*, April 6, 1998; and Stephen Steinberg, "Nathan Glazer and the Assassination of Affirmative Action," *New Politics* 9:3, New Series (Summer 2003), www.wpunj.edu/~newpol/issue35/Steinberg35.html.

24. Nancy Kauffman, Gary Miller, and Kevin Ivey, "Affirmative Action and the White Male in America," *Labor Law Journal* 46 (November 1995): 692; and Scott Canon, "Cries of Reverse Discrimination Build to Chorus," *Kansas City Star*, July 27, 2009.

25. Naomi Levine to Abraham Goldstein, February 25, 1978, box 1, folder: Affirmative Action, 1977–79, Records of the White House Office of Counsel: Robert Lipshutz Files, Jimmy Carter Presidential Library, Atlanta.

26. James T. Kloppenberg, *The Virtues of Liberalism* (New York: Oxford University Press, 1998), 154.

The scholarly literature on affirmative action is vast; so too the approaches to studying it. Few of the authors of the many books and articles that have appeared in the past forty years, however, focus in a sustained way on opposition before *University of California v. Bakke* (1978). The broad surveys of the period and the history of affirmative action tend to look only at "blue-collar" opposition, treating working-class conservatives as a vanguard for the rising New Right. They capture the growing divisions within the Democratic Party, but there is little or no effort to distinguish between the different kinds of "reverse discrimination" protests. These works include James T. Patterson, *Grand Expectations: The United States, 1945–1974* (New York: Oxford University Press, 1996); William H. Chafe, *The Unfinished Journey: America since World War II*, 7th ed. (New York: Oxford University Press, 2010); Bruce Schulman, *The Seventies: The Great Shift in American Culture, Society, and Politics* (New York: Da Capo, 2002); Terry H. Anderson, *The Pursuit of Fairness: A History of Affirmative Action* (New York: Oxford University Press, 2004); and Ira Katznelson, *When Affirmative Action Was White: An Untold History of Inequality in Twentieth-Century America* (New York: Norton, 2005).

Scholars in the fields of sociology, political science, and policy history concentrate on the way that the civil rights and feminist lobby "captured" federal agencies and the judiciary and gave shape to emerging equal employment opportunity policies. Although they do not present a specific understanding of the diverse origins of opposition, their insistence that the changing nature of political institutions in the period framed what was politically possible informs this book. In *The Civil Rights Era: Origins and Development of National Policy* (New York: Oxford University Press, 1990), Hugh Davis Graham offers an encyclopedic understanding of the influence of civil rights machinery; Graham acknowledges the efforts of opponents, but in his analytic framework they do not have sufficient political capital in the executive branch to turn back race- and gender-sensitive programs. John David Skrentny, *The Ironies of Affirmative Action: Politics, Culture, and Justice in America* (Chicago: University of Chicago Press, 1996); Paul D. Moreno, *From Direct Action to Affirmative Action: Fair Employment Law and Policy in America, 1933–1972* (Baton Rouge: Louisiana State University Press, 1999); and Anthony S. Chen in *The Fifth Freedom: Jobs, Politics, and Civil Rights in the United States, 1941–1972* (Princeton: Princeton University Press, 2009) represent the view that political culture and partisan politics shaped the contours of what was possible in the development of equal employment policies.

Labor and working-class historians offer the most substantial treatment of "reverse discrimination" protests. Their efforts lie in chronicling the long, sometimes violent, struggles to overcome racism and sexism in diverse industries such as steel, tobacco, meat packing, and communications. Rank-and-file activists, sustained by civil rights and feminist leaders and sympathetic policymakers and judges, pushed for changes in collective bargaining agreements, wage scales, seniority lists, and internal union structures in order to achieve workplace equality. Although allowing for the occasionally sympathetic union official, historians portray labor leaders as either paralyzed by the resistance of white unionists on the shop floor or eager to collude with members to obstruct the implementation of affirmative action plans. Thomas J. Sugrue's comprehensive study on the broad political and economic transformations occurring outside the South in the decades following World War II in *Sweet Land of Liberty: The Forgotten Struggle for Civil Rights in the North* (New York: Random House, 2008) is a nuanced study of policy and social struggle. The most comprehensive treatment of these changes in the American workplace since World War II is Nancy MacLean, *Freedom Is Not Enough: The Opening of the American Workplace* (Cambridge: Harvard University Press / Russell Sage Foundation, 2006). Dorothy Sue Cobble takes up the rise of union feminism and support for antidiscriminatory measures in *The Other Women's Movement: Workplace Justice and Social Rights in Modern America* (Princeton: Princeton University Press, 2004). In my book *"Rights, Not Roses": Unions and the Rise of Working-Class Feminism, 1945–80* (Urbana: University of Illinois Press, 2000), I focus on both the emergence of support for gender equality as well as its uneven development within specific unions. The other works on individual unions include Nancy Gabin's *Feminism in the Labor Movement: Women and the United Auto Workers, 1935–1975* (Ithaca: Cornell University Press, 1990); and Mary Margaret Fonow's *Feminism in the United Steelworkers of America* (Minneapolis: University of Minnesota Press, 2003).

There is growing scholarly interest in taking up the history of opposition to race- and gender-sensitive programs in specific industries. Two recent works on affirmative action in the skilled trades and construction are Nancy A. Banks, " 'The Last Bastion of Discrimination': The New York City Building Trades and the Struggle over Affirmative Action, 1961–1976" (PhD diss., Columbia University, 2006) and a volume edited by David Goldberg and Taylor Griffey with essays by Erik Gellman, Brian Purnell, Julia Rabig, and John J. Rosen entitled *Black Power at Work: Community Control, Affirmative Action, and the Construction Industry* (Ithaca: ILR / Cornell University Press, 2010). For the steel industry, for example, in addition to Fonow's book, John Hinshaw, *Steel and Steelworkers: Race and Class Struggle in Twentieth Century Pittsburgh* (Albany: SUNY Press, 2002) and Ruth Needleman, *Black Freedom Fighters in Steel: The Struggle for Democratic Unionism* (Ithaca: ILR / Cornell University Press, 2003) detail the shop floor struggle of activists and give some attention to those who resisted equal employment opportunity.

Not surprisingly, the South has received considerable attention, in particular from Timothy J. Minchin, who has authored several important studies on race and southern labor in the period after World War II. They include *Hiring the Black Worker: The Racial*

Integration of the Southern Textile Industry, 1960–1980 (Chapel Hill: University of North Carolina Press, 1999); *The Color of Work: The Struggle for Civil Rights in the Southern Paper Industry, 1945–1980* (Chapel Hill: University of North Carolina Press, 2001); *Fight against All Odds: A History of Southern Labor since World War II* (Gainesville: University Press of Florida, 2005); and *From Rights to Economics: The Ongoing Struggle for Black Equality in the U.S. South* (Gainesville: University Press of Florida, 2007). There have been fewer studies that deal with labor and affirmative action in regions and cities outside the south; a worthy exception is Robert O. Self's *American Babylon: Race and the Struggle for Postwar Oakland* (Princeton: Princeton University Press, 2003).

Many of these labor historians focus on the economic and psychological privileges union men enjoyed as a result of their "whiteness" and "masculinity." Some scholars deploy these conceptualizations strategically, less as a sweeping indictment of the whole labor movement and more, as Thomas Sugrue puts it, as "niches of whiteness" within a labor movement with an uneven and sometimes-contradictory approach to civil rights. Others operate out of an exclusively "whiteness" framework, such as Herbert Hill in his "The Problem of Race in American Labor History," *Reviews in American History* 24 (1996). Hill, a longtime labor director at the National Association for the Advancement of Color People (NAACP), argued that white racial dominance blanketed the whole the labor movement. At the NAACP and later as an industrial relations professor at the University of Wisconsin, he laid out the case for the pervasiveness of racism in the labor movement, even in industrial unions organized into the Congress of Industrial Organizations (CIO), such as the UAW.

Hill's sweeping view was a kind of proto-whiteness perspective: although he made his case against the labor movement before the emergence of whiteness scholarship in the early 1990s, Hill dismissed episodes of cross-racial cooperation and argued instead that racial identity and privilege were woven into the very social and economic fabric of labor unions. This view has since informed many of the scholarly accounts of campaigns for racial and gender equality, such as Bruce Nelson's *Divided We Stand: American Workers and the Struggle for Black Equality* (Princeton: Princeton University Press, 2001).

These "whiteness" studies have influenced this study, but not as much as a different kind of critique, one that highlights the inadequacy of affirmative action to deal with the mounting unemployment and labor's slide in membership in the 1970s. Judith Stein took the lead in this approach in her study of industrial relations and economic policy-making in the steel industry, *Running Steel, Running America: Race, Economic Policy, and the Decline of Liberalism* (Chapel Hill: University of North Carolina Press, 1998). Even those scholars who view affirmative action in a more favorable light than Stein maintain that the ideological gulf separating full-employment advocates with rights-based liberals resulted in a weakened condition for both sides. Guian McKee concludes in *The Problem of Jobs: Liberalism, Race, and Deindustrialization in Philadelphia* (Chicago: University of Chicago Press, 2008) that the split between the race liberalism and much of the labor movement damaged the potential for improving the economic status of all workers irrespective of race.

Labor and working-class historians have offered sharp critiques of affirmative action that center on both the ill-fitting political priorities of the period and the conflicting systems of industrial relations law and affirmative action. According to Nelson Lichtenstein in his *State of the Union: A Century of American Labor* (Princeton: Princeton University Press, 2002) and Jefferson Cowie in his *Stayin' Alive: The 1970s and the Last Days of the Working Class* (New York: New Press, 2010), there was little political momentum in evidence in a decade marked by chronic economic downturns and an emboldened business and conservative antiunionism. The problem lay deeper than simply the lack of interest in job creation and labor law reform: the arrival of affirmative action cast in disarray a well-established collective bargaining regime whose foundational legislation, the Wagner Act of 1935, created the National Labor Relations Board to oversee disputes. Civil rights activists and liberals had long complained that this industrial relations framework did not adequately address race discrimination and, so, they welcomed a new one that would deliver workplace justice. The dilemma, notes sociologist Paul Frymer, was that the bifurcated system of enforcement bodies and laws wreaked havoc on union solidarity and treasuries as costly lawsuits drained their coffers. Men and women workers of all races suffered as a result. Already in decline, organized labor limped into the conservative Reagan era.

The primary sources for constructing the history of affirmative action and labor unions are diffuse. They come from the collected race and sex discrimination complaints contained in the Department of Civil Rights of the American Federation of Labor–Congress of Industrial Organizations (AFL-CIO) at the George Meany Memorial Archives in Silver Spring, Maryland. There are other important records at the Meany Archives that tell the story of organized labor's shift from opposition to support to affirmative action, especially those of the AFL-CIO Department of Civil Rights and the AFL-CIO Department of Legislation. The other significant repository of labor archives dealing with affirmative action is the Walter P. Reuther Library at Wayne State University in Detroit, Michigan. There, the records of the United Automobile Workers and the American Federation of State, County, and Municipal Employees are housed, as are those of the Coalition of Labor Union Women and the Coalition of Black Trade Unionists. The Reuther Library also contains much of the research material for the chapter on affirmative action opposition in the Detroit Police Department, including copies of the union newspaper *Tuebor*.

On race relations in Detroit after World War II, see Thomas Sugrue, *The Origins of the Urban Crisis: Race and Identity in Postwar Detroit* (Princeton: Princeton University Press, 1996); Sidney Fine, *Violence in the Model City: The Cavanaugh Administration, Race Relations, and the Detroit Riot of 1967* (Ann Arbor: University of Michigan Press, 1989); Joe T. Darden et al., *Detroit: Race and Uneven Development* (Philadelphia: Temple University Press, 1987); Mary M. Stolberg, *Bridging the River of Hatred: The Pioneering Effort of Police Commissioner George Edwards* (Detroit: Wayne State University, 1998); June Manning Thomas, *Redevelopment and Race: Planning a Finer City in Postwar Detroit* (Baltimore: Johns Hopkins University Press, 1997); and Heather Ann Thomas, *Whose Detroit? Politics, Labor, and Race in a Modern American City* (Ithaca: Cornell University Press, 2001).

Although there are no monographs dedicated to the history of affirmative action in higher education, Robert M. O'Neil's *Discriminating against Discrimination: Preferential*

Admissions and the DeFunis Case (Bloomington: Indiana University Press, 1975) offers a thorough and sympathetic account of the trial by a legal scholar who supported the University of Washington position at the time. The relevant court decisions and legal briefs for *DeFunis* can be found in Ann Fagan Ginger, ed., *DeFunis versus Odegaard and the University of Washington: The Record,* 3 vols. (Dobbs Ferry, NY: Oceana Publisher, 1974). The primary sources for the case, and for higher education in general, are varied and scattered. The University of Washington Library is a treasure trove into the early stages of the *DeFunis* case, including Marco DeFunis's attempts to gain admittance to the law school. For Jewish organizations, the three main repositories are the American Jewish Committee Archives and Record Center and the American Jewish Historical Association, both in New York City. In addition, the Library of Congress houses the records of the National Council of Jewish Women, and the American Jewish Archives in Cincinnati is home to a small but important collection relating to the *DeFunis* case.

The presidential papers of Lyndon Johnson, Richard Nixon, Gerald Ford, and Jimmy Carter, as well as those of relevant congressional members, not only offer a top-down perspective of political and policy developments in the 1965–78 period, they include correspondence and organizational information from individual and local anti–affirmation action efforts. The most important of these were for the Committee on Academic Non-Discrimination and Integrity, found in the Gerald Ford Presidential Library in Ann Arbor, Michigan.